Multinational Enterprise and Economic Analysis, second edition, surveys the contributions that economic analysis has made to our understanding of why multinational enterprises exist and what consequences they have for the workings of the national and international economies. Covering both theories and tests of hypotheses, and synthesizing material from social science and applied disciplines, Richard E. Caves develops the logic behind public policies that affects multinational enterprises. He shows the points of harmony and conflict between national policies and sources of discrepancy between national and world welfare. The book summarizes what economists have learned about why multinational firms stretch their activities across national borders and what consequences their presence has for competing local businesses, public policy makers, and the general public.

Professor Caves has completely updated the book to cover contributions appearing through the mid 1990s. Many parts have been rewritten to reflect new ideas and lines of research appearing since the first edition. It remains the only survey volume to draw equally on analytical contributions of both economics and business administration bearing on the multinational firm.

D1627992

CAMBRIDGE SURVEYS OF ECONOMIC LITERATURE

MULTINATIONAL ENTERPRISE AND ECONOMIC ANALYSIS

Second Edition

CAMBRIDGE SURVEYS OF ECONOMIC LITERATURE

Editor
Professor John Pencavel, Stanford University

The literature of economics is expanding rapidly, and many subjects have changed out of recognition within the space of a few years. Perceiving the state of knowledge in fast-developing subjects is difficult for students and time consuming for professional economists. This series of books is intended to help with this problem. Each book gives a clear structure to and balanced overview of the topic, and is written at a level intelligible to the senior undergraduate. They will therefore be useful for teaching but will also provide a mature yet compact presentation of the subject for economists wishing to update their knowledge outside their own specialties.

Multinational enterprise and economic analysis

Second edition

RICHARD E. CAVES

Harvard University

Published by the Press Syndicate of the University of Cambridge
The Pitt Building, Trumpington Street, Cambridge CB2 1RP
40 West 20th Street, New York, NY 10011–4211, USA
10 Stamford Road, Oakleigh, Melbourne 3166, Australia

First published 1996

Printed in the United States of America

Library of Congress Cataloging-in-Publication Data

Caves, Richard E.
　　Multinational enterprise and economic analysis / Richard E. Caves.
　　—[Updated ed.]
　　　　p.　　　cm. — (Cambridge surveys of economic literature)
　　ISBN 0–521–47265–2. — ISBN 0–521–47858–8 (pbk.)
　　1. International business enterprises.　I. Title.　II. Series.
HD2755.5.C395　1996
338.8′8—dc20
　　　　　　　　　　　　　　　　　　　　　　　　　　　　　　95–15937
　　　　　　　　　　　　　　　　　　　　　　　　　　　　　　CIP

A catalog record for this book is available from the British Library.

ISBN 0–521–47265–2 hardback
ISBN 0–521–47858–8 paperback

CONTENTS

v

Contents

PREFACE

The multinational enterprise (MNE) has attracted an immense amount of writing, scholarly and otherwise. Dull treatises instruct business managers on how to run MNEs. Passionate polemics chronicle their alleged misdeeds and call for the regulatory hand of government. Between these poles are found reams of description and comparison. Economic analysis has certainly not neglected the MNE. However, when the first edition of this book was written, the analytical treatments seemed seriously fragmented, as each brand of economic analysis carved its initials into the MNE without worrying much about what other branches made of it. This book's first edition (1982) therefore sought to integrate the research literature in two ways. It characterized the MNE as one form of internalization of transactions, thus placing it in the transaction-cost approach to economic organization, and integrated this core concept with the findings about MNEs reported by each standard functional branch of economic analysis. The second form of integration drew together theory and evidence, the former largely the domain of economics, the latter found adrift in the seas of business administration, political science, and the like. This integrative effort apparently proved useful to readers, which is why this revised edition appears with its organizational structure essentially unchanged.

The other reason for the revision is all too apparent. My informal estimate is that the stock of literature relevant to this survey appearing since 1982 is roughly as large as that published between the birth of Christ and 1982. Although the core transaction-cost analysis has undergone only evolutionary change, significant new theoretical contributions have emerged in the areas of international trade, industrial organization, international finance, and taxation. Analytically informed empirical studies using statistical methods have become much more common, not least from diffusion of the methods of economic research into the realm of business administration. New data sources have emerged, and existing ones have been exploited more thoroughly. The public policy debate has undergone a tectonic shift.

This book is put forth as an analytical synthesis and literature survey, but it suffers many shortcomings in both roles. As literature survey it ignores an enormous volume of descriptive material except as a source of inadvertent tests of hypotheses. Comparisons of Japanese and other MNEs no doubt interest many readers, but they claim attention here only when the differences can be regarded as testing some behavioral hypothesis. This survey also ignores a great deal of literature on public policy toward the MNE. It does cover the normative prescriptions of economic analysis and systematic evaluations of the effects of policy on MNEs' behavior. It attempts (Chapter 10) a stylized interpretation of the typical country's policy debate in the context of political behavior. However, it does not treat policy issues in specific country settings, except as the analytical research literature has been driven by policy issues emerging in the major industrial countries (especially the United States) – a choice necessary for keeping the book's length manageable.

Other limitations arise not from decisions about coverage but from the author's competence. Literature in languages other than English is sorely neglected. However, the premier status of English in the increasingly integrated international community of research scholars makes life ever easier for linguistic free-riders such as myself. Also, Dunning's (1985) country-by-country survey provides some confidence that not too many nuggets have escaped the scholarly metal detector.

Another limitation of this volume derives from the nature of the subject, in that the economic analysis of the MNE, its causes and consequences, spans the whole range of the standard fields of applied economics. The intellectual traveler must therefore pass from the fertile valleys of his scholarly specialty into the featureless plains of general scholarly acquaintance, and thence to the forbidding wilderness of Not My Subject. The balance of the material no doubt reflects my preoccupation with the fields of industrial organization and international economics, although it does so in the conviction that the theoretical tools and research methods of these fields have more to contribute to an understanding of the MNE than do those of other branches.

This book is intended to serve not only the scholar needing an analytical survey of the subject or one of its components but also the advanced undergraduate or graduate student in search of a comprehensive treatment. Every experienced teacher knows that a literature survey and a textbook are very different things. The student does not care much about who are the players in the game, and the professional does not need a basic exposition of simple theoretical concepts. Despite that problem, this book's first edition has apparently found appreciable use as a text, and so this dual agenda was retained. Still included are compact expositions of some important theoretical concepts, especially in international economics and public finance, that lie outside the standard core of undergraduate economic theory and might be unfamiliar to student customers for a course on MNEs. Students will find these expositions terse but (one hopes) adequate when augmented by appropriate professorial armwaving. The hard cases are the sections on general-equilibrium theory in Chapters 2, 5, and 7.

Some users have lamented this book's lack of the descriptive and tabular material that one ordinarily employs to lighten a textbook. That choice flows inevitably from the book's objective of providing a compact literature survey. The teacher wishing to supplement it with descriptive material, case studies, and original scholarly articles now has many resources on which to draw. The United Nations Centre on Transnational Corporations (now Programme on Transnational Corporations) has issued many publications that collect and consolidate much relevant data and information. The Centre also promoted a lengthy series of volumes of reprinted articles and chapters that have been published by Longmans (London) during the past two years. These volumes generally lean toward the less technical part of the research literature and hence prove a likely source of readings for students. The library shelves contain numerous other compendia and conference volumes that hold potential pedagogical material.

The author of any literature survey must select a policy on depth of coverage. I have tried to set the margin high enough to keep the book reasonably compact without omitting works of substantial usefulness. The shadow price is somewhat higher than it was in the first edition, and I have omitted some works that are covered in other literature surveys, replicate but do not extend existing knowledge, or (in a few cases) claim results that are disputable but not worth disputing. Any survey of contemporary literature chases a moving target; this volume's coverage becomes hit-or-miss after the middle of 1994.

I am grateful to many readers of the first edition for their suggestions and especially to those who supplied detailed comments on a draft of this revision – Magnus Blomström, Glenn Hubbard, Bruce Kogut, and Bernard Yeung. Ann Flack skillfully assisted in processing the manuscript.

1

The multinational enterprise as an economic organization

The multinational enterprise (MNE) is defined here as an enterprise that controls and manages production establishments – plants – located in at least two countries It is simply one subspecies of multiplant firm. We use the term "enterprise" rather than "company" to direct attention to the top level of coordination in the hierarchy of business decisions; a company, itself multinational, may be the controlled subsidiary of another firm. The minimum "plant" abroad needed to make an enterprise multinational is, as we shall see, judgmental. The transition from a foreign sales subsidiary or a technology licensee to a producing subsidiary is not always a discrete jump, for good economic reasons. What constitutes "control" over a foreign establishment is another judgmental issue. Not infrequently a MNE will choose to hold only a minor fraction of the equity of a foreign affiliate. Countries differ in regard to the minimum percentage of equity ownership that they count as a "direct investment" abroad, as distinguished from a "portfolio investment," in their international-payments statistics.

Exact definitions are unimportant for this study, because economic analysis in fact emphasizes that at definitional margins decision makers face close trade-offs rather than bimodal choices. However, the definition does identify the MNE as essentially a multiplant firm. We are back to Coase's (1937) classic question of why the boundary between the administrative allocation of resources within the firm and the market allocation of resources between firms falls where it does. In a market economy, entrepreneurs are free to try their hands at displacing market transactions by increasing the scope of allocations made administratively within their firms. The Darwinian tradition holds that the most profitable pattern of enterprise organization should ultimately prevail: Where more profit results from placing plants under a common administrative control, multiplant enterprises will predominate, and single-plant firms will merge or go out of business. In order to explain the existence and prevalence

1

of MNEs, we require models that predict where the multiplant firm enjoys advantages from displacing the arm's-length market and where it does not. In fact, the prevalence of multiplant (multinational) enterprises varies greatly from sector to sector and from country to country, affording a ready opportunity to test models of the MNE.

The models of the multiplant firm potentially relevant to explaining the presence of MNEs are quite numerous and rather diverse in their concerns. It proves convenient to divide them into three groups: (1) One type of multiplant firm turns out broadly the same line of goods from its plants in each geographic market. Such firms are common in domestic industries with fragmented local markets such as metal containers, bakeries, and brewing. Similarly, the many MNEs that establish plants in different countries to make the same or similar goods can be called horizontally integrated. (2) Another type of multiplant enterprise produces outputs in some of its plants that serve as inputs to its other activities. Actual physical transfer of intermediate products from one of the firm's plants to another is not required by the definition; it needs only to produce at adjacent stages of a vertically related set of production processes. (3) The third type of multiplant firm is the diversified company whose plants' outputs are neither vertically nor horizontally related to one another. As an international firm it is designated a diversified MNE.

1.1. Horizontal multiplant enterprises and the MNE

We start by equating the horizontal MNE to a multiplant firm with plants in several countries. Its existence requires, first, that *locational forces* justify dispersing the world's production so that plants are found in different national markets. Given this dispersion of production, there must be some *governance* or *transaction-cost advantage* to placing the plants (some plants, at least) under common administrative control. This abstract, static approach provides the most general and satisfying avenue to explaining the multinational company. The locational question – why plants are spread around the world as they are – we take up in Chapter 2. We assume at first that plant *A* was located in southeast England because that was the lowest-cost way to serve the market it in fact serves. We also assume that this locational choice was not essentially influenced by whether the plant was built by an MNE, bought by an MNE, or not owned by an MNE at all. The static approach also puts aside the vital question of why a company grows into MNE status – something more readily explained after the static model is in hand.

The transaction-cost approach asserts, quite simply, that horizontal MNEs will exist only if the plants they control and operate attain lower costs or higher revenue productivity than the same plants under separate managements. Why should this net-revenue advantage arise? Some of the reasons have to do with minimizing costs of production and associated logistical activities of the firm.

The more analytically interesting reasons – and, we shall see, the more important ones empirically – concern the complementary nonproduction activities of the firm.[1]

Proprietary assets

The most fruitful concept for explaining the nonproduction bases for the MNE is that of assets having these properties: The firm owns or can appropriate the assets or their services; they can differ in productivity from comparable assets possessed by competing firms; the assets or their productivity effects are mobile between national markets; they may be depreciable (or subject to augmentation), but their lifespans are not short relative to the horizon of the firm's investment decision.[2] Successful firms in most industries possess one or more types of such assets. An asset might represent knowledge about how to produce a cheaper or better product at given input prices, or how to produce a given product at a lower cost than competing firms. The firm could possess special skills in styling or promoting its product that make it such that the buyer differentiates it from those of competitors. Such an asset has a revenue productivity for the firm because it signifies the willingness of some buyers to pay more for that firm's product than for a rival firm's comparable variety. Assets of this type are closely akin to product differentiation, a market condition in which the distinctive features of various sellers' outputs cause each competing firm to face its own downward-sloping demand curve. The proprietary asset might take the form of a specific property – a registered trademark or brand – or it might rest in marketing and selling skills shared among the firm's employees. Finally, the distinctiveness of the firm's marketing-oriented assets might rest with the firm's ability to come up with frequent innovations; its proprietary asset then might be a patented novelty, or simply some new combination of attributes that its rivals cannot quickly or effectively imitate. This asset might vary greatly in tangibility and specificity. It could take the specific form of a patented process or design, or it might simply rest on know-how shared among employees of the firm. It is important that the proprietary asset, however it creates value, might rest on a set of skills or repertory of routines possessed by the firm's team of human (and other) inputs (Nelson and Winter, 1982, Chapter 5).

---

[1] This approach developed through the works of a number of authors, including Hymer (1960, 1968), Eastman and Stykolt (1967), Kindleberger (1969), Johnson (1970), Caves (1971), McManus (1972), Buckley and Casson (1976), Dunning (1977*a*, 1981*b*), Magee (1977*a*), and Hennart (1982). For early antecedents, see Southard (1931, Chapter 3) and Pennie (1956).

[2] No single term used in the literature captures all these conditions. "Proprietary assets" seems to come closest, but "intangible assets," "firm-specific assets," and "monopolistic advantages" generally have the same meaning.

The proprietary assets described by these examples evidently share the necessary conditions to support foreign investment. They are things that the firm can use but not necessarily sell or contract upon. Either the firm can hold legal title (patents, trademarks) or the assets are shared among the firm's employees and cannot be easily copied or appropriated (by other firms or by the employees themselves). They possess either the limitless capacities of public goods (the strict intangibles) or the flexible capacities of the firm's repertory of routines. Especially important for the MNE, while the productive use of these assets is not tightly tied to single physical sites or even nations, arm's-length transfers of them between firms are prone to market failures. These failures deter a successful one-plant firm from selling or renting its proprietary assets to other single-plant firms and thereby foster the existence of multiplant (and multinational) firms. Proprietary assets are subject to a daunting list of infirmities for being detached and transferred by sale or lease:

1.   They are, at least to some degree, *public goods*. Once a piece of knowledge has been developed and applied at a certain location, it can be put to work elsewhere at little extra cost and without reducing the capacity available at the original site. From society's point of view, the marginal conditions for efficient allocation of resources then require that the price of the intangible asset be equal to its marginal cost, zero or approximately zero. But no one gets rich selling bright ideas for zero. Therefore, intangible assets tend to be underprovided or to be priced inefficiently (at a net price exceeding their marginal cost) or both.

2.   Transactions in intangibles suffer from *impactedness* combined with *opportunism*. This problem is best explained by examples: I have a piece of knowledge that I know will be valuable to you. I try to convince you of this value by describing its general nature and character. But I do not reveal the details, because then the cat would be out of the bag, and you could use the knowledge without paying for it unless I have a well-established property right. But you therefore decline to pay me as much as the knowledge would in fact be worth to you, because you suspect that I am opportunistic and overstate my claims.

3.   A proprietary asset might be diffuse and therefore incapable of an enforceable lease or sale contract. The owning firm might readily contract with a customer to achieve a specific result using some competence that it possesses, but be unable to contract to install that competence within another firm. Even with well-defined intangibles, various sources of uncertainty can render contractual transfers infeasible or distort the terms of viable deals.

This application of modern transaction-cost analysis underlies a framework widely used in research on the MNE. It asserts the existence of three necessary conditions for the appearance of horizontal foreign investments: (1) The firm can appropriate some value-creating proprietary asset ("ownership"); (2) production processes that employ or apply the value-creating asset are efficiently dispersed among several national markets ("location"); and (3) the decentralized application of the proprietary asset is more efficiently managed within the owning firm than by renting it at arm's length to another firm ("internalization"). This framework, developed mainly in Dunning's (e.g., 1981*b*) writings, is referred to by the oxymoron "the eclectic theory of foreign investment." It is controversial only as to its sufficiency to explain all MNEs' operations; it clearly lacks that sufficiency, as it does not apply to the cases of vertical and diversified MNEs (Rugman, 1985; Teece, 1986).

Some extensions

The proprietary-assets approach yields certain extensions and variants. Although the standard exposition contemplates a goods-producing firm, it evidently applies as well to MNEs in the services sector.[3] The site of production of a service is sometimes indefinite, and accordingly it is not subject to the clear dichotomy between exporting and foreign production that is applicable to a good. While a hotel chain serves customers at the site of the service's consumption, a consulting firm does not (Boddewyn et al., 1986; Enderwick and Associates, 1989; UNCTC, 1989). The proprietary assets of services multinationals seldom result from research investments, but they commonly rest on information and capabilities that effectively yield economies of scale and scope and support goodwill assets. Also, some service MNEs (but not only they) possess an important special type of proprietary asset that is transaction-specific. In transaction-cost economics, a transaction-specific asset exists in some resources, facilities, knowledge, or even merely trust that particular parties can valuably use in repeated transactions with each other. The switching costs that they incur if they change transaction partners supports a persistent supplier-customer relation that can deter either party from taking temporary advantage of the other. As empirical evidence subsequently demonstrates, the proprietary assets that drive foreign investment in some business services seem to be strongly transaction-specific, with service MNEs emerging to preserve and benefit from the parent's ties to customers who themselves have become MNEs.

Another extension pertains to the longevity of proprietary assets. The standard approach is one of comparative statics: A domestic firm is assigned some fixed proprietary asset, and its profitable exploitation through foreign direct investment is deduced. Proprietary assets can be enlarged or improved through investment, however, and such investment decisions should themselves depend

---

[3] The value of foreign investments in services probably accounts for 40 percent of the capital invested in foreign subsidiaries according to the United Nations Centre on Transnational Corporations (hereafter UNCTC, 1989), but the research literature is locked into a goods-production mind-set.

on the firm's opportunities to undertake foreign investments. Foreign investments themselves might be undertaken in order to develop or improve proprietary assets. Such assets are also subject to depreciation and obsolescence, and their deterioration might lead to foreign divestment as a reversal of the foreign-investment process (Boddewyn, 1983). The creation and destruction of such assets and the variance of returns in the investments that firms make in them should be reflected in the longevity and turnover of foreign investments themselves (Caves, 1995).

Studies of domestic multiplant operation (Scherer et al., 1975) indicate a number of economies directly relating to the firm's production activities, and these can apply to the MNE if they do not stop at the national boundary. There can be transaction-cost economies in the procurement of raw materials that go beyond the input needs of the single plant. Economies can arise in the transportation network for outbound shipments of finished goods that extend beyond the single plant's output. Localized demand or cost fluctuations can warrant coordinated use of plants' capacities so that several plants' outputs can be flexibly shipped from the temporarily favored site (de Meza and van der Ploeg, 1987; Kogut and Kulatilaka, 1994). If the industry's output consists of a line of diverse goods, each plant might efficiently specialize in some items rather than each producing the whole array. It is an empirical question how fully these economies are available to a multiplant firm operating across national boundaries, because they depend on the cost of moving goods (inputs or outputs) among plants or the effectiveness of managerial coordination of distant activities.

Another asset of the ongoing firm is its capacity to generate investible funds beyond what it can profitably use for expanding its current activities. One view of the ongoing firm's financial decisions holds that it attaches different opportunity costs to funds from various sources. Externally secured funds – debt and new equity – are costly because of transaction costs and moral-hazard problems and the reduced independence they entail for the managers, as well as the direct cost of paying additional interest or dividends. Internally generated funds – profits not paid out to current shareholders – have a lower opportunity cost, and managers will put them to work in a new activity with an expected profit rate (internal rate of return) lower than what would be needed to warrant external borrowing. Thus, excess capacity in internally generated funds can also motivate foreign investment.[4] Indeed, this point generalizes further to the advantage an established company might have in entering a foreign market simply because excess profits can be earned there, and the firm stands near the front of the queue of potential entrants in terms of its ability to overcome whatever

---

[4] The financial model of the firm that underlies these propositions has less than universal acceptance among economists but agrees with evidence summarized in Section 6.1.

entry barriers sustain the excess profits. The implications of this point for the MNE as a market competitor are discussed in Chapter 4, and empirical evidence appears in Section 9.3's discussion of MNEs originating in less-developed countries.

Finally, the firm's choice of foreign investment for maximizing the returns to its proprietary assets in foreign markets is made against an array of alternative arrangements involving arm's-length deals with other firms. When the proprietary asset is a patent, trademark, or well-defined technology, licensing or franchising it to other firms might be the owner's preferred strategy (technology licensing is reviewed in Chapter 7). When a value-creating activity requires proprietary assets that two (or more) firms must contribute, and outright merger of the firms is not efficient, various alliances, cooperative arrangements, and joint ventures can be employed (Oman, 1984; Dunning, 1984; Buckley, 1985; Hennart, 1989; Mytelka, 1991). For example, a firm might prefer some contractual arrangement to serve a small foreign market where establishing its own subsidiary requires an otherwise avoidable fixed cost (Anderson and Gatignon, 1986). Other cooperative arrangements and management-services contracts can become instruments of choice when host governments cannot credibly commit to eschew expropriation (or its equivalent in taxation) once the MNE has sunk its foreign investment (see Section 4.4). Evidence on these forms of interfirm agreement will be noted subsequently, because they compete with foreign investment as a way to maximize returns on proprietary assets.

Empirical evidence: prevalence of horizontal foreign investment
Hypotheses about horizontal MNEs have received many statistical tests. The usual strategy of research involves relating the prevalence of MNEs in an industry to structural traits of that industry: If attribute x promotes the formation of MNEs, and successful firms in industry A have a lot of x, then MNEs should be prevalent in industry A. These tests have been performed on two dependent variables: foreign operations of firms in a source country's industries normalized by their total activity level in those industries (hereafter "outbound" foreign investment), and foreign subsidiaries' share of activity in a host country's markets normalized by total transactions in those markets (hereafter "inbound" foreign investment). The exogenous variables are chosen to represent features of industries' structures that should either promote or deter foreign direct investment. These econometric studies are prone to at least two types of misspecification that have led to certain modified research strategies. First, foreign investment substitutes for other methods (exporting, licensing foreign producers) of maximizing rents on proprietary assets in foreign markets. A given industry's share of foreign investment might be high either because foreign investment works well or because the alternatives work badly. The most attractive way to address this problem is to measure the extent of use of the

alternative methods and test the determinants of all of them together. Second, the extent to which country 1's firms invest abroad depends not only on the absolute properties or qualities of their own proprietary assets but also on the qualities of assets held by firms competing with them in foreign markets. The data requirements for dealing head-on with this problem are onerous, but some progress has been made in studies of bilateral foreign-investment patterns.

The number of studies embodying these designs has grown large enough to sustain its own monograph-length survey (UNCTC, 1992a). Here the main conclusions will be summarized, with reference only to selected papers. There is considerable agreement on the major results among studies of both outbound and inbound investment, among studies of a given type for each country, and among studies based on different countries. Therefore we offer here some generalizations about the principal conclusions without referring extensively to the conclusions reached in individual studies or about particular countries. Then we take up extensions and qualifications. Findings about the trade-off between foreign investment and exporting are treated in Chapter 2, and about the trade-off between foreign investment and other forms of association between business units in Chapter 7.

First, a roster of the main statistical studies of outbound foreign investment includes these: for the United States, Horst (1972a), Wolf (1977), Pugel (1978, Chapter 4; 1981a), Goedde (1978, Chapter 2), and Lall (1980); for Sweden, Swedenborg (1979); and for Japan, Kogut and Chang (1991) and Drake and Caves (1992). The principal studies of inbound foreign investment include: for the United States, Lall and Siddharthan (1982), Caves and Mehra (1986), and Wesson (1993); for Canada, Caves (1974b), Baumann (1975), Saunders (1982), and Owen (1982); for Great Britain, Dunning (1973b), Caves (1974b), and Hughes and Oughton (1992); for Germany, Yamawaki (1985); for Australia, Parry (1978) and Ratnayake (1993); and for India, Kumar (1990). Their results confirm, first and foremost, the role of proprietary assets inferred from the outlays that firms make to create and maintain these assets. Research and development intensity (R&D sales ratio) is a thoroughly robust predictor. Advertising intensity has proved nearly as robust, even though most studies have lacked an appropriately comprehensive measure of firms' sales-promotion outlays.[5] The literature also consistently finds a significant positive influence for an industry's intensive use of skilled managerial labor; this variable seems to confirm the "repertory of routines" basis for foreign investment, indepen-

---

[5] More and Caves (1994) showed that intrafirm royalty receipts by MNE parents (after controlling for transfer-pricing distortions) behave like cash flows resulting from foreign investments that transplant the MNE's intangible assets. Survey evidence gathered by Bertin and Wyatt (1988, pp. 25–9) showed that MNEs regard technology advantages as their most potent competitive advantage, followed by marketing and managerial assets.

dent of the strictly intangible proprietary assets (Pugel, 1981*a*). (More comprehensive measures of labor skills also exert statistically significant positive effects in some studies, but it is unclear what hypothesis they test.) A third result that also supports a role for the firm's general coordinating capacity is the positive influence of multiplant operation within large countries such as the United States. This hypothesis was advanced and given some statistical support by Eastman and Stykolt (1967, Chapter 4); both Caves (1974*b*) and Saunders (1982) confirmed that multiplant operations in the United States are a significant positive predictor of foreign investment in adjacent Canada, although Caves found that the hypothesis is not confirmed for remote, insular Britain.[6]

Other tests have dealt with sources of entry barriers that might concentrate production in particular locations. Some evidence indicates that extensive scale economies in production deter the dispersion of plant operations and thus retard foreign investment. Also, some investigators have tested the hypothesis that activities requiring (absolutely) large capital investments might favor the multinational activity of existing large enterprises. None of these hypotheses has been supported robustly, although support for the scale-economies hypothesis is noted in Chapter 2. The hypotheses are not finely tuned, and many studies suffer from the inclusion of such variables as an industry's average firm size or the concentration of its producers, which are themselves endogenous, collinear with other exogenous variables, and lead to results that are sensitive to specification choices and generally untrustworthy.

Included in many of these cross-section models are variables seeking to capture the positive influence of tariff protection of the host-country market or (alternatively) the ease or cost-advantage with which a host-country market can be served through exports rather than foreign investment. These are discussed in Chapter 2. The important point is that they have rather little explanatory power compared to variables based on proprietary assets, which embody necessary conditions for foreign direct investment.

Several special issues do need to be noted here:

1. *Development of proprietary assets.* The cross-section tests summarized so far neglect the development and turnover of stocks of proprietary assets. This process is most easily seen in studies of individual firms, but it does exert some influence at the national level. Drake and Caves (1992) showed how the development of proprietary assets in Japan's manufacturing industries in the 1970s and 1980s led to subsequent increases of Japan's share of foreign investments in U.S. industries. Cantwell (1989, Chapters 2, 6) explored the long-run relation between nations' proprietary-asset stocks, reflected in patents, and

---

[6] Juhl (1985) confirmed it for Germany. Useful demonstrations of the nature of proprietary assets other than intangibles lie in studies of MNEs based in "unlikely" source countries such as Canada (Rugman, 1987).

their revealed comparative advantage in gathering rents on world markets. The association is closer for exports and overseas production taken together than it is for exports alone.

2. *Adversary relation between source- and host-country assets.* The relativity of competing companies' proprietary assets can be tested only at a broad national level (see Chapter 2) or through analyzing industry-level flows of investment between pairs of countries. Kogut and Chang (1991) explored the roles of both Japanese and U.S. R&D expenditures in influencing the rate of Japanese foreign investment. It turns out to be positively related to both flows; there is no positive relation to the Japan-U.S. differential, as one would expect if the two expenditure flows create adversary proprietary assets. Apparently spillovers and positive externalities are the dominant factor for R&D, but Pugel et al. (forthcoming) found that Japanese foreign investment is repelled by the marketing outlays of U.S. competitors. Kim and Lyn (1987) found a negative relation between foreign investment in U.S. industries and the market value of U.S. firms with which they compete – specifically, the component of those market values not explained by the U.S. industries' own R&D and advertising levels and their concentration ratios.

3. *Foreign investment to augment proprietary assets.* Related to the result of Kogut and Chang is the hypothesis that (some) foreign investment takes place in order to draw on host-country assets in order to augment the proprietary assets of the entering MNE. Case-study evidence documents extensively this motive for foreign investment, e.g., Japanese foreign investments in research-intensive industries of the United States and Germany (Tsurumi, 1976, pp. 116–17; Yoshida, 1987, pp. 47–8; Alsegg, 1971, pp. 218–30). The United States remains the natural market in which to test the hypothesis. Wesson (1993) argued that a U.S. industry's share of world exports is the best available proxy for intangibles found in the U.S. market that could serve this purpose. He found that foreign investment in the United States increases with several variables that indicate the stock of relevant U.S. assets (such as classes of skilled labor), either directly or interacted with the export-share measure of the U.S. advantage. Consistent with Wesson's results, Pugel (1985) found that R&D/sales ratios of foreign subsidiaries operating in the United States are approximately equal to those of U.S. subsidiaries abroad.

4. *International mobility of proprietary assets.* Some research addresses the international mobility of proprietary assets by explaining why competing firms in an industry differ in their propensities to invest abroad. Horst (1974*a*, Chapters 4 and 5) explored the effects of various corporate assets on the foreign-investment behavior of firms in the U.S. food-processing sector. The proprietary assets held by these firms divide roughly into two classes. Some succeeded on the basis of heavy national advertising, others with extensive and intricate distribution systems for bringing their products to the final consumer

in good condition. The latter group has taken part less extensively in foreign investment, because these complex distribution systems are a drain on managerial resources and are not readily replicated in foreign markets. The advertisers, on the other hand, are heavy foreign investors. The firms with intensive distribution systems also display less extensive multiplant development within the United States, suggesting that the diseconomies of scale in extending their empires constrain them geographically within the United States as well as internationally.[7] Statistical studies (Horst, 1972b; Grubaugh, 1987a) have come to confirm the role of different endowments of competing firms as predictors of their MNE status. Belderbos and Sleuwaegen (forthcoming) in particular showed that predictions based on Japanese firms' endowments extend even to the destinations of their foreign investments.

5. *Evidence from market valuations of firms.* Another method recently employed to test the proprietary-assets approach is by means of information on the stock market's valuation of the MNEs. Morck and Yeung (1991) analyzed ratios of market to book value (Tobin's q) for U.S. MNEs to show that the market's valuation of these firms increases with their investments (R&D, advertising) in proprietary assets and with the extent of their multinational operations. This influence of foreign operations, however, depends on and operates through these outlays on proprietary assets. (Otherwise, multinationality might be valued by shareholders for diversification or tax advantages that it provides instead of for rents on proprietary assets.) Morck and Yeung (1992) studied the stock market's valuation of announcements that a U.S. firm had acquired control of a firm located abroad. Although U.S. markets' reactions to domestic mergers tend to be insignificantly positive or even negative for the acquiring firm, Morck and Yeung found a significant positive response to the average foreign acquisition. Further, the response increases with the firm's rate of spending on proprietary assets – R&D (especially for small acquiring firms) and advertising (especially for large ones). Gupta et al. (1991) similarly observed positive responses to joint ventures announced in the People's Republic of China.

Multinationals in service industries

Horizontal MNEs in banking and other services have received increased attention from researchers. The proprietary-assets hypothesis again makes a good showing – especially when extended to the transaction-specific assets of an ongoing semicontractual relationship between the service enterprise and its customer. A bank, advertising agency, or accounting firm acquires a good deal of specific knowledge about its client's business, and the parties' sustained relationship based on trust lowers the cost of contracting and the risks of opportunistic behavior. The service firm enjoying such a quasi-contractual

---

[7] Similarly, Meredith (1984) demonstrated the pull of foreign direct investment to Canada associated with spillovers of U.S. sales-promotion outlays across the Canadian border.

relation with a parent MNE holds a transaction-cost advantage for supplying the same service to the MNE's foreign subsidiaries. If the service must be supplied locally, the service firm goes multinational to follow its customer.

Much casual evidence reveals this transaction-specific asset behind service industries' foreign investments (e.g., Safarian, 1966, p. 210; Behrman, 1969, pp. 3–4), especially in the banking sector (Grubel, 1977, and references cited therein; Pastré, 1981; Yannopoulos, 1983; Enderwick and Associates, 1989, pp. 61–78). Grubel affirmed the transaction-cost model but also cited two other factors. Some banks acquire particular product-differentiating skills analogous to those found in some goods-producing industries; they can explain banks' foreign investments in less-developed countries (Baum, 1974) and in countries with large populations of migrants from the source country. Also, national banking markets commonly appear somewhat noncompetitive because of cartelization or regulation or both, and foreign banks are well-equipped potential entrants. The Eurocurrency markets' rise can be largely explained on this basis. The traits of foreign banks' operations in the United States affirm these propositions (Lees, 1976; Terrell and Key, 1978). Some propositions about internalization in banking have been tested statistically. Nigh, Cho, and Krishnan (1986) found increases in U.S. bank assets abroad to vary significantly by country with increases in the overall book value of the U.S. foreign-investment position, with the openness of the host country's policies controlled. Sagari (1992) confirmed the same proposition for levels of banking and nonbanking foreign investment. Heinkel and Levi (1992) symmetrically showed the prevalence of foreign countries' banks in the United States to increase with the country's exports and with the value of financial claims that the U.S. holds on the source country's capital market. Li and Guisinger (1992) found that the growth of foreign investment by a source country's service (all services sectors) MNEs increases significantly with the source's total initial stocks of foreign investment; the closeness of the relationship declined from the 1970s to the 1980s.

The prominence of transaction-specific assets as a factor driving foreign investment is apparently matched in other service industries such as advertising agencies, accounting, and consulting firms (Terpstra and Yu, 1988; Enderwick and Associates, 1989, pp. 79–106). Studies of other multinational service industries, however, bring out different factors. International hotel chains resemble other franchise operations in creating centrally a proprietary asset (standardized product image, reservation system) that must be combined with other inputs at the site of consumption. No sharp economic boundary exists between domestic and international hotel franchises, and Dunning and McQueen (1982) showed that international hotel chains' penetration of various national markets is inversely related to the development of franchise systems in the domestic industry. International construction firms rely on repertories of routines and reputation assets resembling those that commonly support MNEs in manufacturing (Enderwick and Associates, 1989, pp. 132–51).

1.2. **Vertically integrated MNEs**

The vertically integrated MNE is readily regarded as a vertically integrated firm whose production units lie in different nations. Theoretical models that explain vertical integration should therefore be directly applicable. Again, we assume that production units are dispersed in different countries due to conventional locational pressures – the bauxite mine where the bauxite is, bauxite converted to alumina at the mine because the process is strongly weight-losing, and the smelter that converts alumina into aluminum near a source of low-cost electric power. The question is, why do they come under common administrative control? The proprietary-assets model is not necessary, because neither upstream nor downstream production unit need bring any distinctive qualification to the parties' vertical consolidation. Some proprietary advantage of course *could* explain which producer operating at one stage undertakes an international forward or backward vertical integration.

Models of vertical integration

Until the rise of transaction-cost economics the economic theory of vertical integration contained a large but unsatisfying inventory of special-case models. Some dealt with the physical integration of production processes: If you make structural shapes out of the metal ingot before it cools, you need not incur the cost of reheating it. Such gains from physical integration explain why sequential processes are grouped in a single plant, but they neither preclude two firms sharing that plant nor explain the common ownership of far-flung plants. Another group of traditional models regard vertical integration as preferable to a stalemate between a monopolistic seller and a monopsonistic buyer, or to an arm's-length relation between a monopolistic seller and competitive buyers whose activities are distorted due to paying the monopolist's marked-up price for their input. Some models explain vertical integration as a way around monopolistic distortions, while others explain it as a way to profit by fostering such distortions.

The theory of vertical integration has been much enriched by the same transaction-cost approach that serves to explain horizontal MNEs. Vertical integration occurs, the argument goes, because the parties prefer it to the ex ante contracting costs and ex post monitoring and haggling costs that would mar the alternative state of arm's-length transactions. The vertically integrated firm internalizes a market for an intermediate product, just as the horizontal MNE internalizes markets for proprietary assets.[8] Suppose that there were pure

---

[8] Williamson (1985) deserves credit for popularizing this approach. For a survey of models of vertical integration, see Perry (1989).

competition in each intermediate-product market, with large numbers of buyers and sellers, the product homogeneous (or its qualities costlessly evaluated by the parties), information about prices and availability in easy access to all parties in the market. Neither seller nor buyer would then have reason to transact repeatedly with any particular party on the other side of the market. When these assumptions do not hold, however, both buyers and sellers acquire motives to make long-term alliances. The two can benefit mutually from investments that each makes suited to special attributes of the other party. Each then incurs a substantial fixed cost upon shifting from one transaction partner to another. Each seller's product could be somewhat different, and the buyer incurs significant costs of testing or adapting to new varieties, or merely learning the requirements and organizational routines of new partners. The buyer and seller gain an incentive to enter into some kind of long-term arrangement.

If transaction-specific assets deter anonymous spot-market transactions, they leave open the choice between long-term contracts and vertical integration. Contracts, however, encounter the costs of negotiation and of monitoring and haggling previously mentioned. These ex ante and ex post costs trade off against one another – a comprehensive contract can reduce subsequent haggling – but the overall cost remains.[9] The problem is compounded because, even in a market with many participants, unattached alternative transaction partners tend to be few *at any particular time* when a party might wish to recontract. Fewness compounds the problems of governance in arm's-length vertical relationships.

One special case of the transaction-cost theory of vertical integration holds promise for explaining MNEs involved in processing natural resources. Vertical integration can occur because of failings in markets for information, as analyzed earlier in the context of proprietary assets. A processing firm must plan its capacity on some assumption about the future price and availability of its key raw material. The producers of that raw material have the cheapest access (perhaps exclusive) to that information. But they have an incentive to overstate availability to the prospective customer: The more capacity customers build, the higher they are likely to bid in the future for any given quantity of the raw material. Therefore, vertical integration could occur in order to evade problems of impacted information (Arrow, 1975).

To summarize, intermediate-product markets can be organized in a spectrum of ways stretching from anonymous spot-market transactions through a variety of long-term contractual arrangements at arm's length to vertical integration. Switching costs and durable, specialized assets discourage spot transactions

---

[9] Economists like to make the point that the uncertainties impelling vertical integration could be averted by resorting to comprehensive forward-contract markets, if they existed (Buckley and Casson, 1976). Because they do not exist for the same reasons that vertical integration emerges, the point has no operational significance.

and favor one of the other modes. If, in addition, the costs of negotiating and monitoring arm's-length contracts are high, the choice falls on vertical integration. These empirical predictions address both where vertical MNEs will appear and how they will trade off against contractual relationships.

Empirical evidence

Far fewer statistical studies address these hypotheses than the ones concerned with horizontal MNEs. Pugel (1978) and Owen (1982) did conclude that American manufacturing industries having greater involvement with natural resources invest larger proportions of their assets abroad. However, the indicator used was nothing but a dummy variable designating the ferrous and nonferrous metals industries. McKern (1976) provided the only comparative examination of the extractive industries themselves. He was left unimpressed with the unimportance of monopoly/monopsony market structures for explaining foreign investment in Australia's extractive industries. Also, he could not accord much importance to the foreign MNEs' motive of assuring themselves access to supplies, because in many cases they did not transfer Australian raw materials directly to their own refining facilities but instead sold them on the open market. Accordingly, he argued that an important motive for vertical integration is the use by MNEs of the knowledge they have acquired about the international market for the raw materials in question. This basis for vertical integration in MNEs adds up to a proprietary-assets explanation, analytically similar to the one that proves so fruitful for explaining horizontal MNEs. Case studies reaching this conclusion include Read (1983) and Chalmin (1986).

A great deal of information exists on individual extractive industries in which MNEs operate on a worldwide basis, and this case-study evidence merits a glance in lieu of more systematic findings. For example, Stuckey (1983) found the international aluminum industry to contain not only MNEs integrated from the mining of bauxite through the fabrication of aluminum projects but also a network of long-term contracts and joint ventures. Market participants are particularly unwilling to settle for spot transactions in bauxite (the raw ore) and alumina (output of the first processing stage). The problem is not so much the small number of market participants worldwide as the extremely high switching costs. Alumina refining facilities need to be located physically close to bauxite mines (to minimize transportation costs), and they are constructed to deal with the properties of specific ores. Likewise, for technical and transportation-cost reasons, aluminum smelters are somewhat tied to particular sources of alumina. Therefore, arm's-length markets tend to be poisoned by the problems of small numbers and switching costs. And the very large specific and durable investments in facilities also invoke the problems of long-term contracts that were identified earlier. Finally, Stuckey gave some weight to Arrow's model of vertical integration as a route to securing information: Nobody knows more about future bauxite supplies and exploration than an existing bauxite producer.

A good deal of evidence also appears on vertical integration in the oil industry. The ambitious investigations have addressed the U.S. segment of the industry, but there appears to be no strong difference between the forces traditionally affecting vertical integration in national and international oil companies.[10] These studies give considerable emphasis to the costs of supply disruption faced by any nonintegrated firm in petroleum extraction or refining. Refineries normally operate at capacity and require a constant flow of crude-oil inputs. Storing large inventories of input is quite costly, and so backward integration that reduces uncertainty about crude supplies can save the refiner a large investment in storage capacity. It also reduces risks in times of "shortages" and "rationing," when constraints somewhere in the integrated system (crude-oil supplies are only the most familiar constraint) can leave the unintegrated firm out in the cold. The hazard of disrupted flows translates into a financial risk, as vertically integrated firms have been found to be able to borrow long-term funds more cheaply than those with exposure to risk (Greening, 1976, Chapter 1).[11]

Country-based studies of the foreign-investment process have also underlined vertical MNEs as the outcome of failed arm's-length market transactions. Japanese companies became involved with extractive foreign investments only after the experience of having arm's-length suppliers renege on long-term contracts, and they also experimented with low-interest loans to independent foreign suppliers as a way to establish commitment (Tsurumi, 1976, Chapter 2).

Vertical integration: other manifestations

The identification of vertically integrated foreign investment with extractive activities is traditional and no doubt faithful to the pattern accounting

---

[10] By "traditionally" we mean before the OPEC cartel became fully effective in the early 1970s. See Penrose (1968, pp. 46–50, 253–9), Greening (1976), and Teece (1976, Chapter 3).

[11] The international iron-ore market in the 1970s provides an example of the attraction of vertically integrated MNEs for reducing risk. Mostly because of nationalization of iron-ore mines, the degree of vertical integration in the international iron and steel industry had been declining. The nationalization and dis-integration had been encouraged by a period of high prices for iron ore. However, as the situation changed in the 1970s, the prices declined and the nonintegrated ore producers began scurrying to secure long-term contracts and restore some of the dismantled integration. See Vernon and Levy (1980). Several international extractive industries have undergone sharp changes in organization associated with shifts in conditions that made feasible the emergence of competitive spot and futures markets, greatly reducing the value of vertically integrated MNEs. For descriptions and a model able to explain the sharpness of the regime shifts, see de Kuijper (1983).

for the bulk of MNE assets. However, it gives too narrow an impression of the role of vertically subdivided transactions in MNEs.

First of all, it neglects a form of backward integration that depends not on natural resources but on subdividing production processes and placing abroad those that are both labor-intensive and footloose. For example, semiconductors are produced by capital-intensive processes and assembled into electronic equipment by similarly mechanized processes, both undertaken in the industrial countries. But, in between, wires must be soldered to the semiconductors by means of a labor-intensive technology. Because shipping costs for the devices are low relative to their value, it pays to carry out the labor-intensive stage in a low-wage country. The relationship of the enterprises performing these functions in the United States and abroad must obviously be a close one, involving either detailed contractual arrangements or common ownership. This subdivision of production processes should occur through foreign investment to an extent that depends again on the transactional bases for vertical integration.

Writers on offshore procurement and the associated international trade always refer to the role of foreign investment in transplanting the necessary know-how and managerial coordination (Helleiner, 1973; Sharpston, 1975). Jarrett (1979, Chapters 7 and 8; also see Helleiner, 1979, and J. Lee, 1986) explored statistically both the structural determinants of this type of trade and the role of MNEs in carrying it out. His data pertain to imports under a provision of the U.S. tariff whereby components exported from the United States for additional fabrication abroad can be reimported with duty paid only on the value added abroad. His statistical analysis explains how these activities vary both among U.S. industries and among countries taking part in this trade. His results confirm the expected properties of the industries that make use of vertically disintegrated production: Their outputs have high value per unit of weight, possess reasonably mature technology (so are out of the experimental stage), are produced in the United States under conditions giving rise to high labor costs, and are easily subject to decentralized production.[12] Among overseas countries, U.S. offshore procurement favors those not too far distant (transportation costs) and with low wages and favorable working conditions. With these factors controlled, the component flows increase with the extent of U.S. foreign investment, both among industries and among foreign countries.[13]

[12] Jarrett measured this last by the extent of multiplant operation of companies in the United States and by the extent to which U.S. producers depend on inputs purchased from other establishments in the same industry.

[13] If the presence of foreign investment is associated with offshore procurement, it should also be true that the factors influencing the proportion of U.S. imports that come from overseas corporate affiliates should include these same determinants of offshore procurement. This proposition is confirmed in Jarrett's analysis (1979, Chapter 2) of related-party imports to the United States.

A considerable amount of vertical integration is also involved in the "horizontal" foreign investments described earlier in this chapter, and the behavior of horizontal MNEs cannot be fully understood without recognizing the complementary vertical aspects of their domestic and foreign operations. Many foreign subsidiaries do not just produce their parents' goods for the local market; they process semifinished units of that good, or package or assemble them according to local specifications. Pharmaceuticals, for example, are prepared in the locally desired formulations using basic preparations imported from the parent. The subsidiary organizes a distribution system in the host-country market, distributing partly its own production, but with its line of goods filled out with imports from its parent or other affiliates.[14] Or the subsidiary integrates forward to provide local servicing facilities. These activities are bound up with the development and maintenance of the enterprise's goodwill asset, as described earlier, through a commitment of resources to the local market. The firm can thereby assure local customers, who are likely to incur fixed investments of their own in shifting their purchases to the MNE, that the company's presence is not transitory. This consideration helps explain foreign investment in some producer-goods industries for which the proprietary-assets hypothesis otherwise seems rather dubious (Tsurumi, 1976, Chapter 4).[15] All of these activities represent types of forward integration by the MNE, whether into final-stage processing of its goods or into ancillary services.

The evidence of this confluence of vertical and horizontal foreign investments mainly takes the form of case studies rather than systematic data. It is emphasized in the study of foreign investments by West German enterprises by Fröbel et al. (1980, Chapter 12). It is implied by the extent of intracorporate trade among MNE affiliates – flows that would be incompatible with purely horizontal forms of intracorporate relationships. Imports of finished goods by Dutch subsidiaries from their U.S. parents (Stubenitsky, 1970, p. 102) are high (as percentages of the affiliates' total sales) in just those sectors where imports might complement local production for filling out a sales line – chemicals (24.9 percent), electrical equipment (35.4 percent), and transportation equipment (65.5 percent). The prevalence of intracorporate trade in engineering industries also suggests the importance of components shipments (U.S. Tariff Commission, 1973, pp. 284, 314–20). The case studies of intrafirm trade in Casson and Associates (1986) showed the importance of this forward integration for innovative and complex manufactured goods.

----

[14] Nicholas (1983) emphasized vertical foreign investment in distribution, following upon failed arm's-length contracts, as a critical step in the development of many British MNEs.

[15] Also, Jarrett (1979, Chapter 3) found that the extent of foreign investment by U.S. industries increases with the percentage of their product lines deemed to require frequent or extensive sales or technical services to customers. This influence is significant with other influences such as advertising and research intensity taken into account.

Statistical evidence on U.S. exports and imports passing between corporate affiliates sheds light on this mixture of vertical and horizontal foreign investment. Lall (1978*b*) analyzed the factors determining the extent of U.S. MNEs' exports to their affiliates (normalized either by their total exports or by their affiliates' total production). He could not discriminate between two hypotheses that together have significant force: (1) That trade is internalized where highly innovative and specialized goods are involved, and (2) that trade is internalized where the ultimate sales to final buyers must be attended by extensive customer engineering and after-sales services. Jarrett (1979, Chapter 2; also see Helleiner and Lavergne, 1979) confirmed these hypotheses with respect to the importance in U.S. imports of interaffiliate trade, which in his data includes exports by foreign MNEs to their manufacturing and marketing subsidiaries in the United States as well as imports by U.S. MNEs from their overseas affiliates. Jarrett also found evidence that interaffiliate trade in manufactures reflects several conventional forms of vertical integration: More of it occurs in industries populated (in the United States) by large plants and companies, capable of meeting the scale-economy problems that arise in the international disintegration of production, and in industries that carry out extensive multiplant operations in the United States.

Sleuwaegen and Yamawaki (1991) showed that the prevalence of Japanese foreign investment in U.S. distribution (relative to manufacturing) is greater for durable and heterogeneous goods that cannot be promoted to buyers simply through media advertising. The productivity of foreign investments into forward integrated distribution activities is shown directly by Yamawaki's (1991) finding that such investments in the U.S. distribution sector contributed substantially to increasing Japanese exports to the United States. As Williamson and Yamawaki (1991) showed, these investments get the foreign MNE over a substantial entry barrier into distribution that provides rents to manufacturers who surmount it.

The entwining of vertical and horizontal relations has important corollaries for the behavior of MNEs that will emerge in later chapters. For example, it suggests why the expansion of output by foreign subsidiaries can coincide with expansion of the parent's production for export to the same market. A purely horizontal relation between parent and subsidiary implies that their outputs will be substitutes for one another, whereas the confluence of horizontal and vertical relations raises the possibility that they are complementary within the MNE. Evidence lending some support to this proposition will be reviewed in Chapters 2 and 5.

1.3. **Portfolio diversification and the diversified MNE**

This section completes the roster of international multiplant firms by accounting for those whose international plants have no evident horizontal or vertical relationship. An obvious explanation of this type of MNE (though not the only one, it turns out) lies in the spreading of business risks. Going multinational in any form brings some diversification gains to the enterprise, and these reach their maximum when the firm diversifies across "product space" as well as geographical space.

Economic analysis normally assumes that individual investors are risk averse and hence seek to compose portfolios of assets so as to eliminate non-systemic risks associated with particular securities (companies), leaving them to face only system-wide risks. For this purpose the international diversification of portfolios holds an obvious attraction, although that process might be inhibited by various factors discussed in Chapter 6.

Given the diversification achieved by shareholders, the value-maximizing firm's management selects a risk/return trade-off that values risk at the market price of residual, systemic risk (Greenberg et al., 1978). It is widely recognized, however, that firms might behave as if averse to risks specific to the enterprise itself. This behavior could result even with optimal principal-agent contracts between the firm's owners and its manager, because risks to the firm's survival threaten its employees with large adjustment costs. Also, the firm as a working coalition of heterogeneous inputs – a characterization notably consistent with the standard model of the horizontal MNE – has a substantial organizational investment at hazard of obsolescence. The likely reaction of MNEs to opportunities for international diversification can be viewed against this background. On the one hand, individual foreign investments might be regarded as particularly risky. Risks arise in the behavior of host-country governments that in many ways can disfavor an alien firm lacking local support (this problem is discussed in Chapter 4). Also, information on the host-country market is more costly to the foreign investor than to the native; even after rational investments in information, the MNE settles for incomplete knowledge and hence exposes its investment to a greater variance of expected outcomes. On the other hand, the firm that makes investments in several national markets should enjoy diversification gains, benefiting not only itself but also shareholders if they are constrained from international diversification (Chapter 6).

Now we consider empirical evidence on diversification as a motive for the MNE. Within a national economy, many shocks affect all firms rather similarly – recessions, major changes in macroeconomic policy. Between countries, such disturbances are more nearly uncorrelated. Also, changes in exchange rates and terms of trade tend to favor business profits in one country while worsening them elsewhere.[16] Statistical evidence confirms that MNEs enjoy gains from diversification: The larger the share of foreign operations in total sales, the lower the variability of the firm's rate of return on equity capi-

---

[16] See Rugman (1979), especially Chapters 2 and 4.

tal (Cohen, 1972; Rugman, 1979, Chapter 3; Miller and Pras, 1980).[17] MNEs also enjoy lower levels of risk in the sense relevant to the stock market – financial risk (beta), according to Hughes et al. (1975), Thompson (1985), and Michel and Shaked (1986). Jacquillat and Solnik (1978) investigated the degree to which large MNEs based in Europe and America can be regarded as "walking mutual funds" that are diversified across national economies. They found that the rates of return on the market values of their firms' equity shares are still quite closely tied to economic conditions in their national home markets, excepting only the MNEs based in the smaller European countries. In general, this evidence supports the hypothesis that the MNE attains appreciable international diversification. However, the diversification might result from investments that were propelled by other motives; whether foreign direct investment yields diversification gains for which shareholders will pay is considered in Chapter 6.

Some further evidence on MNEs' diversification can be found in specific transactions that have potentials for spreading risk. The most diversification should accrue to the MNE that acquires a foreign subsidiary diversified in product line as well as geographical space. If diversification motivates foreign investment, we should find some of this "double diversification" in MNEs' structures. Early surveys (Barlow and Wender, 1955, p. 159) asserted that diversified foreign investment is a rare phenomenon. Caves (1975) and Dubin (1976, Chapter 6) found statistical evidence that MNEs' activities are more diversified among products on their national home ground than in foreign subsidiaries, confirming the impression from surveys (Dunning, 1958, pp. 115–18; Safarian, 1966, p. 211; Saham, 1980, pp. 172–5). Apparently the extra costs and risks of adding activities abroad look unappetizing to the firm that seeks diversification from whatever source;[18] also, minor related products in the firm's line tend to get made at the home base.

Nonetheless, there is evidence that diversifying in domestic product markets and investing abroad are alternatives for mature companies (Caves, 1975; Wolf, 1977) even though in uncontrolled samples the larger and more mature firms will have expanded in both directions (Pearce, 1993). Also, specifically diversified foreign investments are growing more numerous. Kopits (1979) found

[17] Miller and Pras (1980) found that the variability of operating income for U.S. MNEs is negatively related to both their sizes and the numbers of foreign countries in which they have subsidiaries; they also concluded that being diversified among heterogeneous regions offers more stabilization than being in closely similar countries. Oddly, with these influences controlled, they did not find significant stabilization of profits due to the companies' exports and their product-market diversifications in the United States.

[18] If foreign investment typically had diversification value that offset its specific risks, we should expect MNEs to accept lower expected rates of return on foreign investments than on domestic investments. But survey evidence, such as that of Barlow and Wender (1955, p. 114), points to a higher minimum for foreign investments.

that the diversified foreign investment of U.S. MNEs in 1968 was positively related to the extent of R&D activities in the U.S. base industry of the parent (company size and seller concentration were also controlled in this regression analysis but did not prove significant). The result agrees with the hypothesis that a firm's research activities often produce proprietary assets useful outside its base industry; these should lead to international diversification, just as they promote diversification at home (also see Pearce, 1993). In this vein Hisey and Caves (1985) analyzed a sample of international acquisitions by U.S. companies that could be classified as either related or unrelated diversifications relative to the acquirers' U.S. activities. The unrelated ones are significantly associated with risk-spreading properties, the related ones only weakly with spillovers of proprietary assets among product markets. Kim et al. (1993) undertook an elaborate analysis of the means and standard deviations of U.S. MNEs' returns on assets in the 1980s, estimating how each firm's risk/return pattern differs from that of its (U.S.) industry and relating the residuals to the properties of the firms' diversification patterns. They found (consistent with Hisey and Caves) that MNEs that are highly diversified geographically had apparently located an attractive niche of high returns coupled with low risks. Other groups of MNEs reveal the trade-off normally expected: Either low risks and returns (with high unrelated product diversification but low diversification of other types) or high risks and returns (with high related and low unrelated product diversification).

Some other hypotheses not covered in this statistical analysis also help to explain MNEs' diversification. U.S. MNEs make a somewhat larger proportion of diversified foreign investments in less-developed countries (LDCs) than in industrial countries. This is probably due to controls imposed by LDC governments on the remittance of profits by MNEs operating within their boundaries; restricted from repatriating its profits, the MNE's best alternative might be to invest in some diversifying activity within the country. Another explanatory factor is the large wave of conglomerate mergers that took place in the United States in the 1960s and 1970s. Suppose that firm B, either a horizontal or a vertical MNE, is acquired by the larger firm A. If A's base industry remains the principal activity of the merged firm, B's overseas assets will appear to be a diversified foreign investment of the merged firm. Or if A diversifies domestically, whether by merger or otherwise, its diversified domestic division might later sprout a horizontal foreign subsidiary, making the firm as a whole appear (to the statistician) diversified internationally.[19]

---

[19] For evidence, see Horst (1974a, pp. 110–11). That overseas diversification represents some kind of optimizing global calculation is suggested by Gorecki's finding (1980) that the diversification levels of Canadian domestic firms can be explained by Canadian market variables, whereas the diversification levels in Canada of foreign subsidiaries operating there cannot.

1.4. Summary

The existence of the MNE is best explained by identifying it as a multiplant firm that sprawls across national boundaries, then applying the transaction-cost approach to explain why dispersed plants should fall under common ownership and control rather than simply trade with each other (and with other agents) on the open market. This approach is readily applied to the horizontal MNE (its national branches produce largely the same products), because the economies of multiplant operation can be identified with use of the firm's proprietary assets, which suffer many infirmities for trade at arm's length. This hypothesis receives strong support in statistical studies, with regard both to intangible assets and to capabilities possessed by the firm.

A second major type of MNE is the vertically integrated firm, and several economic models of vertical integration stand ready to explain its existence. Once again, the transaction-cost approach holds a good deal of power, because vertical MNEs in the natural-resources sector seem to respond to the difficulties of working out arm's-length contracts in small-numbers situations where each party has a transaction-specific investment at stake. Evading problems of impacted information also seems to explain some vertical foreign investment. The approach also works well to explain the rapid growth of offshore procurement by firms in industrial countries, which involves carrying out labor-intensive stages of production at foreign locations with low labor costs. Although procurement occurs through arm's-length contracts as well as foreign investment, the role of foreign investment is clearly large. Finally, numerous vertical transactions flow between the units of apparently horizontal MNEs as the foreign subsidiary undertakes final fabrication, fills out its line with imports from its corporate affiliates, or provides ancillary services that complement these imports.

Diversified foreign investments, which have grown rapidly in recent decades, suggest that foreign investment serves as a means of spreading risks to the firm. Foreign investment, whether diversified from the parent's domestic product line or not, apparently does offer some diversification value. Diversified foreign investments can be explained in part by the parent's efforts to utilize its diverse R&D discoveries, and certain other influences as well. However, other diversified investments appear specifically aimed at spreading risks through international diversification, especially among geographic markets.

2

The MNE and models of international economic activity

In Chapter 1 we presented a microeconomic view of the MNE based on the theory of economic organization. Yet foreign direct investment was traditionally a concern of international economics, a branch disposed to use general-equilibrium tools for explaining economy-wide or worldwide phenomena: nations' patterns of commodity trade, the allocation of their endowments of factors of production, and the functional distribution of income. Does international economics offer a distinctive and sufficient explanation of MNEs to place against the organizational explanation from Chapter 1? If so, which has the more explanatory power? If not, how can organizational models of the MNE be consistently embedded within models of international production and exchange?

2.1. Foreign direct investment and international capital flows

The key junction between international economics and the MNE is the export of equity capital that occurs when a company starts a foreign subsidiary. International flows of capital are a central concern of international economists, who long explained the MNE as simply an arbitrager of equity capital from countries where its return is low to countries where it is high. If the differing rates of return to capital that induce these movements correspond to differences in the social marginal productivity of capital, then the MNE's activity also raises the world's real income.

This approach ties the MNE to a considerable body of general-equilibrium theory about the interrelationships of international trade, international movements of factors of production, and the distribution of income (see Section 2.3). Furthermore, this body of theory has many empirical implications: MNEs should be based in the countries best endowed with capital (where its domestic marginal productivity is therefore the lowest). They should move capital toward the countries least well endowed with capital (with, presumptively, the highest marginal products of capital). But the theoretical role of the MNE as a capital arbitrager was neither developed analytically nor tested empirically. This tranquil if unsatisfactory situation was assaulted by Hymer (1960), who argued that the capital-arbitrage hypothesis was inconsistent with several obvious patterns in the behavior of MNEs:

1. The United States had long shown net exports of foreign direct investment but net inflows of portfolio capital. How could equity capital be cheap and portfolio capital dear in the United States, relative to the rest of the world, unless American investors were exceptionally keen to take risks?

2. MNEs move in both directions across national boundaries, and some countries are both home bases for many MNEs and hosts to many subsidiaries controlled abroad. If MNEs merely arbitrage capital, then rates of return to capital must be high in some industries in each country and low in others. How could this pattern arise unless national capital markets are balkanized?

3. If foreign direct investment were pure arbitrage of capital, large financial intermediaries should be prominent participants. However, nonfinancial companies make up most of the crowd, and the profits that they earn in particular markets hardly have an intimate relationship to the long-term rate of interest – which should represent a nation's marginal product of capital.

Hymer not only decked the capital-arbitrage explanation for foreign direct investment but also laid the foundations for a microeconomic explanation of the MNE by pointing out that they are not randomly distributed among industries and that competitive conditions, in particular product markets, clearly influence foreign investment. His and subsequent microeconomic explanations of foreign direct investment still assume that the MNE goes abroad to raise its total profit, but they recognize that differences between countries in some overall marginal product of capital are neither necessary nor sufficient. Specifically, the capital-arbitrage hypothesis runs into trouble on two points.

First, an international difference in expected profits does not suffice to induce foreign direct investment. Suppose that a given industry in each of two countries is organized on the classic model of pure competition. Let demand for the industry's product increase abroad, so that the price rises there and the existing firms make excess profits in the short run. Do the firms in the domestic industry now turn themselves into horizontal MNEs? The proprietary-assets model of Chapter 1 says no. A purely competitive industry has ample new local entrants to compete down the windfall profits in the foreign market. And purely competitive firms by definition lack any unique rent-yielding assets that offset the intrinsic disadvantages and transactions costs of operating in a foreign environment. As Hymer (1960, Chapter 1) and Kindleberger (1969, Chapter 1) argued, MNEs are logically incompatible with purely competitive organization of an industry. There must be something else to account for the rise of MNEs, so the capital-arbitrage hypothesis is not sufficient. Hufbauer (1975, pp. 261–3) showed formally that foreign investment depends on demand elasticities and production-function parameters, not just capital-cost differences.

One can also argue that the capital-arbitrage hypothesis is not necessary. From habits of thought and accounting, we identify the rents earned by proprietary assets as excess returns to capital. However, they are pure rents (or quasi rents) that are tied to capital only in the sense that risks associated with their use and transfer are borne by equity capital. That function is consistent with equity capital earning the same (risk-adjusted) return in all uses in every country.

For all these reasons the capital-arbitrage hypothesis was swept from the field by the transaction-cost approach set forth in Chapter 1. Empirical investigations resting solely on the arbitrage hypothesis accordingly have not fared well. Capital intensity per se is never a significant predictor of which industries are prone to heavy involvement with foreign direct investment.[1] When the flow of foreign investment from the United States to Europe increased considerably from the 1950s to the 1960s, D'Arge (1969) and Bandera and White (1968) sought to determine whether this increase corresponded to an increase in the profit rate on U.S. investments abroad relative to that at home. They found the statistical relation insignificant or even perverse: the foreign profit differential seemed to fall just as foreign investment was increasing. However, that pattern naturally reflects the low short-run cash-flow profits expected for new foreign investments: some subsidiaries fail in these risky ventures, and others run substantial shakedown losses.[2] Rapidly increasing foreign investment raises the proportion of the population of subsidiaries that is young and still in the shakedown period or fated to exit, and average accounting profits appear to be falling. Better controlled studies have confirmed the expected positive relationship of foreign investment to profit differentials; at the same time, theoretical research on corporate finance has shown that the risk-averse MNE need not do all its borrowing in the cheapest place (see Chapter 6). Finally, Wilkins (1986) examined the histories of some MNEs that had operated purely as arbitragers of finance and showed their success rate to be negligible. Clearly, the capital-arbitrage hypothesis, without something more, is neither satisfying theoretically nor confirmed empirically.

Nonetheless, once we accept the necessary role of the transaction-cost approach, international economics helps in several ways to explain the existence and behavior of MNEs. Section 2.2 is concerned with the relationship between exporting and direct investment at the level of the individual enterprise. Sec-

---

[1] There is no difference in capital intensity between foreign-investing sectors and others in either source countries (U.S. Tariff Commission, 1973; Juhl, 1979) or host countries. (O'Loughlin and O'Farrell, 1980, did find MNEs in the more capital-intensive Irish industries, but they are no more capital-intensive than Irish firms in those industries.)

[2] This pattern has been suggested by many surveys such as Ågren (1990) and demonstrated statistically by Lupo et al. (1978). See Caves (1994).

tion 2.3 takes up general-equilibrium models that are useful for understanding the causes and consequences of MNEs. Section 2.4 considers the relevant empirical evidence on the distribution of MNEs' activities among countries.

2.2. The choice between exporting and foreign direct investment

This section develops an important extension of the proprietary-assets model from Chapter 1. The firm equipped with such an asset enjoys several possible ways to claim rents in a foreign market. The product embodying the asset can be produced by a foreign subsidiary for local sale. It can be licensed for local production by an independent firm. Or it can be produced in the asset-holding firm's base location and exported. The proprietary-assets model thus identifies exporting and direct investment as alternative strategies for the potential MNE. An immediate corollary is that forces restricting trade encourage foreign investment in those sectors where foreign investment is an option. Tariffs protecting a national market from imports therefore encourage direct investment.

Theoretical models of the firm's decision

The behavior of the profit-maximizing MNE in the face of tariffs was worked out by Horst (1971; see also Copithorne, 1971), and a simple version of his analysis is presented here (based on Horst, 1973).[3] Assume that the MNE can sell its product in two countries, Home and Foreign, and faces a downward-sloping demand curve in each market. Its costs of production in each country depend on the amount produced there, and we are interested in cases of both diminishing returns (marginal costs increase with output) and increasing returns (marginal costs decline as output increases). The firm is assumed to maximize its total profit. Home is the MNE's base, and Figure 2.1 is constructed so that the firm will always maintain production there; the question is whether it supplies Foreign by export or local production. Panel A of Figure 2.1 shows the market in Home and the firm's marginal cost (c_1), demand (p_1), and marginal revenue (r_1) curves. If it sold only in the domestic market, it would produce the quantity indicated by the intersection of r_1 and c_1. Panel C similarly shows demand conditions in Foreign and the firm's marginal cost function (c_2) if it becomes a MNE and undertakes production. Panel B contains a construction that brings this information together. First, if the firm starts to export from Home, it will incur rising marginal costs as output expands and higher marginal revenue as the number of units sold to Home's buyers contracts. Suppose (contrary to assumption) that the firm faced a fixed price of M at which it could sell abroad. Then it would choose to produce Q_1 in 1, selling S_1 of it at home and exporting S_1Q_1. The domestic price would become P_1 instead of the lower price that would prevail if there were no exports. Curve c_x in panel B is what Horst

---

[3] Also see Hirsch (1976) and Rugman (1980*b*, Part I).

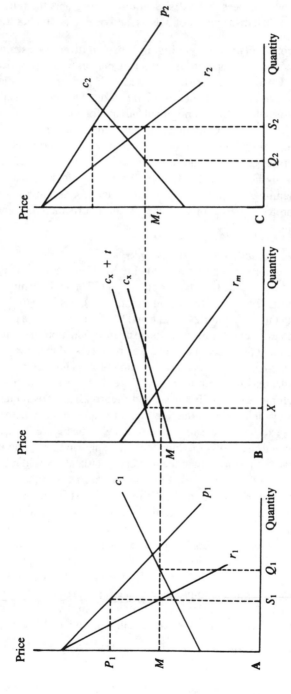

Figure 2.1. A: Revenue and cost functions in Home country. B: Intrafirm trade. C: Revenue and cost functions in Foreign country.

calls the marginal cost of exporting from the home country, and it illustrates the quantity that would be exported for each price like M. From panel C we derive an analogous construction by allowing the firm the (imaginary) possibility of importing various quantities of its product for resale at prices such as M_t. If M_t is less than the firm's no-imports level of marginal cost in local production, it transfers some imports, cutting back its local production and expanding its sales. Given M_t, the firm would produce Q_2 locally, sell S_2, and import Q_2S_2. The lower is M_t, the larger are its imports, and the more does its production in Foreign contract (eventually disappearing). By experimentally varying M_t, we construct the schedule r in panel B, which is the marginal revenue from importing into Foreign.

Only one more step is needed to complete this construction. Assume that Foreign imposes a tariff that elevates the delivered price of imports over their foreign price by an amount indicated by the shift from c_x to $c_x + t$ in panel B.[4] Now we have constructed schedules showing the firm's marginal revenue from importing (r_m) and its tariff-adjusted marginal cost of exporting ($c_x + t$). Just as it sets its domestic price in each market by selling the quantity that equates marginal revenue and marginal cost, so does it determine the amount of intracorporate exports. Equilibrium exports are X, and the quantities sold (S) and produced (Q) are shown in the Home and Foreign markets.

As Figure 2.1 is drawn, the firm serves Foreign partly by local production and partly through exports from Home. If Foreign raises its tariff, the MNE responds by increasing its local production and reducing its exports. But the MNE's locational decisions also reflect the difference in real costs between the two markets – the classic forces of comparative advantage (as costs affect the production pattern for the country as a whole) and absolute advantage (as these costs appear to producers in a particular industry). One other factor influences the outcome: The MNE cannot set prices in the two national markets so different that other parties find that it pays to arbitrage between them.

Horst also explored the case in which the MNE enjoys scale economies in production, so that the marginal cost curves slope downward rather than upward. In that case the firm will not both produce in a market and transfer exports to it. It might produce only in Home and export to Foreign, produce only in Foreign and export to Home, or produce in both but not export. Suppose that the firm initially produces only in Home. Foreign then imposes a high tariff. The firm might find that Foreign's market is most profitably served entirely by local production. Indeed, it might even shift *all* of its production to Foreign, serving Home's market with imports from Foreign (this would depend on Home's tariff). Another consequence of scale economies is that where the MNE

---

[4] This potential flow of exports, of course, is trade within the MNE, and so there may be no identifiable market price. That may be a problem for the tariff collector if t is expressed as an ad valorem tariff. Transfer pricing will be discussed in Chapter 8.

locates its production depends not just on tariffs and absolute advantage in production costs (at any given scale) but also on the sizes of Home's and Foreign's national markets. Make Home a large market, Foreign a small one. The firm could rationally locate all its production in Home, serving Foreign through exports, even though Foreign has an absolute advantage in production costs at any given scale. For this pattern to emerge, Home must impose a tariff high enough to discourage the location of all the firm's production in Foreign.[5]

Horst's partial-equilibrium approach was extended in a series of papers by Horstmann and Markusen (1987a, 1987b, 1992). They represented the MNE's proprietary-asset advantage by assuming that the firm incurs a fixed cost of operation as a company (F) and another fixed cost (G) for a plant in any national location; a potential local competitor in a host country must incur $F + G$ to start production, the MNE only F. Horstmann and Markusen (1992) developed the implications of Horst's decreasing-cost case, showing how the relative sizes of F, G, variable production cost, and transport costs (and tariffs) can determine whether a two-country world industry consists of two single-plant exporting firms, one MNE with two plants, or two MNEs. (Other results of Horstmann and Markusen will be noted subsequently.) In a similar paper Motta (1992) showed how unexpected shifts in the organization of such a world industry can occur as the size of the host country's market exogenously increases. Also, Ethier (1986) focused on the fact that the MNE's operation intrinsically requires incurring costs in two different countries (the proprietary asset in one, the good embodying it in another, when trade is infeasible). MNEs' activities can then be deterred when cost structures differ too much between the two countries, rendering unprofitable this two-stage process that starts with investment in the proprietary asset.[6]

Exports and foreign investment: joint determinants

If the (potential) MNE chooses the cost-minimizing way to serve any profitable foreign markets, then it should take simultaneous account of all the factors favoring the one or the other. Anything that favors foreign investment (such as tariffs) discourages the use of exports, and vice versa. As was noted in Chapter 1, many cross-section statistical studies of the determinants of foreign direct investment took some account of factors affecting the alternative flows of exports.[7] Others more properly regarded exports and foreign investment as

---

[5] Accordingly, research on production scales in Canada often has blamed the small scales prevailing there in part on the U.S. tariff (Wonnacott and Wonnacott, 1967).

[6] Itagaki (1987, 1991) developed the implication of risk aversion for the MNE's investment choice when foreign investment involves incurring first a fixed and then a variable production cost in a foreign market subject to a random outcome.

[7] Tariffs and other trade-related variables proved statistically insignificant in many of these studies. The misspecification of the model from not endogenizing exports is no doubt one explanation, but another misspecification is also common: relating the stock

jointly determined variables or analyzed determinants of the *relative* use of exporting and local-market production through affiliates.

Horst (1972*a*) originated this methodological approach, and Swedenborg (1979) used data on Swedish exports and foreign investment to provide a thorough application. She found that those Swedish industries with high levels of foreign investment tended also to have high levels of exports. However, the ratio of exports to total production for Swedish industries and the ratio of foreign production by subsidiaries to Swedish domestic production were influenced in opposite ways by certain forces. Notably, she found that industries whose plants are capital intensive and exhibit extensive economies of scale tend to export rather than invest abroad. She also concluded that both exports and foreign production are positively related to R&D activities and workers' skill levels in Sweden – indicators of the importance of proprietary assets. This finding agrees with various studies summarized in Chapter 1. A paper that is methodologically noteworthy in this literature is Grubert and Mutti (1991*a*), who demonstrated the appropriate use of exogenous policy instruments – host-country corporation income tax and tariff rates – to identify the models determining U.S. foreign investment in and exports to various host countries.

Other studies have confirmed and extended these results. Horst (1972*a*) found that the ratio of U.S. MNEs' exports to Canada divided by local sales by their subsidiaries was higher the smaller was the Canadian market relative to that of the United States, presumably indicating the deterrent effect of scale economies on Canadian production. Buckley and Pearce (1979) analyzed the exports and foreign-subsidiary sales of the world's largest manufacturing enterprises, noting that those most active in exporting and least active in foreign investment are based in sectors with the greatest apparent scale economies. Their data also confirm Horst's theoretical finding that scale economies can pull the MNE's production abroad rather than concentrating it at home. MNEs in some small countries (Benelux, Switzerland) exhibit high ratios of foreign-subsidiary sales to total sales (Sleuwaegen, 1988). Many studies have confirmed this finding indirectly by demonstrating that minimum efficient scale puts a lower bound on the size of the foreign investment transaction.[8] Andersson and Fredriksson (1993) demonstrated another aspect of this scale-efficiency effect: foreign subsidiaries of large MNEs export more, the fewer the countries in which their parents have subsidiaries. Presumably the relation re-

of foreign investment at a given time to tariff rates at that time. When foreign investment has accumulated over many years and is subject to sunk costs, it can appear unrelated to tariffs (or other current determinants of trade flows) even if that causal relation was active when the original investments were made. Studies that analyzed flows rather than stocks of foreign investment have been more successful (e.g., Caves and Mehra, 1986).

[8] For example, in the smaller industrial countries, foreign subsidiaries are on average larger than their national-firm competitors (Caves et al., 1980, Chapter 4, on Canada; Deane, 1970, pp. 64–5, on New Zealand; O'Loughlin and O'Farrell, 1980, on Ireland).

flects variation in the extent of scale economies and the incentive to locate production close to the site of consumption or use.

Other results link the relation between exports and foreign investment to specific structural differences among industries. Lall (1980) found that the ratio of U.S. MNEs' exports to the sum of their exports and foreign-subsidiary sales increases with the importance of their R&D expenditures but is negatively related to the importance of advertising expenditures; high advertising levels indicate traits of buyers' behavior that encourage local production and discourage serving the market from abroad. Kravis and Lipsey (1992) confirmed these results and added labor intensity as a negative factor. Caves et al. (1980, Chapter 4) analyzed imports into Canada and subsidiaries' shares in the Canadian market as jointly determined parts of a larger cross-sectional model. They reported at least weak evidence that advertising intensity discourages imports and encourages direct investment (see also Owen, 1982); scale economies (inferred from U.S. production patterns) favor imports, whereas tariffs and transportation costs deter them (the statistical significance of these last findings is marginal). However, the R&D level is positively related to both exports and foreign investment, a finding echoed by Buckley and Pearce (1979) and Lall (1980).

Brainard (1993c) provided a capstone to this line of research with an investigation in cross section of flows of trade and subsidiaries' sales in both directions between the U.S. and 27 other countries in 64 industries. For the typical country/industry cell she found that sales by subsidiaries of U.S. MNEs (as a proportion of those sales plus U.S. exports) increases significantly with the cost of transporting goods between the United States and the foreign country, tariff protection of the foreign market, and the host nation's openness to foreign direct investment. It decreases with production scale economies and recent appreciation of the host's currency relative to the U.S. dollar. U.S. R&D levels and physical distance strongly affect whether *some* subsidiary sales are recorded for a country/industry cell, but they do not appear in the model of the subsidiaries' sales share. For flows into the United States the same relationships generally hold. Brainard regards these findings as strongly confirming the MNE's trade-off between the cost saving from concentrating production at one location and the artificial and natural transportation cost that such concentration entails.

Much research has addressed trade flows within MNEs (intrafirm or interaffiliate trade – see Hipple, 1990, and UNCTC, 1988b, p. 92, on its importance). The results are difficult to interpret, because they usually amount to correlations among jointly determined variables, but they shed some light on how location factors determine foreign investment. Zejan (1989) studied the imports by Swedish MNEs' subsidiaries from their parents (normalized by the subsidiaries' sales), finding that they decrease with the proportion of the parent's global assets that are located outside of Sweden; this relation can reflect simply the degree to which the parent has substituted host-country production for production in Sweden as a way to serve local markets. Similarly, a foreign subsidiary's dependence on imports from its parent increases with the parent's capital intensity, an indicator of the degree to which scale economies deter the decentralization of production (Zejan's own interpretation of these results is rather different). Zejan, like nearly all other researchers, found intrafirm trade to increase with the parent's research intensity, presumably indicating the parent's disincentive either to decentralize production of innovative goods (see Chapter 7) or to trade them at arm's length. Sleuwaegen (1985) traced the positive influence of R&D intensity on interaffiliate trade in both intermediate and final goods.[9]

Another general finding is that subsidiaries are more likely to be involved in exporting and/or importing than are comparable domestic host-country enterprises (e.g., van den Bulcke, 1985, pp. 271–2; MacCharles, 1987; Willmore, 1992). A sufficient explanation is that multinationality lowers the fixed cost of engaging in international transactions, which presumably exceeds that of establishing a comparable flow of transactions in the business's domestic market. Whether the involvement entails exporting, importing, or both depends on the business's activity (within its MNE's family of affiliates) interacting with the nation's comparative advantage structure. The heavy participation of foreign subsidiaries in trade and the complementarity of interaffiliate trade with their local production (and sales) activities is well established. Using Swedish data Swedenborg (1985, pp. 233–6) showed that Swedish exports to foreign affiliates increase significantly with the affiliates' production, while Swedish exports to unaffiliated parties decrease with the affiliates' output.

Interaffiliate trade attracted the rather ill-conceived hypothesis that it would adjust tardily to short-run disturbances, compared to interfirm trade, because of the bureaucratic sloth of large enterprises. One could just as well hypothesize more rapid adjustments as a corollary of efficiently internalized transactions. Rangan and Lawrence (1993) demonstrated the responsiveness of intrafirm trade to exchange-rate movements. Goldsbrough (1981) noted that intrafirm trade flows are likely to involve more distinctive and less substitutable goods than arm's-length trade, so that it should differ not in its elasticity but in its predictability; that hypothesis was confirmed.[10]

[9] Also see Pearce (1993, Chapter 3) and Siddharthan and Kumar (1990). Benvignati (1990) is an exception, but she did not control for the extent of (U.S.) parents' assets placed abroad to receive the intrafirm trade.

[10] There have also been studies indicating that MNEs' total trade flows are no less sensitive to macroeconomic variables than those of domestic firms (Lipsey, 1993; Blomström and Lipsey, 1993). It is not obvious why any difference should be expected.

Differences in production costs: comparative statics

The MNE's decision where to locate production should be determined by differences among candidate locations in production costs (converted to a common currency). This hypothesis has not been much tested, perhaps because it is obvious, perhaps because appropriate unit-cost data are seldom available. The hypothesis is a bit less obvious than it seems. Maki and Meredith (1986) pointed out that MNEs might transfer production from a low-cost to a high-cost location if their proprietary assets embrace the ability to transfer their source-country cost advantages. Maki and Meredith's measurement of cost advantages is biased in favor of this hypothesis, so their confirmation of it should be discounted, but the possibility that proprietary assets' effects might swamp nominal cost differences remains. The most useful evidence on cost differences and location choices comes from studies of changes due to exchange-rate movements. Cushman (1985; also Batra and Hadar, 1979) showed that how exchange-rate changes affect foreign investment depends on the activity that the subsidiary will undertake: permanent depreciation of the host's currency encourages investments in facilities to produce exports from the host and discourages investments in fabricating externally sourced inputs to supply the host market, while temporary depreciation encourages arbitrage-type transactions.

Empirical research on actual changes in nominal or real effective exchange rates has generally confirmed that depreciation of a host-country's currency encourages foreign-investment inflows while depreciation of a source country's discourages outflows. Goldsbrough (1979) found that foreign-investment inflows and outflows of the major industrial countries depend significantly on movements of relative exchange-rate adjusted unit labor costs. Caves (1989) observed that, among source countries, flows from the smaller and newer foreign investors were more sensitive to the dollar exchange rate than were established investors engaged mainly in plowing back funds to existing foreign investments. Other empirical confirmation of exchange-rate sensitivity include Kohlhagen (1977), Ray (1989), and Brainard (1993c).

Evidence on tariffs and foreign investment

A great deal of survey and anecdotal evidence confirms the influence of tariffs on MNEs' locational decisions, not least because many trade restrictions have sought just that result. Countries such as Canada and Australia used tariff increases to encourage the growth of local production. Firms that had established markets for their exports then found it more profitable to establish production facilities behind the tariff wall than to write off their investment in the local market or continue to serve it from lower-cost locations abroad. This pattern was confirmed in numerous studies, such as those of Brash (1966, Chapter 3), Deane (1969), Saham (1980, pp. 69–70), Nicholas (1986), and

Ågren (1990). Studies of import restrictions by the United States repeatedly conclude that they induce large inflows of foreign investment, sometimes on the basis of mere threats (Burton and Saelens, 1987; Yoffie, 1993). Wilkins (1974, pp. 172–3) found the effect operating even in the depths of the depressed 1930s, when foreign countries elevated tariffs by enough to cause many U.S. MNEs to create or expand subsidiaries behind the tariff barriers. The influence has been confirmed in some statistical studies of the shares of host-country markets held by MNEs through exports and through local production. The higher the host country's tariff protecting the industry, the larger the fraction of MNEs' sales should be accounted for by local production. Horst (1972*a*) reported this result for U.S. exports to Canada,[11] and Swedenborg (1979, Chapter 5) confirmed the finding for Swedish exports and foreign investment. Brainard (1993*c*) provided a broad confirmation for U.S. inflows and outflows.

Many less-developed countries have followed the policy of attracting MNEs first with tariff protection and quantitative restrictions on imports, then inducing them to expand their investments by means of domestic-content requirements and other such devices (see Chapter 9). For example, Reuber et al. (1973, pp. 120–32) and Guisinger et al. (1985) found that substantial proportions of foreign investments had benefited from tariff or quota protection on their outputs and tariff concessions on their imports of inputs or machinery.

This relationship between trade barriers and foreign investment has also been explored through the analysis of changes over time – especially in the formation of the European Community (now European Union), whose members eliminated trade restrictions among themselves while maintaining a standardized set of trade barriers against imports from the rest of the world (see Yannopoulos, 1990, for a general survey). For potential multinational companies based outside the Community, the creation of this enlarged internal market should have increased the desirability of producing within the Community relative to exporting to it. That is because the enlarged market permitted some firms to attain efficient scale in European production and thus lower net costs of goods sold in Europe, even if the tariffs charged on imports from outside the Community were unchanged (their average level in fact did not change). Schmitz and Bieri (1972; see also Schmitz, 1970) examined the share of U.S. foreign direct investment going to European countries that took part in tariff-preference arrangements, finding an acceleration of the upward trend in U.S. foreign direct investment and a deceleration of the trend in U.S. exports. Scaperlanda and Balough (1983) found that (with other forces controlled) U.S. plant and equipment investment in Community manufacturing industries increased with an indicator of the Community's tariff discrimination against imports from

---

[11] Horst's results were not confirmed in a replication by Orr (1975), and several other studies failed to confirm the hypothesis; however, misspecifications are common in this literature.

outside. Blair (1987) concluded that accession to the Community by the United Kingdom (a mature host country) diverted U.S. investment toward the continental countries,[12] and Sleuwaegen (1984, 1988) demonstrated how the Community's formation directed foreign investment to small countries such as Belgium which now gained a locational advantage for serving the whole Community (see also Cantwell, 1989, Chapter 4).

A seeming corollary is that among Community countries internal free trade should cause production to expand at efficient locations and exports to substitute for foreign subsidiaries' production. The evidence does not support the prediction, but for explicable reasons. Sleuwaegen (1988) showed that intra-Community subsidiaries commonly were started by means of acquisitions and receive heavy interaffiliate imports from their parents; hence, their principal role is as marketing arm for parents not previously serving the market. Cantwell (1988) also associated intra-Community investments in some industries with rationalizing locations and concentrating production for scale efficiencies. Molle and Morsink (1991) confirmed the complementarity between foreign-investment flows and trade among Community members but also found that physical and cultural distance deter foreign investment. The further unification that occurred with the creation of the European Union in 1992 greatly increased rather than decreased cross-border foreign investment within the Union (UNCTC, 1990).[13]

In summary, we have combined the transaction-cost model of the MNE from Chapter 1 with locational forces identified by international economics to deduce that exports and horizontal foreign investment should be substitutes for one another. The evidence confirms the proposition, subject to two qualifying comments. First, this substitution does not apply to interaffiliate trade, which is a complex consequence of both organizational and locational forces. Second, an alternative to foreign investment and exports among the ways to serve foreign markets remains to be considered: licensing the firm's proprietary assets to an arm's-length producer in another country (see Section 7.2).

2.3. Foreign investment and resource allocation in the world economy

International economics does not offer a fundamental explanation for MNEs, but it does contribute substantially to explaining their scope of operation through the trade-off between exports and foreign investment. More than that, the general-equilibrium models of international economics provide a

---

[12] Community nontariff barriers exerted some pull on British (preaccession) foreign investments in the Community, according to Millington and Bayliss (1991), although a weak influence relation to transaction-cost factors.

[13] Useful studies of individual industries appear in Dunning and Robson (1988).

framework for understanding certain aggregate causes and consequences of the MNE's international movement of resources that are implied by the partial-equilibrium transaction-cost models. For example, they explain the price adjustments that ultimately limit profitable flows of direct investment.

Basic general-equilibrium tools

Most of the model building that allows us to pursue the MNE into the context of general equilibrium builds on the Heckscher-Ohlin model, a textbook staple in international economics. The model's advantage for this purpose is that it concentrates on the interrelationship between a nation's pattern of international trade and its endowment of factors of production (including capital). It can therefore be used to explore the consequences of international movements of factors of production – the MNE's transfer of capital – by identifying them as changes in the factor endowments of the sending and receiving countries. The relationship between trade and foreign investment can be fully developed and effects deduced of foreign investment on rewards of factors of production and thus the distribution of income.

In its simplest form the Heckscher-Ohlin model assumes that the world consists of two countries, Home and Foreign. Two commodities, food and clothing, are produced and traded. Each nation has a given endowment of two factors of production, labor and capital. A crucial assumption of the model is that the production functions of food and clothing differ in their requirements of capital and labor; let us suppose that for any given prices of these factors, food production uses proportionally more capital per worker employed than does clothing. The Heckscher-Ohlin model also assumes that a good's production function is the same in each country: A given number of units of capital and of labor produce the same number of clothing (or food) units, both at home and abroad. Markets for products and factors of production are assumed to be perfectly competitive, and transportation costs are ignored.

Some key features of the model's treatment of the domestic economy can be reviewed in terms of the transformation (or production possibility) curve for the home country, shown in Figure 2.2. That curve shows all combinations of food and clothing that can be produced efficiently with the home country's assumed stocks of labor and capital – "efficiently" meaning that any increase in the output of one good can be accomplished only by cutting production of the other. One condition for efficient production is that the value of the marginal product of labor in food be the same as the marginal product of labor in clothing, and the same for capital. In the absence of international trade, the amount of each good produced equals the amount consumed, and demand conditions determine which point is chosen on transformation curve *FC*. Let us suppose that it might be either *A* (much food consumed, little clothing) or *B* (much clothing, little food). In order to see how output and factor use are interrelated, assume that

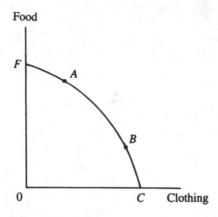

Figure 2.2

equilibrium was at *A* but now shifts to *B* because of a change in consumers' tastes. The shift in preferences toward clothing raises the price of clothing relative to that of food. Output declines in food, the capital-intensive sector, and expands in labor-intensive clothing. Whatever wages (to labor) and rentals (to capital) levels prevailed at *A* will be thrown out of equilibrium by the change, because the contracting food industry discharges a lot of capital, whereas the expanding clothing industry seeks to hire a lot of labor. Therefore, wages rise relative to capital rentals. This link between production (product prices) and factor rewards obviously has some significance for the incentive to undertake foreign investment.

If the home country in fact trades with the foreign country, equilibrium in the model is depicted in Figure 2.3. Each country produces at some point *P* or *P** on its own transformation curve, but the processes of international exchange determine some equilibrium point *T* that describes the (different) bundle of goods that each country consumes. As Figure 2.3 is drawn, the transformation curve for the foreign country *F*C** is shown upside down, with its production point *P** superimposed on *P* for the home country. The home country produces a lot of food and a little clothing (*P*), exporting food and importing clothing to achieve the bundle of goods consumed depicted at *T*. Likewise, from the foreign country's viewpoint, a high level of domestic clothing production (*P**) is converted through trade into the consumption bundle *T*.

We have not explained exactly how the equilibrium associated with *P*, *P**, and *T* gets established; we simply assume it is an equilibrium and note some of its properties. A sufficient reason for the equilibrium to involve this trade pattern is that the home country is relatively well endowed with capital (used heavily in food production) and the foreign country in labor (used heavily in

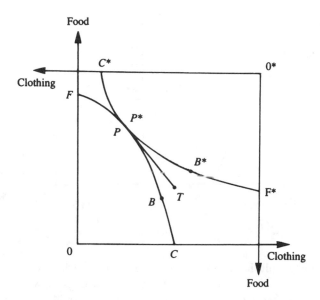

Figure 2.3

clothing). Home has a comparative advantage in food, Foreign in clothing. If *P* and *T* represent an equilibrium for Home, consumption without any international trade would occur at a point like *B* (Home consumes more of both food and clothing at *T* than at *B*; those are the "gains from trade"). When production shifts from *B* to *P*, as trade is established, the relative price of food rises in Home, and therefore capital rentals rise relative to wages. In Foreign, the opposite process takes place: At *B**, clothing was cheaper than in equilibrium with international trade at *P**, and the shift of production from *B** to *P** raises wages relative to capital rentals. Indeed, with further assumptions, it can be shown that introducing trade not only pulls factor rewards in different countries in opposite directions but also brings them into absolute equality – that Home and Foreign wages become equal in equilibrium with unrestricted international trade, as do Home and Foreign capital rentals. If foreign investment took place in such an equilibrium, it would leave world output unchanged.

These fundamentals support some propositions about international factor movements and the MNE. Suppose that no international trade takes place, so that both countries are consuming outputs indicated by *B* and *B**, and factor payments are in equilibrium accordingly. Now, permit capital to move internationally. Without trade, capital earns less in capital-rich Home than in capital-short Foreign. Therefore, foreign investment is induced to flow from Home to Foreign. Because the transformation curves depend on the factor endowments,

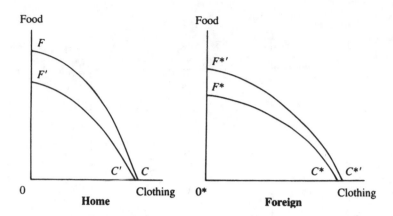

Figure 2.4

the capital transfer will shift them as shown in Figure 2.4, from FC to $F'C'$ and from F^*C^* to $F'C'$. The discrepancy in capital's earnings between the two countries will be reduced, possibly eliminated. The shift provides a real-income gain for whatever owners move their capital from Home to Foreign, and it indeed raises the rentals accruing to *all* capital in Home. But the erstwhile scarce units of native capital in Foreign lose – the inflow from abroad bids down their reward. Labor is also affected in both countries. Home's labor finds less capital to collaborate with in production, and so its wage falls; Foreign labor finds more capital clamoring for its services, so that wages there rise.[14]

We could investigate international factor movements by starting not with trade absent but with a free-trade equilibrium (T in Figure 2.3). Assume that sufficient conditions hold in this trading equilibrium for each factor's reward to be equalized in the two countries. Now suppose that Foreign imposes a tariff on imports of food from Home. The tariff reduces its international trade (and Home's) and shifts its production point from P^* some distance toward B^*. The reward to capital rises in Foreign and falls in Home. Capital tends to move from Home to Foreign, and trade between them continues to diminish as its factor-endowment basis is eroded.[15] Eventually trade ceases, except for exports from Foreign needed to repatriate the profits from Home's foreign investment. Thus, this model shows dramatically the substitution between trade and foreign investment (see Section 9.2 for normative implications). Just as

[14] This summary omits a number of refinements to the analysis; in particular, demand conditions might be changed by international factor movements.

[15] Mundell (1957) developed this analysis. We omit some details. It matters, for example, whether or not Foreign's terms of trade (shown by P^*T) are affected by the tariff that it imposes.

the individual firm chooses between exporting and investing abroad (Section 2.2), so are trade and capital movements alternatives for the economy in the large. In general equilibrium, though, they are not always substitutes. Suppose that factor-endowment differences were extreme, with Foreign having very little capital and therefore specializing completely in the production of clothing in the free-trade equilibrium. Purvis (1972) showed that a movement of capital from Home to Foreign can then lead to a new equilibrium with more trade between the two countries. That is because the marginal product of capital in Foreign may then be much greater than in Home, so that the capital transfer increases Foreign's gross domestic product much more than it reduces Home's. Markusen (1983) developed a series of cases in which capital flows to the country exporting capital-intensive goods, so that trade expands (also see Wong, 1986).

Foreign investment and specific factors of production

The standard general-equilibrium trade model lies far afield from the theoretical basis of the MNE developed in Chapter 1, in which international capital movements serve only to loft proprietary assets across national boundaries, and competition is presumed to be imperfect. Two classes of general-equilibrium models have sought to bridge this gap. The first seizes on the horizontal form of foreign investment, in which the firm based in the source country's food industry transplants its capital to that same industry in the host nation. The assumption is therefore made that capital is *specific* to that sector: It can move from country to country, but not between the food and clothing industries in either country. The assumption is extreme, but it captures the notion that the MNE transfers a bundle of assets when it invests abroad; the capital itself might not be tied specifically to that sector, but the managerial skills and intangible assets are. Furthermore, all types of capital are specific in the short run, and the assumption of short-run sector-specific capital gives theoretical results more reasonable than the contrary assumption that capital is continuously mobile between industries (Neary, 1978).

Labor as before is assumed to be immobile between countries, although freely mobile between each country's food and clothing industries. If labor markets are purely competitive, the marginal products of labor should be equal in the Home food and clothing industries, and also in the Foreign food and clothing industries, but not in general between countries. Similarly, if MNEs move capital between countries to eliminate arbitrage profits, the marginal products of capital become equal in the Home and Foreign food industries, and in the Home and Foreign clothing industries, but not between the two sectors.[16]

---

[16] Suppose the necessary assumptions are satisfied for the strong result mentioned earlier: Trade flows alone suffice to equalize factor prices between countries when there are two factors and products, not specific factors. Now, with specific factors we need make only

Specific factors change some properties of the standard model. Suppose that a MNE moves some capital from Home to the Foreign clothing industry. As before, the rentals to clothing capital are driven down in Foreign, and labor's wage is raised. Capital specific to Foreign's food sector also loses. That happens because Foreign's expanding clothing sector attracts labor from Foreign's food sector, raising the marginal product of labor there and hence reducing the marginal product (and rental) of food specific capital. Even though capital is sector-specific, an increase in Foreign's stock of clothing capital depresses the rentals there of food capital as well as clothing capital. Indeed, the rental of food capital in Foreign could fall more than the reward to clothing capital there. The effects of the capital outflow on factor rewards in Home are the opposite of those in Foreign: Labor loses and specific capital gains in both sectors. This model predicts that direct investment will be cross-hauled between countries. If the MNE transfers clothing-specific capital from Home to Foreign (an exogenous disturbance), the rentals to food-specific capital in both countries change so as to encourage it to migrate from Foreign to Home.

In the specific-factors model as in the standard model, a tariff can serve to attract foreign investment. Foreign's tariff on food imports raises rentals to food-specific capital, food capital flows in, and Foreign labor shifts toward the food sector. But clothing-specific capital suffers. In practice tariff policy often seems designed to protect or enhance the rentals received by factors of production specific to a sector.[17]

Batra and Ramachandran (1980) developed a slightly different version of this model in which multinational capital is freely mobile between countries in one sector, but local capital in the other sector is immobile between countries as well as between sectors. Many of their results deal with corporation income taxes and will be noted in Chapter 8. Their other conclusions closely echo those just set forth. For example, make the food sector the one occupied by MNEs and Foreign the net importer of MNE capital as well as the importer of food. Foreign's tariff on food imports attracts more MNE capital, raises wages in Foreign, and lowers the return to local capital in Foreign's clothing sector. Wages fall in Home, and the returns to local capital in Home's clothing industry rise.

one industry's specific capital mobile between countries, and that – along with free trade in commodities – suffices to equalize wages, rentals to food capital, and rentals to clothing capital between countries. If *both* types of capital are made mobile, there is in general no longer an equilibrium with incomplete specialization in international trade: Either production of one good ceases or all international trade ceases except for international factor payments. See discussion in Caves (1971), Amano (1977), and Neary (1980).

[17] The analysis of the preceding paragraphs is based on the work of Caves (1971, pp. 17–19) and Jones (1971). Certain problems with countries' sizes and abilities to influence world prices are neglected here; see Falvey (1979).

They showed that the returns to MNE capital may either rise or fall as a result of this tariff-induced capital movement.

Another modification of the model is due to Burgess (1978; also see Tsai, 1987), who introduced goods that do not enter into international trade (non-traded goods). Suppose that Foreign's economy contains two sectors. Its clothing sector produces an internationally traded good – perhaps primary fibers used as an input by textile-based MNEs elsewhere in the world. Its other (food) sector is now assumed to produce a good consumed domestically and not entering into international trade. A disturbance in the form of an inflow of direct investment to the traded-goods (clothing) sector shifts factor rewards in the same manner as before – capital loses in both of Foreign's sectors, and labor gains. However, a new element enters into the adjustment process in the form of a rising price of food, Foreign's nontraded good. That rise occurs because labor is drawn from the food sector to the clothing sector, while demand remains basically unchanged. This increase in the relative price of food can offset the initial fall in rentals for food capital – indeed, more than offset it, leaving this specific factor better off. And the rise in the relative price of food puts workers' welfare gain in doubt. The smaller is the increase in wages relative to the increase in food prices, and the more of their incomes workers spend on food, the more likely is their real-income gain to be erased. Other results can be mentioned briefly. Jones et al. (1983) developed the specific-factors model for the case in which one good is nontraded in each country. Panagariya (1986) injected the element of trade based on increasing returns in production.

Specific-factor models can also imply that the presence of internationally mobile capital (through the agency of MNEs) alters the basic pattern of comparative advantage. Make sector-specific capital a necessary input to food production, along with labor, whereas clothing production requires only labor. Workers do not move internationally, but capital moves freely to wherever it can earn the larger rentals. Which country exports clothing and which exports food depends not only on David Ricardo's comparative labor productivity but also on the absolute advantage that mobile capital has for producing food in the two countries. Home labor could be relatively more efficient in textile production than in food, and yet the food productivity of capital in Home might attract so much capital as to co-opt enough of Home's labor supply to make food Home's export good.[18] In general, the more mobile are factors of production, the less does comparative advantage have to do with patterns of production.

In the standard Heckscher-Ohlin model (no specific factors), similar results emerge when technology differs between countries, so that a given bundle of

---

[18] This model was developed by Jones (1980); also see Jones and Dei (1983).

capital and labor produces more clothing (or food) in one country than in the other. Make Foreign's food industry technically more efficient than Home's (no difference in clothing). Even though factor endowments favor Foreign to export clothing, the technology difference permits Foreign to export food as well as attracting more MNE capital. If *both* of Foreign's industries are more efficient, the capital transfer from Home is further enlarged, and Foreign definitely exports food if her efficiency advantage is as great in food as in clothing (Jones, 1970; Purvis, 1972).

Mobile proprietary assets in general equilibrium

Another line of research has absorbed into general-equilibrium trade theory two implications of the MNE – that its international transfers of resources raise productivity, and that its proprietary assets dispose it toward impurely competitive markets – monopolistically competitive or oligopolistic. Markusen's model of the MNE's proprietary advantage (the fixed cost required to start the firm need not be duplicated when it adds another plant) can be applied to the gains from trade due to this costlessly traded asset. Markusen (1984) also assumed that the associated scale economy causes markets to be either monopolized or duopolistic, with scale economies never permitting more than two producers in either country. The other good in this two-good model is produced competitively, and the two economies are identical except with regard to foreign investment. Without foreign investment national welfare levels will be affected by the competitiveness of national producers, who might either monopolize their respective home markets or engage in Cournot competition. Now replace Home's national enterprise with a MNE which, using its mobile proprietary asset, can serve Foreign's market through local production more economically than a Foreign national firm. The MNE's costless resource transfer expands Foreign's production opportunities, but whether it raises Foreign's welfare depends on how much more rivalrous would be a world duopoly consisting of two national enterprises. (Home gathers the rents from the proprietary asset and clearly benefits, regardless of how national enterprises compete.)

A second approach on different lines was undertaken by Helpman (1984, 1985) and Helpman and Krugman (1985, Part IV). This approach also embraces the MNE's proprietary asset in the form of an intermediate input that is produced in one country and then (due to scale economies in production) used to turn out a final product in just one location, either Home or Foreign. Potential MNEs produce differentiated goods (manufactures) in markets that are monopolistically competitive. The second product (food) is produced under pure competition. The other assumptions of the standard Heckscher-Ohlin model are retained, with the intermediate proprietary asset requiring only capital as an input (the final differentiated product uses labor along with the asset). A principal concern of Helpman is how the presence of MNEs affects the possibility of factor-price equalization, which (in the standard model) can be precluded if (given identical tastes) the two countries' factor endowments differ so much that they are incompletely specialized in equilibrium. Factor-price equalization might be feasible without any foreign direct investment, in which case (on Helpman's assumptions) none will occur: each country is likely to produce some number of varieties of manufactures using homemade proprietary assets, and manufactures flow both ways between the two countries to supply consumers who (on Helpman's assumption about their tastes) each consume all available varieties of manufactures. If factor endowments differ too much, however, foreign investment (exports of the intermediate proprietary asset) takes place, expanding the domain of factor endowments for which factor-price equalization is possible.

Another factor important for foreign investment and trade is the relative size of the two countries. Suppose that Home is small and well endowed with capital. It will export proprietary assets and some manufactures, importing other manufactures and food. Make Home a larger part of the world economy, still capital-rich, and all manufactures made in Foreign might emanate from Home's MNEs (proprietary assets).

Brainard (1993a) shifted away from the emphasis of Helpman and others on factor proportions and treated the MNE's international expansion as a trade-off between the advantages of concentrating production in one location (due to scale economies) and of producing at the site of consumption (due to transportation costs). Two countries are given identical factor endowments and tastes for manufactures and food. As in Markusen's model, a separate fixed cost is incurred to create each firm's proprietary asset and to start each plant (which also has constant variable costs). Exports of manufactures incur a transport cost, while trade in proprietary asset services (and food) does not. With the economies' sizes, endowments, and tastes identical, each country supplies its own food in equilibrium, but they undertake balanced international trade in some combination of differentiated manufactures and proprietary assets' services. Specifically, each manufacturer is more likely to operate a single-plant firm (no foreign investment), the higher is the plant's fixed cost and the lower are the transport cost and the firm's fixed cost. The reverse of these conditions can yield an equilibrium in which all manufacturers are MNEs and balanced international trade occurs in proprietary assets' services. Intermediate between these cases is an equilibrium with some MNEs and some single-nation firms, causing balanced trade flows in both manufactured goods and assets' services. The model thus indicates substitution between exports and foreign investment. In any of these cases the number of companies depends on consumers' elasticity of demand substitution between manufactures and the height of transport and fixed production costs.

2.4. Distribution of foreign investment among countries

The preceding sections of Chapters 1 and 2 supply many predictions about the allocation of foreign investments (headquarters, subsidiaries) among countries. Some predictions are straightforward to test, even though the empirical literature on national and intranational location choices is not particularly rich. Other propositions resist empirical test. One of them holds that discrete jumps occur sometimes in response to small changes in parameters when scale economies are present (Horstmann and Markusen, 1992). Another is the anomaly of an increase in activity in Home when wages rise in Foreign, despite unchanged product prices, because the contraction of the MNE's activities in Foreign relaxes the constraint of scale diseconomies in administering the MNE's plant in Home (Ethier and Horn, 1990).

General-equilibrium theory of international trade suggests two main propositions:

1. Just as patterns of international trade depend on comparative advantage and the factors underlying it, so should the distribution of MNEs. The MNE arises when an enterprise finds itself with opportunities to start or link up with an establishment in another country. Some countries may be relatively well endowed to support these opportunities, just as they might be well endowed with capital, forests, or sunshine.

2. The general-equilibrium theory of international trade (Section 2.3) shows how factor endowments and trade flows are interrelated. It offers some specific testable propositions and provides a framework for thinking about how everything goes together.

The first of these points needs some elaboration. One can imagine that industry characteristics completely explain the distribution of foreign direct investment among countries. A certain proportion $p(i)$ of industry i's activity is carried out in establishments linked to MNEs, and $p(i)$ varies among countries only because of random factors. The proportion that industry i makes up of country j's economic activity (call it $v_j(i)$) depends only on classical comparative-advantage and locational forces. Then the MNE activity in j would be fully explained by $v_j(i)$ and the $p(i)$ values, which do not depend on j. Notice that the proportion $p(i)$ does not distinguish between j's role as a home base for MNEs and as a host to their foreign subsidiaries.

This scheme, which admits no direct relationship between country characteristics and the extent of foreign direct investment, contradicts none of the preceding analysis. The firm-specific proprietary assets and transaction-cost factors giving rise to foreign investment unquestionably bear a significant relationship to industry characteristics, so that the prevalence of MNEs varies systematically among industries. However, these assets and the MNEs they support could be distributed among a world industry's successful companies randomly with respect to their national origins. We can certainly imagine something more: that national qualities influence the prevalence of MNEs directly, and not just through engendering a mixture of industries that is favorable (or unfavorable) to their emergence. Consider these possibilities:

1. Some countries' endowments of real resources or culture provide a yeasty environment for the development of potential MNEs. Others' endowments lack just these traits. The former countries become disproportionately important as home bases for MNEs, the latter as hosts of their subsidiaries. The identities of these natural source and host countries might not be independent of one another: Given that country j is endowed to be an important source for MNEs, transaction-cost and locational factors could make country k a natural place for its MNEs to alight. In formal terms, the $p(i)$ now vary with country traits and, furthermore, must be disaggregated into source and host components.

2. The mixture of activities carried on within a country may not be independent of the extent of MNE activity in its various industries. In the notation used previously, the $V_j(i)$ may be causally influenced by the $p(i)$ and not independent of them.[19]

In terms of the preceding general-equilibrium models, the standard Heckscher-Ohlin and specific-factors models link country characteristics to MNEs' operations solely through the industry mix determined by the endowment (and other factors). The models that inject product differentiation, however, open the possibility that country traits – those of one country, or interacting traits of pairs or groups of countries – wield an influence independent of the industry mix. Although they have not found a home in general-equilibrium models, country traits favoring or impeding the organization of complex business enterprises could have the same effect.

As a last preliminary, consider the research strategies for explaining the international location of foreign direct investment. Its international distribution is described by a matrix in which each country appears as a source (row) and as a host (column). One might seek to explain the overall prominence of the various countries as sources (the row totals) or as hosts (column totals). One country's distribution might be studied (a particular row or column, or the net flow measured by differences between corresponding row and column elements). Analogous to intraindustry (two-way) trade, two-way intercountry for-

---

[19] We can note some statistical evidence that bears directly on this point and the underlying approach to the international distribution of foreign investment. Dunning's (1980) study of the international distribution of U.S. foreign investments found that the share of U.S. sales in foreign markets (whether through exports or subsidiary production) is larger the larger is the foreign market. If there are substantial fixed costs to each bilateral international transaction (whether trade or investment), one would therefore expect the $p(i)$ to be higher in larger countries. Caves (1980b) found grounds for rejecting the hypothesis that the extent of foreign investment in a national industry is independent of the scales and productivity levels of the establishments operating within it. Because these variables in turn affect an industry's overall size, these relationships can be taken to mean that the $p(i)$ and the $V_j(i)$ interact with each other.

eign direct investment might be analyzed (absolute difference between cells *ij* and *ji* normalized by their sum). Each design has been used in the research literature. Rather than review them mechanically, we start with those aligned with the preceding theoretical models and then draw in the other lines.

Empirical tests: theoretical models and international location

If foreign direct investment is identified with the international movement of capital, or if proprietary assets are regarded as capital assets (Helpman, 1984), the implication follows that foreign investment should flow "downstream" from capital-rich to capital-poor countries. If it is closely involved with product differentiation, two-way investment should occur, with the degree of bilateral balance depending on countries' sizes and the reciprocal attraction that their differentiated varieties hold for each other. A hypothesis due to Burenstam Linder (1961), for example, holds that countries with similar levels of income per capita will tend to find each others' varieties attractive. The differentiation and Heckscher-Ohlin models give competing predictions if Burenstam Linder's hypothesis is maintained, but in general they are independent.

Dunning (1981*b*, Chapter 5) provided a useful setup for this literature by analyzing countries' gross outflows and inflows per capita. A pure Heckscher-Ohlin pattern would involve large gross and net outflows from capital-rich (high-income) countries, large inflows to capital-poor (low-income) countries. The actual pattern is otherwise. Gross outflows are high for the highest-income countries but then drop off sharply; gross inflows also decline systematically with income per capita, though not as fast as outflows. Only the richest countries have net outflows; countries with middling incomes per capita exhibit the largest net inflows; and two-way foreign investment is substantial for all the industrial countries. Evidently the simple Heckscher-Ohlin hypothesis does poorly. It is also rejected by the many simple regression analyses that have tested the hypothesis that foreign investment is attracted to low-wage countries and obtained perverse results (e.g., Wheeler and Mody, 1992), although some confirm an attraction to low unit labor costs or wages normalized by literacy (or other human-capital indicator) (Schneider and Frey, 1985; Culem, 1988; Koechlin, 1992). In the distinctive case of Japan Wakasugi (1994) demonstrated that rising relative land rents in Japan contribute significantly to propelling foreign direct investment from the country. Clearly some life remains in the Heckscher-Ohlin hypothesis, but it seriously needs integration with the role of product differentiation and perhaps other national characteristics.

The most focused treatment of this integration comes from Brainard (1993*b*), who analyzed two-way foreign direct investment between the United States and 27 other countries (overall, or aggregated over 64 industries). She found that the total value of subsidiaries' sales in a pair of countries (combined sales of country *i*'s subsidiaries in *j* and *j*'s subsidiaries in *i*) increases with their combined national incomes and with the similarity of their sizes – as predicted by models of monopolistic competition in international trade. The same holds for two-way exports to unaffiliated parties – that is, trade flows not passing between affiliated businesses. Two-way foreign direct investment decreases (that is, the imbalance of reciprocal flows increases) with the difference in a country's skilled-labor endowment from that of the United States and with the difference in normalized arable land endowments. She concluded that something like the product-differentiation model is important for explaining the activities of MNEs, but that the factor-proportions model "explains some portion of their activities."[20] Two-way foreign investment has been analyzed in the setting of the European Union. Cantwell and Sanna-Randaccio (1992) found the incidence of two-way investment closely associated with reciprocal patent holdings, and Savary (1992) showed how French-Italian two-way patterns reflect the reciprocal strengths of the national industries' proprietary assets.

With this framework established, conclusions can be incorporated from other studies of MNEs' distribution among host countries.[21] Aside from their mixed findings about wages and labor availability already noted, they largely agree on several other results. More foreign investment is found in larger countries, but in most studies this result is not tied to any specific hypothesis (such as justifying the fixed cost of foreign investment over exporting). It typically also increases with national income per capita, as Dunning (1981*b*, Chapter 5) observed. Nankani (1979) and Wheeler and Mody (1992) controlled the congeniality of the host country's mixture of industries for MNEs' activities. Some studies confirmed the positive influence of host-country tariffs documented in Section 2.2. However, more interesting are general indicators of the host country's riskiness for foreign investors or of the liberality of policy toward foreign investment, merchandise imports, or both. Openness to foreign investment (Lecraw, 1984; Li and Guisinger, 1992; Koechlin, 1992; Brainard, 1993*c*) and good economic infrastructures (Root and Ahmed, 1978; Wheeler and Mody, 1992) increase it, while a difficult language and/or remote culture decrease it (e.g., Hjerppe and Ahvenainen, 1986). Risk factors and political instability de-

---

[20] Also see Wickham and Thompson (1989) who, in an otherwise interesting paper, were less successful in relating two-way foreign investment to two-way (intraindustry) trade. Several other pieces of evidence weigh in against the Heckscher-Ohlin or capital-arbitrage explanation of foreign investment. No difference is found between foreign-investing industrial sectors and others in source countries (U.S. Tariff Commission, 1973; Juhl, 1979), although differences sometimes turn up in host countries (O'Loughlin and O'Farrell, 1980).

[21] These are quite numerous and include Root and Ahmed (1978), Nankani (1979), Swedenborg (1979), Schneider and Frey (1985) who summarized preceding studies, Clegg (1987), Culem (1988), Yamawaki (1990), Lecraw (1991), Veugelers (1991), Li and Guisinger (1992), Koechlin (1992), Wheeler and Mody (1992), Woodward and Rolfe (1993), and Schroath et al. (1993).

crease it in some studies (Schneider and Frey, 1985; Lecraw, 1984) but not in others (Wheeler and Mody, 1992).[22] The legal firmness of industrial property rights increases investment in host countries (Lee and Mansfield, forthcoming); this relation is discussed further in Chapter 7.

Source-country attributes

Other research identifies attributes of MNEs' source countries or bilateral source-host affinities that explain their presence. These affinities resemble the findings motivated by the product-differentiation hypothesis (Brainard, 1993b, summarized previously), but they also cover factors that reduce the MNE's cost of entering a foreign market or increase the cost-effectiveness of its internal control mechanisms. Many of the more interesting findings come from informal and historical inquiries rather than statistical tests of hypotheses.

Krainer (1967) and Franko (1976, Chapters 2 and 3) argued that the paucity of raw materials in the European industrial countries, coupled with their high levels of industrialization, brought into being a large stock of MNEs integrated backward into the acquisition of raw materials. High raw-materials costs and risks to the continuity of overseas supply also promoted the rise of chemical firms specializing in man-made substitutes for natural materials; their discoveries then provided the intangible assets that floated subsequent foreign investments (also see Davidson, 1976). On the other hand, Swedish multinationals tended to build their proprietary assets in manufacturing activities that draw on natural resources abundant (or once abundant) in Sweden (Swedenborg, 1979; Olsson, 1993). Franko (1976, Chapter 4) argued that the small national markets of some European countries induced heavy foreign direct investment because the narrow domestic-market base provided successful firms with only limited opportunities to diversify their risks.

The literature of economic history (e.g., Hertner and Jones, 1986) shows how periods of rapid national economic development and reverses to them (e.g., wars) have led to expansions and contractions of countries' status as sources of MNEs.[23] This can be seen in the rapid growth of MNEs based in the United States after World War II, followed by successes for the revived European countries and subsequently Japan in raising the relative outflows of foreign invest-

---

[22] Corresponding to the negative effect of host countries' political instability on investment from abroad is its positive influence on their own foreign investments in the United States (Tallman, 1988). Political instability thus should be distinguished from a host government's purposive expropriation of sunk foreign-owned assets, discussed in Chapter 4. Akhter and Lusch (1991) concluded that political instability does not directly deter foreign investment; rather, high productivity (and incomes) and social infrastructure favor both foreign-investment inflows and political stability.

[23] The effects of Germany's military ventures and German companies' attempts to deal with lost subsidiary assets were traced in essays by H. Schröter and V. Schröter in Teichova et al. (1986).

ment from those countries (UNCTC, 1988*b*, pp. 28–31; Dunning, 1988, Chapter 8). Although Porter (1990) focused not on foreign investment but a generalized inference about national industries' successes in garnering rents in foreign markets, his research shows clearly how lucky accidents of institutional development and successful agglomerations in particular industries generate national firms' proprietary assets. Finally, on the down-side of the development process, Blomström and Lipsey (1989) and Kravis and Lipsey (1992) showed how the rent-yield potential of its foreign subsidiaries can outlive a country's exporting success when it faces increased international competition.

Japan, a latecomer to foreign investment, is a strategic case for testing hypotheses about national characteristics and their changes. The cultural distance of Japan from the Western industrial countries and its substantial net dependence (until recently) on foreign technology left successful Japanese companies with little basis for going multinational. Indeed, the important intermediary role of the Japanese general trading companies in economizing on the country's scarce skills for business transactions with foreigners – direct investment included – clearly identifies cultural distance as a negative predictor of a nation's participation in foreign direct investment.[24] Drake and Caves (1992) showed statistically that the development of proprietary assets (R&D, sales promotion) in Japan came to exert an increasingly strong influence on Japanese investment abroad.[25]

A final line of analysis for explaining countries' prominence as parents of MNEs concerns the well-known product cycle (Vernon, 1966, 1974*b*), which predicts both the point of origin for MNEs and something about the pattern of their international spread. Innovations tend to be labor saving, and so their value increases with the cost of labor, whether the production labor saved by a process innovation or the household labor time saved by a new consumer durable good. Innovators perceive the needs and opportunities in their immediate vicinity, and so innovations appear in the countries with the highest labor costs and incomes per capita. Initial production also takes place near the point of innovation because of communication costs within the innovating enterprise and uncertainty about the production process in the early stage. Thus, proprietary assets resting on innovations fall into the hands of firms in the highest-income countries. The model continues by tracing the innovation's diffusion to foreign markets, first through trade, then through foreign investment, propelled by forces discussed previously in this chapter. It implies that foreign investment

---

[24] See the work of Yoshino (1976), Tsurumi (1976), and Ozawa (1979*a*).

[25] Ray (1989) investigated inflows of direct investment to finely disaggregated U.S. industries during 1974–85, testing for affinities between industry traits and investing firms' source countries. He found, for example, that Japanese firms shun diversifying activities, while (small) Canadian firms avoid industries with extensive scale economies in production.

flows from richer to less wealthy countries, but not necessarily reaching the lowest in income per capita, because the innovation eventually loses its proprietary character and escapes from the hands of the originating MNEs.

The model helps to explain the prominence of the United States as a progenitor of MNEs, especially in the two or three decades following World War II, as well as the recent reversal associated with a declining advantage in income per capita over the other major industrial countries (Vernon, 1979). For explaining broad foreign-investment patterns, however, it faces competition from the role of organizational innovations that have diffused from the most successful industrial countries (Kogut, 1992). Also, in its first version the model missed the point that if labor-short countries make labor-saving inventions, materials-short countries should equally make materials-saving innovations that then underpin MNEs. Davidson (1976) showed that innovations in the European countries are substantially more materials saving than those in the United States.

Affinities between source and host countries

Evidence set forth on source and host countries separately can be supplemented by findings on affinities between pairs of countries that promote investment flows between them. Such an affinity might come from product differentiation, consistent with Brainard's (1993*b*) link between two-way foreign direct investment and similarities in countries' incomes per capita. Affinity also results from factors that reduce communication and information costs associated with transborder transactions or otherwise create common interests, even in the political and social realms. Nankani's (1979) statistical study showed that foreign investment is enlarged between those pairs of industrial nations and LDCs that were formerly connected by a colonial tie. Not only did the colonial ties offer political protection and lower transaction costs to MNEs, but also their termination posed a threat to the industrial nation's remaining exports to its former colonies and promoted foreign investment – an effect that eventually eroded as other source countries gained access to the now-independent LDC (Svedberg, 1981). Several statistical tests found that (cet. par.) foreign investment in host countries is increased by their political alliances with the source (Schneider and Frey, 1985; Tallman, 1988; Koechlin, 1992).

An especially ample literature suggests that bilateral affinities in foreign investment arise because they minimize transaction costs or risks for firms making foreign investments. The pattern is commonly documented in the series of moves made by a nascent MNE on its way to the status of a large "global" company. Davidson (1980) showed that low-information cost countries such as Canada, Mexico, and the United Kingdom bulk disproportionally large as destinations for U.S. MNEs, and they were even more prominent in earlier times.

Davidson established the existence of a typical sequence of moves that starts with Canada (also see Horst, 1972*b*) and proceeds with the United Kingdom, West Germany, Mexico, Australia, France, Brazil, etc. Kravis and Lipsey (1980) pointed out that the rankings of destination countries by the numbers of U.S. subsidiaries that they contain vary too little among industries to reflect perfectly informed static cost-minimization decisions by MNEs. The implication is that low-information-cost stepping-stone host countries will remain disproportionally prominent even after some MNEs go on to (as it were) bigger and better things.

This pattern of bilateral affinities is repeated regularly for other source countries that have been studied. Italian MNEs start with neighboring southern European countries and the LDCs that received heavy immigration from Italy (Onida and Viesti, 1988, pp. 49–74); Japan goes to Southeast Asia (Yoshihara, 1978, pp. 24–31; Tsurumi, 1976, Chapter 3), Australia to New Zealand (Deane, 1970, pp. 61–2), Sweden to neighboring European countries and the United States (Swedenborg, 1979, pp. 56–60), France to French-speaking lands and adjacent European countries (Michalet and Delapierre, 1976, pp. 8–9). From the viewpoint of host countries, O'Loughlin and O'Farrell (1980) noted that Ireland, which provides public services that reduce risk and transactions costs for the MNE, has thereby attracted MNEs that are smaller than typical of the breed. In a useful statistical test Veugelers (1991) not only confirmed the positive effects of common language and neighbor status but also showed how fully they dominate production-cost factors – unit labor costs, tariffs.

Unfortunately, none of these studies of affinities parcels out the various types of determinants: demand-side factors associated with product differentiation, cost-side factors associated with initial fixed costs of search and investigation or continuing (flow) costs of transportation or coordination. Each is clearly involved, but the only evidence to give some feeling for their respective roles comes in studies of the location choices of export-oriented foreign subsidiaries. Product-differentiation and other demand-side factors are irrelevant for them, and so cost factors should and do dominate the determinants of their locational choices. Kravis and Lipsey (1980) hypothesized that the exports of majority-owned foreign affiliates of U.S. MNEs tend to be concentrated where unit labor costs are least and access to material inputs is easy.[26] They also controlled for country size (scale economies). Their results confirm the hypotheses about access to materials and economies of scale; for unit labor costs, the coefficient is not significant. Jarrett (1979, Chapter 8) analyzed the distribution among foreign countries of U.S. imports under tariff provisions that allows goods of U.S.

---

[26] Their proxy for this is "residual openness": A country is assumed to have better access to material inputs if the ratio of its total trade (exports plus imports) to its GNP is higher than its population and density would suggest.

origin processed abroad to pay duty only on the processing.[27] He found that this activity favors countries near to the United States (lower shipping costs) as well as those with low wages and low incidence of labor disturbances. Riedel's (1975) findings on foreign investment in Hong Kong are similar.

Interregional choices of location

A footnote to this section is provided by the many studies of MNEs' locational choices within countries (chiefly the United States): Glickman and Woodward (1988), Coughlin et al. (1991), Woodward (1992), Ondrich and Wasylenko (1993), and earlier works cited in these. They agree closely on the statistical significance and economic importance of most location determinants. Agglomeration effects are important, although land availability is a positive influence. Infrastructure (highways, railroads, airports) attracts foreign investors; state and local taxes deter them, although government promotion and assistance is a positive factor. Findings on labor are complicated by the lack of data on productivity or unit labor costs, but human-capital resources are clearly an attractive factor, the incidence of union membership a deterrent, while the effect of wages as such varies from study to study. Foreign investors tend to locate in parts of the United States nearest to the source country – Canadians in the north, while the Europeans avoid the West Coast and the Japanese avoid the Southeast (also see Harrington et al., 1986). Hines (1993*a*) showed that state corporate tax rates are a strong influence; a 1 percent higher rate causes a decrease of 7 to 9 percent in the share of manufacturing investment by MNEs from source countries that do not give credits against taxes paid abroad.

Little formal evidence is available on location patterns within other host countries, but van den Bulcke and de Lombaerde (1992) illustrated the working of similar location forces within the European Union's metal-working sector.

2.5. Summary

If the field of international economics offers a sufficient explanation for the MNE, it would seem to lie in the arbitrage of capital between countries where its marginal product is low and those where it is high. However, this is inconsistent with many obvious facts about the distribution of foreign investments, and neither necessary nor sufficient in light of the transaction-cost model of Chapter 1. Nonetheless, foreign investment generally does involve some net transfer of capital, so it is desirable to draw on the relevant theory of international capital movements.

Horst (1971) first presented a microeconomic model of the choice that the MNE faces between investing abroad and exporting from the home base. If it

---

[27] Recall that the foreign processor often is an affiliate of the U.S. importer, but need not be.

faces a downward-sloping demand curve in each market and its production is subject to scale economies, the MNE chooses to concentrate production in one location, unless trade restrictions block this choice, and it can wind up producing only in a large national market even though it would enjoy lower costs in a smaller one. The most sophisticated empirical studies regard MNEs' exports and foreign investments as jointly determined. Abundant empirical evidence confirms the value-maximizing locational choices made by MNEs, taking account of production and transport costs, scale economies, and product differentiation and other demand-side factors. Historical evidence strongly confirms the effect of a tariff to lure the MNE's production behind the barrier, and the market enlargement effected by the European Community had the same consequence. Exchange-rate changes also affect foreign investments when they are expected to be long-lived (i.e., to change the real terms of trade). It is important to distinguish arm's-length trade from interaffiliate trade, which is complementary with foreign production activities.

General-equilibrium concepts from international economics also address the causes and consequences of foreign investment, even though they commonly presume perfectly competitive markets and equate the MNE's activity with capital arbitrage. The Heckscher-Ohlin model establishes a link among the factor endowment of a country, its structure of production, and the rewards to its factors of production. A capital-rich country tends to export goods that use capital intensively. When its exports expand, the rentals to its capital rise and workers' wages fall. In a free-trade equilibrium, under specialized assumptions capital will earn the same at home and abroad, leaving no incentive for MNEs to move capital internationally. Conversely, where trade is restricted, capital flows can effectively substitute for it; trade and foreign investment thus are alternatives in general equilibrium as well as for the individual company.

Some efforts to bring general-equilibrium theory closer to the MNE have centered on the concept of specific factors of production, sector-specific capital that is mobile between countries but not between industries. The sector-specific model has its own implications for foreign investment and income distribution, and it has attractively realistic properties such as an ability to explain the cross-hauling of foreign investments. One broadly important implication of sector-specific mobile factors is that they tend to locate wherever in the world their reward is greatest, causing absolute advantage and not classical comparative advantage to determine patterns of commodity trade. Other efforts incorporate models of imperfect competition – oligopoly or monopolistic competition – in order to capture the effects of MNEs' proprietary assets and to relate foreign investment to two-way trade in differentiated products.

These elements of international-trade theory help to explain the distribution of foreign investments among countries. Although foreign investment does tend to flow from capital-rich toward capital-poor countries, the prevalence of two-way foreign investment and the importance of a nation's human capital as a factor attracting foreign direct investment sharply confine the predictive power of the standard trade model. Bilateral affinities among countries are important for explaining the international location of foreign investment. These affinities come from many sources. Countries with similar incomes per capita probably tend to demand similar varieties of differentiated goods. More readily documented, languages and cultures shared between countries reduce MNE's transaction costs, just as neighboring countries reduce their communication and coordination costs. The influence of pure production-cost factors dominates MNEs' locational choices only in the case of foreign investments in export-processing facilities.

3

Organization and growth of the MNE

Economic analysis traditionally treated the firm as a single decision-making center, as if one mind were absorbing all relevant data and making all decisions on the basis of well-considered objectives. In fact, decision making is decentralized within firms, and the decisions reached can be colored by the structure of internal organization chosen by the firm and the incentives and resources that it provides to its various groups of functional specialists. This coloration arises from precisely the costs of information and transactions discussed in Chapter 1. The MNE enjoys certain advantages over the arm's-length market, but they must trade against the organizational costs and constraints that the firm encounters in coordinating multinational operation. Therefore, an examination of the MNE's internal structure is a logical extension of the transaction-cost model of the MNE's underlying rationale. This should aid understanding of how the firm will respond to both market stimuli and public policies.

3.1. Expansion processes in the firm

A valuable starting point is the process of the growth of the firm, as it pertains to the MNE. We can link the transaction-cost model of the MNE to constraints on the firm's process of growth and adjustment and to evidence on riskiness and turnover in multinational activities.

Expansion of the MNE subject to adjustment costs

The transaction-cost approach to the MNE can explain the course of the firm's development over time, as well as the prevalence of MNEs at a given time. If the MNE can sometimes seize an advantage to displace a market and reduce transactions costs, the firm's costs of securing information and arranging transactions shape its behavior. The transaction-cost approach makes an elementary point about why MNEs are not ubiquitous. The typical entrepreneur, a native of some particular country, brings to his or her business activities a general knowledge of its legal and social system and its peculiar "ways of doing

57

things." The business firm (possibly excepting some mature MNEs) has a clear-cut national base and identity, with its internal planning and decision making carried out in the context of that nation's legal and cultural framework. When the entrepreneurial unit founds or acquires subsidiaries in foreign lands, it must incur a fixed cost of learning how things are done abroad. Home-office personnel sent to run and develop the subsidiary will (for a time, at least) be less effective than at home. Foreign nationals can be hired to run the shop, but then a different fixed cost must be incurred to teach them the firm's way of doing things. Either choice leaves the potential MNE facing a virtual disadvantage in the foreign market with respect to its local competitors, who access that social and cultural milieu as a spillover without explicit cost. The transaction-cost advantages of the MNE are necessary to get it over this intrinsic disadvantage.

The transaction-cost approach also implies that firms' proprietary assets are first developed in some national market. These assets influence a series of investment decisions taken over time by successful firms, including decisions to begin and expand foreign investments, subject to various adjustment costs and constraints. First, the firm cannot instantaneously undertake all the profitable projects utilizing that asset which it can locate. Constraints limit the firm's growth, such as how rapidly it can expand its management cadre and its equity-capital base.[1] The firm considers various plans for using its distinctive assets so as to maximize the expected present value of its future profits. Suppose that its proprietary advantage over (at least some of) its rivals becomes clear when it is a single-nation firm holding only 10 percent of its national market. Its next most profitable move might be either to expand into foreign markets or increase its share of the domestic market. Although the choice could go either way, information costs create a bias toward continuing domestic expansion, which does not necessitate the new information and search costs associated with going abroad.

As the firm's share of its domestic market grows, the marginal returns to further expansion at home eventually decline. Given the elasticity of the market demand curve and its competitors' expected reactions, the higher an expanding firm's market share, the lower the demand elasticity that it perceives. Also, its increasing market share might come at the cost of dislodging stronger and stronger competitors. Expanding to serve overseas markets becomes more and more attractive.

Once expansion abroad tops the list of profitable investments for the firm, the choice of destination should be affected by information costs as they vary among foreign destinations. The first site for overseas investment is likely to be the national market where the entrepreneur faces the least disadvantage of lan-

[1] Penrose (1959) first emphasized the constraint on growth due to the firm's limited ability to expand its management; Horst (1974b) summarized the literature on financial constraints on the firm's growth in the context of MNEs (see Section 6.1).

guage and culture (see Section 2.4). Successful foreign investments themselves can augment the firm's proprietary assets, making the course of international expansion highly path-dependent (Kogut, 1983, emphasized the sequential process of multinational expansion).

Firm-specific determinants of foreign investment

The first body of evidence bearing on this expansion process links foreign-investment decisions to proprietary assets accumulated by the firm. Horst (1972b) first compared firms within industries to test what traits discriminate between those that go abroad and those not yet holding MNE status. The only significant difference he found was in the size (market share) each had already attained in the domestic market. This result supports the hypothesis that the firm runs through its opportunities in the domestic market before incurring the transactions cost of going abroad. Horst (1974b) later found that overseas expansions by successful U.S. food-processing firms could be explained by qualitative differences among their proprietary assets. Subsequent statistical studies detected a number of differences among firms that significantly affect their contemporary decisions whether or not to undertake foreign investments. Caves and Pugel (1980, Chapter 2) confirmed Horst's result on firm size but also associated differences in firms' advertising outlays with their foreign-investment choices (also see Wolf, 1975, and Swedenborg, 1979, Chapter 6). Grubaugh (1987a) revisited Horst (1972b), finding significant positive influences not only for market share (size within industry) but also research intensity, product diversity, and the importance of selling and administrative expenses (weakly significant). Several statistical studies have recently added to this literature: Ball and Tschoegl (1982) on international banks' entries in California and Japan, Marion and Nash (1983) on foreign food-retailers' entries into the United States, Kimura (1989) on foreign investments by Japanese semiconductor firms, and Belderbos and Sleuwaegen (forthcoming) on foreign investments by destination of Japanese firms. The innovations made by the semiconductor firms and the breadth of their product lines and extent of "downstream" integration into consumer electronics promote their foreign investments in industrial host countries, as well as their sizes in the Japanese market. Marion and Nash, however, found that not absolute size but share already claimed in the firm's home market predicts investment in the United States. Other investigators have tied the firm's foreign-investment decision or the extent of its foreign operations to its age and/or accumulated experience.[2]

Several authors investigated the relation between product-market diversification and foreign investment (see Section 1.3 and Galbraith and Kay, 1986). The results are somewhat diverse and reflect differences in samples and mea-

---

[2] Swedenborg (1985); B. Beaudreau in a dissertation summarized in Enderwick and Associates (1989, p. 47).

suring methods, but they are consistent with the short-run trade-off hypothesized previously (Caves, 1975; Wolf, 1977; Davidson, 1984; Kimura, 1989; cf. Marion and Nash, 1983). Other studies that compare product-market and geographic (international) diversification levels achieved by firms of varying sizes and maturities (e.g. Grubaugh, 1987*b*) usually find positive correlations: given time and resources, a firm can exploit opportunities for diversifying in both directions, and the sorts of proprietary assets that support foreign investment are the same ones associated with "related" diversification.

Foreign investment decisions

The clinical literature of business administration contains investigations of the process by which firms make their decisions about foreign investments, and conclusions from these bear on the adjustment and information costs hypothesized previously. Commonly stressed is the random fashion in which firms initiate investigations of opportunities for foreign investment, perhaps as a parochial response to a problem perceived somewhere down in the firm's administrative hierarchy (Aharoni, 1966; Brooke and Remmers, 1970, Chapter 4; Michalet and Delapierre, 1976, pp. 27–9). An unfortunate conclusion sometimes drawn is that the foreign-investment process itself is highly random, which ignores the likelihood that many firms ill-endowed for foreign investment similarly toy with but reject the idea of venturing abroad.

Section 2.4 shows that each source country's MNEs pick foreign markets for their debuts so as to minimize the information and transactions costs associated with foreign investment. The new MNE can accommodate to a not-too-challenging environment while it is learning the ropes – acquiring knowledge that reduces the cost (or risk) of future expansions into more alien terrain. And its intangible assets provide it with some offsetting advantages at the earliest stages. It can work its plant at designed capacity sooner than a comparable independent firm (Forsyth, 1972, pp. 60–2), and a product innovation borrowed from its parent involves fewer shakedown difficulties for the subsidiary (Dunning, 1958, p. 120). This accumulation of experience has been modeled theoretically as paying a fixed cost to improve one's ability to distinguish between low-return and high-return opportunities (Casson, 1994).

The process by which the firm investigates the foreign-investment option shows certain important properties (Aharoni, 1966, Chapters 4 and 5). Information and search costs are quite high for foreign investment as compared with other investment decisions, what with overseas site visits, the cost of acquiring the necessary approvals from foreign governments, and the like.[3] These high

---

[3] Aharoni (1966, Chapter 5) suggested that the commitment to invest abroad often comes not from a conscious strategic decision but from a series of investigative steps (investigation and market development) that bring the incremental cost of foreign investment down to a level that finally seems attractive.

fixed costs of decision making constitute an important reason for expecting that foreign investment will be mainly an activity of firms whose accumulated resources could support a large capital commitment abroad.[4] Closely related to these fixed costs of search is Aharoni's finding that the perceived risk of foreign investment is quite high. The more costly is information, the less of it one acquires, and the more risky is the outcome perceived to be. At least one survey of MNEs' experience confirms that firms' foreign subsidiaries perform better when they initially choose sites with low information costs and gather information roundabout by first exporting or licensing independent foreign producers than when they proceed "cold turkey" with the foreign-investment decision (Newbould et al., 1978, Chapters 4 and 6). Because the firm's previous stock of knowledge holds little value for the foreign-investment process itself, an incremental investigation of foreign markets clearly is likely to be an efficient procedure (Johanson and Vahlne, 1978).[5]

The pattern described here can be traced through many historical and case studies. Indeed, the early process of expansion of firms to national-market status in the nineteenth-century U.S. economy was apparently quite similar to their evolution to multinational status more recently (Kindleberger, 1969, pp. 33–5). We have evidence on the behavior of early MNEs such as Singer Sewing Machine Co. (Wilkins, 1970, Chapters 3 and 4; Nicholas, 1983), which became foreign investors through a process of incremental problem solving, such as dealing with the unsatisfactory performance of foreign licensees or sales agents. The historical case studies also show that the evolution of the decentralized multiplant and multinational firm depended on nineteenth-century innovations in communications (telegraph and telephone) that allowed the firm to achieve economies of integration.[6]

The historical evidence also confirms the incremental approach that companies have taken to the countries they have chosen for foreign investments. Wilkins (1970, Chapters 6 and 7) stressed that the initial investments undertaken in Canada and Mexico during the 1890–1914 period represented cheap, natural extensions of domestic activities for many U.S. companies. Dubin (1976, Chapter 5) found that the smaller the firm and the less diversified its portfolio of overseas assets, the more likely are its foreign assets to be con-

---

[4] An indirect indication of these fixed costs appears in Antonelli's (1985) analysis of diffusion among MNEs of computer-based management of international data telecommunications. Larger MNEs with more internationalized operations and more centralized management structures tended to be the earlier adopters.

[5] We note a purely tax-based incentive for starting foreign subsidiaries with a small dowry of capital and letting them grow by retained earnings (Sinn, 1993): this practice maximizes expected profit to the extent that profits are taxed when they are repatriated rather than when they are earned (see Chapter 8).

[6] Vernon (1977, Chapter 1) made the same point about the expansion of MNEs after World War II.

centrated in familiar countries. Wells (1983, Chapter 7) explained how the expansion of MNEs from third-world countries is strongly influenced by the presence of expatriate communities that reduce the incipient MNE's costs of securing reliable information. Evidence reviewed in Section 2.4 shows how strongly this pattern is imprinted on the aggregate distribution of foreign direct investments. For example, Davidson (1980) showed how the distribution of U.S. foreign investments among host countries is affected by the sequences of moves by which MNE empires are extended from more to less familiar countries.

Several other types of evidence indicate the effects of information and adjustment costs on the expansion of MNEs. Exporting activity serves as a low-cost source of specific learning to potential foreign investors (Denis and Depelteau, 1985). The expansion process also uses experience gained in one host to support investment in similar hosts (Benito and Gripsrud, 1992). The method of entry into foreign markets (discussed in Sections 3.3 and 3.4) is picked with an eye to minimizing the costs of inexperience or making repetitious use of a systematized procedure (Caves and Mehra, 1986; Franko, 1989; Zejan, 1990*a*). Firms proceeding through a series of incremental steps have emerged more successful than those that take discrete jumps (Newbould et al., 1978; Buckley et al., 1983). Some tests of experience effects, however, have turned out negative (Yu, 1990; Benito and Gripsrud, 1992).

Foreign investments are clearly risky ventures, so that prolonged processes of international expansion can pay off for MNEs in improved chances for success (and thereby a higher expected value of future profits). The research literature on MNEs has paid little attention to the probabilistic nature of foreign investments' outcomes and the churning that occurs in the distribution of MNEs due to the random outcomes of initial and subsequent investment actions (or inactions) (Caves, 1995). Bane and Neubauer (1981) found that the mortality rate is higher for a foreign subsidiary that specializes in products different from its parent's original product. Mitchell et al. (1992) confirmed that the risk of business failure is reduced for firms that have already achieved MNE status, but is inflated for firms that are changing (either increasing or decreasing) their multinational presence. Mitchell et al. (1994) concluded that the odds of survival are improved for the foreign entrant that waits for the information revealed by the fates of early entrants, although not so long that competition squeezes out the prospect for rents; and Mitchell et al. (1993) showed that in an industry in transition to increasing multinationalization the domestic firm tends to enjoy more success (both abroad and at home) if it expands its international operations, and also a greater risk to its domestic survival if it does not. There is also evidence (Lee and Kwok, 1988) that the financial leverage selected by large companies decreases with their degree of multinationality, consistent with greater risks from foreign investment and inconsistent with the predominance of diversification benefits.

Indirect evidence of these business risks appears in various studies of longevity and turnover among MNEs. New foreign investments are subject to high risks, evident in the low aggregate profits regularly reported for foreign subsidiaries after a recent burst of foreign investment (e.g., Ågren, 1990). These risks then decline with age, as is shown by strong associations between its subsidiaries' age and a firm's extent of MNE development (Swedenborg, 1985) and by the strong relation between the profit rates of foreign affiliates and their ages, with the country and industry of the subsidiary controlled (Lupo et al., 1978). On the other hand, smaller and newer MNEs that prove profitable apparently grow faster than do large and mature, profitable ones (Rowthorn and Hymer, 1971; Droucopoulos, 1983). This conclusion also emerges from studies of firm size and growth that compare domestic firms and MNEs (Siddharthan and Lall, 1982; Cantwell and Sanna-Randaccio, 1993). Similarly, the average profitability of MNEs usually exceeds that of domestic firms (e.g., Benvignati, 1987), presumably because of rents to the MNEs' proprietary assets, and increases in multinationality are accompanied by increases in profit (e.g., Grant, 1987), but profitability does not increase with size outside of small firm-size classes, and growth if anything decreases with (initial) size (Kumar, 1984).

Another aspect of turnover that has been little studied is the decline and demise of MNEs. The transaction-cost approach suggests that it should reflect the depreciation and obsolescence of MNEs' proprietary assets (Boddewyn, 1983). Data analyzed by Torneden (1975) and Wilson (1979) suggest that hazard rates for foreign investments are high (during 1967–71 Torneden found divestments were 16 percent of newly founded subsidiaries), and the evidence in both studies seems consistent with high rates of infant mortality. Yamawaki (1994b), however, observed lower rates for Japanese foreign subsidiaries. Subsidiaries closely integrated with the MNE parent are more likely to survive, as are larger new subsidiaries and those with more diversified outputs. Yamawaki (1994b) observed that divested subsidiaries are significantly more likely to have been acquired rather than built *de novo*: a business once separably marketable can more readily be sold again. The same pattern is evident in the data of the Harvard Multinational Enterprise Project (Curhan et al., 1977, pp. 21, 168). Divestments are not concentrated in less-developed countries, and the data suggest that normal market hazards and not "country risks" are the main factor (Glickman and Woodward, 1989, pp. 129–35). Divested subsidiaries are commonly sold off to domestic host-country enterprises, consistent with their demise being associated with the random hazards specific to foreign investment (Wilson, 1979).

3.2. Organizational structure

Once a firm undertakes its first foreign investment, it must devise ways to integrate that activity with its overall decision-making structure. The devices used build on the organizational structures that have evolved in large enterprises of all types. These organizational devices are economically significant for several reasons. Their design depends on the structures of the markets in which the firm operates, and they influence firms' market behavior; therefore, a knowledge of organizational structures helps explain the behavior of MNEs as economic actors. Finally, the ease with which MNEs adapt to certain policies imposed by governments depends on their organizational structures.

Organizational forms and foreign subsidiaries

Once an enterprise grows large enough to have a formal hierarchical organization, two principal forms are available to it. The *functional (F) organization* consists of a group of functionally specialized departments reporting to a chief executive. The *multidivisional (MD) organization* places two or more *F* organizations under the supervision of a single top executive. The *F* organization attains the virtues of specialization: Members of each department concentrate on their own tasks without any redundant communication with other departments. The *F* organization is good at doing one thing as efficiently as possible. The *MD* form evolved when business enterprises found that they could profitably undertake diverse activities (diversify in products or geographically) so that it grew inefficient to place all production activities, say, within a single production department. The *MD* firm benefits from making each division a "profit center," responsible for turning a profit on its own designated activities. If profit performance gives top management an efficient means of supervising its divisions, then chief executives can concentrate on longer-run strategic matters – anticipating environmental changes, allocating capital among divisions, devising methods for the best use of the firm's resources. The more diversified a firm's activities, the more likely that it employs *MD* organization. The *MD* form, incidentally, evolved in the United States around 1920 and subsequently diffused widely throughout the United States and other countries.

Stopford and Wells (1972, Chapter 2) found that U.S. companies usually are organized in the *F* form at the time they acquire their first foreign subsidiaries. The first foreign venture commonly is tied to the parent by loose organizational links because of the risk and uncertainty surrounding it, and because nobody knows what performance level to expect from it. Also, it simply does not pay at this stage to establish an elaborate apparatus to administer foreign subsidiaries: Steuer et al. (1973, Chapter 7) found that they are more loosely supervised the smaller their parents (also see Baglini, 1976). As foreign operations mature, the enterprise establishes an international division to coordinate such functions as transfer pricing, finance, and the distribution of exports among production units. That event often accompanies or follows the evolution of the parent's overall organization from *F* to *MD*. Adoption of the *MD* form provides the enterprise with a flexibility for entering and coordinating new areas of business that makes the proliferation of foreign subsidiaries more likely. Nonetheless, coordinating foreign operations through an international division is problematical for the *MD* enterprise. Its domestic divisions usually are organized by product, whereas its international division is concerned with overseas production of these same products. Domestic product managers have no direct incentive to give the international division access to assets helpful to foreign units producing the same line, a problem of "suboptimization" for the MNE. Firms therefore cast about for other organizational structures to contain this problem. One solution is to organize the whole company into worldwide product divisions, but that invites a different problem of suboptimization: common aspects of overseas operations are handled in separate divisions. A different solution is to divide an international division into area divisions, each responsible for all operations in some overseas region. This solution is popular where the foreign subsidiaries supply one another with components or intermediate products, requiring close coordination.

The choice of an organizational structure thus represents a balancing of advantages among discrete alternatives. Consider the choice between global product divisions and international or area divisions. The economic principle behind this choice is to place within a division those activities that require extensive communication or coordination with each other and to keep separate other activities not needing continuous or regular interchange. The more diversified are the outputs that a firm produces abroad, and the more international are the markets for its inputs and outputs, the more likely it is to choose global product divisions. Without them, too many interchanges over product-specific problems must pass across divisional boundaries. Also, with an international division or area divisions, a highly diversified company grows entangled keeping track of internally heterogeneous product lines. A single international division is seldom used if the firm makes 40 percent or more of its sales abroad, because the power structure of claimants for the top executive's ear then grows imbalanced.[7] Davis (1976) noted the prevalence of global product divisions in firms with heavy research spending, demanding close global management of their product-specific proprietary assets. International area organizations flourish where mature product lines are supplied to common end-user markets, so that the MNE's chief coordination problem lies in its regional marketing organization. Egelhoff (1988) recently confirmed these patterns.

Getting its organizational structure properly matched to its pattern of activities is important for a firm's efficiency and profitability. A firm with *MD* organization and diversified operations abroad that are supervised by an inter-

---

[7] Perhaps reflecting the same factor of intracorporate political balancing are the results of some studies of MNEs based in small countries, whose individual foreign subsidiaries might exceed the size of the parent firm. Forsgren (1989) described the units' interaction as a political relationship among equals rather than as a managerial hierarchy.

national division probably suffers a mismatch. Stopford and Wells (1972, pp. 79–82) found that the mismatched MNEs they studied were, on average, less profitable than those they deemed properly matched. They also concluded that for a MNE the *F* form of organization is typically less effective than *MD*.

Brooke and Remmers (1970, Chapter 3) took a somewhat different approach to explaining MNEs' organizational structures but obtained conclusions consistent with those of Stopford and Wells. They classified management systems in MNEs as "close" or "open," depending on the intensity of the parent's supervision of the subsidiaries and the density of communications and information links between them. The close structures occur in vertical MNEs, where interruption of the product flow through one affiliate promptly affects the operations of others. They also occur in horizontal MNEs that extensively share common technologies or that distribute an identically branded good in several regions, so that malfunction of one affiliate impairs the profitability of others. Another condition for close control is that differences between national markets do not impel local adaptation of the product (Alsegg, 1971, pp. 120–1, 175). Similarly, de Bodinat (1975) and Hedlund (1981) related the closeness of control to several traits of the enterprise's technology, strategy, and market environment. Supervision is more centralized where the plant sizes and activities of parent and subsidiaries are similar, where technology is complex, where many transactions occur between parent and subsidiaries, where idiosyncratic dealings with national governments are not important, and where the market environment (specifically, level of demand) is relatively more predictable. Young et al. (1988) and Jarillo and Martinez (1990) demonstrated the sharpness of the distinction between close (centralized) and open (localized) subsidiaries.[8]

MNEs based in different nations made different organizational choices, due to differences in national cultures and especially to the gradual diffusion of organizational innovations that originated in the United States. European MNEs once commonly used informal supervision of subsidiaries through nothing more than a personal reporting relationship between the presidents of the subsidiary and parent (Franko, 1976, Chapter 8; Jedel and Kujawa, 1976, pp. 60–2; Jones, 1986a, pp. 13, 16). As late as 1971 more than a third of European MNEs surveyed by Franko retained a "mother-daughter" system, whereas the rest used organizational patterns similar to those of American MNEs (global product divisions, international divisions). Hulbert and Brandt (1980, pp. 11–23) observed this differential diffusion in Brazilian subsidiaries of U.S. and European MNEs. Similarly, Chandler (1980) found that U.K. firms became multinational

---

[8] Ghoshal et al. (1994) investigated how the volume of communication between parent and subsidiary varies with the subsidiary's autonomy. Either sign is plausible: The autonomous subsidiary looks after its own problems, or alternatively it substitutes informal communications with the parent for formal authority links. In the event, no relation was found.

later than their U.S. counterparts because family control survived longer among U.K. firms. The rate at which the family firm can expand without slipping from its owners' control is limited by the family's thrift and fecundity, and the absolute scale of investment in and management of international expansion presses hard on the family's capacities.

Because the basic organizational structures open to firms are discrete, a dilemma confronts the MNE that needs the types of coordination supplied by both international divisions and global product divisions. Should it live with an impure but imperfect form? Should it attempt the formal synthesis offered by the novel matrix organization? Or should it muddle through with various coordinating devices to patch up the cracks that appear in a traditional organization? Surveys (Business International, 1981) suggest a drift toward global product divisions, but with copious use of patchwork devices. Egelhoff (1988) found worldwide product divisions prevalent among European-based MNEs, international and area divisions among U.S. MNEs – a natural reflection of the geography of their continents of origin. The matrix organization did not realize its potential (Pitts and Daniels, 1984). The cross-coordination problems that it addressed have not gone away, however, and perhaps for that reason research has shifted to coordinating mechanisms within the MNE and away from general organizational structures (Martinez and Jarillo, 1989).[9]

Economizing on internal coordination

What matters economically for these relationships between the MNE's market environment and its internal organization is not so much the substantive details (which can be left to business practitioners) as the general economizing process that takes place. MNEs lavish extensive resources on internal coordination when close coordination pays, as when the profits of different affiliates are strongly interdependent and inconsistent policies would be costly. Fewer resources are devoted to control when it is costly (for a subsidiary in a remote location), when the affiliate's local environment is unstable or highly distinctive (making coordination ineffectual) (Alsegg, 1971, pp. 9–11), or when dealings with governments are especially important (Prahalad and Doz, 1987) although not highly interdependent (Mahini and Wells, 1986). Fewer resources are used on coordination with a small subsidiary than with a large one, or one in a large and potentially lucrative market.[10] Consistent conclusions come from field studies of the relative influence of parent and subsidiary on various classes of deci-

---

[9] Kobrin (1994) investigated whether the relationship among strategy, organizational structure, and profits in MNEs needs to be mediated by observing the extent of their global "mind-set," meaning the unimportance of nationality in the staffing of executive positions. He found that MNEs indeed differ in this regard, and global mind-sets are correlated with measures of the internationalization of the firm's activities, but none of this turns out to interact with its choice of strategy and organizational structure.

[10] See Alsegg (1971, pp. 209–10) on the effects of formation of the European Community.

sions (Negandhi, 1983). Such comparative-statics evidence also appears in the consequence of temporal changes in environmental costs and benefits of MNEs' coordination policies. The mother-daughter organization held greater attraction when international communication and travel were slow and costly (Jones, 1986*b*), and the decreased impediments (both natural and artificial) to the international movement of goods since the 1950s have raised the payout to inter-affiliate trade and close coordination (instead of each subsidiary doing its best within an insulated national market) (Martinez and Jarillo, 1989).

Research on coordinating mechanisms used by MNEs clearly shows that they seek to make value-maximizing choices. There is wide agreement that MNEs systematically centralize some functions, especially finance (uniform financial reporting, budgeting, accounting, and forecasting) and usually research and development (e.g., Goehle, 1980), while decentralizing others. Given this difference, various control mechanisms can be used together to achieve greater or lesser degrees of centralization as the MNE's situation warrants. Hedlund (1981) equated centralization with the formalization of controls (manuals, written reports, etc.) as distinguished from informal or behavioral controls (visits between subsidiary and parent personnel, long-run transfers of personnel, etc.). He found formal controls more prevalent where subsidiaries' environments are more predictable, other owners are present (i.e., joint ventures), or subsidiaries are regarded as being in trouble. Hulbert and Brandt (1980) and Egelhoff (1984) similarly found a strong contrast between these types of controls and noted that formality increases with the subsidiary's size. Ghoshal and Nohria (1989) distinguished between centralized and formalized control systems, expecting that environmental complexity would increase formality but reduce centralization; however, their data did not support the distinction (complexity reduces both), although subsidiaries in strong bargaining positions within the firm (large, cash-rich) are subject to high formality but low central control. Hulbert and Brandt (1980) observed that parents enjoy scale economies in applying parallel controls to all their subsidiaries that limit optimization to each subsidiary's situation.

Not much research links MNEs' positions on this trade-off to their industry bases or other such readily quantified data, but Goehle (1980) showed that the expected sorts of strong contrasts are observed among industries. Attempts have also been made to associate the trade-off with differences in national culture and business practice that might make either formal or informal controls relatively more effective. Among source countries Japan attracts the most interest in this regard (Yoshino, 1976, Chapter 5). No particularly clear patterns emerge, however; Hulbert and Brandt (1980) found that U.S. MNEs use more of both formal and informal controls than do other countries' MNEs, and Japanese MNEs do not rely strongly on informal controls. Where subsidiaries of MNEs with diverse national origins operate in similar host-country environments, their control arrangements show no obvious imprint of their differing source countries (e.g. Safarian, 1966, pp. 85–6).

A standard question of research on business administration is whether one organizational choice yields more profit than another. Since each option's choice should be based on a proper match to the firm's economic environment, one would expect no unconditional difference in profit associated with the control mechanism chosen, but firms with control systems properly aligned to their environments might be more profitable than others. Roth and Morrison (1990; also see Goehle, 1980) found no unconditional differences among business units that could be cluster-analyzed into locally responsive, globally integrated, and bifocal. Leksell (1981) stressed how much organizational idiosyncracy could prevail in MNEs without seeming to affect their relative performance. Habib and Victor (1991) tested whether MNEs' profits suffer where mismatches occur in the major organizational choices, finding that "fit" considerations affect organizational choice about as strongly for MNEs in services as in manufacturing, but that only in manufacturing is there appreciable evidence that mismatches impair profits.

3.3. **Effects of organization: new venture or acquisition?**

These relationships between the market environment of the MNE and its internal organization hold economic interest because they affect economic efficiency, but they do not directly engage the issues of public policy that motivate most economic analysis. In this and the following sections we consider some business policy decisions flowing from MNEs' organizational structures that are significant for public policy. Public opinion sometimes takes offense when a national enterprise is acquired by a MNE domiciled in a foreign land. The stir might result simply from the nationalistic urges that motivate so much policy toward MNEs, but also from a more rational concern for competitive effects (among other national interests): so-called green-field entry by the MNE adds a new enterprise unit to the national market, whereas entry by acquisition does not.

The organizational costs and patterns of MNEs suggest a series of hypotheses about circumstances in which the foreign firm is more likely to enter a market by acquisition. Influences on MNEs' decisions to acquire rooted in the market for control of business units are also taken into account. Entry via a joint venture with another enterprise cuts across this choice and is discussed in Section 3.4.

Risk, size, and experience

Evidence presented previously established the riskiness of foreign subsidiaries. They require fixed and variable costs of administrative coordination, and MNEs incur these only where the expected payout warrants. Both risks and coordination costs affect the choice between acquisition and green-field entry. To start a subsidiary by acquisition, the prospective parent goes into the market for corporate control and acquires equity shares in a going business. There it must compete with equity shareholders (persons and institutions) in general, and their rivalry forces the buyer to pay a price that would let a non-controlling investor earn only a normal or competitive rate of return on the ac-quired business. The MNE might expect positive payoffs, of course, if running the acquired business increases rents to its proprietary assets, or if the MNE en-joys a lower cost of capital. The MNE that instead starts a new venture avoids paying the going-concern value for an acquired business, which it may not value highly if it wants to install its own management practices (a strong pref-erence of Japanese MNEs, according to Tsurumi, 1976, pp. 194–5).[11] However, high start-up costs penalize the outsider relative to a native entrepreneur. Hence, no general presumption favors either method of entry. Extraneous factors can prove quite important: when the stock market is depressed, for ex-ample, picking up physical assets by buying companies grows cheaper relative to building plants.

Entry by starting a new business unit might also be more risky than acquisi-tion. The going business is a working coalition. From the viewpoint of the for-eign MNE, it possesses an operating local management familiar with the national market environment. The MNE that buys the local firm also buys ac-cess to a stock of valuable information. These factors surely reduce the uncer-tainty about the new subsidiary's subsequent case flows. Therefore, in general, to choose acquisition rather than a new venture is to choose a lower but less un-certain expected rate of return.

That conclusion can now be linked to the evidence about MNEs' organiza-tional structures. When a firm first goes abroad, it faces an especially high level of uncertainty and hence craves the information stock and lower riskiness of entry to a foreign market via acquisition (or a joint venture with a knowledge-able partner). Of course, the firm launching into MNE status with an innova-tive proprietary asset might not locate a going concern suitable for its purposes, but otherwise acquisition is attractive. This hypothesis was confirmed by Du-bin (1976, Chapter 5) and Stopford (1976). The MNE past its first steps abroad apparently does not balk at the uncertainty associated with a new foreign ven-ture, as Dubin found that large MNEs are more likely to add new subsidiaries

---

[11] Michalet and Delapierre (1976, pp. 33–4) suggested that acquisition is more likely in sectors where the advantages of MNEs rest in general organizational ability and not technology or other specific assets. One might expect that the survival rate of sub-sidiaries founded by acquisition would exceed that of newly founded subsidiaries, be-cause of the risk difference, but evidence mentioned in Section 3.1 shows that the easier salability of an acquired business is the dominant influence. The paradox might be re-solved if failures leading to closure could be distinguished from those that end in sale of the business unit.

through new ventures than are small ones.[12] Finally, the MNE's rate of growth can affect its preferred method of expansion overseas. The evidence suggests that the novice MNE's stock of information increases with the time it has been in the business. If age brings wisdom, the fast-growing MNE holds a smaller stock of experience than the equal-size MNE that has reached its current state more slowly. The fast grower will therefore value more the information stock in the hands of a going firm and more likely add to its subsidiaries through acquisition. Dubin (1976, Chapter 6) seems to confirm this hypothesis.[13]

Diversity and other influences on acquisition of subsidiaries

The MNE's diversification should also affect the expansion process. First, consider the geographical diversity already achieved by a MNE. This factor, like size and experience generally, increases the MNE's information stock and reduces the premium it will pay for the security of acquiring a going firm rather than building anew. Dubin (1976, Chapter 5) and Wilson (1980) accordingly found that MNEs already highly diversified among overseas regions are less likely to add new subsidiaries through acquisition. Diversity also enters in the degree to which the product line of a new subsidiary differs from the MNE's established activities. The more remote the new activity, the greater its uncertainty and potential for costly mistakes, and the more likely is the MNE to pay for the greater security of entry by acquisition (Dubin, 1976, Chapter 6). Cutting across these results, however, is evidence that some widely diversified companies set up a process of expanding via acquisition, whether in their national home markets or abroad, and reap administrative scale economies in that process itself.

Although the effect is ill-documented, product-market competition can influence the entry mode. Hörnell and Vahlne (1986, pp. 97–101) suggested that acquisition is cheapened when the MNE can credibly threaten product-market competition that will impair the target's value. Also, acquisition can occur as a defensive measure to keep the target assets from falling into the hands of a rival.

Some influences on the MNE's method of expansion come directly from the market for corporate control. The net advantage of buying a going concern depends on the price one must pay. The more going concerns that are available to

[12] Two points of qualification: First, Dubin examined his hypotheses about acquisition behavior one at a time, and so his finding that x and y are related could be because z is not controlled. Second, there has been a clear trend over time for more subsidiaries to be added through acquisition (Wilson, 1980; Hörnell and Vahlne, 1986, pp. 34–6), and this trend could color conclusions reached by comparing MNEs that have started their subsidiaries at different points in time.

[13] Similarly, in a fast-growing national market, it is more costly to forego profits because of the longer delay associated with building a subsidiary from scratch. Dubin (1976, Chapter 9) reported higher acquisition rates in faster-growing foreign markets.

be bought, the lower the market price the acquiring MNE is likely to pay. MNEs should choose to acquire less frequently in less-developed countries, where few suitable firms can be found (Wilson, 1980), and in small economies generally (Dubin, 1976, Chapter 9). The latter result is striking, because the smaller the market, the more does the firm entering with new efficient-scale facilities stir up competitive rivalry.

The market for corporate control also shows up in the traits of the local firms that MNEs select for acquisition. Little (1981) found U.S. acquirees to be slightly less profitable than other firms in their industries and notably heavy on long-term debt, suggesting that they were constrained for supplies of capital. Similarly van den Bulcke (1985) observed that Belgian targets suffer internal finance problems (38 percent) or capital shortage (29 percent) or need infusions of product technology (17 percent). Other studies have indicated similar patterns. Erland (1980) found that Swedish firms with foreign participation started out with technology intensity below average for their industries, but the majority showed increases after their foreign infusion. Stubenitsky (1970, pp. 73–7) learned that Dutch entrepreneurs who sell control of their firms to MNEs need specific assets brought by the MNEs (technology, capital) as well as new managerial talents. Reuber and Roseman (1972) stressed the illiquidity of Canadian firms, which would tend to depress their market values, as a cause of international mergers.

Statistical tests

The one-by-one tests of hypotheses just summarized have given way to multivariate statistical tests, which also inject some new hypotheses. Caves and Mehra (1986) analyzed decisions of foreign MNEs entering the U.S. market. They found that the larger the business started or acquired relative to the parent's size, the more likely is the security of acquisition sought. Their results on the parent's diversity, however, clash with previous findings based on U.S. investments abroad: The likelihood of acquisition increases with the parent MNE's geographic and product diversification, so large MNEs have apparently routinized the process of entry by acquisition. Specialized parents adding undiversified subsidiaries show no statistically significant preference for a green-field approach. Acquisition is chosen when the U.S. market is growing rapidly, but also when it grows very slowly (which presumably devalues the existing business assets). Competitive considerations matter: The MNE opening a large business in a concentrated industry is more likely to acquire, avoiding the competitive consequences of new capacity added in a green-field entry. Also, a weak tendency toward acquisition is seen when the MNE is joining a rush to the U.S. market of others based in its industry and country. No evidence was found that the number of potential targets (independent firms in that industry and size class) affects the entry method. Nor does the type of proprietary assets brought by the parent (R&D, advertising-related) except that durable-goods producers significantly favor green-field entries.

Other multivariate studies have probed these and other relationships. Kogut and Singh (1988), who also analyzed entries into the U.S. market, added the role of host countries' cultural characteristics. Cultural distance from the United States weakly deters green-field entries (and significantly promotes joint ventures), while a cultural aversion to uncertainty significantly deters green-field entries (the latter result is driven by Japanese entries). Zejan (1990a) determined that diversified Swedish MNEs also tend to obtain new subsidiaries through acquisition, and that acquisition grows more likely in high-income host countries (larger supply of business units? liquid market for corporate control?). Zejan (1989) added the conclusion that acquired subsidiaries subsequently undergo less integration into the MNE's operations (interaffiliate trade). Hennart and Park (1993) analyzed Japanese MNEs' entries into the United States, confirming the findings of Caves and Mehra about industry growth and the size of the U.S. business, but also observed that R&D intensity disposes the Japanese MNE toward green-field entry, while entry into a diversifying business is effected by acquisition. They found no influence for financial factors (stock prices or the parent's leverage) or for the parent's past experience. Ågren's (1990) results are consistent with the preceding studies but not strong statistically.[14]

Healy and Palepu (1993) pointed out that host countries differ greatly in foreign MNEs' access to the market for corporate control, because either regulations are discriminatory or shareholdings are concentrated in financial institutions so that the market for corporate control is generally inactive. Both factors influence the total value of (normalized) international acquisitions, but the authors did not investigate the substitutability of green-field investments.

3.4. **Joint ventures and other agreements between firms**

The joint venture provides one choice on the MNE's menu of organizational options, along with acquiring a going firm or starting a new business unit (covered in Section 3.3) and entering into some other sort of alliance or contractual arrangement with another firm. In this section the joint venture is considered as a principal example of international alliances or contracts between firms. It is readily addressed by the transaction-cost approach to MNEs' activities.

The large empirical literature on joint ventures is best not treated chronologically. That is because a confusion persisted until recently between two outcomes: (1) the MNE shares equity in a business activity with another enterprise or agent, as the preferred way to maximize its profits; (2) the MNE is forced to

---

[14] A useful paper on the limits of our ability to explain choice of entry mode is Yamawaki (1994a).

share equity control by policies of the host government. The former outcome is discussed here, the latter in Chapters 9 and 10. A related confusion prevails because of researchers' emphasis on the turnover of or MNEs' problems with joint ventures: Such phenomena dispose the researcher with a business-normative viewpoint to regard joint ventures as mistakes and to neglect the possibility that like other investments they represent bets on uncertain outcomes that could turn out well or badly.

Properties of joint ventures

The transaction-cost approach regards the MNE as a coalition of heterogeneous resources that include its distinctive proprietary assets. In this context a joint venture, by definition a sharing between active partners of equity control over a business activity, represents a partial merger of selected assets controlled by two (or more) enterprises (Beamish, 1988, Chapter 7). Firms could find such alliances productive because the assets in question are heterogeneous in quality, lumpy in capacity, and capable of use in several locations and/or activities. Optimal combinations of such assets are therefore idiosyncratic and specific, and the best available combination for pursuing some activity might well require teaming assets that belong to different firms.

Such teams can be formed in several ways. Firm *A* can rent or buy the asset that is needed from firm *B*, although *A* then runs into the market failures that explain why such assets are integrated into firms' coalitions of resources in the first place. Firm *A* can merge with firm *B*, although that might well tax a single management to coordinate their many combined assets that are not complementary in use. The partial merger or alliance represented by a joint venture thus offers an option plausible in light of the transaction-cost approach. That approach also suggests, however, what problems or constraints should limit joint ventures. While a rental or purchase contract simply transfers control of an asset, a joint venture links the partners through an incomplete contractual relation in which their shared equity commits them to negotiating how to handle whatever disturbances or opportunities subsequently arise. Relative to a complete contract, its incompleteness implies high ongoing costs of haggling and monitoring, subject to little contractual foundation beyond the parties' defined contributions of inputs and equity shares. The hazards are clear enough: if one party gains managerial influence over the deployment of the other's proprietary asset, the manager gains less than 100 percent of the benefits from making best use of the asset and incurs only part of the cost of degrading or undermaintaining it; even worse, an intangible asset might be appropriated by a joint-venture partner.

Modern theory of contracts (Hart and Moore, 1990, and earlier references cited) makes important points about the optimal structure for such agreements. Suppose that the parties are asymmetrically informed about the consequences of combining their assets, or about the best action to take after the assets are combined: one party observes the outcome of the combination, or subsequent outside events that determine how the combined assets are best deployed, more cheaply than the other. Then the maximum value of the combined resources is realized if decision rights are placed in the hands of the party who is better informed or better able to act as the ongoing decision maker. This sharp-eyed party will, however, also have an incentive to make decisions along the way so as to slide the maximum benefit into its own pocket. Both parties recognize this incentive at the outset. Therefore, the best contract assigns the decision rights to the sharp-eyed party but requires an initial payment to the other party calculated on the assumption that its partner will behave opportunistically once the venture is under way and the external information in hand.

This contract-theory model provides an attractive framework for studying joint ventures in which the partners hold unequal equity shares. Equal-share joint ventures by implication presume that the parties can bring qualities (knowledge, skills) to the ongoing management process such that the costs of haggling are more than offset by the valued created through using what each party can contribute to the management of the venture's distinctive combined assets. The partners' initial commitments of resources may effect a stabilizing exchange of hostages (Buckley and Casson, 1988).

An implication of the preceding discussion is that wholly owned subsidiaries, joint ventures, and still less formal collaborations among firms differ in their fixed and organizational start-up costs. Auster (1992) argued that as we proceed from the more mature and certain market environments to the most fluid and uncertain, we should expect wholly owned subsidiaries to give way in turn to joint ventures and informal collaborations. By implication the average longevities of these ventures should decline along the same spectrum.

These theoretical considerations hold a number of empirical implications for situations in which joint ventures will be selected, the likely lifespan or turnover of such ventures (related to the duration of the productive sharing of resources), and the specific sharing of equity control. The predictions are not necessarily simple, however. Should joint ventures prevail in industries where intangible proprietary assets are important (signaled by heavy R&D and sales-promotion expenditures)? Such assets can create greater value if combined with complementary assets in the hands of other firms, but also they are most vulnerable to appropriation and impairment through suboptimal maintenance and development. The empirical evidence says a good deal about each of these issues, although most of it in fact predates the preceding theoretical framework.

Empirical evidence
The first empirical studies of joint ventures fastened onto the governance problems that can cause their termination or reversion to single-firm con-

trol. Franko (1971, Chapter 2) found that the reversion of joint ventures to single control is positively associated with perceived importance to the parent of internationally standardized product quality, design, and style. MNEs whose strategies depend on standardization fear that a poor quality product sold under their brand in one country will impair their goodwill asset elsewhere, a circumstance that can bring conflict with a host-country joint-venture partner who has only a local stake in the asset.[15] Franko did not find that R&D activity predicts the abandonment of joint ventures, however, because the research results often are exactly what one partner contributes to the joint venture, taking a share of equity in return. Stopford and Wells (1972, pp. 119–23) found a negative relationship between the MNE's rate of R&D spending and the proportion of its subsidiaries organized as joint ventures. However, that could indicate either the avoidance of joint ventures by research-rich firms or their effective use to minimize the cost of innovation by less active research spenders.

Franko also found evidence of intolerance of joint ventures by the MNE that seeks to integrate its subsidiaries' operations. If either its subsidiary A or its subsidiary B can serve market X, the MNE parent will pick the lower-cost supplier (call it A). But if B is a joint venture and can earn a positive profit from serving X (but a smaller profit than can A), a conflict arises between the MNE and its local B partner, who will want B to get the assignment. Similarly, if the MNE's subsidiaries supply components to each other, joint-venture status exacerbates the problem of pricing these intracorporate transfers. On the other hand, joint ventures are less troublesome for nontraded goods or products made behind prohibitive tariff walls.[16]

Franko (1971, Chapter 3) related the MNE parent's tolerance of joint ventures to its organizational structure. He noted that a MNE organizing its subsidiaries into geographical area divisions no longer treats each subsidiary as a local profit center and hence finds joint ventures inconvenient (also Stopford and Wells 1972, pp. 114–17). On the other hand, the MNE with worldwide product divisions and a high degree of product diversification might welcome joint ventures to develop certain products or markets that the parent counts as

---

[15] Also see Stopford and Wells (1972, pp. 109–10), Tomlinson (1970, Chapter 2), and Deane (1970, pp. 75–8).

[16] However, Franko (1971, Chapter 2) could not confirm this statistically. The data of the Harvard Multinational Enterprise Project seem to match the pattern. Of subsidiaries wholly owned by their parents in 1975, 12.1% were heavy exporters; the share is 9.4% for majority-owned subsidiaries, 8.2% for joint ventures, and 8.3% for minority-owned subsidiaries. Subsidiaries making heavy sales to other MNE affiliates are about equally numerous among wholly owned subsidiaries (10.5%) and joint ventures (10.4%), but less among majority-owned subsidiaries (8.2%) and minority-owned subsidiaries (7.2%). If the population is confined to subsidiaries based in manufacturing, the predicted patterns concerning joint ventures become clearer still (calculated from Curhan et al., 1977, pp. 386, 394).

peripheral, thereby letting it economize on managerial and other contributions to the venture. Kim and Hwang (1992) confirmed the link between organizational structure and propensity for joint ventures.

Many of the positive factors that cause firms to seek out joint ventures were documented in case-based research. They are especially evident in the extractive industries where the project is risky or involves a large minimum efficient scale of operation or both. Partnership among several vertical MNEs interested in acquiring the project's output lets them spread the risk and the financial burden and limit the output they receive from the venture to the needs of their downstream facilities. (Such firms often wish to draw vital inputs from several sources to minimize the risks of being cut off from a single supplier.)[17]

Joint ventures are also sought by MNEs lacking some capacity or competence needed to make the investment succeed – a straightforward prediction of the transaction-cost model. In contrast to the preceding evidence on joint-venture failures, technology assets seem often to provide an important basis for firms' entries into joint ventures – either because different firms' technologies need to be combined, or because one's technology needs the cooperation of a different sort of asset (such as marketing skills).[18] Sometimes these ventures involve sharing the costs of pursuing some innovation that both partners hope to use (a goal often imputed to cooperative R&D projects). Beamish and Banks (1987) found that appropriation is not typically a problem when the partners contribute disparate technologies. Mariti and Smiley (1983) found such technological-complementary agreements to account for 41 percent of the cooperative agreements in their sample, and Stopford and Turner (1985), pp. 112–16) give a similar impression. The fact that joint ventures commonly serve to exploit technology assets remains consistent with MNEs having concern for leakage and appropriation, for some surveys find that technology-rich companies tend to use fully controlled subsidiaries more than do other MNEs.[19] A strong case for sharing confronts the MNE that is diversifying in product as well as geographical space and thus is doubly lacking in managerial know-how

---

[17] Stopford and Wells (1972, pp. 117–19). Stuckey (1983, Chapter 4) made an intensive investigation of joint ventures in the international aluminum industry. He found considerable support for the scale-economies argument, the rapidly proliferating joint ventures in aluminum being concentrated in bauxite refining, where both scale economies and risk are greatest. He also pointed out that joint ventures provide a simple method of sharing the company-specific intangible technological knowledge common in this sort of industry. He did not find much support for competing hypotheses, such as that joint ventures serve to foster collusion.

[18] A way that firms protect their technology assets from appropriation, according to Blodgett (1991), is by taking a large ownership share in the venture.

[19] Southard (1931, pp. 136–7) long ago noted this preference, and Dunning and Pearce (1977, p. 13) found that subsidiaries under less than 100 percent parental control accounted for a majority of all subsidiaries in low-technology British industries but only 11 percent in the high-technology industries.

for competing in the new market (Stopford and Wells, 1972, Chapter 9).[20] MNEs based in extractive sectors therefore might seek partners when they start foreign subsidiaries to process their output, because the parents lack the needed marketing skills (Stopford and Wells, 1972, pp. 132–3). Stopford and Haberich (1978, Table 6) determined that the larger the subsidiary, the more likely it is that the parent has majority control, which suggests that the joint ventures are in small, sideline activities.

Another positive reason lies in the MNE's occasional need for specific resources possessed by local joint-venture partners. These include knowledge about local marketing or other environmental conditions, as well as general assistance in risk bearing (e.g., Tomlinson, 1970, Chapter 2) and in dealing with the host government (Phillips-Patrick, 1991). Joint ventures economize on the information requirements of foreign investors and are thus likely to appeal where these are more onerous. Besides their prevalence in subsidiaries producing diversified products (described earlier), joint ventures are used more often by small and/or new MNEs, who presumably need both the information and companionship in sharing risk.[21] When thrust into MNE status by their main contractors' ventures abroad, Japanese subcontracting firms often seek joint ventures, despite large spillover benefits handed to their foreign partners (Horiuchi, 1989). The prevalence of joint ventures among foreign subsidiaries of Italian MNEs is attributed to these firms' small sizes relative to MNEs from other industrial countries (Viesti, 1988).

Joint ventures also seem to be more prevalent as MNEs proceed toward more unfamiliar host countries. For example, the less "global" U.K. MNEs increase their use of joint ventures once outside the Commonwealth countries (Stopford and Haberich, 1978, Table 7). Michalet and Delapierre (1976, pp. 35–6) observed that the French MNEs' proportions of ownership in their subsidiaries increase with the host country's level of development and with the importance in the industry of commercial marketing factors. Joint ventures are uncommon in culturally familiar LDC settings, such as British firms in Malaysia (Saham, 1980, pp. 150–1). Japanese MNEs at least initially were more prone to joint ventures than are other MNEs; one 50-company sample found fully 82 percent of the foreign subsidiaries to be joint ventures (Yoshino, 1976, Chapter 5). One explanation is that the great cultural distance between Japan and foreign markets induces Japanese firms to seek expertise on local conditions (Tsurumi, 1976,

---

[20] Also see Blomström and Zejan (1991), who found a higher propensity for joint ventures among product-diversified Swedish MNEs and those having little experience with foreign production.

[21] Stopford and Wells (1972, pp. 138–41); Tomlinson (1970, pp. 74–86); Yoshihara (1978, pp. 39–40). However, in their study of foreign investment by smaller U.K. MNEs, Newbould et al. (1978, Chapter 5) found that subsidiaries 75% or more controlled by their parents were significantly more profitable than those under diluted control.

pp. 204–6). Other explanations are more economic: Many of the subsidiaries engage in extracting raw materials; Japanese firms that have been expanding rapidly find their resources (capital and local management talent stretched); Japanese foreign investment runs heavily to countries that require local partners.[22] Echoing Franko (1971), Tsurumi (1976, pp. 206–12) found a tendency for Japanese MNEs' subsidiaries to revert to full control once established.

Recent statistical research on joint-ventures choices complements these findings from field and case research (Fagre and Wells, 1982; Lecraw, 1984; Kogut and Singh, 1988; Gatignon and Anderson, 1988; Contractor, 1990; Gomes-Casseres, 1989, 1990; Hennart, 1991; Agarwal and Ramaswami, 1992; Kim and Hwang, 1992). Its interpretation requires some caution because of the conflation of MNEs' choices and public-policy constraints mentioned previously. Some studies dichotomize subsidiaries' ownership as full or shared, while others embrace more categories or take one parent's share as the dependent variable. Some sample so as to focus on bargaining with the host government, others to avoid or distinguish this factor from MNEs' private optimizing choices. Consistent with the ambiguous role of R&D assets already noted, the studies disagree on their affinity for shared control. Gatignon and Anderson (1988) found that they dispose subsidiaries toward full control.[23] Lecraw (1984) concurred that they increase control in the face of host-government demands, but Kogut and Singh (1988) that they dispose MNEs toward joint ventures. Gomes-Casseres (1989) found no simple relationship but confirmed that R&D favors joint ventures when the subsidiary is diversified from the parent; indeed, proprietary product technology significantly deters joint ventures in undiversified subsidiaries while encouraging them in diversified subsidiaries.[24] There is more agreement that advertising and buyer-goodwill assets point away from joint ventures and that less experienced MNEs and MNEs going to unfamiliar destinations are more attracted to joint ventures. Cultural distance between source and host countries and uncertainty avoidance as a cultural characteristic of the source country both promote joint ventures (Kogut and

[22] Tyebjee (1988) sampled Japanese joint ventures in the United States, finding that they engage in activities related to the parent's, such as forward vertical integration and complementary products. Mutual benefits are clear: The Japanese MNE seeks market experience or U.S. technology, but half of the U.S. partners also seek Japanese technology or production skills.

[23] Gatignon and Anderson were quite successful in discriminating between joint ventures and wholly owned subsidiaries but, like the rest of the literature, quite unsuccessful at explaining the varying proportions of equity taken. Aside from Blodgett (1991) a major gap in the literature is the application of contract theory to explain the ownership division in joint ventures.

[24] Consistent with Gomes-Casseres's complex story is Hladik's (1985, Chapter 5) success in predicting whether a joint venture would itself undertake research on the basis of attributes of its parents and its host-country setting.

Singh, 1988), and both industrial and regional experience deters them (Gomes-Casseres, 1989). Shared control is more common in rapidly growing host-country markets. MNEs undertaking more interaffiliate trade and coordination of subsidiaries shun shared control (Gomes-Casseres, 1989). The sharing of control in order to enjoy economies of scale is probably reflected in a disposition toward joint ventures in large-size activities and activities involving natural-resource extraction. The specific statistical interaction between traits of the MNE and of the market that it contemplates serving, as determinants of the choice of entry mode, was established by Agarwal and Ramaswami (1992).

Functionally similar to the preceding statistical studies is Geringer's (1988) investigation of the qualities that U.S. MNEs value when they seek joint-venture partners in other industrialized countries. Knowledge of the local market and good relations with the host government top the list, followed by various sorts of asset complementarities and factors implying compatibility between the two partners (e.g., similar size and organization). Geringer (1988) gives a somewhat different impression from the survey of Mariti and Smiley (1983), in which marketing agreements play a minor role relative to sharing and transferring technology.

Finally, the subject of joint ventures' failures and reversions (introduced by Franko, 1971) has recently received more attention. Auster (1992) confirmed her hypothesis that joint ventures should occur in less mature and more uncertain markets, which itself implies that they will be short-lived. Kogut (1988a, 1988b) provided data on the longevity of joint ventures, showing them to be quite short-lived (peaking sharply at 5–6 years), with international joint ventures more short-lived than domestic ones (also see Beamish, 1988, Chapter 2). It remains an open question whether this pattern reflects the governance costs and problems of opportunism stressed by Franko (1971) or a more natural form of turnover: If joint ventures represent selective combinations of their parents' assets, and those assets are subject to change and obsolescence, it follows that joint ventures should on average have shorter lives than their MNE parents and other free-standing firms that hold portfolios of such assets and can readily refurbish the stock and add new assets. Harrigan's (1988) evidence supports this view, as does the thin harvest reaped by investigators who sought to test the determinants of joint ventures' success (Geringer and Hebert, 1989). Kogut (1989) tested the exchange-of-hostages mechanism, finding that joint ventures are indeed more likely to survive when the partners share other contractual links as well (licensing, supply contracts, other joint ventures). He also found longevity reduced where the industry in general is undergoing structural change and where the venture undertakes R&D in a sector that is not R&D intensive in general.

Other interfirm agreements

Joint ventures represent one type of interfirm agreement, and a good deal of interest currently extends to others. Some of these are vertical contracts:

technology-transfer agreements (see Chapter 7), franchise contracts, and input-supply arrangements. Others represent various forms of cooperation that seem to resemble looser versions of joint ventures (Ghemawat et al., 1986; Porter and Fuller, 1986). The objectives listed for these agreements generally seem to be obvious extensions of the factors explaining the selection of joint ventures. Informal devices seem important to the successful governance of these cooperations: reputations of the parties as hostages to their good behavior, interperiod balancing of equities in uncertain outcomes (Perlmutter and Heenan, 1986). In the computer industry Gomes-Casseres (1993) identified complex multifirm alliances that seem explainable by numerous coincident sources of market failure. The limited lifespans associated with joint ventures also seem to be present, although Johanson and Mattsson (1988) reported an average 13-year lifespan of sampled informal customer-supplier relationships, which commonly persisted over sequences of foreign-investment decisions by one or both parties. These coalitions are found in industries with the same structural properties that are correlated with MNEs' activities overall – research intensive, capital-intensive, highly concentrated, export-intensive in the United States, and risky in the sense of intertemporal variability of firms' rates of return on equity.[25]

3.5. Summary

The transaction-cost model of the MNE implies that the firm is a contractual coalition of heterogeneous assets – long-term employees, physical capital, intangibles. Although ownership links avert market failures in transactions in these proprietary assets, the internal organization of the MNE itself incurs costs and "organizational failures" that color its market behavior and affect important issues of public policy. Evidence on growth processes in MNEs affirms this characterization. The firm takes on ventures abroad only after it has accumulated some critical mass of assets. Because of the novice firm's lack of information and experience, the intrinsically risky first venture usually is into a relatively familiar, low-risk foreign environment. The risks of foreign investment are evident in the (limited) evidence on high turnovers.

The foreign subsidiary, although first held aloof, must be integrated into the parent's administrative structure – often a functional organization when the first foreign venture occurs, but likely to gravitate into a multidivisional one. Overseas activities can be integrated either through international or foreign area divisions or through product divisions that span both domestic and foreign markets. The MNE's choice tends to devolve from the principle that activities sharing the same problems and needing the most communication should be closeted within the same division. How large an investment the MNE makes in administrative apparatus to coordinate its members depends on whether or not its activities yield a high return to close integration (subsidiaries in unfamiliar or

---

[25] Other studies that identify and describe various "new forms" of international cooperation among firms include Oman (1984), Mowery (1987), and Mytelka (1991).

unstable environments tend to be left on their own). MNEs vary greatly in regard to what decisions are centralized in the parent; finance is always centralized because it provides the nerve system for the parent's efforts to maximize global profits, and it appears that other decisions are centralized to whatever degree is warranted by the technical and market structure of the firm's activities. Nationality-based differences in MNEs' organizational structures reflect the diffusion of organizational innovations from the United States and the persistence of family control and loose organization in noncompetitive markets.

Whether the MNE enters a foreign market by acquiring a local firm or by starting a new business depends on these organizational traits. Making an acquisition gains the entrant MNE a going local management and represents a low-risk strategy for quick entry, but the market for corporate control capitalizes any rents already accruing to the business into the purchase cost. Greenfield entry preserves access to these rents but is slower and riskier. We expect that novice MNEs or those diversifying into unfamiliar product lines tend to make acquisitions, whereas those with extensive experience abroad in their base activities prefer to start their own businesses; the evidence is mixed, in that mature MNEs seem to routinize the process of expanding by acquisition. Among host countries the available supply of local firms and the state of the market for corporate control make a difference.

Some MNEs choose to operate foreign subsidiaries as joint ventures with another partner or partners, and some host governments require MNEs to take on local partners. MNEs vary greatly in their propensity for joint ventures. These may prove welcome where minimum efficient scale is large, risk is considerable, or the MNE lacks some vital input (such as knowledge of host-country conditions). Joint ventures are shunned by the MNE that cherishes appropriable proprietary assets or extensively transfers components among its subsidiaries, but joint ventures are welcome for the firm exploiting an intangible asset in a market diversified from its base. Novices and small MNEs are more likely to welcome joint ventures. The lifespans of joint ventures on average are short, reflecting the transient opportunities and/or depreciable proprietary assets that they possess. So-called new forms of cooperation and alliances among MNEs in many ways resemble joint ventures and supply agreements between buyers and sellers.

4

Patterns of market competition

Among areas of popular concern with the MNE, not the least confusion arises over its relationship to monopoly and problems of competition policy. The MNE that attracts attention is a large company holding a large share in at least some of the markets where it operates. However, properly analyzed, the normative issues raised by monopoly, large size (or diversification), and international ownership links are quite different. In this chapter we investigate the extent and character of the relationships between the MNE and market competition.

4.1. Foreign investment and oligopoly

Entry barriers and bases for foreign investment

The transaction-cost analysis of MNEs implies their prevalence in industries with concentrated sellers (Caves, 1971), because the influences giving rise to MNEs are identical to the bases of several barriers to entry into industries, and entry barriers cause high seller concentration. The theory of entry barriers has been controversial at a normative level (Is it socially undesirable that X should shield incumbents' profits from entry?), but there is fairly general agreement about where and how entry barriers limit the number of market occupants, our concern here. These are the types of barriers normally recognized:

1. *Advertising outlays* are associated with an entry barrier in certain types of industries where advertising dominates the information sought by buyers and its dissemination is subject to scale economies.[1] Advertising is also a good indicator of the prevalence of proprietary and goodwill assets likely to support foreign investment, as we saw in Chapter 1.

---

[1] Without the scale economies, the entrant would be at no disadvantage. Without the dominant role of advertising as an information source, the entrant could use other marketing tactics (lower price, salespersons, etc.). With these conditions, incumbents can enjoy a substantial first-mover advantage.

2.   *Capital-cost barriers* arise where very large outlays are required to enter an industry at an efficient scale of production. It is not clear how much these entry barriers arise from the sunkenness of incumbents' capital investments (making the market noncontestable) and how much they devolve from capital-market imperfections. The latter might result from problems in asymmetrical information between would-be entrants and the financial markets – problems that incumbent firms have already somehow solved, bettering their costs of capital. The capital-markets interpretation implies an advantage for firms established elsewhere, including MNEs, as potential entrants, but the sunk-capital case yields them no such advantage.

3.   *Scale economies* in production limit the number of sellers who can earn positive profits. They have the least affinity for foreign investment because they induce firms to centralize production and export to foreign markets rather than to decentralize and acquire MNE status (Section 2.2). However, scale-economy barriers favor multinational operations in some instances. For an assembled product such as automobiles, scale economies might be modest in the final assembly stage but large (relative to the national market) in the production of certain components. If there is no smoothly working international arm's-length market for the components, the MNE can gain an advantage against single-nation firms by producing these components at a single location and assembling them in individual national markets.

4.   *Research and development* acts as a source of entry barriers because in some settings research activities involve scale economies and provide first-mover advantages to successful innovators.[2] The MNE's advantage for overcoming such barriers lies in the possibility of centralizing R&D activities worldwide, just as in the production of components subject to scale economies in production. But the centralization of R&D has a further advantage in that shipping intangible research results around the world may be less costly than shipping physical components.[3]

5.   *Organizational complexity* is an underworld candidate (Vernon, 1970; Lippman and Rumelt, 1982). If entry into an industry entails organizing a complex coalition of inputs, that task entails a scale economy or fixed cost of its own and more uncertain prospects for the would-be entrant. Many of MNEs' proprietary assets are bound up in the capabilities of just such complex coalitions, which both protects them against entry and favors them as entrants into other markets.

In short, each source of barriers to entry is linked to the reasons why MNEs exist in the first place. And MNEs hold some advantage over newly organized

[2] Like advertising, R&D is not associated with appreciable entry barriers in every setting. See Mueller and Tilton (1969) and Klepper and Graddy (1990).

[3] See Teece (1977) and the discussion in Chapter 7.

and/or single-nation firms in getting over these barriers to entry (implications to be considered subsequently).[4] Therefore the height of entry barriers and the extent of foreign-investment activity should be highly correlated. And because entry barriers mostly determine an industry's level of seller concentration, we expect foreign investment and seller concentration to be closely associated.

The empirical evidence clearly supports this conjecture. Dunning (1958, pp. 155–7) found two-thirds of surveyed U.K.-based foreign subsidiaries operating in highly concentrated markets. Steuer et al. (1973, p. 94; also see Dunning, 1973*b*) also observed a significant correlation between seller concentration and foreign subsidiaries' shares of U.K. industries' sales; industries with high concentration and substantial subsidiaries' shares usually contain three or more foreign subsidiaries among the leading firms. Fishwick (1981) reported high correlations between seller concentration and foreign investment in the United Kingdom for later years as well as for France and West Germany, and the pattern also appears for Guatemala (Willmore, 1976), Mexico (Blomström, 1989, Chapter 6), Australia (Parry, 1978), New Zealand (Deane, 1970, pp. 300–3), and Canada.[5] Pugel (1978, p. 68) found a close relationship for U.S. manufacturing industries between seller concentration and the share of activity carried out abroad.[6]

Several investigators probed the bases for this well-established correlation. Fishwick (1981) and Globerman (1979*b*) suggested that little or no correlation between concentration and foreign investment in the United Kingdom remains once other determinants of concentration are controlled. Rosenbluth (1970) showed that the prevalence of foreign subsidiaries in concentrated Canadian industries could be explained by the facts that subsidiaries tend to be big firms and the leading firms in concentrated industries are large. In the same vein, Steuer et al. (1973) and Fishwick (1981) noted that foreign investment is never prominent in unconcentrated industries, whereas it might or might not be in concentrated ones. (Concentrated industries can lack foreign investment when concentration rests on scale economies in production that national firms have fully exploited.)

---

[4] For a particularly clear empirical analysis of how proprietary assets serve to overcome entry barriers, see the study by Hawawini and Schill (1994) of Japanese banks' entry into the European financial services market.

[5] Caves et al. (1980, p. 87); Baumann (1975). The exceptions to this generalization hold some interest. Baba (1975) found no correlation for Japan and suggested that the reason might be the government's solicitous protection of concentrated domestic sellers.

[6] Also see Newfarmer and Mueller (1975) on Brazil and Mexico. Connor (1977, Table 3.19) gave a distribution of estimated minimum four-firm concentration ratios in the industries where these subsidiaries operate. In Brazil, 83% are in industries whose concentration exceeds 50%, 58% in industries where it exceeds 90%. For Mexico, the corresponding figures are 84% and 21%.

Effects of concentration on foreign investment

Even if oligopoly and foreign investment share common structural causes, either one could still wield some causal influence on the other. But we must tread cautiously when specifying the causal mechanisms and testing them so as to control for their common causes. What causal links can be established theoretically and empirically?

Take first the effect of concentration on foreign investment. Knickerbocker (1973) argued that the extent of foreign investment depends on the form that oligopolistic interdependence takes in certain U.S. manufacturing industries. If an oligopoly is "tight-knit," its members will share their plans and allocate resources within the industry approximately as will a single monopolist; investment abroad will take place only to maximize joint profits for the industry as a whole. In a loose-knit oligopoly, by contrast, firms recognize interdependence with their rivals but lack sufficient contractual consensus to coordinate their activities. They might then adopt simple imitative behavior: A leading firm raises its price, and others follow; someone expands capacity, and the rivals imitate lest they be disadvantaged in some ensuing price war (or other strategic interaction). Knickerbocker argued that imitation can occur in foreign investments. Rival *A* establishes a subsidiary in France. Rivals *B* and *C* recognize that this investment might knock out their export business in France and give *A* first-mover advantage if the investment should prove successful. Still worse, *A* might discover some competitive asset in France that it could repatriate to torment *B* and *C* on their native soil. These considerations dispose *B* and *C* to imitate *A* and found their own subsidiaries in France. Their combined expansions of capacity of course should cause excess capacity and/or depress prices in the French market – a deterrent. On the other hand, if the investments turn out badly for all parties, they do share *some* oligopolistic understanding and hence excess profits (worldwide) that will make the losses bearable.

This pattern had been noted in surveys and descriptive studies (Hellmann, 1970, p. 244; Hu, 1973, pp. 105, 137–8), but Knickerbocker first tested it statistically. Using data on subsidiaries founded by U.S. MNEs in 23 countries during 1948–67, he calculated "entry concentration indexes" indicating the extent to which the MNEs in a particular manufacturing industry bunched their investments in particular host countries and periods of time. Of course, entry could be concentrated because of common responses to the same favorable development in France, and some bunching would occur on a random basis. However, such factors cannot account for the significant relationships that Knickerbocker found between the extent of entry concentration and seller concentration in the U.S. parent industries: Entry concentration increases with seller concentration up to a point (eight-firm concentration around 60–70 percent), then declines. His oligopolistic-reaction model indeed predicts that imitative behavior should occur in moderately concentrated industries, not unconcentrated ones (no interdependence recognized) or highly concentrated ones (tight-knit oligopoly). Bunching is also more evident in industries whose U.S. parent firms went abroad for the first time after World War II, so that stable patterns of mutually dependent behavior were less likely to have matured. Less bunching occurs in industries in which oligopolistic rivalry is blunted by advertising or diversified product lines. Finally, some evidence suggests that imitative behavior is discouraged in industries where scale economies in production are important;[7] imitation then entails either onerous excess capacity in the newly entered foreign market or facilities that are inefficiently small.

Other studies have lent some statistical support for Knickerbocker's main hypothesis. For example, Caves et al. (1980, pp. 86–7) found that the extent of foreign investment in Canadian manufacturing industries (where U.S. companies account for about four-fifths of all foreign investment) is more closely associated with seller concentration in the corresponding U.S. industries than with concentration in the Canadian industries themselves; also, the relationship has the shape predicted and found by Knickerbocker – rising to a maximum at concentration levels that correspond to loose-knit oligopoly. Caves and Pugel (1980) found that in U.S. manufacturing industries the middle-size firms are more likely to be foreign investors in the more concentrated industries. Jarrett (1979, Chapter 3), however, did not confirm Knickerbocker's hypothesis in his analysis of the factors determining foreign investment by various U.S. manufacturing industries, perhaps because of multicollinearity among his explanatory variables. Flowers's (1976) study of foreign MNEs found simply that entry concentration rises with seller concentration in the home industry at a rate that differs from one source country to another. And Caves (1991) applied Knickerbocker's methodology to the horizontal mergers that took place across national boundaries during 1978–88; no link was confirmed between entry concentration and structure in a broad sample of industries, although imitative waves had apparently occurred in industries with selected common traits. These traits are such that the real options acquired in such mergers are adverse (when exercised) to the profits of competitors, who best respond by imitative mergers to acquire their own bundles of options.[8]

Effects of foreign investment on concentration

The relation between entry-barrier sources and foreign investment indicates that foreign investment can affect concentration, but with the direction of effect unclear. On the one hand, MNEs are the most favored potential en-

---

[7] Rather weak statistically; see Knickerbocker (1973, Chapter 6).

[8] Also see Yu and Ito (1988). We omit here a number of poorly specified studies that claim to test Knickerbocker's hypothesis without carefully conditioning it on market structure, as he did.

trants into national markets that are likely to be highly concentrated and profitable, implying that in equilibrium these markets will be less concentrated if MNEs may enter than otherwise. On the other hand, the scale economies inherent in their proprietary assets and their cost or revenue-productivity advantages over single-nation competitors can raise concentration by driving the latter from the market (or into a fringe corner of it). The pro-concentration potential of MNEs' operations can also be regarded as the outcome of random processes. Investments in developing proprietary assets have high-variance outcomes, which tend to increase concentration if the big winners greatly increase their market shares and are not systematically pulled back by subsequent reverses. These diverse possibilities make the specification of empirical tests and the interpretation of their results a delicate matter.

The most straightforward proposition to test is the ability of MNEs to surmount entry barriers that block most other firms. Gorecki (1976) first showed, using Canadian data, that structural entry barriers significantly deter domestic entrants but do not affect the inflow of MNEs. Shapiro (1983) replicated Gorecki's study with better data, finding that MNE entrants tend to be deterred by scale-economy and capital-cost entry barriers, but actually encouraged by barriers related to advertising and research and development (however, advertising and R&D also accelerate rates of market exit for MNEs). Geroski (1991) employed United Kingdom data to discriminate between the entry behavior of MNEs and domestic firms, concluding that the maximum profit that incumbents can take while forestalling entry by MNEs averages about one-tenth less than the maximum that precludes entry by domestic firms.

If MNEs enjoy some advantages in surmounting entry barriers, their arrival could still leave the entered market either less or more concentrated than before. Negative relationships between MNE entries and changes in concentration seem to be the rule. Knickerbocker (1976, pp. 77–8) found a significant negative correlation between numbers of entries into the U.S. market by non-U.S. MNEs and changes in concentration in U.S. manufacturing industries in the 1960s. The same pattern holds for industries in Italy, France, West Germany, and Canada.[9] Also, some studies (Steuer et al., 1973, p. 97; Fishwick, 1981, Chapter 2) found a negative relationship (significant for Fishwick) between the *level* of foreign investment and change in concentration for Britain. However, positive relationships between levels of both concentration and MNE activity persist for some countries (see Lall, 1979a, on Malaysia; Petrochilas, 1989, Chapter 8, on Greece) even after other determinants of concentration are controlled.

The evidence thus tends to suggest that MNEs' prevalence and concentration remain positively correlated, but in industries prone to foreign investment their

[9] See Rosenbluth (1970) for the evidence on Canada. The available case studies generally lead to the same conclusion. See Dunning (1974b) on various British industries.

roles as actual and potential entrants reduce the maximum price-cost distortions that concentrated participants can achieve. Other evidence amplifies this somewhat ambiguous conclusion. First, Knickerbocker (1976, pp. 38–59) and Vernon (1977, pp. 73–8) showed that the total number of MNEs increased greatly in the past half century, a growing population of both actual competitors in particular national industries and potential entrants to those industries. Knickerbocker (1976, pp. 64–74) also pointed out that the increasing extent of product-line diversification among MNEs' foreign subsidiaries implies that the potential MNE entrants into an industry are not restricted to foreign firms in that same industry. However, the industries with few diversifying MNE entrants are, as expected, those with high entry barriers due to product differentiation, research, or high capital costs and extensive scale economics.

Second, the method of the MNE's entry (green-field entry or the acquisition of an existing national firm) affects its competitive consequences, because green-field entry adds another seller to the market in question, whereas acquisition initially leaves concentration unchanged. The competitive significance of green-field entries should be greater, although entry by acquisition can have a pro-competitive significance if the MNE vitalizes a failing business or uses its nonproduction assets to make the acquired company more effective (see Section 3.3). Entry occurs more often by acquisition when MNEs are hastening to match their oligopolistic rivals' foreign investments (Dubin, 1976, Chapters 10–12): Rates of entry through acquisition rose during the episodes of bunched entry into foreign investment that Knickerbocker (1973) uncovered. Green-field entry is more common when the industry entered abroad is the same industry in which it is based at home (where it should, in any case, be an effective competitor). MNEs do make acquisitions to avoid the alternative of adding capacity to a concentrated industry (Caves and Mehra, 1986; compare Dubin, 1976, Chapters 6–8). However, acquisitions and other changes in corporate control occur more frequently in concentrated industries and industries in which MNEs are prevalent; they also have larger positive effects on the productivity of the affected business units, regardless of whether MNEs are involved in the control changes as buyers, sellers, or not at all (Baldwin and Caves, 1991).

Overall, these conclusions follow: The substantial overlap between the sources of entry barriers and the sources of foreign investment implies that the two should be highly correlated across industrial markets, as indeed they are. These correlations do not themselves prove that any direct causal relationships exist between foreign investment and concentration. Some relationships have been found, however. Rivalrous behavior in loose-knit oligopolies tends to promote foreign investment. And the occurrence of new entry by MNEs tends at least initially to reduce the level of concentration, even though entry is often effected by acquiring a local firm. Thus, neither of these causal chains simply amplifies the positive correlation between concentration and foreign investment that derives from their underlying common causes.

4.2. Market behavior with MNEs present

The conclusions of Section 4.1 leave us some distance to go with the relation between foreign investment and imperfect competition. The MNE's affiliate is a rival in an ongoing national market. The MNEs that compete in one national market might face each other in many markets and therefore recognize their mutual dependence more fully. If the *new* subsidiary tends to reduce seller concentration, the established subsidiary might elevate entry barriers. This section is concerned with such issues of ongoing behavior: Does the presence of MNEs increase, decrease, or simply alter patterns of oligopolistic interdependence in the world market? The question is difficult to answer, not just because of a scarcity of hard empirical evidence but also because the answer depends on what alternative we have in mind. Would markets be more rivalrous if all transnational ownership links existing among national companies were severed? The answer is almost an automatic yes, because many more companies would populate the world market than before. Would markets be less oligopolistic if no MNE had ever founded or expanded a foreign subsidiary? The answer depends on how many non-MNE companies would have arisen in the absence of competitive pressures from MNEs – no easy matter to determine. Cutting across these issues is the problem of the geographical scope of "the market" in which oligopoly elements may or may not exist. We follow custom in thinking of the nation as the first approximation to the geographical market, consistent with tariffs, international transportation costs, and shared legal and cultural systems that make economic communication easier within nations than between them. Still, some products are clearly sold in international markets, others in markets localized within nations.

Mutual dependence among MNEs

Do large MNEs collude with one another in individual national markets? Do they collude in recognition of their recurrent contacts in numerous national markets? Theoretical models of imperfect competition in single markets are numerous; they will not be reviewed here, except to note that they identify both the incentive of small numbers of rivals to collude for joint monopoly profits and the difficulty of sustaining cooperative contracts. The models specifically helpful here are those able to relate multilateral foreign direct investments to competitive environments in which they occur:

1. *Product differentiation* in a model of monopolistic competition suffices to explain why countries both export and import the same products (Helpman, 1981) and by extension why two-way foreign investment would occur (think of the foreign subsidiary as finishing and marketing its parent's distinctive product variety). This model explains why MNEs would face each other in sev-

eral markets, but it assumes that large numbers of them are present and that no strategic interactions take place (Brainard, 1993*a*).

2. *Intraindustry trade with Nash behavior* entails firms treating each national market as isolated from others and competing with local rivals in the manner of nonstrategic oligopolists. The specific outcome depends on the decision variable that firms employ: quantity-setting (Cournot) or price-setting (Bertrand) behavior (Brander and Krugman, 1983; Dei, 1990; Krugman, 1989, for a survey). As with the monopolistic competition models, extension of the model's insights from intraindustry trade to intraindustry foreign investment seems straightforward.

3. *Strategic interactions* can affect both firms' decisions to operate in several national markets and the competitive consequences of their presence in multiple markets. Horstmann and Markusen (1992) and Rowthorn (1992) analyzed the two-stage game in which duopolists based in separate national markets determine whether each will sell in the other's market through exports, a foreign subsidiary, or not at all. Campa and Donnenfeld (1994) showed that endogenous reactions of domestic rivals make it possible that the likelihood of foreign investment to circumvent a protective tariff need not increase monotonically with the tariff, once domestic rivals' optimal reactions are considered. Given the numbers of MNEs operating in a set of national markets, Bernheim and Whinston (1990) demonstrated how their multimarket contacts could make a cooperative (effectively collusive) outcome feasible, even though it might be infeasible in single markets taken one at a time (see also Cowling and Sugden, 1987, pp. 36–53).

It was shown in Chapter 2 that a great deal of mutually penetrating foreign investment exists among the industrial countries (Norman and Dunning, 1984, and Erdilek, 1985, treated various aspects of the subject). The empirical evidence to be reviewed here bears on the occurrence of collusion and other strategic interactions among MNEs. By implication, if not directly, it addresses the scopes of strategic and nonstrategic interactions among MNEs.

Much of what we know about collusive and cooperative contacts among MNEs comes from the first half of the twentieth century, perhaps because the significant multinational companies in many industries were fewer than today. It was noted that one natural form of international collusion – an agreement that firms will not compete in each others' territories – actually implies the absence of foreign direct investment or its limitation to individual firms' allotted spheres of influence. Vernon (1974*a*, pp. 276–7) argued that agreements not to compete can explain the almost complete lack of foreign investments by certain U.S. industries in the period between World Wars I and II. Most of the evidence, however, bears on the interactions of MNEs following the occurrence of foreign investments. In the worst case markets could wind up less competitive after the peace treaty is signed than they were before the initial aggressive move. An example is supplied by the British tobacco market after the entry of American Tobacco in 1901, induced by the British tariff, American purchased a leading British producer. That event caused 13 dismayed British rivals to merge into Imperial Tobacco. After a year of duopolistic rivalry, a peace treaty gave Imperial a monopoly of the British and Irish markets, and American got a guarantee that Imperial would not sell in the United States or its dependencies. British-American Tobacco was organized as a joint venture to handle business in the rest of the world.[10] Usually, however, it is unclear that the ensuing oligopolistic rapprochement sufficed to offset the competitive thrust of initiating foreign investments. Rivalry among foreign investors or exporters sometimes led to agreements not to compete, perhaps cemented by licensing agreements or other devices to neutralize competition among established subsidiaries.[11] Some agreements were forged by means of joint-venture subsidiaries or fractional shareholdings exchanged among the parent companies themselves.[12] International cartels were worked out to mitigate competition among established MNEs during recessions.[13] Jones's (1986a) analysis of the profitability of British MNEs attributed some successes to proprietary assets but others to membership in effective cartels.

International collusive arrangements among MNEs or potential MNEs evidently prevailed at some time before 1940 in a majority of industries where MNEs were active. Why does the record since World War II offer no such chronicle of successful collusive arrangements? We cannot rule out, of course, that such arrangements exist but remain concealed successfully. Examples do still turn up. Kudrle (1975, Chapter 10) documented parallel action of the farm-equipment MNEs to price-discriminate against the North American market for farm tractors (also see Newfarmer, 1980, Chapter 4). However, some old cartels clearly faltered or gave way to aggressive rivalry (Newfarmer, 1985, Chapters 3, 4). There are several reasons why the extent of effective international collusion should have decreased markedly. During 1945–55 many U.S. MNEs were successfully prosecuted under the antitrust laws for their earlier collusive behavior (Wilkins, 1974, Chapter 12). After World War II many countries passed antitrust laws, and if these varied in toughness and degree of enforcement, they were still tougher than nothing at all. Partly in response to antitrust prosecutions, partly seizing the opportunity opened by the wartime destruction of their European competitors, U.S. MNEs shifted from cooperative behavior

---

[10] Dunning (1958, pp. 30–1); Wilkins (1970, pp. 91–3). The explosives market during 1896–1914 provides a similar example (Wilkins, 1970, pp. 89–91), the metal-container industry a more recent one (Wagner, 1980). Also see Hu (1973, pp. 163–5) on the automobile industry.

[11] Wilkins (1974, pp. 79, 80, 82, 86–8, 151); Wilkins (1970, p: 87). See Dunning (1958, pp. 158–60) for more recent experience.

[12] Wilkins (1974, pp. 68, 78–9, 292–4); Franko (1976, Chapter 4).

[13] Wilkins (1974, pp. 173, 175).

to aggressive behavior during 1955–65 and rapidly expanded the number of standardized product lines (i.e., not intensive in R&D) that they produced in Europe.[14] With the successful recovery of Europe and Japan, far more "significant" companies (actual and potential MNEs) came to operate worldwide in most industries than before World War II, and seller concentration measured at the *world* level probably declined in many of the more concentrated industries (Vernon, 1977, p. 81).[15] Finally, the mix of important industries has shifted from those producing homogeneous primary materials (wherein the gap between collusive and rivalrous profits is apt to be large) toward those producing differentiated or heterogeneous goods (in which the differentiation supplies natural insulation to the individual seller while complicating the maintenance of collusion).[16]

Whatever the roles of these changes, recent evidence suggests not so much successful collusion among MNEs as the sort of imitative rivalry that Knickerbocker (1973) associated with loose-knit oligopoly among American multinationals. This behavior can lead to the formation of subsidiaries to preempt rivals or to punish a rival for an aggressive move undertaken elsewhere. Although examples of such behavior go back many years,[17] it has been systematically documented only by Graham (1978) for the years 1950–70. He hypothesized that a large company in MNE-prone industries, finding its domestic market invaded by a new subsidiary of a foreign MNE, is likely to retaliate by invading the foreigner's home turf. The affronted firm's proprietary assets can aid the subsidiary to earn a normal profit once its strategic value is counted. The strategic value arises if a subsidiary on the invader's turf establishes both a means of retaliation and a hostage that can be staked out in any subsequent understanding between the two parents. In a group of manufacturing industries, Graham determined the dates when European MNEs established subsidiaries in the United States and tested whether or not they were bunched in ways that significantly suggested a response to a previous bunching of American investments in Europe. He found such associations for a number of industries, and the lagged re-

[14] By contrast, the growth rate of these lines produced in Europe during the next decade (1965–75) was no more rapid than in the rest of the world (Vernon 1977, pp. 63–5).

[15] Stopford and Baden-Fuller (1988) investigated the interesting case of the European major home appliance industry in the 1970s and 1980s, when the formation of the European Community should have caused an increase in Community-wide concentration (because of great scale economies) but did not. They hold that exchange-rate turbulence supplemented by political pressures against exit kept most of the European firms in the game and precluded the expected concentration.

[16] Evidence from the United States and the United Kingdom rather strongly associates price fixing and market-division agreements among domestic producers with the traits of product homogeneity. See Hay and Kelley (1974) and Swann et al. (1974, Chapter 4), as well as Vernon (1974*b*).

[17] Wilkins (1970, pp. 89–90); Wilkins (1974, pp. 78, 83); Franko (1976, Chapter 4). Arthur D. Little (1976, p. 103) discussed some other reasons for this type of behavior.

sponse seemed to be more clearly evident in those industries with higher levels of seller concentration, high R&D outlays, and extensive product differentiation (which tends to set aside nonstrategic explanations).

Franko (1976, Chapter 6) reached conclusions similar to Graham's from reviewing the rapid proliferation of subsidiaries of European MNEs in other European countries after World War II.[18] Tariffs were then being eliminated within the European Community, a move that by itself should have promoted the concentration of production at the most efficient sites. However, it was also a time when the "negotiated environment" of soft competition under complaisant government supervision was giving way to more aggressive rivalry among European firms – both those based in the same and in different national markets. Of course, some of these proliferating subsidiaries might have served as hostages to the parent's cooperative behavior.[19]

MNEs and other market rivals

The concept of *strategic groups* helps us to understand the competitive role of MNEs and their subsidiaries. Firms can compete as active rivals without being identical as peas. They can differ in their participation in other markets: Some are vertically integrated or diversified, others not. They can differ in how they compete in the market at hand: Some produce a full product line, whereas others specialize; some advertise heavily, whereas others do not. Research on industrial organization has shown that, other things being equal, the more complex an industry's strategic-group structure, the more competitive is the market (Newman, 1978). This is because strategically similar firms readily recognize their interdependence with one another, pursue similar proximate goals, and react alike to disturbances. Members of different groups lack these natural harmonies.

The strategic-group concept suggests the hypothesis that MNEs might take part in different strategic groups than their national competitors, or that MNEs domiciled in different source countries might comprise different strategic groups.[20] A few industry studies seem to confirm this hypothesis. Sciberras (1977), for example, divided the U.K. semiconductor industry into two groups that are largely congruent with MNEs and national firms. Statistical evidence has also supported the hypothesis. Studies of both Canadian and Spanish manufacturing industries found that the structural forces determining the profitability of national enterprises and MNEs' subsidiaries are quite different, the latter being much less fully explained by conditions in the local market.[21] The

---

[18] Also see Tsurumi (1976, pp. 64–7, 121–3) on the experience of Japanese MNEs.

[19] Franko (1976, pp. 149–50) reported circumstantial evidence that a network of joint ventures in the plastics industry serves to give hostages against price cutting.

[20] These possibilities are discussed in more detail elsewhere (Caves, 1974c).

[21] Caves et al. (1980, Chapter 9); Donsimoni and Leoz-Arguelles (1980).

same two countries also supply evidence that the profits of domestic companies are lower the larger is the MNE group with which they compete.[22] That difference is of course implied by the proprietary-asset hypothesis about the basis of MNEs, and many studies have found MNE parents or subsidiaries to be more profitable than their domestic competitors. Shapiro (1980), for example, found U.S. (though not other MNEs') subsidiaries in Canada to be more profitable than Canadian firms after controlling for industry concentration and firms' sizes and financial structures.

The strategic-group concept might also apply to the rivalry between home-based and foreign MNEs in an industrial nation. Because of the national differences analyzed in Section 2.4, one would expect substantial variation among industries in the relative strengths of the home and foreign MNEs. Evidence from Sweden (Swedenborg, 1985, p. 232) and Britain (Hughes and Oughton, 1992) suggests a negative cross-industry correlation of their market shares and an adverse effect on each other's profits.

Anecdotal evidence confirms MNEs' distinctiveness as competitors. They compete in ways that use their proprietary assets to best advantage (Vernon, 1974*b*, 1977, Chapters 3–5). A MNE new to a national market likely proves a disturbing competitive force. Any entrant is likely to disturb an industry with few sellers, but the MNE, lacking familiarity with local folkways, is less likely to fall in with any prevailing pattern of cooperation, a prediction documented by the complaints of its national rivals (Behrman, 1970, pp. 43–52, provided examples). Domestic competitors' reactions will include attempts to emulate or offset the proprietary assets brought by the foreign investor; Dunning (1986, Chapter 8) chronicled U.K. firms' product competition and cost-cutting that followed the entry of Japanese competitors. On the other hand, as the subsidiary ages and "goes native," its competitive manners improve as its market conduct becomes less distinguishable from that of domestically controlled enterprises. A final point of distinctiveness was established by Williamson (1986), who investigated the effect of foreign subsidiaries' presence on the competition between imports and domestic output in Australian industries. The sensitivity of domestic producers' margins to import prices is lower where MNEs prevail (even with product differentiation controlled), but imports' market shares adjust more sensitively to gaps between domestic and import prices where MNEs are active (which suggests that they internalize sourcing decisions effectively).

Profitability and market performance

Concentrated market structures and collusive conduct raise normative concerns about the allocative efficiency of markets. Those concerns have motivated research on the profits reported by MNEs (parents, subsidiaries) simi-

---

[22] Caves (1974*a*); Donsimoni and Leoz-Arguelles (1980).

lar to those addressed to price-cost markups in general. Both in general and in its applications to MNEs this research runs into problems of interpretation. That concentrated sellers as a group mark prices up above marginal costs has a clear normative interpretation – a deadweight loss of welfare is occurring. Whether some policy intervention can effectively retrieve the loss remains a separate question. What if particular sellers in a market (possibly MNEs) earn excess profits but others do not? There is no market-level problem of deadweight losses. However, a different normative question might arise as to why the profitable sellers' proprietary advantages do not diffuse (so that other sellers can become equally cost-effective), and whether public policy should encourage that diffusion. Let us turn to selected evidence.

Connor (1977, Chapter 5) applied the standard research procedure to subsidiaries of U.S. MNEs operating in manufacturing industries of Mexico and Brazil. He expected their profits to depend on the concentration of all sellers in the host-country markets, the subsidiaries' own shares, and their local investments in proprietary assets (advertising, R&D). His findings were not robust and varied between the two hosts, but they do yield a few generalizations. For Brazil a subsidiary's profits increase with both industry concentration and its own market share, but are unrelated to the subsidiary's outlays on advertising or research. Lecraw (1983) studied subsidiaries operating in light manufacturing industries in Southeast Asian developing countries. He similarly found each subsidiary's profits to increase with both its own share and market concentration (leading firms' shares). These results confirm the conventional wisdom about industry concentration and profits. They also reveal the rents to MNEs' proprietary assets, because the more productive the asset (something that cannot be observed directly), the higher are both the subsidiary's market share and its profit rate. The normative issue raised by the latter result is exactly the one mentioned in the preceding paragraph.

Lecraw reported other noteworthy results. Profits decline with the number of source countries represented by subsidiaries in the market – a direct test of the hypothesis that a market's strategic complexity is hostile to collusion and monopoly rents (Newman, 1978). Profits increase with tariff protection and decrease with capital intensity and the recent change in the subsidiary's share (suggesting that aggressive competition does not increase short-run profits). Unlike Connor he found some significant influence of a subsidiary's R&D and advertising on its own profit rate; a nonsignificant result here, however, is no surprise, because the MNE's proprietary asset probably results mainly from current and past outlays of the parent and not its subsidiaries.

Kumar (1990) analyzed the determinants of price-cost margins of both foreign and domestic firms in India, where policy interventions likely have strong effects. Concentration and tariff protection are not significant influences, but foreign subsidiaries' margins increase with their reliance on nonproduction la-

bor (presumably involved in deploying their proprietary assets) and their reliance on imported technology, and domestic competitors apparently do better
where they are large and can employ labor-intensive production techniques.

Bergsten et al. (1978, Chapter 7) were concerned with the effects of foreign
investments by U.S. companies on the profitabilities of their domestic operations. Assuming rational investments by these parties in their foreign subsidiaries, the parents' profitability could be augmented through their foreign
investments, in three ways with quite different normative implications. First,
proprietary assets discovered or developed at home and then used abroad can
yield rents.[23] Second, the MNE's diversification allows it to undertake riskier
activities than firms with fewer options for spreading their risks, and therefore
might earn higher average worldwide profits. (Of course, with *enough* MNEs
around, these rents will be competed away.) Third, assets picked up in its overseas activities might allow the American MNE to blockade entry, intimidate rivals, or otherwise make the American market less competitive than otherwise
(see Horst, 1974*a*, Chapter 5). Bergsten et al. found that the domestic profits of
firms in U.S. industries increase (i.e., with profits from abroad controlled) significantly with the extent of their overseas activities, as well as with their research and sales-promotion outlays. However, a company's absolute size
(including overseas assets) is not a determinant of its profits. Bergsten et al. asserted that this statistical result points to the third link between MNE activity
and profits, but it is unclear how the third is distinguishing from the first in that
the better proprietary asset yields both more domestic revenue and more profitable foreign investment.

In conclusion, MNEs are large firms that typically operate in concentrated industries and earn both monopoly profits and rents to their proprietary
assets. However, there is no decisive evidence that multinational status either
does or does not feed back to make industries still more concentrated or less
competitive.

4.3. Competition policy and national welfare

Because transnational ownership links can affect the competitiveness
of markets, the MNE's competitive behavior raises issues of public policy.
Every industrial country has some form of competition policy on its statute
books – enforced with some degree of vigor, and pursuing objectives that usually, but not always, are pro-competitive. Welfare economics affirms that competition policy can help to avert some market failures. The details are
complex, and dilemmas definitely arise in which more competitive markets
bring society closer to one normative goal while taking it further from another.
Nonetheless, the case for the normative superiority of competitive versus non-

---

[23] Severn and Laurence (1974) concluded that the profits of U.S. MNEs were augmented
by their ability to amortize the cost of their research activities over worldwide markets.

competitive markets is broad enough that we assume more competitive markets to be desirable for purposes of the following discussion.

In competition policy we encounter for the first time, but not the last, the dilemma of national objectives in policy toward the MNE. Welfare economics usually assumes that the proper and expected goal of national economic policy is to maximize the national income – expected because the government is elected by those who receive the national income, proper because a maximized income can *potentially* be distributed so as to make everyone better off. If each nation acts to maximize its own national income, however, world income need not be maximized, because many policies can potentially raise one country's income while lowering that of another. Such redistributions naturally require some transmission belt that links market conditions in the two countries, and this the MNE can provide. If such links exist, the policies that will maximize national incomes taken separately are not globally efficient, and they also become bases for conflict when they redistribute welfare internationally.

In competition policy, the core of the dilemma is quite clear. Within the national economy, optimal competition policy calls for competitive markets. In order to maximize national income in international transactions, however, the nation should extract the maximum monopoly rents from foreigners: charge the monopolist's profit-maximizing price on everything they sell and pay only the monopsonist's profit-maximizing price for anything they buy. The MNEs, along with the exporters and importers, are citizens whose activities invite interference in pursuit of these objectives. Of course, just as each nation rationally seeks to gain monopolistic advantage over others, it also seeks to repel their efforts to wrest the same types of rents from its own citizens. MNEs, especially because their incorporated subsidiaries are legally citizens of their countries of residence, are inevitably caught in the conflict. We summarize a few theoretical points concerning competition policy with MNEs present, then briefly explore the encounters that have taken place between MNEs and U.S. antitrust policy.

MNEs and the theory of competition policy

The normative criteria that welfare economics provides for competition policy in the open economy are a simple translation of those it provides for tariff policy. Domestic markets should be competitive, with the social marginal value (generally equal to market price) in each market set equal to social marginal cost. On foreign sales, however, the social marginal cost should be equated to the nation's marginal revenue. On purchases from foreigners, social marginal value should be equated to the extra revenue expended on the last unit bought. In the context of tariff policy, and with all markets assumed to be competitive, these prescriptions call for a series of taxes on imports and exports calculated so as to exploit any monopoly or monopsony power that the nation possesses. An alternative, equivalent under some circumstances, is simply to allow and encourage the nation's international sellers and buyers to do the monopolizing themselves. The two policies differ only in whether the revenues turn up in the public treasury or in private hands. This prescription of monopoly/monopsony applies to MNEs as well. MNEs that produce and sell abroad should be encouraged not to compete with one another in foreign markets. National MNEs acquiring goods abroad for domestic sale should be discouraged from competing as buyers.

The plot thickens if the rival MNEs that invest and sell (or buy) abroad also do business in the domestic market. Conceivably the government could allow them to behave as monopolists abroad but admonish them to behave competitively at home. Indeed, most countries attempt just this strategy by allowing their exporters to collude on their foreign transactions in ways that would be illegal at home (Organization for Economic Cooperation and Development, 1974). How a given set of firms can cooperate to different degrees in different markets is unclear; Auquier and Caves (1979) showed what compromise competition policy should choose if the same price-cost markup must prevail in both international and domestic transactions. The more international an industry's business, the higher the degree of monopoly that should be allowed by competition policy. Indeed, under restrictive assumptions, the degree of monopoly should be set equal to the fraction of sales made abroad.

The nation that buys goods from a foreign monopolist, whether MNE or not, can wield policies to improve its national welfare. If the monopolist profitably supplies the country's market through imports, imposing a tariff can improve the home country's welfare. The welfare gain does not depend on the monopolist producing under increasing cost, as it does when the foreign industry is competitive, although it does depend on the shape of the demand curve (Corden, 1967; Katrak, 1977). But that optimal tariff could induce the monopolist to switch over to serving the home market through a local subsidiary. Svedberg (1977, Chapter 3; 1979) showed that this switch can leave the home country better off because it can then tax the subsidiary's profits. But the home welfare level associated with a taxed subsidiary can fall short of that attained when a tariff captures part of the monopolist's profits from selling imports. If so, the home country should ban the foreign investment. Bardhan (1982) developed a similar comparison of cases.

Competition policy as well as tariffs can be used with monopolistic foreign sellers. Indeed, a policy of enforcing competition successfully applied to foreign subsidiaries by a host government has a greater welfare payout than an application to an otherwise identical domestic firm (or industry), because foreign producers' surplus is shifted to domestic pockets. If competition policy cannot force prices into equality with marginal costs, national welfare can be raised by shifting business (and producers' surplus) to foreign subsidiaries' domestic competitors – even if the latters' costs are higher.

Competition policy might also address the normatively significant entry-deterrence games that have been studied by Horstmann and Markusen (1987*b*, 1989) and Smith (1987). First, a MNE might invest strategically in a small market in order to preempt a potential local competitor; such preemption can be profitable because the MNE incurs a transport cost serving the host market with exports, and it gains a cost advantage over the local rival from recycling its proprietary asset. The host nation's welfare might be impaired by this preemption: In such a setting the host is better off with foreign investment if competition suffices to drive prices down to average costs or if the local firm would not enter in any case; but it might lose if the host market can support a local firm only with no foreign competition (cannot support one engaged in Cournot competition with a foreign subsidiary).

"Profit-shifting" policies have been studied extensively in the setting of international competition in third-country markets between duopolists based in different countries, and the conclusions apply as well to production by foreign subsidiaries as by exporting (see the survey by Krugman, 1989, pp. 1201–7). Suppose that the two duopolists compete as either Cournot or Bertrand sellers. If one government can commit itself to subsidize (in the Cournot case) or tax (Bertrand) its national duopolist, the national firm adjusts its decision variable in light of the subsidy or tax, and the other duopolist responds. The net effect is that profits are shifted from the foreign to the home seller. In some cases a country might want to subsidize a foreign enterprise if the resultant expansion of its output brought a sufficiently favorable change in the nation's terms of trade (Barros, 1994). Such models of strategic trade policy attracted much attention during the 1980s. However, their shortcomings make them poor bets for serious policymakers: the indeterminacy of whether tax or subsidy should be used (unless the primacy of price or quantity competition can be observed empirically), the possibility of retaliation by the foreign government, and the unclarity of why a government can effect a commitment to boost its firm into a Stackelberg leadership position (which is what the tax or subsidy is supposed to do).

Suppose that national authorities eschew all these nationalistic policies and turn a blind eye to the parentage of firms in the national market. MNEs still raise problems for optimal competition policy. One national firm acquires a company selling the same product line in another country. If the two nations' officials detect monopolistic tendencies by watching the concentration of domestic *producers*, the usual practice, neither authority sees anything amiss. That is because producer concentration remains unchanged (at least initially). But the merger leaves one less independent firm in the world market, and so international *seller* concentration has necessarily increased. And seller concentration rises in one or both of the countries if either of the now-combined firms formerly exported to the other nation. The world's interest in competitive markets is therefore not automatically served by national authorities, even if they forswear taking monopolistic advantage of each other. Having each national competition-policy authority promote effective competition among whatever firms operate in its own national market is still not worldwide first-best.

U.S. antitrust policy

A thorough survey of national competition policy toward MNEs is beyond the scope of this volume, but a brief sketch will illustrate the relationship between theory and policy.[24] Perhaps because of its large and relatively closed economy, the United States traditionally applied antitrust policy more vigorously than did other industrial nations with smaller and more open economies. U.S. policy has allowed its domestic producers less freedom to collude when selling abroad, fearing that foreign-market collusion is likely to spill onto the domestic market. Several threads of U.S. policy tend to maximize world rather than domestic welfare. International mergers have come under fire several times because the foreign firm acquired by a U.S. enterprise was a significant potential (if not actual) competitor in the U.S. market, or even when the probably anticompetitive effect lay partly or even wholly outside the United States. A series of cases after World War II attacked joint ventures that U.S. MNEs had formed with their overseas competitors. Some of these ventures implemented agreements to divide markets and exclude foreign competitors from the United States, in which case domestic economic welfare was the main issue. Other joint ventures, however, had bolstered U.S. MNEs' ability to extract rents from foreign markets. The courts specifically rejected the contention that laws allowing U.S. producers to collude on export sales justified joint or collusive behavior in establishing subsidiaries overseas. It is not clear that the world-welfare perspective would survive if antitrust were an active policy area today, as the U.S. government has cast about for ways to weaken the proprietary assets of foreign firms competing with U.S. MNEs.[25]

4.4. **Vertically integrated MNEs and competition for resource rents**

The other major issue of competition for MNEs is their interaction with host-country governments over rents to the host nations' natural resources.

---

[24] Brewster (1958) undertook the classic study of international aspects of U.S. antitrust policy; Wilkins (1974, pp. 291–300) offered a convenient summary of the major cases and some of their consequences. Organization for Economic Cooperation and Development (1977, pp. 17–34) summarized recent cases in other countries.

[25] "U.S. Sues British in Antitrust Case," *New York Times*, May 27, 1994, pp. A1, D2. Issues of national courts' jurisdictional reach over MNEs are always present; see Hymowitz (1986) and Williams (1987).

Issues of expropriation and confiscatory taxation have, we shall see, revolved largely around the division of natural-resource rents. These interactions worked themselves out in a complex process over many decades of the twentieth century, but only recently have the theoretical models useful for interpreting them been clearly set forth. Nonetheless, we start with the models.

Models of natural-resource development with sunk costs

Assume that the host government holds sovereign rights to subsurface deposits of some nonrenewable natural resource. The government's objective is to maximize welfare for its citizens. To realize the value of the resource, a mine must first be dug, the (large) cost of which is sunk and irretrievable. A foreign MNE is the economic agent most efficient at constructing and operating the facility. Suppose that the MNE and the government were to reach some agreement that the MNE would build and operate the mine, making fixed and/or continuing payments to the government that divide the rents between them. Once the MNE sinks the investment, the government maximizes national welfare by expropriating the property without compensation and capturing all of the rents. The government cannot credibly commit itself in advance not to expropriate, by the very fact of its sovereignty. The firm understands this second-stage outcome of the game and hence refuses to make the investment in the first place.

This simple case and variations on it were explored by Eaton and Gersovitz (1984) and others, mainly to seek mechanisms that could resolve the dilemma exposed by the simple model. Eaton and Gersovitz assumed that managerial services are a necessary input, along with the (sunk) capital and natural resource. Managerial services are a flow input neither sunk nor capable of expropriation. Then a feasible agreement is for the sovereign host government to incur the sunk cost of the mine while the MNE provides the managerial services. If the capital-supply role remains with the MNE and the government can make limited credible commitments not to usurp the project's cash flow, Bond and Samuelson (1989) showed that the project might be feasible but suboptimally capitalized. Raff (1992) injected the possibility that the host government is uninformed about the MNEs' cost structure and might therefore settle for taxation (making investment feasible) rather than expropriation. Cole and English (1991) and Veugelers (1993) addressed in different ways multiple stages to the game, such that expropriation is deterred by the host's opportunity to lure in more capital and exploit at a later time, or by the threat that no other MNE will come along to serve its needs. Thomas and Worrall (1994) showed the value of organizing the deal so that the MNE takes its cash flows at the outset while the government waits; the government's terminal cash flow is itself a deterrent to expropriation, and this contract form matches the tax holidays in widespread use between MNEs and some host governments (Section 9.1). The presence of a domestic rival to the MNE can complicate the process (Mohtadi, 1990).

Rents and the extractive MNE

Consider a series of competitively organized production processes – one extracting a nonrenewable natural resource, then selling it to the first refining or processing stage, which then passes it along to the next. With each of these stages competitively organized, the equilibrium price paid by the final buyer yields only a normal rate of return to each of the processing stages. At the initial extractive stage, however, the owners of the natural resource might collect scarcity rents over and above the costs of inputs to the extractive process. These rents result from the recognition by all market participants that the ultimate physical scarcity of the resource will cause its net price to be bid up over time. The owner therefore does not extract any unit of the resource if extracting it later is expected to command a price with a higher present discounted value. This action is individually rational; no collusion among resource owners is involved. In addition to these scarcity rents, some resource owners might earn differential or "Ricardian" rents because their resources are of better quality, cheaper to extract, or more conveniently located than other deposits in use.

Now let one or more of these vertically related stages become monopolized. Under certain assumptions (precluding substitutability between the resource and other inputs), one maximum lump of monopoly profits can be extracted from the whole set of vertically related processes. A monopoly operating at any stage can claim it. If a monopolistic tourniquet has been tightened at one stage, monopoly emerging at another stage in the chain cannot generate any larger lump of total monopoly profits, but the two (or more) monopolized stages can misallocate resources worse than does a monopoly at just one stage. Although the single-stage monopolist can grab the maximum profit lump at any stage, the natural-resource owners are in a peculiar position for monopolizing the resource. This is because they hold a stock of the resource, rather than dealing in a flow of output. If they raise price today and reduce demand, units of the resource must have a lower opportunity cost in some future time period. The monopolistic owner of a fixed-stock natural resource plans a different profile of output over time from a competitive industry, and might well choose a slower extraction rate, but the chosen profile depends on complex factors of time horizons and the shape of the demand curve (its elasticity at various prices). Clearly, though, a successful resource cartel such as the Organization of Petroleum Exporting Countries (OPEC) can wallow in short-run monopoly rents when it surprises its customers with an unexpected price rise, and their short-run elasticity of demand is lower than in the long run, when they can substitute other materials for the monopolized resource.[26]

Vertically integrated MNEs enter into this tale of vertically related markets at two points. First, they deal with the ultimate governmental (or other) owners

[26] See Pindyck (1978) on the monopolization of stock resources.

of the natural resources, striking bargains to incur sunk and avoidable input costs. Second, vertical MNEs compete with each other in small-numbers situations. They can be rivals for rights to extract particular natural resources, a factor that should affect the bargain struck with the resource owners. And their rivalry or cooperation can affect the behavior of markets at other stages in the sequence.

LDCs, MNEs, and the division of resource rents

The bargains struck by vertical MNEs with host governments over the shares of rents attributable to natural resources have changed dramatically over time. The story originates in the history of colonialism and political interference by the metropolitan countries with the independence of undeveloped areas. An issue quite central to the vast, ideologically charged debate over the nature and purpose of colonial expansion is whether or not economic objectives related to resource rents were central in the pursuit of colonies. The economic behavior of MNEs, however, became an important issue only in the postcolonial years, when these companies found themselves bargaining with sovereign host governments concerned with the maximum welfare of their own citizens. Surveys of this experience (Vernon, 1971, Chapter 2; Smith and Wells, 1975, Chapter 2; Bergsten et al., 1978, Chapter 5) revealed the changing outcomes of these bargains. The changes affect both the deal struck when the MNE enters and its revision once the resource development is under way.

Deals on initial investments changed with the growing independence and sophistication of LDC governments and, in many markets, the increased numbers of MNEs competing for resource projects. Formerly MNEs got long-term contracts ("concessions") giving them extensive rights in return for fixed and modest royalty payments. The royalty payment (an inefficient device, because it raises the MNE's marginal cost and restricts output) gave way (roughly in the 1950s) to taxation arrangements for sharing the rents, which removed that inefficiency and also shifted some risk to the host government. The hosts also sharply raised their shares of the rents, often taking their gains partly in the form of policy commitments to development objectives (local processing of materials, training nationals, etc.). Host governments increasingly demanded an equity share in the project, which is really no different from taxing the MNE's profits and need not transfer to the host government more of the rents than would a profits tax (Smith and Wells, 1975, Chapter 2; Garnaut and Clunies Ross, 1975; Gillis et al., 1980).

Other changes involve the "obsolescing bargain," a direct empirical counterpart of the strategic interaction with sunk costs outlined previously. The host government with sufficient credibility commits to a deal, and the MNE begins to sink a heavy investment in resource extraction. Apart from any uncertainty about the government's future behavior, there exists great economic and technical uncertainty about the project's future returns, causing the MNE to hold out for high expected returns in the ex ante contract. If the project equals or exceeds the MNE's expectations, the MNE earns economic profits that might be quite visible to host-country citizens. In that event, the host nation is likely to grow dissatisfied with its terms (Kindleberger, 1969). Even if the government that signed the original agreement stands by it, the process of political competition (whether electoral or revolutionary) brings onto the scene government officials who demand renegotiation of an agreement seen to yield "excessive" profits to the foreigner.[27] In the 1950s and 1960s this pressure usually led to the expropriation of the subsidiary by the host government, with the MNE paid off at negotiated terms. The payoff often was at book value, which in principle lets the MNE recoup its investment but not capitalize the stream of rents that it has been enjoying. Surveys indicated that extractive MNEs were far more concerned about the hazard of expropriation than were other MNEs (Barlow and Wender, 1955, p. 128). Kobrin (1982) observed that natural-resource MNEs are more likely to incur the fixed cost of a staff charged with political risk assignment. And Williams's data (1975) (also see Truitt, 1974, and Sigmund, 1980) on the extent of nationalization of foreign investments by LDCs showed the heaviest incidences in agriculture and mining and smelting, along with public utilities.

As host-country governments gained sophistication, they came to recognize that nationalization does not necessarily maximize their national benefits from MNEs' extractive projects. Expropriation, a highly aggressive action, can provoke the victimized MNE to bring its source government to its aid. The host government might be unable to run the operation as effectively as did the MNE, so that the rent stream shrivels appreciably. And the expropriating government could well need the downstream refining and marketing arms of the MNE to process and distribute the output of the nationalized plant.[28] Taxation is a less confrontational and possibly more effective method for the host government to

[27] Picht and Stüven (1991) tested the factors determining whether countries undertook significant expropriations during 1974–5, getting no support for a model resting on national income maximization but substantial support for a behavioral model treating expropriation as a scapegoat strategy. They did find that countries seem to recognize the negative effects of expropriation on good credit ratings.

[28] Williams's (1975) data provide some evidence on this point in the differences among sectors in the extent to which the expropriated companies were compensated for the book value of their investments. Presumably a government that has undertaken to nationalize will compensate the victim only to the extent necessary to maintain some optimal goodwill. The strongest case for compensation comes when the government expects that it will indeed need to maintain future transactions with the MNE. Therefore, the highest proportion of nationalized assets compensated should be in the vertically integrated sectors. Indeed, Williams (1975, Table 6) found the highest proportions in oil production and refining and in mining and smelting; however, the proportion in agriculture was very low.

seize the rents. Therefore, the conflicts with MNEs shifted from expropriation to the obsolescing bargain. The MNE enters under agreed terms for the tax and royalty payments it makes to the host government. If the project yields excess profits, political competition forces the government to demand higher payments in some form. The company curtails its commitment of new funds in response to its revised expectation. However, if the project remains viable, the host government need allow the MNE only the minimum cash flow to cover its variable costs. The host country thus appropriates not just any rents obtained by the MNE but its quasi rents as well – the "normal" profit and depreciation flows from its investment in facilities. In this case the host country can gain more by taxation than by expropriation if nationalization is compensated at book value.[29]

One can charge firms caught in the obsolescing bargain with short-sightedness, but the stylized description does indicate how intendedly rational parties, incompletely informed but without misrepresentation, could fall into such sequences. Government behavior also appears rational ex post.[30] In the aluminum industry, the aggressiveness of various host countries with bauxite deposits varied with the rents and quasi rents potentially available to them. Countries close to the major consuming countries levied higher charges than those some distance away, to collect Ricardian rents due to lower costs of transport to consuming countries. Also, countries with recently developed deposits, where the MNE may be willing to consider additional investments, exercise more restraint (Mikesell, 1975). McKern (1976, pp. 189–93) attempted a comparative analysis of the bargaining outcomes in Australian extractive sectors by calculating approximate ratios of their rates of return to foreign-supplied and domestic capital. The calculation did not impute a rent to the resource itself. He found Australia's profit share lower in sectors that are highly technology-intensive at their downstream processing stages, so that barriers to entry protect the foreign investor from competing bidders. Australia's share increases with the size (relative to world reserves) and quality of the Australian resources, confirming the nation's ultimate access to the rents.

Ultimately other organizational forms replaced the MNE in activities with heavy sunk costs, as the theoretical model predicts. Descriptions of recent practice (UNCTC, 1982, 1983a) emphasize two changes. First, the ex ante contracting process has gained a great deal more sophistication, so that the sharing of risks and rents and the handling of contingencies is more fully anticipated,

---

[29] These taxation practices will be considered further in Chapter 8.

[30] Of course, if the MNE had few rivals when it negotiated its initial contract with the host government, it presumably won more surplus that could "obsolesce" once its fixed capital had been given over as hostage; Diaz Alejandro (1979) surveyed some of the evidence. The effect of MNE competition on the initial bargain will be discussed subsequently.

and the ex post haggling and "obsolescing" processes are substantially reduced. The efficiency of specific contract terms is better judged: for example, output-sharing arrangements induce the managing MNE to produce suboptimal output, but they could still improve on a profit-sharing arrangement that requires monitoring of the MNE's transfer pricing. Second, a variety of ways have been found to avoid the sunk-cost problem. The MNE commonly now supplies not the physical capital but the mobile assets on which its proprietary advantages actually rest: management inputs and downstream processing and/or marketing of the extractive output. The host government organizes a parallel national corporation to provide the physical investment and infrastructure for the project and also to serve as a monitor of the terms of the contract.

Dealings between MNEs and host governments were strongly affected by competition among MNEs. The multinational petroleum companies varied in their rates and patterns of expansion into the international industry, and one can observe repeated strategic moves by each company designed to keep its capacity at the crude and refining stages in balance (Wilkins, 1974). The companies clearly believed their positions highly risky and sought to limit that risk by maintaining an administratively controlled series of production stages reaching from crude extraction to retail distribution.[31] A vitally important development after World War II was the entry of new firms, which had a profound effect on the terms of bargaining for concessions with the oil-producing countries. The triumphant monopolization of the industry by OPEC in 1973 was clearly set on its course by the success of certain countries in wringing better terms from crude-short companies newly entering into the international market, and with nothing to lose from any renegotiation of contracts signed in the past. OPEC's first major across-the-board increase was traced to the effects of competition for concessions in certain North African countries in the 1960s (Vernon, 1976a, pp. 159–78). Even before that, the majors had been willing to go along with tax increases by the producing countries because these taxes were calculated in a way that made them a deterrent to price cutting by the companies in their sales of petroleum (Penrose, 1968, pp. 200–10).

Some features of the international aluminum industry also illustrate defensive strategies and the effects of competition. Stuckey (1983, Chapter 2) observed a slight downward trend in the extent of vertical integration of the leading companies over 1955–77, but newcomers still proceed toward full vertical integration as expeditiously as possible. He voiced some surprise at this

---

[31] The reasons for vertical integration in petroleum have been discussed by Penrose (1968, pp. 46–50, 253–9), Greening (1976), and Teece (1976), among others. Adelman (1972, pp. 94–7) (also see Greening, 1976, Chapter 2) also stressed the role of forward integration into distribution in stabilizing market shares and maintaining points of contact among the majors for evaluating each others' plans. Litvak and Maule (1977) discussed this pattern in another industry.

trend because the industry's total output has grown faster than the efficient scale of facilities in refining, so that one might otherwise expect less integration as well as more competition in the emerging structure. International joint ventures in aluminum grew explosively in the 1960s and 1970s, so that by 1977 they accounted for 36.2 percent of bauxite production, 44.7 percent of alumina, and 38.0 percent of primary aluminum. Stuckey's (1983, Chapter 4) explanations included several transaction-cost factors noted previously (Section 3.4), but he also judged that joint ventures help to restrain competition. After World War II many new entrants came into the aluminum industry, including Japanese firms and state-owned enterprises in countries that were not traditional aluminum refiners. Not only did their entry make the industry more competitive per se, but also their "strangeness" fragmented its strategic-group structure, rendering mutual understandings difficult. Stuckey suggested that the established firms welcomed the newcomers into joint ventures partly to socialize them and to ease communication within the industry.[32]

4.5. **Summary**

The transaction-cost model of the MNE predicts that it will not appear in purely competitive markets. The same features of a market's structure that explain the coming of MNEs also can give rise to barriers to the entry of new firms. Because of these common causes, we expect, and find, high correlations between industries' levels of seller concentration and the prevalence of MNEs. Correlation is not causation, however, and the question of causal relationships between MNEs and concentration is intricate. Knickerbocker (1973) showed that foreign investment in some moderately concentrated industries behaves like other forms of nonprice competition: It is inflated in oligopolies whose leading firms recognize their rivalry but imitate each other defensively rather than cooperating. As a result, an industry's foreign-investment decisions become bunched. The possible effects of MNEs on seller concentration are various, but one is clearly the MNE's role as a favored potential entrant. Influxes of MNEs at least initially reduce the concentration of the national markets that they enter. This pro-competitive role is weakened by MNEs' blossoming taste for entering markets by acquiring established local firms.

Several theoretical models explain why MNEs should interpenetrate each other's national markets for both nonstrategic and strategic reasons, and also why parallel contacts among multimarket firms can increase the feasibility of interfirm cooperation or collusion. Empirical evidence on the aftermath of MNEs' market entries documents collusive outcomes prior to World War II.

---

[32] By a contrary policy of freezing them out of joint ventures, the established firms might have weakened them or deterred their entry. Stuckey suggested that this strategy was not used because entry barriers were in any case no longer sufficient to keep out certain major potential entrants (large copper and oil companies).

Since the war, however, many more MNEs populate most industries than before, and more countries seriously apply competition policy. MNEs make the strategic-group structures of markets more complex, a pro-competitive development. Statistical analyses of MNEs' profits do not effectively test their competitive behavior, because those profits include rents to the MNEs' proprietary assets as well as any monopoly profits.

MNEs pose a dilemma for competition policy insofar as national policy seeks to maximize national welfare, not that of the trading world as a whole. Maximum national welfare calls for competition in home markets but seizure of any opportunity for the nation's MNEs (and other citizens) to lift monopoly rents from foreign pockets. In domestic markets competition-policy authorities should discriminate against foreign monopolists if and only if policy resources are insufficient to go around. Various national policies are identified that might shift profits from foreign to domestic pockets. United States antitrust policy has, for whatever reason, been rather sensitive to international linkages and foreign national welfare in cases dealing with MNEs, apparently closer to maximizing world than national welfare.

Vertically integrated MNEs compete for nonrenewable natural resources, a process that brings them into bargaining with host-country governments seeking to maximize the contributions of resource rents to their national incomes. Given large sunk costs of extracting natural resources, a host government's power to expropriate theoretically precludes foreign investment unless a repeated game or a transfer of the sunk-cost obligation to the government averts the problem. The empirical evidence on expropriation and invasive taxation illustrates the empirical counterparts of these models from contract theory.

5

Income distribution and labor relations

The MNE's relationship to wages and income distribution raises questions at two levels of analysis. In general equilibrium, the MNE reallocates capital between nations. That transfer can alter the income distribution within the source and host countries. In the individual industry (partial-equilibrium analysis) the MNE can affect the labor-management bargain. We shall take up these two levels of analysis in turn; the concluding section will suggest some propositions about the relationship between them.

5.1. Income distribution in general equilibrium

In the early 1970s U.S. labor unions campaigned strenuously to restrict foreign investment by U.S. corporations, in the name of saving American jobs. Nearly two decades later Glickman and Woodward (1989) argued that, while U.S. investment abroad destroys American jobs, foreign MNEs' investments in the United States do not create very many. Similar issues arise periodically in other countries, as in Japan's concern in the 1980s that foreign investment was "hollowing out" its manufacturing sector. Economic analysis does not accept the popular view that foreign investment permanently changes the level of unemployment, but it does affirm that short-run changes in unemployment and permanent changes in real wages can result. Exactly what changes are predicted depends sensitively on assumptions about the nature of direct investment and the structure of the economy. We start with the long-run effects on income distribution and wages, then treat employment effects as their short-run counterparts.

Theoretical models

International-trade theory offers several models that relate international factor movements to the distribution of income. Each abstracts from a great deal, as do all tractable general-equilibrium models. They give very different answers.

Assume we have two countries, Home and Foreign, each with a fixed factor endowment of (homogeneous) capital and labor. Each country produces a single good, and no commodity trade takes place between them. Suppose that (initially) the real return to capital is higher abroad, inducing some domestic capital to migrate to Foreign. In Home, each worker now is assisted by less capital in the production process; the marginal product of capital therefore rises, and that of labor falls. If all markets are competitive, including markets for factors of production, the wage falls. Home's national income rises because the capital that went abroad earns more for its owners than before. The returns to all units of Home's capital rise. Factor rewards go the opposite way in Foreign; the inflow of capital bids up the real wage and erodes the return to Foreign's native capital. Thus, self-interested labor opposes the emigration of domestic capital abroad but welcomes an influx of foreign MNEs.

This theoretical conclusion persists after we allow for commodity trade, so long as each country produces but a single commodity for domestic consumption and export, or all the commodities that each produces utilize capital and labor in the same proportions at any given set of factor prices.

The results do change substantially, however, if each nation produces more than one good, and the production functions differ in their factor intensities (proportions of capital to labor used at any given factor-price ratio). Then we are into the framework of the Heckscher-Ohlin model, reviewed in Section 2.3. The structure of the nation's trade does part of the adjusting to any international reallocation of factors – an important new element in the model. Suppose that Home possesses more capital per worker than does Foreign, so that Home is well suited to produce capital-intensive goods. It tends to export capital-intensive goods, therefore, and import labor-intensive commodities; unless Home's citizens' tastes in consumption lean disproportionally toward capital-intensive goods, these will be cheap in Home in the absence of trade. Now suppose that as an exogenous occurrence some Home capital migrates to Foreign, leaving Home with less capital per worker and Foreign with more than before. This shift in their factor endowments cuts into the international comparative advantage of Home and Foreign and generally predicts a reduced flow of international trade between them.[1] Within each country the change in factor endowments induces a shift of factor services away from the industry supplying exportables and into import-competing activities.

---

[1] See Section 2.3. In different conditions, trade and international factors movements are complementary rather than substitutes. Purvis (1972) showed that a flow of capital from Home to Foreign can expand the trade between them if production functions differ in the two countries so that Foreign's import-competing industry has a relative productivity advantage (even though it has been "disadvantaged" by Foreign's small endowment of capital). Also see Markusen (1983) and the discussion in Section 7.3.

But that shift itself mitigates the negative effect of capital's emigration on the wage of Home's labor. That is because in both of Home's industries the decline in the capital-labor ratio is smaller than for the country as a whole. That seeming impossibility results because the transfer of factors from Home's export-competing industry releases a lot of capital, and only a little labor, relative to the proportions absorbed when Home's import-competing industry expands. The shift of factors of production between industries thereby does part of the job of adjusting to the economy's overall lower capital-labor ratio. Because the capital-labor ratio in each sector falls less, the wage falls less than it otherwise would.

At the limit, the adjustment of Home's output pattern and international trade could account for the system's whole response to an outflow of capital, so that wages (and returns to capital) at Home would be unaffected by the capital outflow. This outcome is possible if Home is a small country whose exportable and import goods' prices are set competitively in a larger international market. Home's terms of trade then are unaffected by the capital outflow. The outflow tends to cheapen Home labor and raise the return to Home capital, as before, but any such tendency generates profits for Home's import-competing industry (which uses relatively much labor) and makes Home's exportables industry (using more costly capital) run losses. Factors are shunted to the import-competing industry, as before. Indeed, because the terms of trade are given, this factor reallocation continues until the capital-labor proportions in all industries are back to their levels before the disturbing capital outflow. Then the former wage and capital-rental levels are consistent once more with equilibrium: Home's markets for labor and capital are cleared, and each of Home's commodity sectors earns normal profits.[2] This adjustment through the shifting of factors between industrial sectors will break down, of course, if Home's exportable industry is actually wiped out before the *ex ante* factor rewards are restored. Should that occur, Home would be in the situation of the one-commodity model described earlier, and the direct relationship between the economy's capital-labor endowment and the returns to its factors of production would prevail.

The preceding paragraph shows that real wages and capital rentals can be left quite undisturbed by exogenous international movements of capital or by other

[2] Chipman (1971) generalized this situation to the world economy. He provided conditions under which, with labor immobile but capital freely mobile internationally, the terms of trade in the world economy are unaffected by shifts in demand among products. Capital rentals are also unaffected, as is the distribution of income. The transformation curve for the world economy as a whole (transformation curves for individual countries were represented in Figures 2.2–2.4 in Chapter 2) must have a "flat spot" on it – meaning that various quantities of food and clothing can be obtained from the world's factor endowment at given terms of trade. However, shifts in world demand from one of these combinations to another may require the reallocation of capital between countries, as described in the text.

"quantity" disturbances such as shifts of demand between products, although factor rewards in a country depend on its terms of trade (the Stolper-Samuelson theorem). A corollary of the Heckscher-Ohlin model is that a country's tariff policy affects international capital movements (Mundell, 1957). Suppose that Foreign imposes a tariff on imports of capital-intensive goods, raising their domestic price and therefore tending to raise capital rentals. If Foreign is a small country, its tariff and the resulting rise in capital rentals attract unlimited capital inflows from abroad that persist so long as the local reward to capital lies above the world level. The increase in its capitalists' income that Foreign's tariff produces is therefore transitory, because the capital inflows from the rest of the world continue until its return is pushed back down to the world level. Foreign winds up with a larger capital stock in residence, but no permanent change in either capital rentals or wages.

In Section 2.3 we reviewed several modern contributions to international-trade theory that have their own implications about capital movements and income distribution. A central generalization of Heckscher-Ohlin holds that, even with factors of production immobile between countries, factor prices (e.g., wages in the two trading countries) can be equalized without any actual labor migration between them. Alternatively, given the stocks of capital and labor in a two-country world, they can be arbitrarily allocated between the countries in a wide variety of ways consistent with factor-price equalization. Within those zones of equalization international capital flows have no effect on income distribution. This proposition yields several extensions:

1.   Regard MNEs as producers of proprietary assets usable either at home or abroad. Helpman (1984) showed that their activity widens the range of allocations of the world factor endowment in which factor-price equalization holds, compared to the simple Heckscher-Ohlin model. If the production of proprietary assets is a capital-intensive activity, in some situations direct investment abroad will raise rewards to Home's capital and lower labor's wage.

2.   Models of production differentiation and trade with monopolistic competition need not change any of the preceding conclusions about factor flows and income distribution, but they explain intraindustry trade that is not naturally related to factor-price differentials. They in general lower the likelihood that international capital transfers are linked strongly to factor prices.

3.   The "specific factors" variant on the Heckscher-Ohlin model (capital is mobile between countries although not between sectors) has been applied to MNEs' distinctive, sector-specific assets. The qualitative implications of that model for income distribution and real wages differ only in some respects from those of the simpler Heckscher-Ohlin model. An outflow of either type of capital from Home will lower Home's real wage, unless factor rewards are locked in to the terms of trade in the way described previously. An exogenous rise in the price of Home's import-competing good (i.e., a deterioration in Home's terms of trade) causes capital rentals to rise in Home's import-

competing sector and fall in Home's export-oriented sector. But now we cannot tell whether Home's real wage will rise or fall.[3] Somewhat in the same spirit is Hartman's (1980) model, in which MNE capital and Foreign's capital are complements in foreign-subsidiary production. Expansion of MNE capital in Foreign then raises the demand for Foreign capital and could lower Foreign wages.

Empirical evidence

The empirical estimates of the effect of foreign investment on U.S. income and its distribution have used the one-commodity model described previously, which makes no allowance for the important role of international trade in curbing the redistributive effects of international capital movements. Musgrave (1975, Chapter 9) simulated the consequences of repatriating to the United States the stock of direct investments that it held abroad in 1968. Her results depend on the measure of capital used and the assumption made about the elasticity of substitution between capital and labor in U.S. production (the lower it is, the more does the repatriated capital drive down capital's share and raise labor's), but the basic story is simple: Although the repatriation does not change U.S. total income much,[4] it substantially increases labor's income (and share) and lowers the income flowing to capital. A study by Thurow (1976), using a similar model, came to the same qualitative conclusion. It is unfortunate that these studies neglected the influence of international trade on income distribution, because, as we have seen, their conclusions would be greatly altered if the Heckscher-Ohlin relationship between the terms of trade and the distribution of income holds empirically (Bergsten et al., 1978, pp. 104–10).

Frank and Freeman (1978, Chapter 8) rested their estimates on a more complex model, although they directed their efforts to taking account of saving behavior rather than international trade. In their model, Home is a single-product economy using labor and capital, but Foreign contains two sectors – one using only imported (MNE) capital, the other using only domestic capital, both employing domestic labor. Productivity may differ between Home's economy and Foreign's MNE sector: The higher Foreign's relative productivity, the greater the incentive for Home's capital to go abroad. Similarly, MNE capital in Foreign may enjoy a capital-specific productivity advantage over domestic capital. At this stage the model yields the same conclusion as that of Musgrave and Thurow: Repatriating all of Home's exported capital will raise the real wage in

---

[3] The marginal product of Home's labor falls in terms of the export good but rises in terms of the other good. Whether or not labor is better off in real terms therefore depends on workers' tastes.

[4] The repatriation is actually estimated to increase the nation's total income, but that is because of consequences of taxation discussed in Chapter 8.

Home, lowering the return to capital.[5] Home's saving rate is next made endogenous, which changes the results strongly. The chance to place capital abroad in high-productivity activities now increases Home's rate of saving. Conversely, requiring the repatriation of Home's MNE capital restricts saving in Home and cuts the capital stock, rather than providing more capital to work with Home's labor. Therefore, the action lowers Home's wages and national income. Thus, Frank and Freeman identified a second significant theoretical omission from those simulated predictions that MNEs' exports of capital lower the domestic wage: the adaptive adjustment of saving, as well as of international trade (also see Koizumi and Kopecky, 1980). The distributional consequences of foreign investment in the long run remain a strictly unsettled issue.

5.2. Employment and wages: short run and long run

The controversies over foreign investments' effect on employment and the balance of payments can be analyzed in a short-run as well as a long-run context. Here we continue to focus the analysis on income distribution and employment, leaving the balance-of-payments question for Chapter 6.

Under certain assumptions, the effect of foreign investment on employment is the short-run counterpart of its ultimate effect on real wages. If foreign investment reduces Home's real wage in the long run, then in the short run Home's export of capital brings labor into excess supply – increases unemployment – at the going wage rate. Some interesting analyses, however, deal with the short run directly, rather than borrowing from the long-run context. They lack standard names in the literature; we shall call them the *investment-substitution* and *export-substitution* questions.

1. When a unit of capital is transferred from Home to Foreign, does it add exactly an extra unit to Foreign's capital stock and subtract one from Home's? This is the investment-substitution question.
2. When a unit of capital has been transferred from Home to Foreign *and* changed the two countries' capital stocks unit for unit, does it reduce the scope for commodity trade as the Heckscher-Ohlin model predicts? This is the export-substitution question.

Both questions turn on the behavior of variables other than employment and real wages, but they certainly affect those variables, and so they are usefully considered here. Although both are concerned with aggregate economic adjustments, they draw on the microeconomic analysis of the MNE built up in the preceding chapters.

---

[5] As in Musgrave's analysis, Home's national income actually expands when all foreign investment is repatriated, because of the effect of the corporation income tax. None of these models considers the loss of rents to MNEs' proprietary assets.

Investment substitution

What makes these short-run models differ from the long-run analysis of Section 5.1 is their recognition of a direct administrative link between international capital movements and commodity-output decisions. This link, the essence of the MNE, is missing from most long-run general-equilibrium models. The standard long-run model is internally consistent, because in perfectly competitive markets the manufacturing firm plays no role as an owner or exporter of capital; capital exports affect firms' production decisions only by altering the prices of their factor inputs. If a competitive firm ran a foreign subsidiary, it would not coordinate its decisions to place capital abroad and its decisions about what goods to produce at home or abroad; each decision should depend solely on market prices.

The investment-substitution question arises from two properties of the firm as a microeconomic organization. First, MNEs and other firms compete directly in particular product markets. If a MNE spots an investment opportunity, it transfers the capital needed to establish a new subsidiary.[6] This action preempts the investment opportunity for any local firms or other MNEs that might have seized it, and they might not make alternative investment plans immediately. Of course, in a neoclassical competitive model we expect the addition of some capital to a nation's stock to drive down capital's marginal product; the investment-substitution problem arises because large, lumpy investments might be involved, and the adversary relationship appears in particular product markets. The second property concerns the firm's ability to finance projects. The competitive model assumes that each firm can borrow (or lend) unlimited amounts of funds at "the" market rate of interest – a property preserved in sophisticated modern models of competitive capital markets. However, there are also good reasons why the individual firm faces a rising marginal cost of borrowed funds; the more it borrows, the higher its opportunity cost (see Section 6.1). This constraint puts alternative uses of the firm's funds in competition with one another in a way not recognized in the purely competitive model. Internally generated funds might be adequate to support an investment in a foreign subsidiary or an expansion of domestic capacity, but not both. If the less profitable opportunity cannot be justified at the higher interest rate demanded for funds borrowed on the capital market, another firm might grab the project.

If a dollar of capital transferred from Home to Foreign need not correspond to the actual change in the two countries' capital stocks, how do we classify the outcomes of the investment-substitution problem? Hufbauer and Adler (1968) described as *classical* the assumption that the amount of capital moved internationally equals the decline in Home's and the increase in Foreign's capital stock. The first alternative that they posed, the *reverse-classical* assumption, rests

---

[6] We neglect until Chapter 6 the possibility that the firm borrows most of its investment in the country where the project is installed.

on product-market competition between the MNE and other firms. The MNE invests one dollar in Foreign. It preempts an investment opportunity that would otherwise have been taken by a domestic firm, which now cancels its investment plans. As a result, total investment in Foreign does not increase. When the MNE invests abroad, the strain on its investment capacity is assumed to make it withdraw from some investment project in Home. However, this abandoned project leaves an opening for some other Home firm, so total investment in Home does not fall. In the reverse-classical case the world's capital stock stays unchanged, as in the classical case; unlike the classical case, each country's own capital stock remains unchanged. The reverse-classical case has an affinity for purchases of existing corporate assets that now make up the major portion of foreign-investment transactions. The liquid assets coming into the seller's hands ultimately exert some effect on real capital formation, but the classical impact of the transfer on wages is surely blunted.[7]

To provide microeconomic underpinning for Hufbauer and Adler's third assumption, suppose that the MNE produces distinctive goods with no close substitutes either at home or abroad. It makes a foreign investment, but without reducing its capital expenditure in Home. No other firm in Foreign finds its market shriveled, and so no offsetting decline in expenditure occurs there. And no other Home firm perceives an investment opportunity left unclaimed, and so Home's capital formation is not further affected. In this, the *anticlassical* case, Foreign's capital stock expands, but Home's remains unchanged.

These three alternative assumptions about international investments and capital stocks rest on conflicting views about the market context of foreign-investment decisions. Each follows from stated assumptions, and each can be spun into a consistent story about general-equilibrium adjustments in the economy.[8] They have quite different implications for employment in the short run and real wages in the long run. In the reverse-classical version foreign invest-

---

[7] Lipsey (1994) recently invoked the reverse-classical case, arguing that U.S. foreign direct investments preclude foreign firms from stealing business that would in any case be lost to U.S. exporters. The U.S. MNE replaces what would otherwise have been some foreign firm's investment abroad, while no U.S. investment opportunity gets passed up.

[8] The chief problem concerns the behavior of saving, if saving and investment decisions are to be in equilibrium. The reverse-classical case requires that supplies of saving in each country be highly elastic in response to expected rates of return. Otherwise, when Home's MNE borrows to invest abroad and its rival borrows to finance the domestic investment that the MNE passes up, the rate of return in Home's capital market will be driven up, and some other firm will abandon its plans. Similarly, the depressed profit expectations in Foreign must reduce saving there, or otherwise the rate of return will fall and tempt some Foreign firm to make an investment. The anticlassical case requires the same assumption about an elastic supply of saving in Home (or wherever the MNE funds its project), but in Foreign either the available investment opportunities (the marginal efficiency of investment) must be quite elastic or the supply of saving must be inelastic.

ment brings no change in nations' capital stocks, only in their ownership, so a capital transfer does not affect real wages. The classical assumption about transfers implies the real-wage effects outlined in Section 5.1. The anticlassical version entails an increase in Foreign's capital stock but no reduction in Home's; its implications for real wages seem to lie between those of the classical and reverse-classical cases.

Export substitution

The export-substitution question stands forth most clearly if we make the classical assumption about capital transfers: Home's capital stock falls and Foreign's rises by the amount of the transfer. What happens to Home's equilibrium level of exports?[9] What does the effect on exports in turn imply for real wages and employment? In the long-run Heckscher-Ohlin model of Section 5.1, capital transfers, on certain assumptions, substitute for exports, reducing Home's equilibrium level of international trade (exports and imports) overall. The capital transfer also lowers Home's real wage under most assumptions. However, the shriveling of trade and the reduction of real wages are not inevitably connected, and indeed a capital transfer can lower wages without affecting trade, or vice versa (see Section 2.3 and Markusen, 1983).

Most discussion of export substitution, however, has taken place in a more microeconomic and political context: Are American MNEs "running away" from American labor to serve their foreign markets through plants abroad rather than by exports from the United States? Are foreign MNEs' investments in the United States really replacing imports? The standard Heckscher-Ohlin model shows that export substitution need not always occur. However, as with the investment-substitution question, standard theory ignores the MNE as an organization and the product-market setting in which it operates. One response to the runaway charge is that capital transfers from the United States are purely defensive, intended to preserve the U.S. company's stake in a market that it can no longer serve profitably via U.S. exports (Kravis and Lipsey, 1992). This case is essentially Hufbauer and Adler's reverse-classical assumption: Somebody puts capital in place abroad to serve the foreign market and oust U.S. exports, and the only question is whether that export-displacing plant is owned by a U.S. MNE or some other firm. This counter to the runaway charge also follows from a congenial set of assumptions. Assume that the U.S. exporter and potential MNE holds a goodwill asset resting on its past exporting and sales-promotion

---

[9] The qualification for "equilibrium level" puts aside a problem of short-run adjustment associated with the capital transfer itself. When Home transfers capital to Foreign, the financial consequence is an increase of total spending in Foreign and a decrease in Home. That change by itself raises Foreign's imports and reduces Home's. But the change in trade is merely transitional, and it dies away once the capital transfer ceases. This "transfer process" is discussed in Section 6.4.

activities in the foreign market, but an asset that will depreciate if product-market rivals increase their local capacity to supply competing goods. Let some disturbance shift production or transportation costs so as to favor serving the foreign market from a plant abroad. It then follows that the foreign market is lost to U.S. exports in any case, and the only question is whether or not the U.S. firm invests abroad in order to defend the cash flow from its goodwill asset.

Another counter to the runaway case focuses not on whether exports fall without the foreign investment but rather on whether they rise after it occurs. In the extreme, exports and foreign investments can be complementary rather than substitutes, as was noted in Chapters 1 and 2. Suppose that high costs of information about foreign markets can be reduced if the MNE opens a plant in the foreign market. Suppose that the plant's presence increases the firm's credibility as a reliable source of supply or reduces the cost of selling locally its full line of goods, including exports from the home base. A foreign investment that initially displaces some of the firm's exports could ultimately raise them to a higher equilibrium level than before. We saw that this outcome is possible and supported by some empirical evidence.[10] That does not make it inevitable, however, and the complementary relationship between exports and foreign investments runs into constraints in general equilibrium that were noted in context of investment substitution. Firm *A* may profitably lay hands on the capital required both to found a plant abroad and to expand its export capacity at home, but the country's capital stock is ultimately limited by its savers' responsiveness to higher expected rates of return. Export complementarity has a close affinity for Hufbauer and Adler's anticlassical case in which foreign investment actually raises the capital stock abroad without reducing it at home.[11]

In summary, the short-run and partial-equilibrium approaches to the effects of MNEs on real wages and income distribution lead into a complex array of considerations that can be grouped around the questions of investment substitution and export substitution. These questions substantially overlap each other

[10] This discussion follows the literature in assuming that the MNE under study is horizontal, producing the same line of goods abroad as at home. Other types give different results. Forward vertical integration in the foreign investment can prove complementary with exports if the subsidiary secures inputs from its parent for further processing. On the other hand, integration backward to secure an input from abroad can expand imports and reduce the demand for labor at home. Finally, a diversified foreign investment is unlikely to affect the investing firm's trade activities directly.

[11] For critical surveys of literature on the export-substitution question, see Bergsten et al. (1978, Chapters 3 and 4) and Frank and Freeman (1978, Chapter 2). For a more recent example, consider Graham and Krugman's (1991) deploring of the averse effect on U.S. terms of trade of foreign MNEs' propensity to import more inputs than do U.S. domestic firms. The position assumes that the choice is between U.S. and foreign management of U.S. production of these goods, although the alternative (with the opposite implication for U.S. terms of trade) could be importing the same final goods from abroad (see Kudrle, 1991).

and lead to a series of models that one by one sound partial and arbitrary, but together help to array possible outcomes. And they show how the transaction-cost underpinnings of the MNE can be related to general-equilibrium models that emphasize the constraints on the economy's overall stock of resources and its influence on resource allocation and factor rewards.

Empirical evidence

Empirical evidence relevant to these models takes several forms. One is simulated calculations that illustrate the consequences of these various models but do not help us to determine which is more nearly correct. Other approaches employ either case studies or statistical analysis to test the predictions directly.

One simulation prepared by the U.S. Tariff Commission sought to determine the short-run effects of U.S. investments abroad on jobs provided by U.S. industry under various assumptions about export substitution or complementarity. U.S. Tariff Commission (1973, pp. 651–72) concluded that all foreign investments that had occurred through 1970 had cost the United States 1.3 million jobs, on the assumption that all foreign production by MNEs (whether U.S.-based or foreign) could instead have been replaced by production at the MNE's national base – full export substitution. However, this large loss could be turned into a small gain by shifting to the following assumption: If foreign production by U.S. MNEs were eliminated, U.S. exports would retain only that proportion of the displaced subsidiaries' market equal to the share of U.S. exports in exports to that market from all sources. Also, an allowance was made for the increased jobs provided in the United States by investments from abroad associated with the gain that had occurred in foreign countries' share of world exports. This case can be described either as limited export substitution or as a partial embrace of the reverse-classical assumption about investment substitution. Frank and Freeman (1978) extended the analysis, estimating what share of foreign markets would be lost if U.S. companies had to serve them from higher-cost domestic production facilities (1978, Chapter 3). They also pursued domestic job losses due to foreign investment through reduced purchases of domestic inputs (1978, Chapter 5). Useful though they are, these calculations pursue the implications of their own assumptions rather than discriminating among the competing models.

That brings us to the case studies and statistical analyses. The case studies, in the nature of things, represent small and nonrandom samples. From a collection of nine cases Stobaugh et al. (1976) concluded that foreign investment by U.S. MNEs is not generally hostile to jobs in the United States. Some foreign investments have little to do with American exports or imports; others keep the investing firm from losing its foreign market entirely. The only foreign investments deemed to displace U.S. exports serve markets that would have grown noncompetitive for U.S. exports anyhow. Case studies from this and other sources support no clear-cut conclusions.[12]

Statistical approaches have also led to diverse results, but together they do leave fairly clear conclusions. One way or another, they sought to determine whether exports and foreign investments of the United States are substitutes or complements for one another. Several studies such as U.S. Tariff Commission (1973, pp. 334–41) and recently Kravis and Lipsey (1992) noted that exports and imports undertaken by U.S. MNEs were growing faster than other U.S. trade or that U.S. domestic output and employment were growing faster in industries with more foreign investment. But neither finding really bears on what would happen to exports or employment if the industries making foreign investments made fewer of them. Several cross-sectional statistical studies described in Chapter 2 concluded that elevated tariffs around a national market promote an inflow of foreign investment and reduce imports. That result suggests that exports and foreign investments are substitutes, but it does not preclude the possibility that the foreign subsidiaries, having taken root, can *later* draw in enough complementary imports to offset the initial substitution.[13]

The most revealing statistical analyses are those that examine the net relationship between exports of U.S. companies and the sales of their foreign subsidiaries after controlling for as many as possible of the variables that should affect both (such as the advertising and research activities of the U.S. industry, scale economies in production, and various other factors relating to U.S. comparative advantage in international trade). Bergsten et al. (1978, pp. 73–96) concluded that investment abroad is complementary with U.S. exports up to a point: U.S. exports increase with net local sales of U.S. subsidiaries until the latter reach a certain level, but the further overseas capacity starts to displace exports.[14] This conclusion accords well with the organizational model of the MNE: Foreign subsidiaries' role in promoting exports should depend on the subsidiaries' existence, but not especially on their own scales of operation.

Lipsey and Weiss (1981) concurred with Bergsten et al. (1978) about the general complementarity between U.S. exports and the net sales of overseas affiliates. The complementarity relationship holds for most major commodity

[12] For critical surveys, see Bergsten et al. (1978, pp. 59–65) and Frank and Freeman (1978, Chapter 2).

[13] Adler and Stevens (1974) tried to estimate cross-elasticities of demand between American exports and the output of foreign subsidiaries that would directly reveal complementarity or substitution by their signs, but no significant results emerged pointing in either direction.

[14] This conclusion holds both for exports of U.S. multinationals to their own foreign affiliates (where the complementary relationship is especially likely) and for the total exports of U.S. manufacturing industries, whether sold to affiliates or sold at arm's length. Also see Swedenborg (1979, Chapter 7) on Sweden and Reddaway (1968, pp. 282–97) on the United Kingdom.

groups and for both developed-country markets and LDCs. Orr (1991) found that foreign investment inflows to the United States significantly raise U.S. imports (with a two-year lag), but they raise U.S. exports by almost as much. Blomström et al. (1988) got similar results for Sweden; their findings for U.S. manufacturing industries were more mixed but showed that any substitution involves subsidiaries' sales to the local market and not subsidiaries' sales to third markets (for which complementarity prevails). Lipsey and Weiss (1981) found that the sales of U.S. subsidiaries abroad are substitutes for exports to their local markets coming from industrial countries other than the United States, and there also is weak evidence (Glejser, 1976) that the subsidiaries of foreign MNEs have a negative effect on U.S. exports. However, Blomström et al. (1988) found exports to the host countries from sources other than the United States to be positively related to U.S. subsidiaries' sales. If one writes this unlikely result off to omitted-variable bias (as its authors do), the evidence suggests that the complementary export and subsidiary sales by U.S. MNEs are both in a competitive relationship with sales by other exporting countries and their MNEs.

None of these statistical inquiries into export substitution addressed the general-equilibrium problem, and thus they cannot be generalized to the overall effect of foreign investment on real wages. For example, if foreign investments and exports are complementary up to a point, that could merely mean that the U.S. capital stock is diverted toward industries that undertake foreign investments (which place capital partly at home, partly abroad) and away from those uninvolved in foreign investment. Whether real wages rise or fall will then depend in part on the relative capital intensities of the two sectors, a question with no obvious empirical answer.

Recently Feldstein (1994a) addressed the investment-substitution issue in a macroeconomic context. The analysis is based on his earlier finding that the level of capital formation in a country is closely tied to its domestic rate of saving: National capital markets may allocate savings well among domestic investment opportunities, but by inference they falter in arbitrage across national boundaries. That led him to expect that foreign direct investment proves a macroeconomically significant form of arbitrage, reducing capital expenditure in the source country (given its saving) and increasing it abroad – Hufbauer-Adler's classical assumption. Feldstein's final estimates indicate that direct investment from and into the United States both correspond roughly to dollar-for-dollar investment substitutions for current direct-investment flows, although one dollar of U.S. foreign investment funded by MNEs' retained earnings depresses U.S. capital expenditure by at most 25 cents. Older macroeconomic studies using Canadian data (Lubitz, 1971a; Van Loo, 1977) agree with Feldstein's results, finding that capital formation in Canada expands by at least one dollar when a dollar inflow of foreign investment is received. Lucas

(1993) used a more neoclassical approach to model the time series of U.S. foreign investment to seven newly industrialized countries. Treating MNEs' capital as an input into host-country production along with local labor and capital, he found that host wages normalized by export prices exert a significant negative influence on inflows of direct investment, but the effects of capital rentals for foreign and domestic capital (in both source and host) are mixed at best. Overall, the evidence tends to support the sensible conclusion that full investment substitution prevails in the aggregate whatever complementarities and reverse-classical patterns might appear for individual firms or industries.

5.3. **Labor-management relations and collective bargaining**

Beyond its effects on overall wages and income distribution, the MNE might change the welfare of workers through its employment policies and its stance in collective bargaining. Indeed, its prowess in labor relations allegedly suffices to explain the MNE's existence, an idea that appears in different versions to match one's politics:

1. The MNE can make credible threats to remove production activities to a location abroad and thereby exploit its labor force in settings where a single-nation firm could not (Cowling and Sugden, 1987, pp. 61–79).

2. Trade unions capture some fraction of the monopoly rents available to employers (e.g., Pugel, 1980*a*), and thus firms' multinational status can affect the wage bargain by placing rents imputed to the MNE within the union's reach. Multinational scope then aids the MNE in fighting off appropriation of its rents or quasi rents (Huizinga, 1990).

The MNE's influence on the labor bargain might devolve simply from its large size or the size of its plants, not its international operations. Research suggests that workers' pay increases with the size of the plant that employs them, and on some evidence their discontent with the job also increases.

Study of this subject is complicated by the diversity of objectives that trade unions pursue and differences among countries in collective-bargaining practices. For example, in Germany labor possesses important statutory rights of codetermination – to be represented in decisions concerning the enterprise. American unions, although they might seek to influence some decisions of MNE managers, have a tradition of confrontational relationships with management and show interest in codetermination only in special situations.

Organization of labor relations within the MNE

How far the MNE decentralizes its labor-relations activities provides useful background to the analysis. The large differences between countries' legal and cultural environments of labor relations suggest a high degree of decentralization. So do the organization structures typically found in MNEs, described in Chapter 3. Because labor markets are, at the outside, national in scope, and because the firm's labor-market decisions are largely, if not entirely, tactical and short-run, most decision-making responsibility should devolve to the national subsidiary or even to the plant. The empirical evidence clearly supports this prediction. A Conference Board survey (Hershfield, 1975) of both U.S. MNEs and foreign companies operating in the United States found that subsidiary managers in nearly three-fourths of the companies could conclude formal labor agreements without seeking parental approval.[15] Their independence increases with the physical and cultural distance of the subsidiary from its parent: Only the labor relations of U.S. MNEs' Canadian subsidiaries are closely integrated with those of their nearby parents. Most large British MNEs similarly stay out of actual collective bargaining by their subsidiaries (Roberts and May, 1974). The more countries in which the MNE operates, the more likely is a hands-off policy. But 63 percent of the U.K. firms occasionally advise subsidiaries on labor-relations matters, and four-fifths are at least sometimes involved with subsidiaries' changes in pensions and other investment-type decisions.[16]

This evidence of decentralization need not imply that the MNE's labor relations are indistinguishable from those of a neighboring national enterprise. Rather, the pattern simply accords with the evidence that labor markets are nationally distinctive and independent of one another, so that MNEs typically see little advantage in the transnational coordination of their collective-bargaining activities. But bargainers on labor's side may nonetheless find it useful to recognize and exploit the MNE's international affiliations. Furthermore, labor relations are a "latently transnational" issue (Kujawa, 1975, Chapter 7), because they may involve investment-type commitments that significantly affect the expected future cash flow of the subsidiary and thereby trespass on the MNE's centralized financial functions.

Hypotheses about MNEs

The descriptive literature on MNEs' labor relations suggests a number of hypotheses about how a company's MNE status might affect the outcome of collective bargaining. The following are representative:

1.   The successful MNE generally holds some firm-specific rent-yielding assets. The more closely does the cash flow approximate a pure rent, the more

---

[15] Jedel and Kujawa (1976, pp. 32–41) reported similar conclusions for foreign subsidiaries in the United States. For a description of the decentralized system of a major U.S. MNE, see Kujawa (1975, Chapter 6).

[16] Apparently, there is not much evidence on why some companies decentralize more than do others (see Roberts, 1972). Kassalow (1978) pointed out a key trade-off at issue: the company can sustain either the communications costs of a centralized system or the employee costs of staffing the subsidiaries with high-quality labor-relations personnel. As a point of perspective, Enderwick (1985, pp. 113–14) found more decentralization in foreign subsidiaries in the United Kingdom than in affiliates of domestic multiplant firms.

attractive a target it is for trade-union bargaining efforts. To the extent that national wage-setting processes permit bargaining at the level of the firm (rather than industry-wide or economy-wide), employee-compensation levels should be elevated where such rents can be appropriated.

2. Multinational status can carry a variety of advantages in the bargaining process that counter the MNE's attractiveness as a target. Transfer pricing can obscure the appropriable cash flow of any one subsidiary and thus frustrate the appropriation effort. The MNE enjoys bargaining ploys that national firms lack. If the MNE maintains capacity to produce the same goods in different national markets, output curtailed by a strike in one market can be replaced from another subsidiary's plant. The cash flows of corporate affiliates permit a given subsidiary greater discretion about taking a strike. More readily than a domestic firm, the MNE can credibly threaten to close down a given plant, or shelve any expansion plans there, and choose another national market for any additions to capacity.

3. Apart from the substance of the labor bargain, the bargainer's presence as a MNE can affect labor relations and productivity. These effects run in various directions. The MNE's management comes equipped with a repertory of labor-relations practices that, at least initially, reflect conditions in its national base and might harmonize poorly with those in the host nation. Even without foreign gaucherie, long lines of bureaucratic communication could impair the MNE's responsiveness to local labor problems (to the extent that the delegation of authority to subsidiaries is incomplete). And the universal suspicion of foreigners can afflict any of the MNE's transactions in the host economy. Counter to these disadvantages, the MNE can arbitrage successful practices and innovations from one labor market to another.

These hypotheses flow largely from theory and evidence already reviewed on the nature and organization of the MNE. However, one model was developed that usefully integrates them. Carmichael (1992) proposed that foreign subsidiaries might be more strike-prone than comparable domestic competitors because of the possible presence of rents coupled with the firm's lack of transparency to a trade union. In general we do not expect strikes to occur when both union and management are well informed about each other's reservation prices and costs of enduring strikes. If the union is uncertain about whether the subsidiary is "weak" (willing to sacrifice some rents rather than incur the cost of taking a strike) or "strong," in a multiperiod interaction between the union and the firm the weak subsidiary might choose to resist in the hope of convincing the union that it is strong. Carmichael showed that if the probability that the MNE is strong is not too high, and not all MNE-union bargaining games that we observe are in their early stages, some unions will choose to strike, and both weak (probably) and strong firms (with certainty) will resist. MNEs will take more strikes than other firms. The model is consistent with MNEs' rates of pay being either the same as or higher than those of national firms.

With this conceptual background we turn to the evidence on MNEs' pay, the harmony of their labor relations, and the plant productivity that they attain.

Evidence on labor relations

The available studies of MNEs' wages and working conditions have controlled for too few extraneous influences to shed much light on these hypotheses, but they merit a brief review.[17] Whichard (1978) showed that U.S. affiliates of foreign companies pay compensation per employee 7 percent higher than that for all U.S. companies. However, nearly all the difference can be explained by differences in the industrial and regional distributions of the subsidiaries; with these controlled, no clear difference remains. Leonard and McCulloch (1991) and Graham and Krugman (1991, pp. 70–1) confirmed this finding. Outside the United States, the U.S. Tariff Commission (1973, Chapter 7) analyzed data (from diverse sources and not necessarily comparable) on the wages of U.S. MNEs and national enterprises in the United States and in six other countries. The MNEs' wages exceed those of indigenous firms in the United States and Canada, are about the same in Belgium-Luxembourg, France, and West Germany, and are a little lower in the United Kingdom. These comparisons did not control for industry mix, region, or other variables. Without control for industry or other compositional factors, Blanchflower (1984) found blue-collar wages in foreign subsidiaries in Britain no different but compensation higher for managerial and clerical employees. Dunning and Morgan (1980) found that control for industry mix halves the excess of MNE parents' wages in the United States but still leaves them significantly above national firms; the same holds for Canada. In the European countries, however, control for industry mix pushes the U.S. MNEs' wages significantly below those of national firms. Company size differences could explain the pattern. United States MNEs are the largest firms (and often operate the largest plants) in the United States and Canada, whereas on average they are smaller than the leading national firms in the European countries. Much evidence suggests that wages increase with size of plant and company within national labor markets. Unfortunately, only one Canadian study (Globerman et al., 1994) controlled for both industry mix and plant size (also capital intensity), and so we know little about the size or sign of any residual difference that could be attributed to MNE status per se.[18]

For less-developed countries (LDCs) casual evidence that MNEs pay higher wages than national firms is fairly abundant. The pattern held for Mex-

---

[17] Numerous fragmentary studies of wages were summarized by the International Labour Organization (1976*b*).

[18] Dunning and Morgan (1980) employed a crude test of association between the wages paid by U.S. multinationals and their profitability. A positive association would confirm the hypothesis that unions intercept some of the rents accruing to MNEs. No association was found – which may mean either there is no association or the data are inadequate.

ico in the U.S. Tariff Commission study, for example, and Reuber et al. (1973, pp. 175–6) found quite a strong effect on wages of skilled and semiskilled labor. This difference in the setting of LDC labor markets suggests another feature that is not often controlled in comparisons between MNEs and other firms. One reason suggested why large plants and companies pay higher wages is to secure "better" workers, meaning those more readily accepting responsibility or direction and thus cooperating harmoniously in a large and complex organization. In LDC labor markets there is probably great variance in individuals' experience with the discipline of a complex organization. This would increase the differential advantageously paid by large companies, especially those with alien management, to buy improved supervision at the plant level. They might also benefit by buying lower turnover of labor (Enderwick, 1985, p. 61). Taira and Standing (1973) tested this hypothesis by inquiring whether or not the wage differentials paid by MNEs are proportionally greater in LDCs where quality differentials in the worker population (as defined earlier) are greater – indicated by low literacy rates and average income per capita. The hypothesis was confirmed.

The incidence of labor disputes in MNEs has been studied, particularly in the United Kingdom. Steuer and Gennard (1971) found the MNEs to experience fewer strikes than their industrial competitors in Britain. The distribution of strikes by duration indicated that in particular the MNEs incur fewer of the short, unpredictable strikes that then seemed so costly to industrial productivity in Britain. However, Forsyth (1972, Chapter 7, 1973) failed to confirm that pattern for U.S. MNEs in Scotland over the decade of the 1960s, and subsequent studies tended to concur (Enderwick, 1985, pp. 120–1). The different result might be due to different size distributions of foreign-controlled and domestic plants, or to regional differences. Creigh and Makeham (1978) controlled for two relevant variables – the labor intensity of the industry and the average size of its plants (both predict increased incidence of strikes) – and found no relationship between strike proneness and foreign ownership. Carmichael's (1992) test of his model controlled for union coverage and several variables related to bargaining power. He confirmed his hypothesis that MNEs take more strikes, and foreign subsidiaries more than U.K.-based MNEs. Although his measures of bargaining power behaved somewhat erratically, Carmichael's core finding seems more credible than previous results. An analysis by Enderwick and Buckley (1983) previously concluded that strikes taken by U.S. MNEs' subsidiaries in Britain increase with the firm's size and profitability and with vulnerability revealed by its trade interdependence with its parent.[19]

---

[19] Little comparable evidence is available for the United States, but Greer and Shearer's (1981) survey found no major difference in labor practices between domestic firms and foreign subsidiaries, and Sanyal (1990) concluded that U.S. unions win a proportion of representation elections that is no different for foreign subsidiaries than for domestic

Evidence indicates that MNEs make some innovations in labor relations as one aspect of the international arbitrage of skills and proprietary assets.[20] An example is the introduction into British labor relations of productivity bargaining – negotiations to remove work rules that drain productivity in exchange for higher wages. In Europe the presence of MNEs accelerated a trend toward more labor bargaining at the plant level rather than at industry and national levels (Gunter, 1975, pp. 150–1; Enderwick, 1985, pp. 109–10).[21] Foreign subsidiaries in the United States seem generally to have integrated themselves successfully into the American labor-relations system (Jedel and Kujawa, 1976, pp. 49–56; Beechler and Yang, 1994), and Japanese MNEs evidently had a major effect. In LDCs, the foreign subsidiaries sometimes prove more adept at dealing with trade unions than do inexperienced domestic companies (Kassalow, 1978).

Multinational union activity

Unions' apparent lack of broad success in winning above-market wages from MNEs in the industrial countries led to an effort to coalesce labor's bargaining power across national boundaries. Would labor gain from extending the bargaining process across national boundaries? If so, are transnational union coalitions an actuality or a likely prospect?

First, some analytical points. In the case of the horizontal MNE a monopolistic seller of labor clearly gains from a bargaining coalition across national boundaries. If the firm can (actually or potentially) serve a given market from plants in several countries, its demand for labor is more elastic in any one country than over the whole set, and so monopolizing its labor supply internationally should yield larger rents than monopolizing it country by country. But the gains to unions from international bargaining with MNEs should not be oversold. The monopoly power of internationally coordinated labor actually does not depend on transnational ownership links among companies. Unions that coalesce to force up widget-industry wages in both Home and Foreign will reduce

establishments. Cousineau et al. (1989) estimated a model of strike determinants in Canada that, although differently motivated, resembles that of Carmichael. After controlling for various uncertainties surrounding the bargaining process and for seller and buyer concentration in the market, they obtained a significant negative influence for foreign ownership. This result might depend on the control for concentration, which itself takes a positive coefficient that exceeds its standard error.

[20] For evidence, see Steuer and Gennard (1971), Gunter (1975), International Labour Organization (1976*b*, especially p. 50), Enderwick (1985, pp. 116–19), and Stopford and Turner (1985, pp. 145–7).

[21] Another effect of the MNE is to complicate the legal arrangements for worker participation in management that prevail in a number of European countries, because the centralization in the parent of certain important decisions on finance, investment, and employment puts them outside the reach of workers' representatives in the subsidiary. Still, the overall judgment holds that MNEs have not worked any transforming effects on national systems of labor relations (Banks and Stieber, 1977, pp. 6–9, 120–34).

the elasticity of the derived demand for labor whatever the organization of the industry. Also, the short-run equilibrium with established horizontal MNEs differs from that in an industry of non-MNE national producers only if the efficacy of short-run supply adaptation differs between the market and administrative channels.[22]

Suppose nonetheless that MNEs do in fact increase the rents unions could potentially extract from transnational bargaining. How likely, then, are the necessary coalitions of unions across national boundaries? The theoretical models set forth in Section 5.1 make the point that sellers of labor in different countries face the same dilemma as any potentially colluding sellers: Although they benefit from acting jointly, each has an incentive to cheat on the coalition and undercut the price demanded by the others. In the general-equilibrium model, capital transfers from Home to Foreign lower Home's real wage (under some conditions) and raise that in Foreign. The same proposition holds for the single industry: If Home's union demands a higher wage but Foreign's does not, the MNE shifts resources to Foreign and increases the demand for labor there. In short, the international solidarity of union bargaining has the same built-in tendency to self-destruct as any collusive arrangement.

Discussions of transnational bargaining in the field of labor relations stress not this theoretical stumbling block but rather the differing institutions and legal systems of national labor markets. National unions differ in their goals. Some are concerned with the paycheck and immediate working conditions, others with broader social and political goals. Bargaining takes place at different points in the market – the individual plant or company, across a whole industry, or even for the whole national labor force. There is little room for international cooperation in bargaining when labor's claims are targeted to an industry that contains assorted MNEs and also a roster of national firms. Labor-relations systems differ on the issues bargained over. Fringe benefits that dominate the bargaining in one country might be mandated by legislation in another, and thus removed from contention. These examples establish the general point that differences among countries in general and specific objectives, labor-market structures, and legal frameworks are formidable deterrents to the international coordination of labor's bargaining power.[23]

---

[22] That MNEs' choices of plant location are sensitive to labor costs is implicit in the large amount of evidence on their location choices reviewed in Chapter 2. Cushman (1987) analyzed two-way flows of foreign direct investment over time between the United States and five principal partner countries, finding them significantly and sensitively related to movements in wages and productivity. He controlled for exchange rates, capital costs, and demand factors.

[23] The many authors addressing this issue include Kujawa (1971), Roberts (1973), Curtin (1973), Flanagan and Weber (1974), Gunter (1975), Banks and Stieber (1977, Introduction), Bergsten et al. (1978, pp. 110–18), Kujawa (1979), Northrup and Rowan (1979, pp. 535–44), and Enderwick (1985, pp. 128–57). All reached essentially the same conclusion.

With the dice loaded against transnational coordination of labor's demands, how far has the process actually gone? These coordination efforts cost real resources for the unions involved. Like other rational economic actors, unions can be expected to make only modest investments in games with low expected payouts. American unions have in general encouraged labor organization in other countries, but not with specific coordination in mind. They have urged their counterparts abroad to demand U.S.-level wages and working conditions in the overseas plants of U.S. MNEs, but in light of the high levels of real productivity prevailing in the United States, that posture is surely intended more to deter foreign investment than to maximize labor's income internationally once the foreign investment is in place. American labor has also tried to use the machinery regulating labor-management relations to wield some influence on companies' decisions to invest abroad (Kujawa, 1973, pp. 253–8), but apparently to influence the substance of the decisions, not from a desire for codetermination.

What international coordination does take place adds up to much less than internationally coordinated bargaining. Exchanges of information seek to determine the joint profitability of a MNE's various arms and the effects of a strike in one country on its operations in another. Gestures of sympathy in one country occur over a labor dispute taking place in another. Efforts are made to get a MNE's labor contracts to expire at the same time in several countries, to pave the way for parallel international wage demands. But actual successes in bringing about international collective bargaining with a single MNE seem essentially nonexistent.[24]

These generalizations accord with survey evidence for the United States (Hershfield, 1975) and the United Kingdom (Roberts and May, 1974). The U.S. survey determined that 10 percent of U.S.-based MNEs had been contacted by unions on a transnational basis. These contacts had not actually led to transnational bargaining, only to union representations on transnational issues. Another 10 percent of companies knew of union efforts to undertake international coordination but had not yet been confronted with the results. Of non-U.S. MNEs contacted in the U.S. survey, somewhat larger proportions had encountered international union activity – one-fifth being contacted about transnational issues, another one-quarter aware of coordination efforts. In the survey of British MNEs, 10 percent indicated some international coordinating mechanism in place among their unions, and another 10 percent expected to face this prospect in a few years.

These surveys also convey some evidence that transnational efforts at labor coordination take place where the expected rewards are highest. Hershfield

---

[24] For descriptions of coordination efforts in the labor movement, see Blake (1972), Roberts (1973), Curtin (1973), Kujawa (1975, Chapter 5, 1979), Weinberg (1978, especially Chapter 3), Prahalad and Doz (1987, p. 109), and the exhaustive investigation of Northrup and Rowan (1979).

(1975, pp. 10–11) found that target companies tend to be larger and more involved internationally, which would increase the return expected of unions' investment in coordination efforts. Target companies also are much more centralized in their labor-relations policies, so that unions might find it easier to hammer out coordinated demands with some hope of their acceptance. International unionism has made some headway in those industrial nations where one would expect it. They are the United States and Canada, with similar language, culture, and productivity levels (Crispo, 1967), and the European Union, with its rapid expansion of international business (Gunter, 1975, pp. 151–7).

One notices that the evidence on international coordination is showing its age, perhaps reflecting the poor fortunes of organized labor in the past decade or so.

5.4. Summary

The effects of MNEs on real wages and income distribution can be examined in both general equilibrium and the partial-equilibrium context of the individual industry. In the simplest model of general equilibrium, capital export by MNEs reduces the real wage, and capital import increases it. In the Heckscher-Ohlin model, however, international trade does part of the adjusting to an international capital flow. In the limit, it can do all the adjusting and insulate the real rewards to factors of production from any effect of capital flows. Simulation studies that have neglected this trade-adjustment effect show, not surprisingly, that repatriation of the stock of capital invested abroad by U.S. MNEs will redistribute income substantially toward labor.

These general-equilibrium models can be given a short-run content by supposing that any change that lowers real wages in the long run lowers employment in the short run. However, empirical controversies over the effects of foreign investment on employment and the balance of payments have flushed out some additional theoretical considerations. The investment-substitution question addresses the possibility that a transfer of capital does not actually lower the sending country's stock or raise the recipient's by the full amount. If it does not reduce the domestic capital stock, then wages should not be adversely affected. The export-substitution question asks whether or not, in the MNE's own sourcing decisions, its foreign investment necessarily substitutes for export sales. The nature of the MNE's activities suggests that a complementary relationship might prevail – up to a point, and in some settings. The statistical evidence gives appreciable support to the complementary relationship (with its "up to a point" qualification attached), and that weakens the prediction that investing abroad will depress real wages in the source country or raise them in the host. In the aggregate, nonetheless, classical investment substitution seems to prevail.

The effect of MNEs on wages can also be analyzed in the partial-equilibrium context of the MNE's bargaining with its own employees. MNEs' access to alternative production sites overseas should make their demand for labor more elastic than other companies' and thus more resistant to unions' wage demands. The MNE's rents themselves tempt capture by labor. MNEs decentralize their wage and employee-relations decisions, reflecting the local and highly institutional character of labor markets. Studies of wages paid by MNEs have suggested that they do not generally differ from those of comparable local firms, once other factors are controlled, except that in LDCs the MNE is likely to pay higher wages to acquire better "quality" labor. MNEs' foreignness is a disadvantage and might be expected to render MNEs' employee relations less harmonious than those of local firms, and their rents attract bargaining efforts; on the other hand, they can arbitrage innovations in labor relations across national boundaries. On some evidence MNEs face more strikes, partly explained by rents available for capture. They also are responsible for some innovations, although their presence has not transformed national labor-relations systems. Potentially, trade unions can gain from international coalitions to bargain with MNEs and have made some efforts, but there are strong reasons why such coalitions are unlikely to succeed.

6

Investment behavior and financial flows

Previous chapters investigated why MNEs invest resources in overseas facilities at all. The focus now shifts to why they undertake capital expenditures abroad at the rates they do, and what explains their choice of methods of financing these expenditures. Their investment and financing behavior might differ from domestic firms' for several reasons. Demands giving rise to their investments are geographically dispersed, based in imperfectly competitive markets, and raise important questions of option values. Their financing decisions are made in imperfect international capital markets that may be balkanized by variable exchange rates. In the long run, does the MNE enjoy an opportunity to arbitrage between national capital markets that are cleaved by transaction costs? In the short run, how do its money-management decisions respond to variations of exchange rates and short-term credit conditions?

The firm's balance-sheet identity and its changes over time provide a helpful framework for the analysis that follows (Stevens, 1972). A growing foreign subsidiary chooses to expand its assets – fixed (plant and equipment) or liquid (receivables, working capital). This expansion must be financed from some increase in its liabilities: retained earnings from its previous profits, new equity or loans from its parent, and borrowing from external sources (call it local borrowing). Similarly, the subsidiary's parent can expand its fixed or liquid assets in its home base, but also its investment in or claims on its subsidiaries. This expansion of the parent's assets can be financed by retained earnings (either its own earnings or those of its subsidiaries) or by securing new debt or equity funds outside the firm. These balance-sheet identities organize several issues that recur through the following discussion. In empirical research, a good deal of emphasis has been placed on explaining subsidiaries' acquisitions of fixed assets and parents' investments in increased net worth of their subsidiaries. The latter – the increase in foreign direct investment – is an increase in the subsidiary's liabilities and is not necessarily identical to the subsidiary's increase in fixed (or even total) assets. That is because local borrowing can also change. When the subsidiary expands its plant and equipment, or when the parent raises its investment in the subsidiary, some increase generally occurs in the liabilities on one or both balance sheets. How closely tied are these changes? Does the firm make its investment decision simply by comparing its expected yield to some uniform opportunity cost of capital? Or do the changes in fixed-asset holdings depend on the firm's particular structure of liabilities? They might, because existing liabilities influence the firm's ability to raise new funds. Finally, does the balance sheet of the subsidiary have a life of its own? Does anyone care about the relationship between its various assets and liabilities? Or does only the parent's fully consolidated balance sheet matter, with shareholders, lenders, and other onlookers watching the global structure of its assets and liabilities but attaching no importance to the composition of assets and liabilities lodged in a particular subsidiary or country?

In the first section of this chapter we summarize empirical research on subsidiaries' fixed investments and parents' changing financial interests in their subsidiaries. Then we shall proceed to the theoretical and empirical questions raised by the (nonfinancial) MNE's liability structure in relation to the international capital market. The chapter then continues with an analysis of the MNE's management of short-term financial assets and certain public-policy issues that surround its international financial transactions.

6.1. Capital formation and foreign direct investment flows

We expect the MNE, like any other business, to plan its investment outlays by selecting from the stock of projects open to it those whose expected internal rates of return exceed the firm's cost of capital. This rule applies to the MNE that maximizes global profits; although other hypotheses about the firm's motives clamor for attention, profit maximization seems to explain most of the action.[1] Although we assume that the MNE maximizes its long-run profits (specifically, its stock-market value to its ultimate owners), we must deal with the hypothesis that the MNE also avoids risk when making its investment decisions. It might shun risk either on behalf of its owners or to maximize utility for its managers and other stakeholders. Interdependent with the question of objectives is the issue of whether the MNE faces a rising short-run cost of capital or hierarchy of funds sources.

Determinants of foreign investment and overseas capital formation

The assumption that profit guides MNEs' investment decisions merely indicates how the MNE reckons, using its information about capital

---

[1] Horst (1974*b*) reviewed the candidates in the context of multinational activity. He pointed out that the alternatives do supply some specific and potentially testable predictions about MNEs' investment behavior.

costs and investment projects' expected cash flows. The outside observer must search for observable variables that are correlated with the variables governing the firm's expectations and thus driving its investment decisions. Several models of investment behavior have been applied to flows of direct investments or capital-formation rates by overseas subsidiaries.[2] One approach is Jorgenson's (1963) neoclassical model, which identifies investment as adjustment to or toward the capital stock that will be optimal for a competitive firm or industry. That stock depends on the desired or expected output level, the capital-output relation, and the price of output relative to the user cost of capital (interest and depreciation rates).

Although the neoclassical model has proved popular in statistical studies of MNEs' investment decisions, its foundation in purely competitive markets raises some doubts. It does not apply to discrete projects – the foreign-investment opportunity in which the MNE finds itself facing a downward-sloping demand curve for the project's output. The outside observer might assume that the firm applies an efficient project-selection rule but is ill-positioned to explain or second-guess the firm's actual decision or test the decision rule against some alternative. Researchers can dredge up only such coarse indicators as the level of GNP or sectoral output in the intended foreign market or some measure of the growth rate of output formulated in the spirit of the "accelerator" relation.

Several time-series statistical investigations proceeded along this line, aiming to explain flows of foreign direct investments by U.S. MNEs or plant and equipment spending by their subsidiaries. They tested various predictors, although usually not in a directly comparative way; the studies differ in how they deal with the lag between a firm's decision to make an outlay and the expenditure of the funds. Stevens (1969) analyzed the investment behavior of 71 individual well-established foreign subsidiaries, using a modified version of Jorgenson's model. He found (pp. 174–6) that investment outlays increase significantly with the subsidiary's sales (as an indicator of its desired capital stock), the subsidiary's profits (indicating the marginal profit of additional investment), and its depreciation allowances (indicating the erosion of its existing capital stock). Kwack (1972) examined aggregate data for changes in overseas assets of U.S. companies. He also found support for a Jorgenson-type formulation, using a weighted average of the gross national products of principal host countries of U.S. MNEs to proxy the movements of the subsidiaries' desired output levels.

Stevens (1972) similarly addressed the aggregate data on plant and equipment expenditures of U.S. MNEs' overseas affiliates, getting somewhat unsatisfactory results for the Jorgenson model and better ones for a simple flexible accelerator (investment depends on past sales, their rate of growth, and past

---

[2] For surveys and discussion, see Richardson (1971) and Stevens (1974).

capital stock). Lunn's (1980) methods and results resemble those of Stevens. Severn (1972), working with data on individual firms, found overseas gross fixed capital formation to be related to the lagged change in overseas sales – the accelerator relation, again. Rather weak evidence emerged to support two other indicators of investment opportunities – the firm's overseas income and the price of the parent's equity shares (a high price embodies the stock market's rosy forecast of future profits to be realized by investment either at home or abroad). Boatwright and Renton (1975) analyzed changes in the stock of MNE capital moving both into and out of the United Kingdom. For both inflows and outflows a neoclassical formulation of the desired capital stock proved statistically significant. However, the lag structure of the relationships was not estimated precisely, and at an intermediate step in the analysis the authors had to resort to assuming an implausibly high elasticity of substitution in production between capital and labor.

Goldsbrough (1979) took up a different aspect of the MNE's investment demand – one congenial to the transaction-cost model of the MNE. He included not only measures of activity in foreign markets but also international shifts in unit labor costs as affected by exchange-rate changes. He confirmed that MNEs' allocations of funds among four major industrial countries have apparently sought to place production facilities in the lowest-cost location.[3] Barrell and Pain (forthcoming) analyzed data on aggregate U.S. quarterly outflows, confirming the influence of relative user costs of capital as well as unit labor costs.

Consistent with this evidence is the finding of several studies (Rowthorn and Hymer, 1971; Buckley et al., 1978) that the growth rates of large MNEs are correlated with the growth rates of their home national economies and their chief industrial bases within those economies (the relation's tightness decreases with the size of the source economy; see Caves, 1990). For large firms this is hardly a surprise. Buckley et al. (1978) found that their firms' growth during 1962–72 was at least weakly correlated with the extent of their multinational operations in 1972. Again no surprise, because increasing overseas assets is one way for the firm to grow. Buckley et al. (1984) found the growth of large multinationals during 1972–7 related to their industry and country of origin but not their size or multinationality. Aliber (1993) argued the broad importance of national growth patterns for major long-run variations in foreign investment.

An important new development in the analysis of MNEs' investment opportunities is application of the theory of real options. It can explain the occurrence of foreign investments, for example, to obtain alternative production sites and profit by switching production between them to take advantage of shifts in lo-

[3] In this context recall the studies described in Chapter 2 that associate shifts in MNEs' investment decisions with major changes in tariffs, such as the formation of the European Community. See Hufbauer (1975, pp. 278–80).

cal costs (Aizenman, 1994; also see the early discussion by Kogut, 1983). It can also explain the deferral of investments subject to volatile underlying returns (Campa, 1994). Caves (1991) sought to test (not very successfully) the role of international horizontal mergers as acquisitions of bundles of real options that are strategic complements among rival international firms. Campa (1994) undertook an elaborate study of investment decisions of MNEs in the chemical-processing industry. Controlling for the levels of variables determining the steady-state profitability of investments (exchange rates, capacity utilization, oil prices), he found that investment is deterred by the volatility of demand (although not that of exchange rates or oil prices). Comparing MNEs to domestic firms in the industry, he concluded that MNEs do not postpone investments in response to country-specific volatility, but their domestic rivals do.

Finance and capital costs

From the demand-side influences on the MNE's desired capital stock, we turn to the financing of MNEs' investments. Boatwright and Renton (1975) incorporated international capital arbitrage by the MNE, making the adjustment of overseas capital stocks depend on international differences in interest rates (long-term government bonds). The statistical significance of this term is somewhat erratic. Cushman (1985), in a paper discussed subsequently, found U.S. direct investment appropriately sensitive to U.S. and foreign real costs of capital as well as investment-demand variables. Petrochilas (1989, Chapter 5) argued (to justify his econometric result) that host-country capital costs could even have a negative effect on foreign investment inflows because of the prevalence of complementary local borrowing. Most research on the financing of MNEs' investments, however, has not relied on a simple capital-arbitrage hypothesis. It has instead traveled two other avenues. One, the adaptation of financing practices to the variability of real and nominal exchange rates, will be considered in Section 6.2. The second is the hypothesis that the MNE operates as if it faces a rising marginal supply price of funds in the short run, with the upward slope due at least partly to the firm's treatment of internally generated funds (retained earnings) as having a lower opportunity cost than does newly issued debt or equity. This hypothesis has broad implications for the MNE's behavior, so we weigh the evidence on it before turning to issues concerning the international capital markets themselves.

Stevens (1969, 1972) and Severn (1972) both treated the MNE's overseas capital-formation outlays as determined jointly with its domestic capital-formation and global financing decisions, as the funding-hierarchy hypothesis implies. Severn supposed that the firm's internal funds (depreciation allowances and retained earnings) represent a preferred form of financing and that its access to borrowed funds deteriorates as it becomes more highly leveraged (i.e., as its debt-equity ratio increases). Accordingly, he expected the MNE's rate of capital formation abroad to decline with the parent's debt-equity ratio (confirmed statistically) and its capital formation at home to increase with the income it has recently earned abroad (also confirmed). Severn's results are roughly consistent with the assumption that the MNE makes its investment decisions around the globe as a package, taking into account the funds it has generated in all of its current operations. Stevens (1969) explicitly tested the hypotheses that plant and equipment outlays of subsidiaries are decreased by the parent's global alternative investments and increased by its global supply of liquidity, and both hypotheses were, in general, confirmed. Ladenson (1972), starting from the flow-of-funds identity for the firm, built a model that reveals a good deal of interdependence among financial flows and changes in assets in the form of systematic processes of lagged adjustment of one variable to another. Kwack (1972) allowed the adjustment of overseas assets of U.S. companies to depend on their retained earnings and depreciation allowances in the recent past as a source of liquid funds; this influence was confirmed statistically. And McClain (1974, Chapter 7) found that changes in British MNEs' assets are related positively to their foreign subsidiaries' cash flows but negatively to investment opportunities in British domestic manufacturing; their domestic (U.K.) cash flows do not wield a significant influence. Symmetrically, McClain found that capital stock in U.K. manufacturing expands less rapidly, the better are the investment opportunities of British MNEs' subsidiaries in the United States. Recently Stevens and Lipsey (1992) reconfirmed these findings, showing that foreign and domestic investments of a sample of large MNEs are limited by the firm's debt-asset ratio and have the expected interdependence with each other. Barrell and Pain (forthcoming) showed that aggregate U.S. foreign direct investment increases with real aggregate corporate profits a half-year previously, presumably a cash-flow effect. Belderbos (1992) demonstrated that MNEs arbitrage capital between countries on the basis of their relative growth rates of local production and rates of return on investment.

An indirect test of the funding-hierarchy hypothesis can be based on the liquidity levels of MNEs relative to their domestic competitors. Reuber and Roseman (1972), analyzing takeovers of Canadian companies by foreign enterprises, found this financial-investment decision to depend on corporate liquidity. Low liquidity in Canada puts more enterprise units on the market and also reduces the bid tendered for them by other Canadian firms, thus increasing foreign takeovers. They also found that U.S. liquidity is positively related to these takeovers. Reuber et al. (1973, Chapter 4) reported that MNEs' internal cash flows strongly affect their investments in ongoing subsidiaries, but the parent's liquidity has little influence on the decision to start a subsidiary. This adversary relation has implications for the effects of exchange-rate changes that are developed in Section 6.2.

If the MNE's global investment and funding decisions are fully interdependent, they also appear highly flexible in response to constraints and disturbances. This is illustrated by the responses of U.S. MNEs to the U.S. Foreign Direct Investment Program (1968–74), which sought to restrict outflows of direct investment in the absence of offsetting borrowing abroad. Scaperlanda (1992; also earlier studies cited therein) documented a large swing from U.S. domestic to foreign and equity to debt funding of U.S. MNEs' foreign subsidiaries. Beenstock (1982) reported similar conclusions from experience in the United Kingdom.

These conclusions from economists' analyses of MNEs' behavior can be checked against evidence on the internal decision processes reported in the literature of business administration.[4] Kelly (1981) surveyed the practices of large U.S. MNEs, finding that most of them follow discounted-cash-flow procedures to evaluate individual projects and then apply a hurdle rate of return, although a few select projects in descending order of expected rates of return until a constrained supply of funds is exhausted. Half the respondents use the parent's worldwide cost of capital as a hurdle, but 23 percent distinguish a local cost of capital; some employ a payback-period analysis, especially as an informal risk premium for investments in developing countries. Oblak and Helm (1980) reported a similar prevalence in use of the weighted-average cost of capital as a hurdle rate, but did find that 52 percent of respondents use different hurdle rates for foreign projects.

Kelly concluded that most adjusting for the riskiness of individual projects is done informally. Oblak and Helm (1980) reported that 72 percent of respondent companies consider risk specifically in evaluating projects (the same fraction reported experiencing greater actual variation in the returns to foreign than domestic projects). Methods used to deal with foreign projects' risks are adjusting the required rate of return (19 percent) or payback period (13 percent) and borrowing funds locally to deal with the specific risk of exchange-rate fluctuations (22 percent).

The preceding analysis implies that when the wholly owned subsidiary receives funds from its corporate affiliates, their delineation as debt and equity is economically arbitrary.[5] Tax and regulatory factors govern the choice. Where

---

[4] Giddy (1981) provided a convenient summary of the decision rules that would be applied by a value-maximizing multinational.

[5] This assertion assumes, it should be noted, that the MNE guarantees the debt of its subsidiaries, so that a subsidiary cannot go bankrupt independent of the MNE as a worldwide legal entity. Although such a guarantee is not a legal necessity of the MNE's operation, empirical research has suggested that it is close to universal practice. Stobaugh (1970) reported that not one of 20 medium-size and large U.S. MNEs would let a subsidiary default on its debt (even if it were not formally guaranteed), and only one of 17 small MNEs would contemplate this event.

the host country's rate of corporate tax exceeds the source country's, the MNE should denominate the maximum proportion of its subsidiary's liabilities to the parent as debt in order to siphon revenues as tax-deductible interest past the foreign tax collector (Shapiro, 1978). Also, should the host country restrict payments made abroad by residents, interest payable abroad by subsidiaries might claim a higher priority than profit remittance. Although these motives will not apply to every set of bilateral relationships between host and source country, data on U.S. MNEs suggest that they do prevail in the aggregate (Brooke and Remmers, 1970, pp. 194–9). The leverage of all majority-owned foreign affiliates of U.S. MNEs in 1966, measured by the ratio of assets to net worth, was 2.15, versus 1.69 for their U.S. parents. In 1970 these figures for a smaller sample of respondents were 2.41 and 1.88 (Leftwich, 1974).[6]

A preliminary assessment of this statistical research on MNEs' investment and financing suggests the following conclusions: Subsidiaries' plant and equipment outlays depend on expected cash flows, as extrapolated from both general market trends and indirect indicators of future profitability (earnings, exchange-rate changes, etc.). However, researchers have not sorted out exactly what variables are the best predictors. It appears, consistent with evidence presented in Chapter 3, that the MNE coordinates its long-run capacity decisions centrally; subsidiaries do not function as separate investment-decision centers, as has sometimes been suggested, even if subsidiaries' financial transactions with their parents on average are quite a small part of the subsidiaries' overall finance (U.S. Tariff Commission, 1973, p. 424). This coordination is consistent with the extensive evidence that MNEs behave as if a hierarchy of funds sources links all of their short-run financing and investment decisions. The parent's global capital-formation decisions are influenced by its global capacity to generate internal funds for reinvestment, and the allocation of capital expenditures among countries depends on relative and not just absolute expected payouts. This financial constraint on the growth of the firm is notably consistent with the analysis of real constraints on the MNE's growth process (Section 3.1).

6.2. **Long-term financing decisions and financial-asset markets**

Although this evidence marks the MNE as a global coordinator of its financing activities, it does not locate the MNE's practice within the world's capital markets. The capital-arbitrage hypothesis (Chapter 2) implies that the firm simply borrows in the world's cheapest capital market, without regard to the location of its own physical assets. The hypothesis that the MNE avoids risks has many implications; for example, the risk of exchange-rate changes implies that the currency of denomination of its liabilities is related to the location

---

[6] Parallel to the denomination of interaffiliate debt and equity is the decision on currency of invoicing in interaffiliate transactions. Mirus and Yeung (1987) showed how this otherwise indifferent decision can be driven by effects on taxes and ad valorem tariffs.

of its physical assets. We establish some theoretical properties of international markets for financial assets in order to determine the options open to the MNE in making its global financing decisions. Then we consider theoretically and empirically aspects of the MNE's financial decisions that interact with international capital-market imperfections.

Theory of international capital markets

The financial behavior of the MNE is clearly the context for examining the capital-arbitrage hypothesis. It quickly takes us into deeper waters – the modern theory of financial-asset pricing. The model's characterization of how financial assets are priced extends to the liabilities of MNEs, yielding conclusions about their costs of capital and financing decisions.

The capital-asset pricing model (CAPM) explains how risk-averse financial investors behaving as pure competitors set prices for financial assets conveying claims to uncertain streams of future income. The asset holders seek to compose diversified portfolios in order to avoid risk as well as to maximize their wealth. In adding an asset to the portfolio, they are therefore concerned with its incremental effect on the riskiness of the portfolio as a whole. The security's effect depends not on its own riskiness but on how closely its returns are associated with fluctuations in the returns to other securities. This analysis leads to the conclusion that the financial rate of return set by the capital market on any given security – that is, on the uncertain stream of income to which its ownership conveys title – is equal to the risk-free rate of return (e.g., on short-term government securities or some such riskless asset) plus a risk premium that depends on the correlation or covariance between the asset at hand and the "market portfolio." How well a given security comes off in the riskiness ratings thus depends not just on how uncertain is its own income stream but also on how closely its fluctuations coincide with those of other financial-asset income streams in the economy generally.

The CAPM emphasizes the behavior of financial-asset holders in the market for outstanding securities, not that of the nonfinancial companies that issue new assets, but the model has many corollaries for the borrowing firm's behavior. The value-maximizing firm does not please its shareholders by acting in a risk-averse fashion, because they can themselves diversify away any nonsystemic risk to which the firm is exposed. If the projects open to the firm offer a choice between those expected to prove profitable but risky and the less profitable but safe projects, it should choose so that the marginal trade-off between risk and return is the same as the price that the financial-asset market places on risk. The classic Modigliani-Miller theorem held that the firm's value is not affected by its choice of the debt-equity composition of its liabilities; the prevailing view today, however, is that an optimal (value-maximizing) leverage ratio for the firm is indeed defined by governance, tax, and transaction-cost factors.

The model's conditions for the pricing of financial assets define a hypothetical world capital market in which MNEs would enjoy no opportunities for profitable arbitrage. Conversely, such opportunities arise from imperfections that open the way to arbitrage between different securities or classes of securities, or even the same security trading at different prices in different submarkets. Consider these possible violations of a perfectly integrated global capital market:

1.   *Risk-free asset.* A formal problem troublesome for the asset-pricing model is the variability of exchange rates and deviations of national price levels from an equilibrium purchasing power parity relation (Adler and Dumas, 1983; Stulz, 1984). Investors residing in different countries then have different yardsticks for measuring real returns and their risks (so that a given security could have different betas in different markets), and the standard theorems of portfolio theory at the least require modification. If different national financial markets are assumed to reach asset-pricing equilibria in isolation, then the price that investors will pay for a given MNE security can evidently vary from one market to the next.

2.   *Barriers to trade in securities.* International transactions in some or all securities might be subject to high taxes, transactions costs, or (at the limit) outright prohibitions. It then becomes possible (although not necessary) that the MNE can undertake profitable arbitrage simply by selling to Home's shareholders claims on productive assets located wholly or partly in Foreign. Discussion in the finance literature indicated that this arbitrage need not be welfare-maximizing for Home's investors if Home's MNEs have monopoly power in Home's capital market, but that problem goes away if borrowers (MNE and other) are numerous enough to make the capital market competitive (Adler, 1974; Adler and Dumas, 1975, 1983; Lee and Sachdeva, 1977).

Recent theoretical research has turned to modeling the effects of particular constraints that might be imposed on the full global optimization of portfolios. Errunza and Losq (1985) addressed the case in which Home's securities can be held by any investor but Foreign securities are excluded from Home portfolios. They found that Home securities are then priced as in an unrestricted model, but Foreign securities command a special risk premium that firms constrained to issue Foreign securities must pay. This premium increases with the risk aversion of Foreign's investors. Eun and Janakiramanan (1986) instead constrained the maximum proportion of any Foreign company's shares that may be held by Home investors. Foreign securities now sell at different prices in the two countries (higher in Home, lower in Foreign relative to the unconstrained equilibrium), with the Home premium increasing with Home investors' aggregate risk aversion.

MNEs' financial decisions

These imperfections of international capital markets identify arbitrage possibilities for multinational enterprises (Naumann-Etienne, 1974). We consider briefly some models that focus on these choices by the firm, then turn to some relevant empirical evidence.

Taxes and transaction costs limit international financial arbitrage, and it is useful to see how they affect the activities of the MNE relative to individual investors. Hodder and Senbet (1990) employed a two-country model with a locked-in exchange rate but different rates of taxation levied by Home and Foreign on both corporate profits (not subsequently taxed at the personal level) and personal income (applicable to investors' income from corporate debt). Taxation apart, individuals can freely invest in either debt or equity in either country, so that their after-tax returns from investing in debt or equity of either Home or Foreign are equalized. The resulting asset prices give the MNE an incentive to do its borrowing in the country with the higher rate of taxation on corporate profits and lend the proceeds as equity to affiliates in the other country. This incentive is independent of the MNE's country of legal domicile.

Another specific model of the arbitrage process deals with the variability of the exchange rate and its effect on the risk-averse MNE's choice of how much output to produce abroad (Siegel, 1983, Chapter 4; Calderon-Rossell, 1985; Broll, 1992). The MNE commits to production levels in the countries before it knows the random realization of the uncertain exchange rate. Its net foreign revenue position is thus risk-exposed, and it has access to no forward market for hedging the risk. In each market its unit costs of production are constant in local currency, and it faces a downward-sloping demand curve for its product. If unit production costs were the same in each country at the mean expected exchange rate, the MNE would follow a perfect hedging strategy of producing abroad enough output to serve demand in the foreign market and remit the profits in kind. If production costs (in this expected sense) are not equal and traded goods incur zero transport costs, some output (net of remitted profits) will be exported from the low-cost to the high-cost country. Compared to a risk-neutral MNE, the international allocation of production will be less sensitive to production-cost differences. The MNE's incentive to undertake demand shifting expenditures such as advertising is also affected (Broll and Zilcha, 1992). Implications of the exchange-rate regime and source of macro-disturbances for the production-arbitraging MNE were developed by Aizenman (1992).

The MNE's risk-bearing strategy can also be related to its borrowing decisions. Consider the case in which Home's risk-averse investors are unable to diversify their wealth directly against fluctuations in the foreign-exchange rate. The MNE might find that Home investors will pay more for its securities if the real assets bound up in its Foreign subsidiary are hedged by borrowing some of its funds in Foreign's currency. If lenders are costlessly diversified, they will pay no more for the firm's securities once this hedge is accomplished.[7] Hart-

---

[7] If the constraint on international diversification is the transaction cost for the diversifying party, the question then becomes whether asset holders can diversify more economically by themselves or by buying securities of MNEs that have done the job for

man (1979) showed how a MNE serving risk-averse home-country investors determines its optimal foreign borrowing (given its foreign assets, and assuming foreign and domestic interest rates are the same). The best amount to borrow depends on how the home-currency rate of return on foreign assets varies with the exchange rate. If it is unaffected by exchange-rate changes, no borrowing need be done abroad. If it changes proportionally with the exchange rate, foreign borrowing should finance all foreign assets. Shapiro (1975a) considered somewhat similar issues. Siegel's (1983, Chapter 5) related model shows clearly that factors which induce the shifting of production abroad also tend to induce borrowing abroad (important for the empirical evidence reviewed subsequently on MNEs' alignment of their foreign-currency assets and liabilities).

Even if MNEs in some circumstances optimally tie local borrowing by their subsidiaries to the stock of assets at risk in a given currency, that does not mean each subsidiary should do its own financing. Value maximization still requires that the MNE coordinate its financing activities worldwide (Adler, 1974; Shapiro, 1978).[8] The capital market is expected to heed the risk exposure of the MNE's assets and liabilities worldwide. Both in making its financing decisions and in determining its cost of capital (to guide its capital-formation decisions), the MNE should make best use of all specific capital markets available to it.

Empirical evidence: MNEs and financial diversification

These theoretical aspects of international capital markets raise questions about the MNE's financial behavior that reach beyond the evidence surveyed in Section 6.1. They lead to evidence on the MNE's contribution to investors' financial diversification, its role in the market for corporate control, and its investment and funding behavior in the face of varying and uncertain exchange rates.

The first question raised in the preceding section is the MNE's role in supplying diversification gains to the holders of its liabilities and thereby inte-

them. Several authors addressed this issue. Soenen (1979) explored the MNE's trade-off between exchange risk and hedging costs. Adler and Dumas (1975) distinguished between imperfections in the international money market (avoidable by an efficient forward-exchange market) and imperfections in international securities markets (due to more intractable forces). Gilman (1981) argued at length that the MNE fails to maximize global profits by treating its home currency as safe and foreign-currency net assets as risk-exposed; however, if shareholders' portfolios are undiversified internationally and their consumption streams include domestic nontraded goods, that policy can represent optimizing behavior by the MNE on behalf of its owners.

[8] Adler (1974) presented a model in which financial decisions can be decentralized efficiently to the MNE's subsidiaries, but it requires that the MNE be able continuously to adjust its ownership shares in the foreign subsidiaries, including taking short positions. This practice is hardly consistent with the MNE's central role as an administrative coordinating device.

grating international capital markets. Holding shares in an internationally diversified MNE offers the shareholder an alternative to holding an internationally diversified portfolio of national securities.[9] Systematic study of this question was launched by Agmon and Lessard (1977) (also see Hughes et al., 1975). The diversification value that a company's shares offer to investors in its national capital market depends, according to CAPM, on the covariance of its returns with the market factor – the general, undiversifiable risk attached to all income streams originating within that nation. The shares of a MNE, to an extent that increases with the fraction of its assets placed abroad, should exhibit a lower covariance with the domestic market factor. By the same token, its income stream should exhibit some covariance with the market factors of the foreign nations in which it operates. Agmon and Lessard confirmed this hypothesis statistically, their results implying that MNEs' securities do offer a special diversification value to shareholders.

A number of papers followed Agmon and Lessard, testing the relationship between a firm's multinationality and its beta, price/earnings ratio, or both (Errunza and Senbet, 1984; Aggarwal and Soenen, 1987; and references cited therein). The results have not been entirely consistent, although they lean toward the conclusion that MNEs' shares provide their holders with both lower risks and lower rates of return (Fatemi, 1984).[10] The findings also suggest that the empirical relationships might not be stable over time. An analytical problem recognized in the literature is that whether the risk-adjusted price of a MNE's shares includes a premium depends on supply as well as demand factors: any cost advantage that the MNE has in providing diversification services over the investor adding foreign stocks to a portfolio; but also the number of home-based MNEs whose shares offer this diversification service. The paper by Errunza and Senbet (1984) represents the current state of this research. They regressed a measure of excess valuation of a U.S. firm's security (essentially a market-to-book ratio) on its systemic risk (beta), firm size, and any of several measures of the extent of its involvement abroad. Excess value indeed proved positively related to multinationality, although to a degree that declined over their sample period (1971–8). When they substituted the security's price/earnings ratio for the excess-returns measure, no relation was found. Taking this study and others together, one conjectures that increasing supplies of MNE

---

9 We note Aliber's (1970) argument in a very different vein that MNEs arise not to supply international diversification but because investors in the securities of their nation's MNEs myopically fail to notice the exchange-rate risks to which their overseas assets are exposed – risks they would not welcome should they add foreign securities to their personal portfolios.

10 For evidence that the MNE can maximize firm value by exploiting restrictions-based differences in the demands of domestic and foreign investors for its securities, see Stulz and Wasserfallen (1992).

securities and decreasing costs of direct international diversification by investors might have eliminated a once-extant premium.[11]

Researchers' interest has lately turned from investors' valuations of the shares of ongoing U.S. multinationals to their valuations of organizational changes in the form of foreign acquisitions (Fatemi and Furtado, 1988; Doukas and Travlos, 1988). This research line was noted in Section 1.3 in a context that immediately shows its key limitation: Investors could attach positive value to a domestic firm's expansion abroad either because it will bring rents to the firm or because it supplies valued diversification services. The evidence shows that the variance in valuations of foreign acquisitions clearly reflects rents but might also reflect diversification services. Although unrestricted samples of foreign acquisitions yield no significant market reactions, a MNE's first entry into a host country does elicit a significant positive excess return. However, so do conglomerate international acquisitions (the target's activity lies outside the principal two-digit industry of the acquirer) and acquisitions made in developing countries (arguably better prospects for diversification than for direct rents). That research approach can also be applied to the market's valuation of foreign acquirers' willingness to pay for U.S. target firms. Both Harris and Ravenscraft (1991) and Swenson (1993) found that foreign acquirers' bids for U.S. firms are valued significantly higher than are those by domestic acquirers. The differential is due at least partly to foreign MNEs' propensity to acquire in research-intensive industries. Foreign MNEs are less likely to compete with other bidders for these targets, suggesting that they pursue specific synergies. Again, there is evidence that the differential foreign premium has declined over time.[12] Morck and Yeung (1991) analyzed a large sample of U.S. companies to determine

[11] Also relevant to this question is the general substitutability between foreign equity and portfolio investments for domestic investors. The macroeconomic study of Ruffin and Rassekh (1986) found a close dollar-for-dollar substitution. The expansion of Japanese foreign investment during the 1980s in particular illustrates these portfolio considerations. It was strongly influenced by the removal of regulations that had kept large financial intermediaries from diversifying their portfolios internationally. That diversification amounted to a gigantic stock adjustment of Japanese portfolios that included large purchases of controlling interests in U.S. real estate, but these direct investments involved no element of the MNE based on transaction-cost considerations (Makin, 1989; Glick, 1990).

[12] Jorion (1990) investigated the degree to which the market returns to U.S. companies' stocks are sensitive to changes in the dollar's foreign-exchange value. Dollar depreciation should directly increase the valuation of foreign monetary assets, although its effect on real assets abroad depends on the firm's configuration of activities. Empirically he found that stock returns increase with dollar depreciation in proportion to the MNE's foreign activity. The size of this effect, however, plummeted between 1971–5 and 1981–7, consistent with a shift from predominantly monetary to predominantly real shocks between the two periods. Luehrman (1990) explored the degrees to which a MNE's value is affected by its exposure to competition from rivals based in different countries and thereby affecting the MNE's exchange-rate exposure.

whether their market valuations (Tobin's q) increase with their multinationality. They found that multinationality has a significant positive influence only in the presence of proprietary assets, thus tending to rule out diversification (except in the presence of these assets) and also tax advantages as primary bases for MNEs.

The MNE plays a two-sided role in dealing with risk: as a supplier of diversification services to risk-averse creditors and as itself a risk-averse actor in a risky international setting. Lee and Kwok (1988) sought to untangle these two roles by analyzing the leverage chosen by MNEs relative to U.S. domestic companies. They controlled for company size, the importance of outlays on intangibles (research and advertising, which increase the agency cost of debt and deter leverage), and the intertemporal variance of cash flows (which increases the likelihood that bankruptcy costs will be incurred and thereby deters leverage). MNEs choose lower leverage than the control sample of domestic companies (also see Shaked, 1986), suggesting that risk-aversion within the firm prevails over the higher debt levels expected of risk-neutral firms engaged in risk-diversifying groups of activities.

Empirical evidence: exchange-rate risks

Harris and Ravenscraft (1991) and Swensen (1993) both addressed a hypothesis put forth by Froot and Stein (1991). Assume the correctness of the financial-hierarchy hypothesis, explained (and supported for large MNEs) in Section 6.1. Exchange-rate movements then cause a wealth effect on the willingness of firms to pay for acquisitions abroad. When the U.S. dollar depreciates, the liquidity of foreign MNEs (held mostly in foreign-currency assets) increases relative to the reservation prices of current owners of U.S. corporate assets. The foreigners bring more funds with low perceived opportunity cost to compete in the U.S. market for corporate control, and should pay higher premia and/or win more auctions. Each study confirmed the effect, with Harris and Ravenscraft reporting that a 10 percent dollar depreciation begets a 2.7 percent gain to the U.S. target's shareholders. Further support is offered by Klein and Rosengren (1992, 1994).

Other empirical evidence bears on MNEs' investment-type decisions in general as they relate to variable exchange rates. First, do firms investing abroad behave as if averse to the risk of exchange-rate fluctuations? Both survey and statistical evidence suggest that they do. Behrman (in Mikesell, 1962, pp. 95–8) found that the vast majority of the U.S. MNEs interviewed seek to minimize the dollar equity invested abroad, and many try to borrow as much as possible in the host country. This motive and decision rule also appear in the survey evidence of Brooke and Remmers (1970, pp. 182, 195) and Robbins and Stobaugh (1973, Chapter 4) – a study dealing with investments in LDCs. A study of the expansion of large foreign subsidiaries in India over 20 years found that only

5.3 percent of their acquisitions of assets were financed from foreign sources (Martinussen, 1988, p. 147). Finally, there is some suggestion that MNEs have used local borrowing as a form of off-balance-sheet financing, to make the parent's leverage look less than a full enumeration of its worldwide debt would indicate – a procedure that may be deceptive if the parent does in fact guarantee the local currency debt of its subsidiaries. Robbins and Stobaugh (p. 127) noted that subsidiaries show higher aggregate ratios of current liabilities to current assets than do their parents' domestic operations, consistent with a risk-induced reliance on local-currency financing.

Stevens (1972) tested the hypothesis that MNEs relate their borrowing abroad to the assets and earnings of subsidiaries that are exposed to depreciation of the host country's exchange rate. He found a quite stable relationship between changes in assets overseas and changes in foreign borrowing, but the relationship is not dollar-for-dollar at the margin, and his test does not seem finely honed to support this particular hypothesis about foreign-exchange risk. Goldsbrough (1979) addressed this question more directly, deriving a formal model that shows how the proportion of a MNE's borrowing done abroad will depend on international interest-rate differentials, the distribution of its capital investments between countries, and the covariation of cash flows from those investments with exchange-rate changes. Goldsbrough's model is consistent with a constant proportional relation between assets and liabilities denominated in foreign currency. Gilman (1981), similarly concerned with foreign-exchange risk and the liability structures of subsidiaries' balance sheets, found that foreign-currency financing is more closely related to changes in subsidiaries' total assets than to their current assets, implying that all assets abroad are viewed as subject to the risk of exchange-rate changes.

Variable exchange rates raise the issue of the financing of foreign investment, but also the quantitative response of MNEs' decisions on capital expenditures abroad to changes in current and expected exchange rates. Kohlhagen (1977) and Cushman (1985) showed that any predictions must be highly conditional. Responses to changes in real and nominal exchange rates by the value-maximizing firm depend on whether change responds to some disequilibrium or embodies a new shock, and responses also depend on how the current (recent) change affects expectations of future exchange rates. Even with these questions settled, the MNE's response depends on the configuration of its activities in the host country. A permanent real depreciation of its currency makes the host country more attractive as a site for production to serve the world (or source-country) market but less attractive as a site for assembling products for host-market sale that contain substantial source-country components.

Kohlhagen's analysis covered investment spending abroad by U.S. MNEs during the 1960s, when fixed exchange rates were subject to occasional devaluations or revaluations, typically to cure large and widely recognized disequilibria. The MNEs' responses (both anticipatory and reactive) confirmed a preference to undertake capital expenditures abroad after a currency is cheapened, or before its price rises. Cushman (1985) covered the period 1963–78, embracing both fixed and flexible exchange rates, and used foreign investment rather than foreign capital expenditures as the dependent variable. Again, the results indicate that foreign investment is attracted to a host country whose currency has depreciated, but also takes account of expected future exchange rates (in his result extrapolative expectations, consistent with the pegged exchange rates that prevailed over half of his period).[13] Given the exchange rate's level, Cushman concluded that an increase in exchange-rate risk actually increases foreign investment; that outcome is consistent with the displacement of source-country exports by production facilities in the host, and also a real-options model.

Campa (1993), analyzing foreign direct investments in U.S. wholesale distribution, focused on how a risk-neutral foreign firm can regard such an investment as a real option. The greater the variance of the U.S. dollar exchange rate, the more likely does the firm gain by waiting for a still more favorable rate (and the larger is the investment it makes when it does exercise the option). Campa confirmed not only that exchange-rate variance deters direct investments in distribution, but also that the deterrent effect is greater, the larger is the sunk cost that the investment entails.

Earlier studies also addressed inflows of foreign direct investment to the United States (Cushman, 1988) or gross acquisitions of foreign-controlled assets in the United States (Caves, 1989). Cushman's results closely parallel those for U.S. outflows in Cushman (1985), including the influences of exchange-rate levels and variability. Caves (1989) also found that depreciation of the dollar attracts foreign investment, but no hypothesis about exchange-rate expectations was supported. Also, given the exchange rate, foreign investment is attracted by lower prices of equity shares, the vehicle for acquiring control of existing business assets.[14]

Goldberg and Kolstad (1994) analyzed risky investment decisions in a sophisticated framework. The MNE that can serve Foreign customers from either Home or Foreign plants faces two sources of short-run risk: the real exchange rate and the level of Foreign's demand. If demand and the Home prices of Foreign currency are positively correlated, the risks of serving Foreign's market

[13] Barrell and Pain (forthcoming), who analyzed aggregate quarterly outflows of U.S. foreign direct investment, found that current appreciation of the dollar causes a speedup to complete foreign investments, while expected appreciation in the next quarter postpones it.

[14] See also McClain (1983). This result has the flavor of the Froot-Stein hypothesis about corporate wealth effects, as does the conclusion that acquisitions of assets in the United States show a strong positive relation to the growth of the source country's real income and thus to corporate funds.

from the Home plant are amplified. They tested aggregate bilateral direct investment flows between the United States and other countries taking account both of exchange-rate variability and its correlation with domestic demand shocks. Exchange-rate variability promotes locating production abroad (as risk-aversion implies), but the covariance of exchange rates and domestic demand has no significant influence.

Subsidiaries' practices in remitting dividends to their parents (versus retaining the funds locally) also call for scrutiny. One probably dominant influence, minimizing the company's global tax bill, will be considered in Chapter 8 (see Hines and Hubbard, 1990). Other influences reflect the general interdependence of MNEs' financial decisions, discussed earlier. For example, susidiaries remit less of their earnings if their desired capital stocks are growing rapidly (Kopits, 1972) or high rates of profits are earned (Mauer and Scaperlanda, 1972). Zenoff's (1966) survey of 30 large U.S. MNEs confirmed the influence of taxes and reinvestment opportunities but also flagged some factors not consistent with profit maximization. For example, parent MNEs that traditionally pay out a fixed proportion of net earnings as dividends tend to require subsidiaries to remit a comparable percentage. The findings of Brooke and Remmers (1970, Chapter 6) are similar. Because the U.S. tax system penalizes the payment of dividends by corporate parents, economists wonder why dividends are paid at all,[15] and that goes for a decision rule imposing the same practice on subsidiaries. A MNE not consolidating its subsidiaries' finances fully into the parent's financial statements might vary dividend remittances so as to "dress up" the financial position that the parent reports to the public, Zenoff suggested. This practice leaves the public partly in the dark about the MNE's global activities and implies some advantage to the company from painting a picture less than completely truthful. Overall, Zenoff distinguished between mature companies with extensive networks of subsidiaries that manage dividend remittance through rules of thumb and MNEs with less experience or less far-flung empires that attune their remittance practices to the needs of the hour.

6.3. Foreign-exchange rates, short-term transactions, and financial reporting

The preceding sections have shown how the MNE and investors in its liabilities respond to the risks of international transactions. These include the political risks of being unable to deter the hostile action of a foreign government, the economic risks implicit in the higher costs of information about foreign environments (one buys less than complete information, and so faces greater risks), and the economic risk of changes in exchange rates and national

[15] Dividends paid are subject to taxation as personal income for the shareholder. If they are plowed back into the enterprise, they become capital gains on the shareholder's equities, taxed only when the shares are sold and then at the lower rate pertaining to capital gains.

prices. In this section we consider how MNEs react to exchange-rate variability in handling their short-term transactions. We shall also review the MNE's problem of evaluating the effects of exchange-rate changes on its value and reporting them to the world at large. This latter problem, "translation" of the changing values of assets and liabilities denominated in foreign exchange into the parent's native currency, gets surprisingly dominant emphasis in the business literature. One might suspect that businesses fret less over how to deal with future exchange-rate changes than over what to tell the public about those past.

Responses to expected exchange-rate changes

To isolate the behavior at issue, suppose that the MNE's decisions about committing resources can be divided cleanly into two groups: Long-run commitments cannot be soon reversed, but short-run commitments can be altered within periods for which the MNE can hedge (or possibly forecast) exchange-rate movements. Long-run decisions by the risk-averse firm might rest on an expectation about how variations in the price of foreign exchange will be correlated with variations in the subsidiary's foreign-currency earnings, but by assumption the MNE cannot anticipate the specific ups and downs. However, exchange-rate exposures three months hence can be covered in the forward market or speculated upon. Various sources describe the many strategies open to MNEs to obtain gains or avoid losses from exchange-rate changes.[16] Some maneuvers involve transactions between branches of the MNE and other parties. The transaction opportunities here are, in general, the same for the MNE as for any other agent; the qualification "in general" allows for the MNE's advantage in holding information acquired in other dealings that may help it to take expeditious action in the foreign-exchange market. Other transactions are internal to the MNE and take place between its various national branches. In internal transactions, the MNE has a clear-cut advantage. Consider speeding up payments due in a currency expected to appreciate and delaying payments denominated in a currency expected to depreciate. In transactions between independent parties, the payment is affected by a precontracted due date and other terms, and rearranging on short notice to take mutual advantage of an expected change in exchange rates might be difficult (Jilling, 1978, pp. 150–2).

Surveys reveal companies' practices for dealing with fluctuations in the foreign-exchange rate.[17] Rodriguez (1980, Chapter 2) found the exploitation of

---

[16] Rutenberg (1970); Robbins and Stobaugh (1973, Chapters 1, 4, and 5); Jilling (1978, Chapters 2 and 3). Itagaki's model (1981) develops several aspects of the MNE's reaction to exchange-market conditions. The long-short distinction made here ignores the emergence of long-term swap agreements that provide a partial substitute for forward markets.

[17] Jilling's survey, taken in 1975, found that the management of foreign-exchange risk, like other financial functions, is highly centralized for most MNEs. Resources committed to the task had been increasing, in reflection of the increasing variability of exchange rates during the early 1970s. This expertise is subject to scale economies and

leads and lags in interaffiliate payments to be the method most commonly used. Next come money-market transactions: Borrow in a currency expected to depreciate; lend in one expected to appreciate. There is the classic maneuver of covering long or short positions in a foreign currency by a sale or purchase in the forward-exchange market or by negotiated swaps. Finally, the MNE can change the currency in which its payables or receivables are denominated. Shifting the terms of a transaction in order to snatch a short-term gain is costly to negotiate with an arm's-length trading partner, and so this instrument is an unwieldy one. Jilling's results (1978, pp. 146–57) generally agree with the priorities found by Rodriguez, as do the findings of Robbins and Stobaugh (1973, Chapter 7).

If the MNE actively pursues expected profits by all possible routes, it will consider taking speculative positions. A good deal of commentary suggests that the nonfinancial company is keener to avoid losses in the foreign-exchange markets than to pursue speculative profits. The majority of Jilling's respondents preferred to make neither gains nor losses; many emphasized minimizing losses, and this attitude was more prevalent among smaller U.S. companies outside the largest 500 (Jilling, 1978, pp. 144, 274, 327). Similarly, Rodriguez (1980, Chapter 2) devised an interview strategy to reveal whether or not managers hold asymmetrical attitudes toward foreign-exchange gains and losses; they displayed a strong allergy to losses. Defensive postures can extend to taking an open position in the short-term forward-exchange market so as to hedge a long-term fixed investment exposed to exchange risk, but this hedge is not self-liquidating and leads to reported short-term gains or losses (Jilling, 1978, p. 64).

That MNEs and other nonfinancial companies should limit their exchange-market activities to defensive maneuvers seems a bit puzzling. If a company is to form the administrative apparatus needed to deal defensively in the foreign-exchange market, why not deal aggressively? The answer probably lies in economies of specializing in the activity of foreign-exchange speculation as well as in nonfinancial companies' attitudes toward risk (Aliber, 1978, Chapter 11). There might be yet another reason why MNEs avoid committing resources to activities in the foreign-exchange market – a reason that harks back to the analysis of Section 6.2. If the MNE finds that the forward market for foreign exchange is already populated by competitive, well-informed speculators, then it cannot hope to "beat the market" with any regularity by speculating outright or entering the forward market only selectively to hedge its exposed foreign-exchange assets and liabilities.[18] True, it can choose to hedge

so increases significantly with size of company. See Jilling (1978, pp. 89–90, 95–6, 113, 314).

[18] Economists have devoted a great deal of effort to testing the efficiency of forward markets. After the event, it often turns out that a speculator could have made profits over a period of time by applying some simple decision rule to forward-exchange transactions

its exposed positions regularly, up to whatever future maturities are available in the foreign-exchange market and through swaps. But the transactions costs cut into its long-run expected profits as the price of avoiding risk. Therefore, the risk-neutral company will avoid hedging if it thinks that the market is efficient (although it might arrange transactions in hope of exchange profits when it thinks it can beat the market).

Rodriguez (1980, Chapter 4) analyzed data on the foreign-currency positions of 36 companies to test hypotheses about their motives and practices in the foreign-exchange market. Nearly all of them experienced substantial changes in exposure to exchange risks, so they could not have followed the "risk-paranoid" pattern of avoiding open positions entirely. Rodriguez also ruled out the possibility that managers think markets are efficient and can never be beaten. The most consistent position, she found, is that managers sometimes think they can beat the market; in fact, during 1967–74 they moved funds toward strong currencies and away from weak ones.[19] The statistical pattern suggests that they acted as if they had noticed that the forward-exchange markets were systematically underpredicting the movements of those currencies. She also found actions to counter foreign-exchange exposures that might lead to losses more common than actions to enlarge those showing promise of gains.

Some researchers focused on the behavior of MNEs at times of major changes in exchange rates, such as the devaluations of the U.S. dollar in 1971 and 1973. Rodriguez's data (1980, Chapter 5) suggest a strong tendency in both the 1971 and 1973 crises for companies to move internally generated funds toward strong currencies, but little evidence of borrowing in weak currencies and lending in strong ones. Klein (1974) and a U.S. Senate study (1975), based on different sets of data, agree in general. Both of these inquiries found that the outflows of foreign direct investment itself were abnormally high during the crisis periods, indicating that U.S. MNEs chose those times to acquire additional long-term foreign assets. And the U.S. Senate study (1975) found that the foreign subsidiaries of U.S. companies increased the share of their payments to third parties denominated in dollars, thereby reducing their dollar balances. Klein (1974) concluded that the MNEs' aggregate contribution to the speculative outflow of funds was proportionally not

(see, e.g., Rodriguez, 1980, Chapter 3). But hindsight beats foresight, and there is no way to show whether or not market participants efficiently used all information and opportunities available to them before the event.

[19] These patterns of intermittent, successful speculation emerged in Rodriguez's data only after she separated the operating accounts from the financial accounts of her companies. The operating accounts reflect marketing considerations, and their foreign-exchange components cannot easily be manipulated in the short run. The financial accounts reflect the firm's opportunities to manage its own liquid assets. Evans and Folks (1979, pp. 19–20) similarly found a strong preference for managing foreign-exchange risk through financial rather than operating transactions.

very large in either 1971 or 1973, but it does appear that MNEs were active in anticipating the exchange-rate changes.[20]

Reporting effects of exchange-rate changes

We noted previously that however successful or unsuccessful are its bets on changes in exchange rate, the MNE faces the problem of translation – reporting to its shareholders and to the world at large how exchange-rate changes have affected its balance sheet. This question holds some economic interest for two reasons. First, observers have noted an appreciable if diminishing tendency for business to confuse translation and transactions aspects of the foreign-exchange problem, undertaking purposive actions on foreign-exchange exposure to improve the nominal results that they report, rather than truly to maximize the firm's value (Rodriguez, 1980, Chapter 2). Second, what asset and liability values are affected by exchange-rate changes is itself essentially an economic question (Shapiro, 1975b; Hodder, 1982).

Suppose that Home's MNE has a subsidiary operating in Foreign, and the price of Foreign's currency (the F$) declines. The subsidiary's balance sheet includes both long- and short-run assets and liabilities denominated in F$. How should the MNE report the depreciation's effect on the home (H$) profits of the whole enterprise? Suppose that exchange-rate changes in general are not thought to predict changes in countries' long-run terms of trade. That assumption implies that the F$'s depreciation probably entails no permanent change in the H$-denominated profits that the subsidiary's plant and equipment in Foreign can produce. By implication, the F$'s nominal depreciation will then correspond to change in Foreign's real exchange rate that is temporary, damped, or both. Then the depreciation will not be the occasion for saying that the MNE's owners have taken a loss on their long-run Foreign assets. But what about the subsidiary's accounts receivable for past F$-denominated transactions? Or what about the subsidiary's short-term borrowing from Foreign banks, now repayable in depreciated F$s? The MNE's Home shareholders would seem to have taken a capital loss on the subsidiary's F$ balances and its explicit contracts to receive F$ payments, but scored a gain on the subsidiary's obligations to pay in F$s. These current, monetary assets and liabilities, however, are the only clear case. What about the subsidiary's inventories, whose future sale value or replacement cost may be affected in diverse ways by the devaluation? What about long-term debts payable in F$, which could undergo further fluctuations in value before ultimately being paid off?

---

[20] Similar evidence has appeared for other currency crises. Brooke and Remmers (1970, pp. 189–90, 199–203) noted that U.S. subsidiaries in Britain, anticipating a devaluation of sterling, in 1964–6 undertook heavy borrowing in sterling and remitted larger-than-average dividends to their parents.

MNEs' accounting practices in treating exchange-rate changes have varied among countries as well as over time. Common practices have included the following (Prindl, 1976, Chapter 2; Evans and Folks, 1979):

1. *Closing-rate method.* All the subsidiary's balance-sheet items are simply converted at the end-of-period exchange rate. If the F$ has depreciated and all the subsidiary's assets and intercorporate liabilities are F$-denominated, then Home's shareholders are told they have taken a capital loss on their equity in proportion to the depreciation.

2. *Current/noncurrent method* (also called working-capital method). All the subsidiary's short-term (under one year) assets and liabilities are translated at the end-of-period exchange rate, long-term items at whatever historical exchange rate obtained when they originally went on the books. When the F$ depreciates, Home's shareholders are told they have taken a loss if the subsidiary's current F$ assets (cash, current receivables, inventories) exceed its current F$ liabilities (accounts payable, short-term bank loans).

3. *Monetary/nonmonetary method.* All the subsidiary's monetary assets and liabilities (of whatever maturity) are translated at the end-of-period exchange rate, everything else at the historical rate. The shareholders are notified of a capital loss if the subsidiary's monetary F$ assets (cash, current and long-term receivables) exceed its F$ liabilities (accounts payable, all F$-denominated loans).

The closing rate method has been popular among U.K. and European MNEs. The practices of U.S. MNEs have been more varied. A 1975 survey (see Evans and Folks, 1979, p. 6) found 35 percent using the current/noncurrent method and 6 percent using a variant on it, 14 percent using the monetary/nonmonetary method and 26 percent using a variant (inventories translated at the current rate). In 1975 the Financial Accounting Standards Board imposed as standardized practice (FAS 8) what was called the temporal method: Items valued on the subsidiary's balance sheet at historical cost should be translated at historical exchange rates; those valued at current or future cost or value should be translated at current exchange rates. This logical-sounding procedure came close to imposing the monetary/nonmonetary method. For most firms it meant that inventory, a current but nonmonetary asset, would be translated at historical exchange rates.

The other important feature of FAS 8 was to forbid MNEs to establish valuation reserves that could be used to segregate unrealized foreign-exchange gains and losses from current operating profits. Previously, unrealized exchange losses could be recognized by a deduction from current income, and a reserve could be created for later use to absorb unrecognized gains. This smoothing of the reporting of unrealized foreign-exchange gains and losses was precluded by FAS 8. Some 37 percent of firms sampled in 1975 had been making some use of deferral.

FAS 8 proved highly controversial because, with exchange rates fluctuating widely and rapidly, the bulk of year-to-year changes in a MNE's reported overseas profits could be due to exchange-rate changes, not changes in local-currency operating profits. Should the F$ be appreciating relative to the dollar while the subsidiary holds an advantageous long-term loan in F$s, the shareholders must be told each period that they are suffering a capital loss, although the interest the MNE is paying is less than otherwise. Should the F$ depreciate, the MNE must indicate a translation loss on its subsidiary's inventories, even though the price level in its market might well rise in proportion to the depreciation, giving the subsidiary a F$-denominated capital gain on the inventories. As Burns (1976) noted, the very diversity of firms' practices before FAS 8 suggests that the translation method giving the least distorted views of a firm's performance varies with its market setting, so that standardization was achieved at the expense of a set of accounting signals noisier than before reaching the public from the average firm. Economic analyses of these problems of accounting practice indicate no simple way to translate an economic evaluation of the effects of exchange-rate changes into accounting rule (see Aliber, 1978, Chapter 8). To determine the most informative method requires forecasts of the future courses of exchange rates and other prices, the structural relation between exchange rates and other variables (prices and nominal interest rates), and specific features of the firm's situation.

FAS 8 forced many companies to change practice, as only 18.6 percent of one survey's respondents had used it previously, and nearly two-thirds had distinguished exchange gains and losses from current profits (Gernon, 1983; Evans and Folks, 1979, p. 8). The complaints of the business community about FAS 8 finally brought its replacement in 1981 by FAS 52. The new standard brought practice closer to the closing-rate method described previously, in that a company's gains and losses from currency translation are distinguished from its operating profits and are shown as a direct gain or loss in the owners' equity. The practice invites the public to distinguish between how well the MNE's foreign subsidiaries do in their real economic transactions abroad and what happens to the fruits of their labors as a result of exchange-rate changes. Although the wealth-maximizing enterprise should consider exchange-rate prospects in making its operating decisions, it seems wise to separate the two kinds of forces in appraising the outcome.

If the public understood perfectly the effects of all economic changes on firms' prospects, it would not matter what the accounting numbers say. If they depend on accounting information, then accounting practices affect their perceptions, and business managers can manipulate the accounts to nurture favorable perceptions. One interesting question about the FAS 8 episode therefore is whether firms changed some of their real economic decisions following the change in accounting practice in order to send favorable signals or curb misperceptions. According to Evans and Folks (1979, p. 15), firms that had to modify their reporting practices spent more on foreign-exchange risk management for self-protection, and they significantly decreased their long exposures in certain currencies.[21] Shank et al. (1979, Chapter 4) suggested that the majority of MNEs had at times incurred real costs in order to avoid reporting translation losses.

A second economic effect is on MNEs' internal evaluation and reward systems, which can affect the efficiency of their operations (Dieterman, 1980). Gernon (1983) reported that during FAS 8's tenure fully 40 percent of respondents did not use it for internal purposes, whereas previously only 19 percent used different procedures for internal and public purposes. About 30 percent of firms rely on untranslated foreign-exchange results for internal evaluation (Demirag, 1988), but the majority use translated results wholly or partly and thus apparently assign foreign-subsidiary managers at least some responsibility for foreign-exchange gains and losses (Lessard, 1986).

If FAS 8 caused MNEs to reveal new information to the public and to incur new economic costs, we might expect the stock market's valuation of these firms to be affected. A number of authors (e.g., Shank et al., 1979; Dukes, 1980) inquired whether or not after 1975 the market shifted its valuation of MNEs forced to change their accounting practices by FAS 8. No significant valuation shifts were found, whether the control group was domestic companies or MNEs whose accounting practices required no change to conform to FAS 8.

6.4. MNE finance and public policy

In this section we shall briefly note some public-policy issues that have risen around the MNE's financial decisions. We argue more generally in Chapter 10 that clashes between MNEs and national governments often arise because governments are unwilling either to accept market allocations of resources as they occur or to impose unambiguous rules (taxes, rationing devices, and the like) to change them. The resulting compromise is a rolling set of informal or limited pressures on economic agents to "do the right thing." The MNE might, for various reasons, not be an easy mark for this moral suasion, and so it gets denounced as a traitor to the national cause. However, our concern here is only with the MNE's financial decisions.

[21] It is not clear that Evans and Folks always distinguished responses to FAS 8 from responses to the general increase in the variability of exchange rates in the 1970s. However, they did find that increased use of forward-exchange markets to hedge exposure was more common among firms that formerly smoothed out their reporting of unrealized exchange gains and losses than among those that always recognized exchange adjustments immediately.

Balance of payments

Governments' concern with the balance of payments was the chief policy issue to bear on MNEs' financial behavior in the 1960s, when almost all the industrial countries chose to maintain fixed exchange rates, and the European Union's exchange-rate arrangements lately revived the issue. To fix an exchange rate at an officially declared value is to forgo using the price of foreign exchange as an adjustment device. Although many prices other than the exchange rate can respond to payments imbalances, the inability of the exchange rate to adjust makes governments more likely to be facing imbalances. In the short run, deficits prove harder to manage than surpluses, and therefore governments with fixed exchange rates often found themselves bending every policy instrument to ward off payments deficits.

With the shadow price diverging from the actual exchange rate and the market signals it supplied, a government facing a payments deficit finds itself picking and choosing among the private sector's international transactions, imposing this control or that voluntary restraint in order to keep the country's external purchases and sales in line. MNEs were promptly fingered for their international capital transfers, and direct investment outflows were restricted by the United States.[22] Much of the surrounding policy discussion was of abysmal cogency, but two pieces of economic analysis proved helpful:

1.   *The transfer process.* In the short run, when a MNE transfers one dollar from Home to Foreign, real spending is likely to expand in Foreign and fall in Home. Extra real spending in Foreign falls on all goods consumed, including those imported from Home, and so Home's exports rise. The reduced spending in Home comes partly out of imports, and so Home's imports fall. Home's balance of trade improves, and indeed could improve enough to "requite" the capital outflow so that it involves no short-run deterioration of Home's overall balance of payments. The analysis of the transfer process developed by Hufbauer and Adler (1968) was summarized in Section 5.2. The net effects of capital transfers on the balance of payments are determined by factors slightly different from those that determine their effects on employment, but the analyses largely coincide.

2.   *The payback period.* Just as one dollar of foreign investment is expected to earn a flow of profits for the MNE, it is expected to bring a reflux of foreign-exchange earnings into the nation's balance of payments. If the government believes that the shadow price of foreign exchange is above the market level, its policy toward investment-type outflows ought to depend on how soon the re-

---

[22] We note the various statistical investigations seeking to confirm that restrictions on foreign-investment outflows did indeed succeed in curbing them. Kwack (1972), Herring and Willett (1972), Boatwright and Renton (1975), Mantel (1975), Goldsbrough (1979), and Scaperlanda (1992) all investigated the question.

turn flows will offset the initial drain. Economists have accordingly measured payback periods for foreign investments (see criticism of the payback concept by Lindert, 1970). The relationships analyzed resemble the questions of investment substitution and export substitution discussed in Section 5.2. For instance, an investment outflow could either support or replace Home's exports – the former effect favoring, the latter harming, Home's balance of payments. And if exports are replaced, their loss may have been inevitable because of the investment-substitution problem. In addition to these effects, payback calculations consider the remittance of dividends by the MNE and perhaps an ultimate repatriation of capital.

Hufbauer and Adler (1968, Chapter 5) sought to estimate these payback periods for U.S. direct investments, as did Reddaway (1967) for the United Kingdom. In some instances the outflows were broken down by individual foreign investing sectors for closer scrutiny (e.g., Makinen, 1970). These measurements by themselves do not prove much about MNEs' behavior. There is no connection between the payback period and the profitability of foreign investment, because the proceeds of a profitable investment may be plowed back, leaving an increasingly valuable but unrepatriated foreign asset; or an unprofitable investment may be promptly dismantled and the salvaged funds brought home. However, some investigations of payback patterns have seized on a "life cycle" of foreign investment. Penrose (1956) considered balance-of-payments effects of foreign investments in the context of subsidiaries' tendencies to expand into new activities as they mature. Prachowny and Richardson (1975) attempted a statistical test of life-cycle effects of foreign investments on the balance of payments, finding that as they mature, subsidiaries rely increasingly on internal funds to finance expansion, earn increasing profits, and generate increasing royalty payments (although these eventually fall off). These results predict something about the time-shape of the payback flow from foreign investment – little at first, but then large as the subsidiary matures.

Investment stability and allocation

The other policy issue touching the MNE's financial decisions concerns the rate of capital formation in the national economy. Governments pursue stable full employment or otherwise adopt macroeconomic goals that touch on gross capital formation and its financing. Two seemingly contradictory hypotheses about MNEs' effects on this effort are common in the literature. The first, pressed by Barnet and Muller (1974) among others, holds that freedom from competitive pressures allows MNEs to delay in adapting their international investment decisions to changed economic conditions (see the discussion by Bergsten et al., 1978, pp. 283–8). The second holds that their access to international financial markets makes them more responsive to investment incentives than are other firms, because they are not constrained by credit conditions in the national market where the investment inducement pops up (e.g., Dunning, 1973*a*). Behavioral evidence leaving toward the latter hypothesis was noted previously.

Stonehill (1965, Chapter 7) concluded that foreign-controlled companies in Norway were not a source of macroeconomic destabilization, relative to domestic enterprises. Hawkins and Macaluso (1977) found some evidence that subsidiaries can substitute retained earnings and external funds from overseas affiliates for local funds when a credit crunch is on. Of course, governments will not always take the same normative view of the MNE's ability to arbitrage funds between national markets. If the credit crunch represents a policy choice, the MNE's access to credit on terms not controlled by the government may be resented. But at times when more investment is desired by the government, the verdict will go the other way.

6.5. Summary

The MNE's financial behavior raises questions about both the macroeconomic and microeconomic environments in which it manages its assets and liabilities. Studies of flows of new investments from parents to subsidiaries and capital-expenditure rates of subsidiaries have sought macroeconomic predictors of these flows. Appreciable support turns up for the neoclassical model of capital formation. However, statistical investigations of MNEs' financial decisions support the conclusion that internally generated funds hold a lower opportunity cost for the MNE than do funds borrowed externally. In any case, the evidence confirms that the MNE makes its investment and financial decisions on a global basis, so that its rate of capital expenditure in one country tends to fall when expected profits rise for investment somewhere else. The theory of real options contributes to explaining its choices.

The capital-arbitrage hypothesis suggests that the MNE borrows wherever in the world funds are cheapest and invests them wherever expected returns are highest. A more subtle view of the MNE's financial decisions must take account of risk and of the degree to which international capital markets are fully integrated without any arbitraging done by MNEs. If this perfection were to be achieved, where the MNE would borrow and how it would structure the riskiness of its liabilities could be indeterminate. But there are grounds for thinking that exchange-rate movements as well as government restrictions and transactions costs leave arbitrage possibilities open to the MNE. The firm will then rationally relate the scale of its borrowing in each country to the amount of capital assets it places there, as well as relative borrowing costs and expected behavior of exchange rates. The empirical evidence on these questions suggests that MNEs do enjoy opportunities for international arbitrage of funds and that investors recognize the value of the international diversification built into the MNE's liabilities. The relationship between local borrowing and investment by the subsidiary, its practices in remitting dividends, and similar financial decisions are generally consistent with the conclusion that the MNE is a present-value maximizer operating in incompletely integrated international capital markets.

The MNE also makes short-run decisions about the composition of its liquid assets in light of expected exchange-rate changes. Although all agents are expected to seek profits or avoid losses from exchange-rate changes, the MNE enjoys advantages in pursuing the goal from cheaper access to information and greater flexibility in manipulating transactions that are internal to it but that would be at arm's length for national companies. The survey evidence confirms that MNEs' hedging efforts center on these internal transactions. It also suggests that corporate risk aversion influences the extent and character of the MNE's exchange-market transactions and that MNEs generally do not embrace the role of pure speculator. But neither do they assume that they can never "beat the market" in anticipating exchange-rate changes.

Exchange-rate variations confront the MNE with problems not only of market response but also of their information systems – how to assess and report changes in their asset values when exchange rates change. The right answer depends on forecasting what today's change in exchange rates portends for future exchange rates as well as for future local-currency prices abroad. The episode of FAS 8 shows that MNEs will expend real resources in order to disseminate favorable signals, and their public reporting requirements can clash with internal evaluation and control.

MNEs' financial decisions sometimes bring them into conflict with government policies, especially those that try to deter responses to current market prices. This form of conflict appears most clearly when governments seek to defend fixed but disequilibrium exchange rates. These conflicts also raise the issue of how the MNE's long-term international transactions affect the balance of payments. The transfer process, outlined in Chapter 5, helps us to investigate the short-run consequences of direct investment for the balance of payments. MNEs' ability to arbitrage capital internationally can make them unpopular with governments seeking to enforce a shadow interest rate that diverges from the cost of capital internationally.

7

Technology and productivity

The MNE's rationale, according to the transaction-cost model, lies in the administered international deployment of its proprietary assets so as to evade the failures of certain arm's-length markets. Premier among those assets is the knowledge embodied in new products, processes, proprietary technology, and the like. Therefore, the MNE plays a role in the production and dissemination of new productive knowledge that is central if not exclusive. Although arm's-length markets for technology are failure-prone, they do exist. Many companies that produce new knowledge are not multinational, and many proprietary intangibles are sold or rented between unrelated parties, or simply copied. The determinants of the trade-off between arm's-length transfers and transfers within MNEs is emphasized because of its role in the necessary conditions for MNEs' operation (Chapter 1).

This chapter starts with empirical evidence on how the MNE makes its decisions about producing and disseminating technology. It proceeds to a treatment of the consequences of this activity for economic change and economic policy. The policy issues are particularly urgent in this case. Not only does the market for knowledge bristle with potential failings, but also international trade in technical knowledge runs into the familiar conflict between the interests of source and host countries.

7.1. The MNE as producer of technical knowledge

Research on the production and distribution of industrial knowledge customarily distinguishes three phases of the process. *Invention* covers the generation of a new idea and its development to the point where the inventor can show that "it works." *Innovation* takes the invention to the point of being placed on the market; this phase includes building and proving out any needed production facilities as well as testing and refining the invention itself. *Diffusion* is the process by which potential users of the innovation actually come to make efficient decisions to adopt. To expose the MNE's role in these stages of technological development, we can collapse the invention and innovation phases but must focus closely on the process of diffusion.

Foreign investment and R&D outlays

The affinities between R&D and the MNE are numerous. We know that the extent of R&D spending is an excellent predictor of MNE activity in an industry (Chapter 1). Most formal R&D is undertaken by firms of at least moderate size; similarly, scale-economy considerations allot foreign investments to the larger firms. Hence, in those industries where most R&D takes place, both the R&D and the foreign investments are likely to be concentrated among the larger firms. Just as R&D promotes foreign investment, foreign investment likely promotes R&D. The established MNE has in hand knowledge that points out paths to profitable innovations in diverse national markets, not just the home market. This advantage from the MNE's information network yields it both a higher and more certain mean expected return from investments in innovation than a similarly placed single-nation company. Therefore, the causation should run both ways between MNE activity and R&D spending.[1]

Mansfield, Romeo, and Wagner (1979) considered the effects of overseas sales opportunities on R&D, finding that the sampled large U.S. companies expect to draw 29 to 34 percent of the returns from their R&D projects from overseas markets via all marketing channels – foreign subsidiaries, licensing, and export of innovative goods.[2] The more research-intensive the company, the larger the share of its R&D returns that comes from outside the United States. The foreign share is greater for research projects in pursuit of basic discoveries than for development projects, which tend to adapt innovations to a particular market's needs. The authors also asked the respondent firms how much they would cut back on R&D if they could collect no rents from abroad. The reductions would be 12 to 15 percent if research results could not be exploited through the firms' foreign subsidiaries, 16 to 26 percent if all foreign rents were cut off. The larger the share of the firm's global sales derived from its foreign subsidiaries, the larger the cut. The more extensive are the firm's sales abroad (both exports and foreign subsidiaries), the higher is the rate of return it expects from R&D activities and the more focused is its R&D on basic research and long-run projects.

[1] Similarly, product-market diversification has been held to favor R&D, and the statistical evidence shows a positive association with causation running both ways (e.g., Caves et al., 1980, Chapters 7 and 8).
[2] The firms included in their sample were not necessarily all MNEs, although the MNE percentage must have been quite high. The statistical results of Severn and Laurence (1974) are consistent with the importance of global profitability to the R&D decisions of MNEs.

Patent statistics also confirm that large firms carrying on research base their R&D investments on the revenues they expect to earn worldwide. The global orientation of research activities is seen in mirror image in the patents taken out in countries that are not themselves major research centers; most such patents are registered by foreign nationals seeking global protection from imitation of their inventions. Bertin (1987) found that foreign patenting is especially influenced by intentions to transfer technology through licensing.

If foreign investment functions partly to garner rents to the parent's R&D assets, it also serves as a method of acquiring knowledge assets abroad, as was shown in Section 1.1. Mansfield (1984) reported that over 40 percent of R&D expenditures in overseas R&D laboratories of sampled U.S. MNEs resulted in technologies that were transferred quite rapidly to the United States. Research outlays and MNE status thus reinforce each other: Hirschey (1981) showed that research expenditures tend to enlarge a firm's (or industry's) multinational activity, and anything (other than research) that expands multinational activity tends to increase R&D spending.

Overseas R&D spending by MNEs

If MNEs take account of worldwide revenue potentials when setting their R&D budgets at home, they also increasingly decentralize R&D activities around the world. Part of the spread is due to inducements offered by host governments (Behrman and Fischer, 1980, Chapter 6), but economic incentives are also at work within the firm. The MNE must determine not only how much R&D to undertake worldwide but also where to do it. This decision sheds light not just on the economics of R&D activity itself but also on the transferability of technical knowledge across national boundaries.

Evidence reviewed in Chapter 2 suggests that the MNE sites its production facilities around the globe so as to maximize the net revenue it earns from serving all accessible markets. If the intangible outputs of its R&D investments could be transferred costlessly among its various plants, the R&D laboratory would simply be placed in the world's cost-minimizing location. However, important forces keep all R&D from settling at some technological Shangri-la. Effective execution of R&D requires a continuous interchange of information with the manufacturing facilities of the company, in order that research be directed to significant economic problems and the solutions be operational. Because of the strategic role of R&D, close contact with top corporate management is also important. These requirements for close communication and interchange, along with any scale economies in the R&D function itself, seem to dominate the decision where to situate R&D activities. They tend to call for centralization at company headquarters, but subject to the centrifugal pull of manufacturing facilities dispersed to serve far-flung markets.

Both statistical evidence and survey evidence on the experience of MNEs confirm this framework.[3] First, the agglomerative tendencies for research to remain at the corporate headquarters remain strong. Not much over 10 percent of most source countries' MNEs' research is carried on abroad, although for Swedish MNEs it reaches 23 percent (Håkanson and Nobel, 1993).[4] That percentage has grown rapidly in the past two decades. R&D abroad is oriented rather more toward development and less toward basic research than is R&D done at home.[5] The pattern confirms that research aimed at adapting products and services to local market conditions often is undertaken in that market. However, there are exceptions: Basic research is more footloose than is applied research, and some of it goes abroad to seek out particular scientific specialists, market conditions, and the like.

Statistical studies have found that the MNE's R&D outlays are more dispersed abroad the larger the percentage of its global sales made by subsidiaries and the less the firm relies on exports to serve foreign markets (Zejan, 1990*b*, found that exports deter adaptive but not innovative R&D abroad). Foreign subsidiaries' R&D outlays increase with their own exports but decrease with their intrafirm trade with affiliates (Håkanson, 1983). Some evidence indicates that scale economies are influential: The more important are scale economies in research, the less is it decentralized overseas; however, the more a firm's production abroad is concentrated in a few subsidiaries (where R&D scale economies can be realized), the more does it decentralize its R&D.[6] With these

---

3 Statistical studies have included Mansfield, Teece, and Romeo (1979), Lall (1979*b*), Parry and Watson (1979), Hewitt (1980, 1983), Håkanson (1981), Hirschey and Caves (1981), Pearce (1989), and Zejan (1990*b*). Survey data and case studies were provided by Safarian (1966, Chapter 6), Creamer (1976), Ronstadt (1977), Germidis (1977), Behrman and Fischer (1980), and Pearce and Singh (1992).

4 Håkanson and Nobel (1993) imputed proportions of overseas R&D employment to various motives: adapt products to local markets, 32%; support local production, 5%; exploit local resources, 8%; political pressures, 34% (the residual due to combinations of these motives).

5 Creamer (1976, Chart 4.2) provided the following data on the functional distribution of domestic and overseas R&D by a large sample of U.S. MNEs. In 1972 the overseas affiliates spent 69.0% for development, 29.9% for applied research, and 1.1% for basic research. The corresponding figures for their U.S. parents were 59.8%, 33.9%, and 7.3%. Parry and Watson (1979) found that in Australia, 42% of subsidiaries' R&D is spent modifying technology from abroad.

6 See also Hood and Young (1976). Mansfield, Teece, and Romeo (1979) presented direct estimates of the minimum efficient scale (MES) of overseas R&D facilities. These estimates vary a great deal, suggesting that MES depends on the exact type of work done by the lab. Quality control and "customer engineering" have small minimum scales relative to the development of new products or components (see also Ronstadt, 1977, Chapter 9). Parry and Watson (1979) reported small scales for most industries, but with some exceptions.

influences controlled, variations in the costs of R&D inputs from country to country exert some effect. Decentralization from the United States accelerated in the 1960s, when U.S. R&D personnel were substantially more expensive than their counterparts abroad, then slowed as that differential disappeared (Mansfield, Teece, and Romeo, 1979, Table 3). Using data on individual subsidiaries of Swedish MNEs, Zejan (1990*b*) showed that more R&D is undertaken abroad in those based in large and high-income host nations. Finally, important confirmation of the sensitivity of MNEs' choices of R&D locations to economic incentives appears in Hines's (1993*b*, 1994*b*) studies of their responses to U.S. tax changes.

7.2. **International transfer of technology**

We now consider the international transfer of technology and the MNE's role in the process, both microeconomic and in the aggregate (the product life cycle and overall patterns in the flow of technology and innovations among countries).

Arm's-length markets for technology

The market for technology entails transfers between firms of technical information (designs, descriptions, plans, etc.), including the right to use or infringe on patents, and frequently the services of the licensor's personnel to install and debug the technology or train the licensee's operators. Agreements can be one-shot, transferring a discrete technology, but commonly they join the parties in a continuous and long-lasting relationship.[7] The agreement includes a royalty rate, frequently some round-number percentage of the licensee's sales revenue or factory costs, perhaps with a minimum payment. The agreement usually contains ancillary restraints: The licensee will grant back to the licensor any improvements made in the process or product; the licensee will not export to certain markets or will otherwise refrain from competing in the licensor's product markets. Licensing is more common the less physically complex are the goods and hence the more easily can technical information be conveyed. It is discouraged in more complex products, such as durable goods, for which research likely involves reconfiguring the product for competitive reasons; the resulting discoveries have little value for licensing to other firms (Wilson, 1977).

The licensing of technologies between competing firms raises complex issues that have been explored theoretically (e.g., Katz and Shapiro, 1985) and empirically. The firm holding proprietary technology and able to write a complete contract with licensees might in some circumstances be indifferent between licensing the technology and itself producing the output that maximizes the resulting profit. If potential licensees hold a cost advantage for serving some

---

[7] Contractor (1980); Herskovic (1976, p. 24); Rosenblatt and Stanley (1978).

customers, then licensing is preferred, but efficient contracts leave them no excess profits. The empirical evidence on licensing convincingly shows, however, that licensors on average can appropriate less than half of the surplus associated with the license transaction – not surprising, given the problem of asymmetrical information between the parties. If the licensee lowers the costs or improves the product of a licensor's competitor, no licensing will occur in some cases (even though a complete licensing contract could be profitable), and in others it will pay the licensor to restrict the licensee's opportunities for use of the technology in order to limit competitive erosion of its own profits.

Evidence supports this proposition in many ways. The closer and more direct is a competitor, the more likely a contract profiting the licensor cannot be written. Competitors in distant countries should therefore be more attractive licensees than local rivals. Apparently much licensing of technology indeed takes place across national boundaries rather than between firms in the same country (Taylor and Silberston, 1973, Chapter 7). Mytelka and Delapierre (1988) noted with surprise the extent to which licenses and other interfirm agreements of European firms are with non-European firms, despite the integration processes of the European Union. The more vulnerable is the licensor's profit to incursions from strengthened competitors, the more will it restrict the licensee's use of the technology. Caves et al. (1983) concluded that licensors exposing their core technologies are indeed more likely to tie the licensee's hands, for example, by restricting where products involving the technology may be sold or obligating the licensee to grant any improvements back to the licensor royalty-free. The licensor's own situation matters: one licensing an established technology is more likely to restrict the licensee's exports than one licensing a novel technology that is likely to grow obsolete before the licensee evolves into a close competitor (Herskovic, 1976, pp. 40–7).[8]

Licensees in the technology market behave in ways consonant with the analysis of corporate strategy presented in Chapter 3. Licensing has its risks for them, but it pays where doing one's own R&D is a poor alternative – for example, where the efficient scale of R&D is large relative to the efficient scale of production (Herskovic, 1976, p. 20) or the licensee is diversifying into an unfamiliar product (Caves et al., 1983). Licensing also pays the firm that is adept at using but not producing the technology. A licensee will take on licenses that require a costly and specific physical investment when the technology lies close to the firm's established competence, but it will avoid large investments in specialized facilities when the licensed technology involves diversifying into unfamiliar territory.[9]

---

[8] Also see Behrman's contribution to Mikesell (1962) and Casson (1979, pp. 20 2).

[9] Also see Taylor and Silberston (1973, Chapter 7) and Herskovic (1976). Katrak (1985) established a complementary relation between technology imports and own R&D for Indian firms.

Competition among licensors influences royalty rates and terms. Regarding royalty revenues overall, one source claimed that U.S. licensors typically shoot for a royalty rate that will relieve an efficient licensee of one-third of its profits (Baranson, 1978*a*, p. 64). Contractor (1980) found that large U.S. licensors typically face competition from other suppliers of technology,[10] but his statistical analysis only weakly confirmed the negative effect of competition on the total (lifetime) returns to a licensing agreement. He did find that they increase significantly with the size of the licensee's plant, which presumably is correlated with the rents that the licensee can earn from the licensed technology.[11] Taylor and Silberston (1973, Chapter 7) observed that the royalty rate decreases as the volume of sales under royalty grows, confirming a fixed component in the charges. Also, royalty rates are positively related to the amount of know-how supplied and the cost of supplying it, and royalties are higher for products subject to price-inelastic demands.

A device commonly used to avert contractual failures is the long-term or repeated deal between two parties such that the reputation loss or switching costs following a terminated deal deter short-run opportunistic behavior. Technology licenses typically run for a number of years. Also, some sources (e.g., Bertin and Wyatt, 1988) indicated that reciprocal licensing among MNEs is itself important, making up 20 percent of the licenses granted by a sample of MNEs and 30 percent of those received (p. 71).

Licensing versus foreign investment

The feasibility of licensing affects the (potential) MNE's choice to serve a foreign market by starting a subsidiary or licensing an established firm. The transaction-cost model attributes the horizontal MNE to shortcomings in arm's-length markets for intangible assets: Just as appropriability is necessary for foreign direct investment, the infeasibility of disimpacting the asset to a licensee precludes the alternative of licensing. We therefore expect the relative advantages and disadvantages of licensing and foreign investment to determine where one stops and the other starts (see Horstmann and Markusen, 1987*a*, for a theoretical model). The empirical evidence on their prevalence ought to confirm these advantages and disadvantages. As Davies (1977; Buckley and Davies, 1979) pointed out, an efficient local firm will see greater present value in a given project than will a foreign entrepreneur, other things being equal, be-

[10] Two to 5 rivals in 34% of the cases in Contractor's sample, 5 to 10 rivals in 10%, 11 or more rivals in 29%. The licensor monopolizes in only 27%.

[11] Contractor (1980) tested a number of hypotheses, usually getting the expected sign but not a statistically significant coefficient. In this sense he found that the returns tend to be higher when the licensee is permitted to export (and thus presumably will pay a higher royalty rate) and when the licensor's patent has a long time to run; they are lower when the technology is old. The gross returns to the licensor increase with the direct costs he incurs implementing the agreement or adapting the technology for the licensee.

cause of the latter's unfamiliarity with the territory. If the foreign firm holding licensable proprietary assets could negotiate licensing terms to extract the local firm's entire rent, it would always license and never choose direct investment. But the choice tilts toward foreign investment when the foreigner cannot collect the full rent or when suitable local firms are not to be found (e.g., in LDCs).[12] Ramachandran (1993) demonstrated directly the restriction of knowledge transfers between unrelated parties, finding that transfers to wholly owned subsidiaries in India involve substantially more reciprocal visits by licensor and licensee personnel than do transfers to partly owned subsidiaries, which in turn exceed the site visits when transfers pass to unrelated Indian firms.

Several empirical studies (especially Baranson, 1978*a*, and Telesio, 1979) exposed the factors that govern this choice between licensing and foreign investment. They suggest, first of all, that companies do contemplate foreign investment and licensing as direct alternatives, preferring foreign investment for its greater rent-extracting potential, turning to licensing only if that potential cannot be realized (Telesio, 1979, p. 37). The following determining forces emerge:

1. Licensing is encouraged where entry barriers deter the firm from foreign investment. Barriers presumably operate when the firm decides that the market is too small, meaning that entry at minimum efficient scale is not warranted given the market's size (Telesio, 1979, pp. 19–20, 38).[13]

2. Licensing is encouraged when the licensor lacks some assets needed for foreign investment. These might include a stock of accumulated knowledge and experience with foreign markets, managerial skills, or capital (meaning that the firm's shadow price of funds is high because of good competing uses). These considerations help to explain why the smaller the firm and the more valuable its internal uses of its resources, the more likely it is to resort to licensing rather than foreign investment (Telesio, 1979, pp. 78–80, 84–6).

3. Licensing is discouraged where arm's-length licenses are costly to arrange because of haggling over complex terms, defining the capability to be transferred, enforcing the agreement, preventing quality deterioration by the licensee when a trademark product is involved, and preventing leakage of a technology from a licensee's hands into those of unlicensed competitors. This conclusion from survey evidence explains the finding of many investigators (Benvignati, 1983; Chen, 1983*c*, pp. 63–6; McMullen, 1983; Davidson and

---

12 The continuum of choice between licensing and foreign investment was illustrated by Kokko (1992, Chapter 4), who showed that among Mexican industries foreign subsidiaries' technology payments to their parents increase significantly with the license payments made by competing, independent domestic firms.

13 Buckley and Casson (1981) modeled the choice among licensing, exporting, and foreign investment as one leading from low toward high fixed costs, trading against high to low variable costs (or foregone rents), disposing them in turn toward markets of increasing size.

McFetridge, 1984; Mansfield, 1984; McFetridge, 1987) that new technologies tend to be first transferred within MNEs or that arm's-length transfers are likely to involve older technologies than intrafirm transfers. Coughlin (1983) showed that countries restricting majority ownership of foreign subsidiaries confine themselves to receiving older technologies.

4. Licensing depends on properties of the technology itself. Kogut and Zander (1993) demonstrated that the codifiability and teachability improve its candidacy for licensing, while its complexity is a deterrent. These factors could underlie the positive effects of a technology's age and number of previous transfers on the likelihood of licensing, as Kogut and Zander's statistical analysis suggests.

5. The lead time required to license an established producer usually is less than that required to start a subsidiary from scratch. If so, licensing is encouraged where the rents to the intangible asset are short-lived, say, because the industry's technology is changing rapidly (Michalet and Delapierre, 1976, pp. 16–17, 24). This consideration probably explains why Telesio (1979, Chapters 5 and 6) found that the proportional reliance on licensing (relative to foreign investment) actually increases with the importance of R&D for a firm: Foreign investment increases with R&D, but licensing increases even more.[14]

6. Risk considerations affect the choice between licensing and foreign investment in diverse ways. The licensor exposes no substantial bundle of fixed assets in the foreign market and so avoids a downside risk (e.g., when expropriation is a possibility) that might deter foreign investment. On the other hand, the risk of leakage of a technology into the hands of competitors deters a firm from licensing its core technology. This consideration probably explains why firms diversified in product markets are more disposed to license.[15] The option of exporting cannot be ignored in this context, because it avoids exposing an appropriable technology abroad by any means. Exporting is favored to protect easily appropriated process technologies (Mansfield, 1984), and Ferrantino (1993) showed that host countries with weak protection of international property tend to be served by exporting rather than by either licensing or foreign direct investment. Lee and Mansfield (forthcoming) found that weak property rights promote foreign direct investment over licensing, and also affect the choice between wholly and partly owned subsidiaries.

7. Licensing is discouraged if the opportunity cost of capital is higher in the recipient country than in the country of the potential licensor, because the licensee then will value the expected stream of rents to the technology less than will the owner of the technology (Jones, 1979, p. 264). This implication of the

---

[14] Clegg's (1987) results based on aggregated data seem to support this finding.
[15] Telesio (1979, pp. 76–7) suggested that diversification may also be associated with shortages of complementary assets needed to start foreign subsidiaries for the purpose of exploiting peripheral technologies.

capital-arbitrage model of foreign investment (Chapter 2) has not been tested on national aggregates, but is supported by case evidence on how the opportunity cost of funds affects companies' choices between licensing and foreign investment.

8. Licensing is encouraged by possibilities for reciprocity: If you license a technology to another enterprise, some day it may in return license one that you require. Telesio (1979, Chapter 4) and Bertin and Wyatt (1988) found this practice quite common in certain industries. It might sustain agreements that are otherwise problematical (as was noted previously) and avoid duplicating fixed costs, but it could have anticompetitive consequences when going firms cross-license each other but decline to license to newcomers, thereby creating a barrier to entry (Telesio, 1979, pp. 62–4).

Some additional light is shed on the trade-off between licensing and foreign investment by Davies's (1977) study of British MNEs' operations in India, at a time when government regulations forced them to choose between licensing and joint ventures with Indian firms. The MNEs were clearly willing to hand over more extensive packages of technologies, provide more extensive auxiliary information, and take the trouble to adapt the technology to Indian conditions when an equity share was retained through a joint venture. Although joint ventures have their own limitations (see Section 3.4), they apparently also avert some of the disincentives to trade in proprietary assets through arm's-length agreements. Kumar (1990, pp. 31–44) showed that during the same period foreign investment in Indian industries was negatively related and the importance of licensing royalty payments was positively related to the R&D-intensity of Indian industries, suggesting a diversion from MNEs to arm's-length licensing.

Finally, Teece (1977) developed unique data on the costs of intrafirm and arms-length transfers of technology that upset the common assumption that information once developed costs nothing to transfer. In the average project that he surveyed, the costs of transferring a production process amounted to 19 percent of the total costs of the project receiving it, with the range (for 26 projects) running from 2 to 59 percent. Teece found that these transfer costs vary from case to case in predictable ways: They tend to be higher the first time the technology is transferred, and higher for newer technologies. They are lower the more prevalent are similar technologies among other companies, and the more experienced in manufacturing is the recipient unit.[16] Transfers to joint ventures

---

[16] Other evidence supports Teece's findings. Tsurumi (1976, pp. 189–92) found that the expatriate personnel needed to transfer a technology increase with its complexity, independent of the scale of the recipient facility. Sekiguchi (1979, pp. 65–7) noted that the effectiveness of transfers of Japanese textile technology has been impaired where recipient countries have restricted the presence of foreign personnel. Ramachandran (1993) showed that licensees who conduct R&D need less input of expatriate personnel to effect transfers.

average 5 percent more costly and to independent licensees 9 percent more costly than transfers to wholly owned subsidiaries.

MNEs, technology transfer, and the product cycle

Vernon (1966) and many followers (notably Johnson, 1968) analyzed the international diffusion of technology under the rubric of the "product cycle." Although primarily concerned with explaining international shifts in production and trade, this model does relate foreign investment and the transfer of technology by the MNE to the diffusion of innovations. The product-cycle model was later laid to rest by its progenitor (Vernon, 1979), although with no surrender of claims for its empirical explanatory power for two to three decades following World War II, and an independent line of research demonstrates a similar relation between the development stage of a product and the number of firms producing it (Klepper and Graddy, 1990).

The model's interest lies in the link it forges between the diffusion of an innovation and the location decisions of MNEs, a link quite consistent with the transaction-cost model of the MNE that emerged in Chapters 1 and 3. Most innovations, the model assumes, are labor-saving. Process innovations substitute capital for labor or reduce input requirements for labor more than they do for capital. Product innovations such as household durable goods substitute capital for labor in the production of utility within the household. The value of such innovations is therefore greatest in countries where wages and therefore the value of people's time are highest relative to the user cost of capital. Invention is an economic search process bestirred (in part) by the inventor's perception of how value can be created. Given the random nature of the search, the inventor is most likely to notice nearby opportunities, so inventions and innovations are concentrated in high-income countries. Early-stage production is also tied closely to the high-income geographical market where the innovation has the best prospects. Methods of producing it are initially fluid and small-scale. Uncertainty about optimal production methods and configurations of the innovation discourages both the development of large-scale production and worldwide search for the most efficient production location. They are also deterred by the low price elasticities of demand, small market sizes, and low levels of competition likely to prevail for a new product. Therefore, production as well as consumption of the innovation initially sticks to the high-income market.

Use of the new technology eventually spreads to other countries as their rising real wages (and values of household labor time) make saving labor more profitable and as the real price of the innovation falls. This demand is at first served by goods imported from high-income areas, a prediction that accords with the high R&D intensity of the export industries of the high-income industrial countries. However, as the innovation's technology and production method stabilize, a search intensifies for low-cost production locations, and this search tends to carry production to lower-wage countries. Increasing price elasticities of demand, as users grow more familiar with the innovation, and increasing competition in the product market pull in the same direction. Exports from the high-income innovating countries are displaced by expanding production in other industrial countries. As the innovation matures, the shifting pattern of production and use might ultimately carry production to the LDCs, with the industrial countries losing their comparative advantage entirely, but the "mature" innovation could get displaced by its successor before this final stage is reached.

Most empirical research on the product cycle has concentrated on patterns of production and trade rather than on the activity of the MNE (Wells, 1972). Yet the prevalence of MNEs in high-R&D industries (shown in Chapter 1) and the disabilities of the arm's-length market for technology transfer both imply that the MNE functions prominently in the international dissemination of innovations. The model explains why the United States has been a fertile source of innovations and a prolific source of MNEs and why U.S. foreign investments have been concentrated in innovative industries both early (Vernon, 1971, p. 85) and late (Gruber et al., 1967) in the twentieth century. As a corollary of the product cycle, the European countries' shortages of native raw materials fostered innovation in materials-saving technologies, a pattern reflected in the industry composition of Europe-based MNEs (Franko, 1976, Chapter 2; Tsurumi, 1976, pp. 174–6), just as congestion in Japan fostered miniaturized innovations (Franko, 1983, pp. 32–5).

Some research has focused on how much difference the MNE's presence makes to the speed and direction of the diffusion process. Extensive evidence that newer technologies are transferred within the firm was cited previously. Tilton's (1971) study of the semiconductor industry emphasized the importance of newly founded foreign subsidiaries in transplanting U.S. innovations to the European countries. Older foreign subsidiaries, however, tend to behave rather like any incumbent firm: An established company will rationally innovate later than a new firm if the innovation makes its facilities obsolete but is not so good that it pays to scrap the existing capacity immediately. Globerman (1975) found no statistical evidence that foreign subsidiaries in the Canadian tool-and-die industry adopt numerically controlled machine tools faster than did domestic firms, but Chen's (1983c, pp. 63–91) study of the diffusion of innovations through four Hong King industries showed a positive association of speed with MNEs' share. Stobaugh's (1972) investigation of petrochemicals and Hufbauer's (1966) study of synthetic materials both suggest that scale economies in production and marketing retard diffusion. The firm that introduces the innovation gains a sustained first-mover advantage and delays taking production outside the country. When diffusion does occur, scale economics point foreign investment toward large host markets. Leroy (1976, Chapter 6) found that overseas transfers of a majority of sampled products followed Vernon's sequence of export-then-produce-abroad; in a minority, however, production started in the

MNE's host country and then remained there. Lake (1979), concerned with the relationship between market structures and the international diffusion of technology among MNEs, weakly confirmed the conclusion from many single-nation studies that diffusion is faster in the more competitive industry. He also found diffusion to be faster when it takes place among firms with previous experience in the process, a result consistent with Vernon and Davidson's (1979) finding that diffusion processes are accelerating over time.

The most comprehensive data on the MNE's role in the diffusion of innovation, assembled by Vernon and Davidson (1979; also see Davidson and McFetridge, 1984, 1985), covered the overseas spread through subsidiaries and licensees of 406 innovations introduced since 1945 by 57 U.S. MNEs. Technologies are indeed first transferred to countries with high incomes per capita, high literacy rates, and proportionally large manufacturing sectors (McFetridge, 1987);[17] recipient countries' severe trade restrictions actually accelerate transfers, while screening restrictions on foreign direct investment retard them. The MNE's information network and ready apparatus for making technology transfers demonstrably affect the diffusion process. The higher the MNE's initial proportion of sales made abroad (through both exports and subsidiary sales), the quicker are innovations transferred for production abroad. Transfer comes more quickly when the innovation lies in the firm's principal product line and when the firm has had previous experience with transfers in this product line. Similarly, the more previous experience with transfers to a given country, the faster is the next innovation transferred to that country. The MNE with a high ratio of R&D to sales (relative either to its base industry or to other MNEs) transfers technology abroad more rapidly. As between subsidiaries and licensees in the diffusion process, subsidiaries predominate in the first few of years of the diffusion of an innovation, but then licensees start to catch up. Licensees play more of a role for true innovations than for new products that imitate other firms' innovations; presumably the imitations are attuned largely to oligopolistic rivalry among firms and hence have little value for licensing (see Wilson, 1977). Firms are more likely to resort to arm's-length licenses when they have had substantial past experience with transfers of technologies of all types, and when the technology lies outside their base industry (Davidson and McFetridge, 1984).

The Vernon-Davidson results are broadly consistent with the preceding analysis of international transfers of technology and the core explanation of MNEs' activities developed previously. Indeed, the consistency of the evidence with rational behavior by well-informed MNEs casts doubt on the original product-cycle formulation, which invoked myopia and uncertainty in the in-

---

[17] Kokko (1992, Chapter 3) similarly found that royalty receipts from technology transfers increase with the capital expenditure rates of the manufacturing sectors of recipient countries.

troductory stage of an innovation to explain the delayed diffusion beyond the innovating country (Leroy, 1976, Chapter 1). Vernon (1979) suggested that the global information network of the established MNE can sever the link between the site where the invention is first proved and the markets where the commercial innovation takes root.

7.3. General-equilibrium and welfare aspects

The international licensing market and the MNE's development and transfer of technology have implications for resource allocation in the overall economy and for economic welfare.

Theoretical contributions

Economists pursuing technology transfer into the realm of general equilibrium have had a difficult task. Such models are traditionally static and do not easily make room for imperfectly marketed assets such as proprietary knowledge. Even with that problem solved, the effects of technical change on production functions can be complex to model. The relevant contributions are complicated, and so the following summary is selective (see Pugel, 1981*b*).

Krugman (1979) presented a model that does not explicitly capture the MNE as a capital arbitrager but does develop the general-equilibrium implications of technology transfers. Krugman's starting point is the product cycle (Vernon, 1966). Suppose that new technology consists of a continuing stream of product innovations that all emerge initially in one country (Home). With a random lag, each new good's technology becomes known in the other country (Foreign). New goods' technologies are known only in Home; old goods can be produced in Foreign as well. Labor is the only factor of production, immobile between Home and Foreign. Under these assumptions, Home's labor may share the rents from the extra value that consumers everywhere place on new goods. Depending on how highly consumers value new goods relative to old ones, Home may specialize completely in new goods, in which case Home workers earn a higher wage. However, if in equilibrium Home also produces some old goods, its labor earns no premium over Foreign's. Product innovations make both Home and Foreign better off – Home by improving the terms of trade, Foreign by making more kinds of goods available for consumption and thus increasing consumers' utility. The transfer of technology, when a new good becomes an old good, also increases the world's real income (because it is then produced by Foreign labor which is cheaper than Home labor). Foreign clearly gains from the technology transfer. Home, however, can either gain or lose: As consumers, Home citizens find that the relative price of the "newly old" good has fallen, but as workers they find that their wage has fallen slightly in terms of all other goods.[18]

---

[18] In a somewhat similar model, McCulloch and Yellen (1976) showed that Home can gain if Foreign turns out to have such a comparative advantage in an innovative good that

Homogeneous, internationally mobile capital can be added to Krugman's model, with its rate of return the same in equilibrium in Home as in Foreign (a case developed further by Dollar, 1986). Innovation tends to raise the marginal product of capital in Home and pull capital in from abroad; the transfer of technology pushes capital abroad to Foreign. Capital movements in Krugman's model are a consequence of transfers of technology, not a cause. There is also a sense in which they substitute for technology transfers in maximizing the efficiency of world production. That is, technology transfers shift the world's production-possibilities frontier outward because they permit producing the existing quantity of the transferred good at a lower resource cost. From such an equilibrium, with Foreign constrained to be completely specialized in old goods, in some cases more efficient world production is attainable by letting enough of Foreign's capital migrate to Home to produce new goods. McCulloch and Yellen (1976) developed this proposition as well as the implications of technology transfers for labor's real income. For example, with capital immobile internationally, Home labor benefits from transfer of Home's technology advantage to Foreign if the advantage is in the capital-intensive good. Then, after the transfer, Home's capital stock must be reallocated toward the labor-intensive industry, raising the marginal product of Home's labor in terms of both new and old goods.[19]

For an effort to show the formal consequences of MNEs as transferors of technology, we turn to Findlay (1978) (also see Koizumi and Kopecky, 1977). In his model Foreign suffers a systematic technology gap. Being backward offers an advantage of sorts: The farther behind the leader you are, the more easily can you pick up the leader's innovations and narrow the gap. Findlay argued, however, that this property of relative backwardness implies not a complete catch-up but an equilibrium lag behind the frontier. He assigned the capital that Home's MNEs invest in Foreign the role of a generalized promoter of technological improvement: The more chances do Foreign's native factors have to observe Home's advanced technology used by Home's foreign subsidiaries, the faster does Foreign's technology level grow. Thus, Foreign's general rate of technical progress is higher, the larger is Foreign's stock of Home-originated MNE capital relative to domestic capital, and the lower is Foreign's technology level relative to Home's. The model contains a complex mechanism that adjusts

production of the newly old good shifts entirely to Foreign. Krugman's model does not allow for comparative-advantage differences among old goods. The McCulloch-Yellen paper will be discussed later.

[19] McCulloch and Yellen also developed the consequences of technology transfers for employment in a Brecher-type model in which the real wage is fixed in terms of the old good. Home's transfer of technology to Foreign can then either raise or lower Home's employment. Segerstrom et al. (1990) demonstrated how tariff protection of Home's industries can raise Home's wages but at the same time reduce the number of new industries that arise to replace older, declining industries.

the stocks of domestic capital and MNE capital in Foreign in relation to the levels of technology in Home and Foreign. When Home's MNEs employ relatively advanced technology in Foreign, they earn high profits, which are taxed by Foreign's government. This tax revenue is channeled to finance expansion of the share of Foreign's domestic capital, cutting down the rate at which the MNE capital promotes the advance of Foreign's technology frontier. Also, Foreign's wage level is assumed to rise with the expansion of that technology frontier, and high wages thereupon cut into the profits of the MNE sector and slow its investment rate. The upshot is that the stocks of MNE capital and domestic capital in Foreign assume long-run equilibrium values that are determined jointly with the technological gap.[20]

MNE capital's "positive contagion" in spreading technological improvement has striking implications for some of the model's comparative-statics properties. An increase in Foreign's tax rate on resident MNE capital raises Foreign's relative stock of domestic capital and lowers dependence on imported capital, but it also enlarges the long-run equilibrium technology gap; so does an increase in Foreign's rate of saving. Whether or not the positive-contagion hypothesis has any empirical validity is, of course, a separate question; the point of Findlay's model is that if technology transfer takes this form it has quite surprising implications for economic policy.

Other approaches to technology transfer have emphasized its relationship to the commodity terms of trade, as did Krugman (1979), but employed a different strategy in building the model. Jones (1979, Chapter 16) allowed Home's superior technology to be embodied in capital goods installed abroad by one of Home's industrial sectors.[21] The capital export is likely to expand world output of the affected commodity, even though risks to Home's foreign investors inhibit the superior technology from driving Foreign's inferior technique totally out of use. Home could lose from this export of technology (and capital) if the transferred technology pertains to Home's export good, lowering its relative price and worsening Home's terms of trade. Home will then maximize its welfare by taxing the export of technology. However, if the exported technology

---

[20] Wang (1990) extended Findlay's model by adding human capital that grows exogenously in Home. Its growth in Foreign has an exogenous component but also depends on spillovers from Home (human capital like raw labor is not directly mobile internationally). Foreign's human capital also enjoys spillovers from Home's MNE capital. An influx of MNE capital to Foreign raises the growth of Foreign's human capital, but that increase narrows the gap with Home's human-capital stock and Foreign's catch-up potential (this latter effect is the dominant one).

[21] Jones (1970) earlier showed in the context of the Heckscher-Ohlin model how technology differences (and thus technology transfers) between countries may affect their equilibrium relative commodity prices in the absence of trade. This model allows for both differential effects between industries and differential biases in the proportional reduction of input requirements for each factor of production.

expands the output of Home's imported good, Home will gain by subsidizing technology exports.

Kojima (1975) was similarly concerned with technology transfer in the context of sector-specific technology and capital, so that technology transfers affect a particular sector and thus the terms of trade. His analysis stems from his empirical observation that Japan's foreign investment in manufacturing has emanated from the country's import-competing sector. When it raises technology levels in the recipient countries (in Southeast Asia, say), it is their export industries that benefit, and so international trade tends to expand. On the other hand, foreign investment by Western countries typically proceeds, he argued, from their export industries to their counterpart industries that are import-competing abroad; capital movements then tend to reduce and substitute for trade (as in the Heckscher-Ohlin model discussed in Section 2.3). Kojima was not so successful in developing formally either a mechanism to induce this transfer of technology or a normative framework for evaluating its effects,[22] but he did usefully suggest that sectorally biased transfers of technology might have important consequences.

The models summarized so far have been concerned chiefly with the effects of free dissemination of Home's technology to Foreign and the optimal policy for Home to follow given that no patent holder collects rents on the exported knowledge.[23] Rodriguez (1975) concentrated on the policy alternatives available to Home's government for maximizing the contribution of the nation's proprietary technology to its own welfare. In a general-equilibrium model he showed that under certain assumptions (notably, constant opportunity costs: the slope of a country's transformation curve does not change as factors are reallocated between sectors) Home's problem of maximizing rents from its technology is identical to the problem of maximizing monopoly rents on its trade with the rest of the world. Suppose that Home produces soft drinks and controls the secret formula for producing their flavoring. Foreign's consumers are assumed to be better off consuming some soft drinks than if they consume only the other goods that Foreign can produce without access to Home's exports or technology. Then Home achieves the same welfare level (and also leaves Foreign in the same welfare position) whichever of the following policies Home's

---

[22] He suggested that technology transfers should be judged favorable to welfare if they expand trade, unfavorable if they contract it. As Jones (1979, Chapter 16) showed, that conclusion might pertain to the welfare of the transferor country in a two-country world, but not to world welfare.

[23] McCulloch and Yellen (1976) did show that free dissemination is never optimal for Home if trade is free of tariffs and Home's resources are fully employed; with unemployment due to a fixed minimum wage, the optimal royalty rate could be anything from zero to prohibitive. Jones (1979, Chapter 16) emphasized the relationship between Home's optimal tax on technology embodied in sector-specific capital goods and Home's commodity terms of trade.

government adopts: (1) an optimum tariff on Home's trade with Foreign; (2) a tax on soft-drink technology licenses that maximizes Home's monopoly profits; (3) authorization of a multinational subsidiary in Foreign to monopolize the soft-drink business in Foreign's market and maximize its profits.[24] Rodriguez's model becomes somewhat more complex if his countries' transformation curves reflect not constant but increasing opportunity costs (as in Figure 2.2); then Home needs to impose both a charge for technology licenses and a tax on trade in order to maximize its real income.

Most of these theoretical studies have treated Home's stock of technology as exogenous. They thus neglect the basic dilemma stemming from failures in the market for proprietary knowledge: One cannot simultaneously distribute the existing stock around the world efficiently and reward inventors so as to induce investments in new knowledge. Pugel (1980*b*, 1981*b*) investigated how induced R&D investments change the consequences of Foreign's natural bent to free-ride on imported technology or tax away any rents collected in Foreign's markets on Home's behalf. Clearly, the globally optimal royalty payment for the use of technology becomes positive, and Foreign may even improve its own welfare by paying royalties so as to induce a continuing flow of cost-reducing research. Foreign's taxes on royalty payments for Home's technology then cause negative externalities for Home, because in cutting R&D investments by Home's producers, they render Home's own (future) unit costs of production higher than otherwise. In the same vein, Koizumi and Kopecky (1980) associated the production of technology with learning-by-doing in the use of the firm's capital stock. The more rents the firm can gather by transferring cost-reducing improvement abroad, the larger capital stock it then chooses to maintain at home in order to generate such experience-based improvements. In this model, transfers of technology abroad can have an adverse short-run effect on the wages of Home's labor for the usual reasons, but a positive long-run effect because of the extra capital formation induced to capture overseas rents from the technology improvements. The endogenizing of technical change has lately been pursued at a high level of generality. The results obtained are generally consistent with the standard general-equilibrium models (Heckscher-Ohlin) and with previous findings (Helpman, 1984) about MNEs and the domain of factor-price equalization (Grossman and Helpman, 1991, especially pp. 197–205).

Recent contributions addressed issues of policy and market behavior for the host country with access to spillovers from foreign technology. Positive exter-

---

[24] The license fee is assumed to take the form of a royalty per bottle of soft drink. If, instead, Home holds out for a lump-sum royalty payment, it is, in effect, making an all-or-nothing offer that can potentially relieve Foreign's consumers of all the surplus they enjoy from soft drinks – not just the part that a simple monopolist would get. Then the technology license becomes superior to the other policies from Home's viewpoint.

nalities can provide a reason for a host country to subsidize inflows of MNE capital (Gehrels, 1983). They can also generate microeconomic interactions between domestic firms that benefit from spillage and MNEs that generate it. Das (1987) treated the case of a subsidiary competing as a dominant firm with a fringe of domestic firms which costlessly increase their productivity in proportion to the subsidiary's output. The subsidiary's optimal response is to reduce its output, elevating the product's price but generating a time path of declining values for both price and the subsidiary's market share. Exogenous (and costless) infusions of the MNE parent's technology into the subsidiary reduce price and raise the subsidiary's share in the host-country market. The rate of growth of the domestic fringe's efficiency increases, but the subsidiary still benefits from the technology infusion (despite the spillover and resulting closer competition). Wang and Blomström (1992) assumed that (beyond a point) a subsidiary's domestic rival must invest in order to siphon productivity gains from its foreign-subsidiary competitor. This spillover increases host-country market demand for the domestic competitor's differentiated product, just as infusions of the MNE parent's technology to the subsidiary pulls demand to the subsidiary's brand. In the model's steady-state Nash equilibrium the two competitors undertake positive rates of investment respectively to infuse and to appropriate knowledge. When the domestic rival narrows the technology gap, the MNE's provoked response is to transfer more technology; this transfer increases with the efficiency of the domestic firm's learning activities and with the sensitivity of market demand to the technology gap.

Empirical evidence

The preceding models together suggest that international transfers of technology might weigh importantly in the welfare economics of foreign investment. If the MNE is a significant agent in transferring technology, the positive effect on world welfare can be large. Therefore, it is important to consider empirical evidence of the MNE's role as a transfer agent. Ideally the evidence will also shed light on the adversary interest of transferor and transferee countries in capturing the associated economic rents. These rents, we have seen, raise policy problems that turn on whether private-property rights in industrial knowledge are feasible and (if so) legally protected. Other influences on welfare are the incidental effects of the transfer on the terms of trade. Most of the empirical evidence bears on two questions: To what extent does seller competition erode the rents potentially accruing to MNEs' technology? Just how superior is the technology used by MNEs, on the average, and how much of it leaks out to competing domestic factors of production?

Some evidence indicates how market competition affects the rent streams generated by international sales of technology and how national governments seek to divert these streams. Can the commercial firms controlling Home's technology monopolize it effectively when they sell in Foreign's markets? Does rivalry among them erode Home's monopoly rents and enhance surplus for Foreign's consumers? Industry studies show a tendency for firms unsuccessful or inactive in foreign investment to license their technology abroad, thereby competing with the foreign-subsidiary sales or exports of other national companies.[25]

Indirect evidence on competition and technology licensing comes from the behavior of governments in this area. If sellers of technology competed as Bertrand price rivals, rents on technologies would tend to yield only a normal rate of return on the resources used in the transfer (not the production) of knowledge. Transferee governments could not intervene so as to better the terms of trade for their citizens. However, if a transferor can exercise monopoly power, a government might usefully intervene to override the bargains struck by its own citizen-licensees and force a cost-minimizing all-or-nothing offer on the foreign owner of the technology. The gains from government intervention should be greater, the more competitively its citizens bid for the license. Peck (1976) concluded that the Japanese government has appreciably raised national welfare by intervening in its licensees' negotiations and suppressing competition among them. Davies (1977) similarly claimed that the Indian government managed to halve average royalty rates and cut the duration of agreements. The alleged success of these interventions does suggest that licensors otherwise command appreciable monopoly power in arm's-length transactions. And, of course, the discrimination in patent policy against foreign applicants, employed by many LDCs and some developed countries, operates to the same end (Penrose, 1973; McQueen, 1975).

Much more evidence bears on the second empirical question: To what degree do technologies and related proprietary assets transferred abroad escape from their owners' control? Given the stock of knowledge, such leakage probably increases the recipient country's welfare and world welfare, while reducing the welfare of the country that invested to produce the knowledge (an exception is leakage that reduces costs and prices of the subsidiary's local suppliers). But in the long run, reduced appropriability lowers investment in such knowledge assets and hence potentially reduces world welfare. For the policymaker in the country generating the technology, there is another question: Do its citizens who use or license technology abroad correctly value the risk to the national welfare of the knowledge thereby escaping from proprietary control? Many such as Baranson (1978b) voiced concern that U.S. MNEs "give away

---

[25] See Tilton (1971, pp. 118–19) on AT&T's licensing policy in semiconductors and Baranson (1978a) on competition among U.S. manufacturers of light aircraft and its consequences for licensing a Brazilian producer.

the store" by licensing their latest and best technologies abroad to dubious customers who are all too likely to make off with the nation's intellectual treasure.[26]

Among empirical studies of the spillover of MNEs' proprietary assets, only Mansfield and Romeo (1980) focused on measuring and evaluating the leakage of specific technologies. From a sample of technologies exported by U.S. firms, they determined the average time elapsed between a technology's introduction by one of the firms and its transfer abroad. The mean lag was 6 years for transfer to the firm's subsidiaries in developed countries, 10 years for transfer to subsidiaries in LDCs, and 13 years for transfer to joint ventures or transfer through arm's-length licenses. Use of the technology abroad was not thought to speed its imitation by a foreign competitor in most cases, but in about one-third the appearance of a competing product or process was advanced by at least 2.5 years.[27] Mansfield and Romeo also secured from domestic firms in the United Kingdom estimates of how often their innovative efforts had been hastened in response to technology transfers from U.S. MNEs to their competing subsidiaries in the United Kingdom. Over half believed that at least some of their products and processes had been introduced (or introduced sooner) to meet the competitive effects of these transfers. There is little evidence on the extent to which innovations diffuse *without* benefit of the MNE or formal licensing arrangements, but De Melto et al. (1980) did report that half of the identified Canadian imitations of external innovations stemmed from independent research, development, and engineering activities of the imitator and not licensing or other commercial transactions with the innovator.

Many studies have touched on the productivity levels and growth rates of MNEs relative to competing domestic firms (especially in host countries). They address issues that range beyond those of technology transfer, such as whether or not MNEs are more efficient than other companies. Early studies examined productivity in foreign subsidiaries and competing domestic enterprises in Australian and Canadian markets.[28] If the two types of firms coexist, and superior

---

[26] Baranson's (1978*b*) case studies yielded little direct support for his normative conclusions because they failed to consider the royalties received from technology licenses by the U.S. licensors and the extent of competition from non-U.S. technology suppliers. Case studies by other investigators (Hayden, 1976) assess the bargaining sagacity of U.S. MNEs more favorably, even in the difficult situations stressed by Baranson where foreign investment is a poor alternative and foreign-government involvement is high.

[27] The acceleration was greater for process technologies. A product innovation usually is imitated by "reverse engineering": Buy the innovation, take it apart, and figure out how it works. This does not depend on propinquity to the factory. Process innovations, however, can be imitated only by observing them, contacting suppliers, hiring away employees, or other methods for which distance matters.

[28] See Brash (1966, pp. 194–202) with regard to MNEs' suppliers and customers as well as evidence of effects on competitors (Dunning, 1958, pp. 224–5; Forsyth, 1972, pp. 145–50).

technology or productivity imported by the subsidiaries progressively spills onto their domestic rivals, the subsidiaries' superiority should appear as a differential-rent component of their value added. And if the gap for domestic firms decreases with their exposure to the subsidiaries, the domestic firms' relative productivity should increase with the subsidiaries' share of the market.[29] Caves (1974a) and Globerman (1979a) both found reasonably strong evidence to support the hypothesis. Neither study had access to data on individual firms or could measure efficiency within the context of fully estimated production functions for the foreign and domestic firms. Other studies of this type for Canada were reviewed by Globerman (1985).

This line of research faces difficult problems of model specification illustrated by the theoretical models summarized previously. Spillovers might increase with the foreign subsidiary presence in an industry, but the spillage itself limits that presence.[30] With spillovers occurring, one might observe either a steady-state difference over time in foreign and domestic producer-groups' productivity levels, with spillovers balancing the influx of new technology to the foreign sector; or one might observe a catch-up process in which spillage eliminates the foreign-domestic productivity gap and reduces the equilibrium foreign share. No empirical studies have had enough data to pin down all these relationships, but recent contributions based on data for individual business units (and including their capital stocks) come closer.

Blomström (1983, 1989) gained access to Mexico's disaggregated data. He found the basic production-function relations quite similar between the foreign and domestic sectors of Mexican industries, except that white-collar productivity appears higher in the foreign units (no doubt, the effect of MNEs' proprietary intangibles) (Blomström, 1989, Chapter 3). On average the productivity residuals of domestic firms are smaller than those of foreign subsidiaries, but they increase with foreign subsidiaries' share of an industry's employment; this positive relationship is robust to controls for labor quality, concentration, and tariff protection (Blomström, 1989, Chapter 4). The gap between productivity of individual plant-size groups and an industry's most productivity plant-size group declines with the foreign units' share of industry

---

[29] The research literature surveyed here assumes that the foreign subsidiary comes endowed with superior technology by its MNE parent. Of equal potential relevance is the foreign subsidiary's performance in picking up new technology from arm's-length sources (Chen, 1983a).

[30] In this sense the positive relation between subsidiaries' industry-level shares and domestic competitors' productivity is a strong result: if firms' individual efficiency levels were exogenous, large foreign shares should be correlated with low productivity levels for domestic competitors (even the best ones that survive). A negative relation is also predicted if the effect of foreign subsidiaries is purely to inject additional competition into the market, destroying rents that otherwise count in domestic firms' productivity levels.

employees (Blomström, 1989, Chapter 5). Kokko (1992, Chapter 5) distinguished industries with large and small average gaps between subsidiaries' and domestic competitors' productivity levels, finding that domestic productivity is more sensitive to the foreign presence where the gap is small (and where the two groups probably engage in more comparable and directly competing activities). Kokko also found this sensitivity to be greater in industries where the foreign share is small, suggesting that the marginal effect might go to zero in industries dominated by foreign subsidiaries.

Other research addressed the dynamics of this relationship. Consistent with the Wang-Blomström (1992) model, U.S. MNEs' transfers of technology to their subsidiaries seem to increase as the subsidiaries' productivity advantage over Mexican domestic competitors declines (Kokko, 1992, Chapters 3, 4; Blomström et al., 1992). Blomström and Wolff (1994) found that domestic producers' productivity increases more rapidly, and the gap from competing foreign producers' productivity grows narrower, the higher the foreigners' initial share and the larger the initial productivity gap. Kokko (1992, Chapter 6) tested the reciprocal dependence of subsidiaries' and domestic competitors' productivity levels on each other's market shares, rejecting the endogeneity of the foreign sector's productivity in general; it was found endogenous, however, where the foreign share is below 50 percent and the industry is "low tech" (that is, the foreign presence then depends on static "comparative advantage" factors). He also found that, in industries with foreign shares below 50 percent and large gaps between foreign and domestic productivity, the domestic units' productivity increases not only with the foreign share but also with foreign productivity (that is, the size of the gap) itself. Overall, Kokko's results suggest a satisfying consistency in the complementary operation of technology spillovers and static cost-based competition.

Similar data for Morocco were analyzed by Haddad and Harrison (1993). They replicated the prevailing positive relation between domestic producers' productivity and foreign competitors' market share, controlling for firm size and the effects of restrictions on import competition. However, they could isolate little if any interdependence between the competing foreign and domestic sectors' rates of productivity growth. In developing countries no clear line exists between spillovers of technology and of general modern business practice. In the People's Republic of China, Liang (1994) observed the productivity of state-owned enterprises to increase significantly with the prevalence of foreign investors in a province; the state enterprises that she analyzed exclude those directly involved in joint ventures with MNEs. The spillovers are geographically localized at the province level but not necessarily intraindustry; also, their significance is strongest in noncoastal provinces, where the foreign presence is smaller and newer.

Identifying the technological (or other) advantages of MNEs by means of data on productivity faces yet another complication. As Hufbauer (1975, pp. 268–71) showed, under some assumptions a MNE's productivity advantage will be exploited through a larger market share and yield no observed differential in productivity. Therefore, interest attaches to studies that juxtapose company size and productivity differentials. Parry (1974*b*) seemed to find that subsidiaries' sizes relative to their domestic competitors in Australia are greater in research-intensive industries. Caves (1980*b*) treated relative size and relative productivity as being jointly determined and also filtered out some influences (scale economies in production, marketing assets of MNEs) that affect revenue productivity but are unrelated to technology.

The conclusion that MNEs play a substantial role in transferring technology requires delicate treatment, because other channels of technology infusion need to be controlled (as few studies have done). Basant and Fikkert (forthcoming) measured the influence on Indian firms' productivity of their own R&D, spillovers from competing foreign subsidiaries, and both licenses and spillovers from R&D in the same industries abroad. Spillovers from subsidiaries have a positive effect that is independent of the other channels, and the productivity of the domestic firms' own R&D lies mainly in absorbing spillovers from abroad (except outside the science-based industries). Also, other hypotheses suggested by the technology-transfer process have fared only moderately well in their statistical tests. If the MNE is a uniquely vital link in transfers of technology, then industrial productivity for countries that are mainly technology importers should be relatively higher in industries congenial to MNEs' operations. This hypothesis was tested on Canada relative to the United States with mixed results (Caves et al., 1980, Chapter 10; Saunders, 1978) and on the United Kingdom relative to the United States with negative results,[31] although Davies and Lyons (1991) did find that MNEs' combined market shares are larger in U.K. industries whose domestic firms suffer greater productivity disadvantages relative to their U.S. counterparts. It is worth recalling that locational and policy-related variables (e.g., transportation costs and tariffs) can lure foreign subsidiaries into markets where they may operate inefficiently, say, at suboptimal scales, but yet be profitable because of the dowry of intangible assets supplied by their parents (e.g., Parry, 1974*a*). These influences are adverse to the productivity of MNEs and of the industries in which they operate.

Similarly, simple comparisons of the relative productivity or profitability of MNEs and their domestic competitors demand careful interpretation. These

---

[31] Caves (1980*a*, pp. 153–4, 170–1); also see Dunning and Pearce (1977, pp. 69–72) and Solomon and Ingham (1977). Katz (1969, Chapter 7) provided positive evidence from Argentina's experience.

will not be considered in detail, but their general thrust has been to find that MNEs are more profitable or display higher productivity than selected single-nation rivals.[32] Researchers have attributed these results to various of the MNE's possible advantages that can raise profitability or productivity, including marketing and managerial skills,[33] product differentiation, and many factors other than technology. In light of the preceding chapters, this whole line of inquiry leaves one unsatisfied. Companies do not become multinational unless they are (or were) good at something. To find that the profit rates or productivity levels of MNEs exceed those for single-nation rival companies is unsurprising, on the one hand, and fails to identify the exact source of the rent, on the other. Therefore, the most revealing study of this type is Vendrell-Alda's (1978) exhaustive analysis of establishment-level data for Argentina. After controlling for many industrial and strategic factors affecting foreign- and domestic-controlled plants in his sample, he found no significant residual productivity differential for the foreign manager per se. His result suggests that any technology or productivity advantages possessed by MNEs are endogenous to the market-structure environments in which they emerge and have no pure residual component.

7.4. Summary

This chapter first examined the microeconomic behavior of the MNE in developing and transferring technology, alongside the arm's-length international market for technology licensing, and then moved to the general-equilibrium theoretical context of these institutions. MNEs tend to be found in research-intensive sectors, and there is evidence that they consciously allocate their R&D activities around the world to best advantage. R&D is pulled toward the parent's headquarters by the need for efficient supervision and scale economies in the R&D process itself; it is dispersed toward the subsidiaries by the advantages of doing developmental research close to the served market and drawing on local resources to enhance its proprietary assets. Empirical evidence confirms that U.S. MNEs would undertake less research if they could not expect to garner rents on it from foreign markets.

The marketing of technological knowledge is failure-prone for the same general reasons as any market in knowledge assets. Nonetheless, a market exists in which licensor and licensee strike agreements. Empirical evidence tells something about the kinds of firms that gain from both licensor and licensee activities, and it also identifies the resource costs of technology transfers that make

---

[32] See, for example, Dunning (1970, Chapter 9), Dunning and Pearce (1977, pp. 69–72), Brash (1966, Chapters 7 and 10), and Forsyth (1972, pp. 64–90).

[33] United States MNEs apparently have served as vehicles for transferring innovations in management and organization as well as technical innovations. See Section 3.2 and Brash (1966, Chapter 5).

technical knowledge something less than the "public good" assumed in most economic analysis. Technical knowledge can be transferred either within the MNE or between independent firms, the division depending on the MNE's assorted advantages and disadvantages. Arm's-length licensing is encouraged by risks to foreign investors and barriers to entry of subsidiaries, by short economic life of the knowledge asset, by simplicity and maturity of the technology, by high capital costs for the potential foreign investor, and by certain product-market settings that favor reciprocal licensing.

The microeconomic evidence on licensing and foreign investment can be fitted into Vernon's product-cycle model, which embraces a number of mechanisms to suggest that as a product's technology matures, its production becomes more footloose and disseminates toward countries less active in producing new technical knowledge. The MNE seems to influence the rate of diffusion at certain stages of the cycle; by implication, the cycle runs its course more rapidly with MNEs active than if technology is diffused only through arm's-length licensing and other channels.

A number of theoretical models aid understanding technology transfer in general equilibrium and its implications for nations' welfare. If Home, the innovating country, cannot collect rents on its technology that is diffused to Foreign, the dissemination generally makes Foreign and the world as a whole better off but leaves Home worse off. But Home might gain from the dissemination if its terms of commodity trade improve enough (e.g., Foreign is very efficient at making the innovation and begins to supply it as a cheap import to Home). If technology disseminates through its attachment to the MNE's international movement of capital, Foreign can benefit from encouraging capital inflows. At the level of competition in the individual industry, spillovers can cause the MNE either to scale back or expand its activities. If technology transfers and capital movements are independent, however, they can be substitutes for one another: Maximum world output can be attained by moving the technology to the capital or the capital to the technology. Home, of course, maximizes its own welfare by charging a monopoly rental for its superior technology; this rental could be an alternative to taxing exports of the innovative good, or Home might need to use both instruments to maximize its income.

Empirical evidence relevant to these theoretical welfare considerations shows that competition among suppliers of technical knowledge serves to beat down the rents they collect. It also indicates something about the leakage of proprietary knowledge from the control of MNEs: Some leakage occurs, but there is no presumption that the MNEs themselves undervalue the risk when licensing or placing their technology abroad. The evidence consistently indicates that the productivity of host countries' domestic firms increases with the prevalence of competing foreign subsidiaries. The marginal effect apparently goes to zero as the MNEs' share grows large, and it varies with the industry's overall rate of technical progress and the closeness of competition between subsidiaries and domestic firms. MNEs' proprietary advantages are taken partly in productivity advantages over local competitors, partly in larger market shares.

8

Taxation, MNEs' behavior, and economic welfare

Beside the great issues of progress, sovereignty, and economic justice that swirl around the MNE, taxation sounds like a matter for narrow minds that warm to accountancy. That instinct is squarely wrong, because it turns out that arrangements for taxing corporate net incomes play an important role in the division of gains from foreign investment between source and host countries. In this chapter we consider the normative effect of corporation income taxes imposed on MNEs – first on global welfare, then on the welfare of source and host countries separately. We take up some empirical aspects of the MNE's responses to taxation in the location and management of its investments. These include how prices on intracorporate transactions can be manipulated so as to minimize the MNE's tax burden.

8.1. Corporation income taxes, market distortions, and world welfare

All countries levy taxes on the net incomes of corporations at marginal rates typically ranging from 30 to 50 percent. Textbooks traditionally identify the profits tax as a levy on a pure economic rent or surplus that has no effect on saving or output decisions. But in practice the tax falls on profits in the popular sense – the sum of the opportunity cost of equity capital plus any rents or windfalls accruing to suppliers of equity capital. Therefore, the corporation income tax drives a wedge between the net return received by savers and the before-tax earnings of their savings when invested by companies. We expect it to depress the amount of saving and capital formation, even though a pure tax on monopoly rents will leave the monopoly with no incentive to change its price or output. How much the tax falls on savers and how much on final buyers of the goods and services provided by capital depends on various elasticities. As always with tax incidence, the inelastic curve takes the drubbing; if the supply of equity capital were perfectly elastic (because people could save in

189

nontaxed forms, or simply consume more of their incomes when a tax reduces the net return to equity capital), the tax would fall entirely on the users of capital's services.

The plot thickens when foreign direct investment occurs, so that Home's savers can place their capital either in domestic industry or abroad, and Foreign's users of capital services can draw upon either local or imported funds.[1] Two concepts of tax neutrality serve to identify the effects of taxes on these allocations. Capital-export neutrality refers to the choice that Home's MNEs make between investing their funds in domestic activities and investing abroad. All relevant taxes taken together are neutral if domestic and overseas investments that earn the same pretax rates of return also yield the MNE the same returns after taxes. Capital-import neutrality addresses the competition between Foreign's domestic savers and MNEs to supply the capital that helps to produce goods in Foreign. The tax system is neutral if equal before-tax returns at the margin to the competing suppliers of capital translate into equal after-tax earnings. Neutral tax systems promote efficient use of resources and also seem fair. Import neutrality places competing domestic companies and foreign subsidiaries on equal footing in that Foreign's tendency to buy capital services from the cheapest source is not distorted by taxes.

Multiple taxing authorities

Neutrality depends on who pays what tax, not which government collects it. Now we consider the implications of various priority arrangements between the Home and Foreign tax collectors. Suppose that Home (the source country) imposes no corporation income tax, but that Foreign (the host country) levies a 40 percent tax on all resident capital, whether of domestic or MNE origin. Capital-import neutrality prevails in Foreign, but capital-export neutrality is violated as Home's MNEs divert their funds toward untaxed domestic investment projects rather than pay Foreign's 40 percent tax. Suppose, instead, that Foreign imposes no tax but Home levies 50 percent on all profits earned by Home's citizens, whether their capital is placed at home or abroad. Capital-export neutrality obviously prevails, but not capital-import neutrality (Foreign's capital use is diverted toward the activities carried on by untaxed local capital).

With both taxes in force, the net effect depends on which tax collector gets first crack at the profits accruing to MNE capital, and what allowance the second one makes for this first exaction. Under the prevailing arrangement, the host country takes the first bite. Home can then choose among the following three policies:

---

[1] The analysis in this section originated in Richman (1963), Krause and Dam (1964, Chapter 4), and Musgrave (1969).

1. *Exemption.* Home can exempt from further taxation any income of MNE capital that has been taxed abroad. Foreign's tax rate then governs the allocation of MNE capital. Where Home's and Foreign's tax rates differ, as in the preceding example, capital-import neutrality will prevail, but export neutrality will be violated.

2. *Tax credit.* Home can tax MNEs' foreign profits at the same rate as Home's domestic capital but give a credit for taxes paid abroad. If Foreign's tax collector relieves the MNE of 40 cents of each profit dollar earned by its Foreign subsidiary, Home's tax collector gives a credit of 40 cents against the 50 cents that the MNE owes to Home, so that the MNE must then pay an additional 10 cents. The effective tax rate is therefore Home's, and export neutrality prevails. The same will be true if, instead, Foreign's rate is 50 percent and Home's rate is 40 percent, so long as Home rebates to the MNE the 10 percent excess of its tax credit over its domestic tax liability. In practice, however, source countries limit tax credits to the company's domestic tax liability on the same income (the *partial-credit* system), so the MNE pays the foreign or domestic tax rate, whichever is higher. Accordingly, either capital-import neutrality or capital-export neutrality prevails, depending on which tax is higher. Import neutrality and export neutrality can coexist only if both countries levy the same corporate tax rates and Home gives a full credit for the tax paid to Foreign. With equal tax rates, the same neutrality will prevail if Home lays the first claim on the MNE's taxable income and Foreign gives the tax credit.

3. *Tax deduction.* Home can allow taxes paid by MNE capital to Foreign only as a deduction from income taxable by Home, so that the MNE's capital placed abroad is subject to double taxation. The overall tax rate on MNE capital is then $t = t_H(1 - t_F) + t_F$ where t_F and t_H are, respectively, the Foreign and Home tax rates. If Foreign's tax is 40 percent and Home's tax is 50 percent, $t = 70$ percent. Obviously, neither export nor import neutrality will be served in this case.

Some major industrial countries employ the exemption procedure (Germany, France, Netherlands, Canada), others the partial-credit system (United States, United Kingdom, Japan). There exists a network of bilateral treaties that preclude double taxation, and so the deduction treatment finds little use in international tax practice. Nonetheless, we shall see that source countries have reason to prefer it.

With capital-import neutrality and capital-export neutrality both prevailing, taxes do not distort the foreign-investment decision. But what arrangement for taxing MNEs imposes the least distortion if Home and Foreign choose to levy their general corporation income taxes at different rates? Musgrave (1969, Chapter 7) and Horst (1980) addressed this issue. If taxes on capital's income fail to depress saving in either Home or Foreign, the tax on MNE profits (whoever levies it) should be the same as Home's general profits tax, so that capital-export neutrality prevails. If the demand for capital services is completely inelastic in both countries, Foreign's tax rate should apply to MNEs, and import neutrality should prevail. If taxation depresses supplies of domestic capital to the same degree in both countries, then the optimal tax on MNE capital should lie between the overall domestic rates levied by Home and Foreign.

Deferral, transfer-pricing regulation, and other complications

The effective rates of taxation influencing MNEs depend on many details beyond those identified so far, such as definitions of taxable income, rules on allowable depreciation, and Home's rules on pooling the MNE's tax position in various Foreign countries. The literature on international taxation raises the worrisome possibility that the practical effects of these details might swamp those of the seemingly general principles already set forth. Alworth (1988, Chapter 5) showed that MNEs' financing decisions can have diverse and important effects on their effective tax rates. One pervasive complication is deferral: the practice of tax-credit source countries to tax MNEs' profits from activities abroad only when the profits are repatriated. If $t_H > t_F$, the foreign subsidiary of a Home MNE can pay t_F on its current profits, reinvest the balance for an unlimited period, and pay the extra $(t_H - t_F)$ only when the profits are repatriated. If $t_H > t_F$, the deferral privilege substantially lowers the effective tax rate paid on capital invested abroad (Horst, 1977).

Deferral has another important property that was identified by Hartman (1985; also see Sinn, 1993). Consider a mature subsidiary abroad that might elect to reinvest some of its profits but has no prospective need for more equity from its parent. Assume that $t_H > t_F$. The subsidiary's decision to reinvest will be affected only by t_F and not by t_H, and capital import neutrality will hold. That is because capital exported from Home becomes "trapped equity" ultimately subject to t_H; it will pay the excess of t_H over its tax credit for t_F sooner or later, whether profits are reinvested or not, and the reinvestment decision does not depend on whether that excess is large or small. By implication, the investment behavior of mature subsidiaries should depend on different determinants from that of others that receive (or might still receive) infusions of equity from their parents. Hartman's conclusion is unchanged if $t_F > t_H$ and the MNE has excess tax credits in Home. Subsequent research (Leechor and Mintz, 1993; papers in Razin and Slemrod, 1990) has qualified Hartman's sharp distinction, but the empirical relevance of t_H to the reinvestment decisions remain an issue. Sinn (1993) formulated the issue in terms of the optimal initial dowry of capital that the parent should provide its subsidiary given the net effect of all taxes on repatriated profits. A higher anticipated repatriation tax induces the MNE to shrink the dowry and let the subsidiary rely more on retentions to reach its steady-state equilibrium size, but the repatriation tax does not distort the equilibrium size unless it is high enough to forestall the whole investment.

The discussion to this point has assumed that the taxing authority cost-lessly observes the real economic values of transactions of the MNE parent and its subsidiaries, for the purpose of determining tax liabilities. Previous chapters showed, however, that current transactions take place pervasively between corporate affiliates (funds injections and repatriations, interest and dividends on interaffiliate financial claims, interaffiliate merchandise trade, royalty payments and management fees, and the like). The transaction-cost model makes it clear that these transactions will often lack counterparts in arm's-length markets, so that neither the tax collector nor the MNE itself has an automatic and costless standard for pricing them. Effective tax rates are clearly altered by the MNE's opportunities for transfer pricing and limits on the tax collector's ability to combat this strategic behavior. Here we consider the theory of transfer pricing (empirical evidence is presented in Section 8.4).

The basic theoretical point (Diewert, 1985; Eden, 1985) is that the MNE facing a nonneutral set of taxes has an incentive to make its profits appear to the maximum extent in the low-tax jurisdiction.[2] Where $t_H < t_F$, the subsidiary in Foreign has an incentive to overstate any purchases it makes from its parent, or understate the cost of goods and services supplied to the parent, until nominal profits earned in Foreign go to zero. That is, the transfer-pricing problem in general has a corner solution, with the firm induced to raise or lower the price on any interaffiliate transaction until all profits have been shifted to the lowest-tax jurisdiction. The corner solution can become an internal one if the tax collector can at a cost determine the true value, and the probability of detection and punishment is a convex function of the distortion entered on the MNE's books (Kant, 1988*a*). Setting an otherwise optimal maximum transfer price on exports to the affiliate is also constrained where the host government imposes an ad valorem tariff on the declared value of the imports, inducing the MNE to limit the transfer price (Kant, 1988*b*). Whether financial flows between wholly owned corporate affiliates are designated as debt or equity is essentially arbitrary, and transfer-pricing incentives (if interaffiliate interest payments are a tax-deductible business expense) can include either maximizing or minimizing the nominal debt-equity ratio of the subsidiary (Hines, 1994*a*). Resource-extraction choices by the MNE can be affected (Samuelson, 1986). Finally, as applications of the literature on optimal policies for incompletely informed regulators, the tax collector can use a national ownership requirement (Falvey and Fried, 1986) or jointly regulate the subsidiary's price and output level (Prusa, 1990; Gresik and Nelson, 1994) to maximize its objective. The tax collector's mandated change in the regulated transfer price can have peculiar effects on the subsidiary's chosen price-output combination (Katrak, 1984).

[2] Significant earlier contributions include Horst (1971), Verlage (1975), Nieckels (1976), Booth and Jensen (1977), Mathewson and Quirin (1979), Itagaki (1979), Samuelson (1982), and Eden (1983).

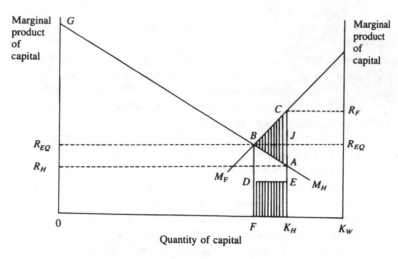

Figure 8.1

8.2. Tax conventions and national welfare

The normative tax-neutrality concepts used so far pertain to world welfare. But these taxes on MNEs can be collected by either Home's treasury or Foreign's treasury, or some combination of the two. Both Home and Foreign have national interests in grabbing the tax revenue, which is part of the country's national income. The tax system that maximizes either Home's or Foreign's national welfare is not consistent with maximum world welfare. Macdougall (1960) pointed out that in a world of competitive industries, and with no externalities, the host country's primary benefit from foreign investment lies in its first crack at the profits accruing to the capital committed locally by the MNE. And that same effect can make Home a loser from foreign investment. Assume that Home applies the partial-credit system for taxes paid to Foreign's tax collector. If Foreign's tax rate is no higher than Home's, capital-export neutrality prevails. But Home is, at the margin, clearly not making the best use of its capital.

Figure 8.1 illustrates the argument. Assume that the world's capital endowment is K_W, measured along the base of the diagram. K_H of this belongs to Home, the rest to Foreign. For each country a function shows the marginal product of capital, decreasing with the amount of capital combined with the rest of the nation's factor endowment (call it labor). Home's schedule is M_H. Foreign's schedule, M_F, is measured from right to left using K_W as the origin. Suppose that no foreign investment has yet occurred. In Home, the marginal product of capital is OR_H, before-tax income of capital is OR_HAK_H, income of labor is R_HGA, and Home's national income is $OGAK_H$. Similarly, the marginal product of capital in Foreign is R_FK_W. Suppose now that capital is made mobile internationally and that each country's corporation income tax rate is 50 percent. When Home's (new) MNEs have shifted the equilibrium amount of capital abroad, FK_H, the pretax return to (and marginal product of) capital becomes FB (or R_{EQ}) in each country, and FD of it ($FD = \frac{1}{2}FB$) is the tax payment. With the first crack going to Foreign's tax collector and Home giving a tax credit, Foreign's tax revenue from Home's MNEs is $FDEK_H$. The gain in world income from the foreign investment is the triangle ABC, the excess of the increase in Foreign's gross domestic product over the decrease in Home's. But Foreign's increase in national income is BCJ, a gain to Foreign's labor, plus $FDEK_H$, Foreign's MNE tax revenue. And Home loses by $FDEK_H$ minus BJA, even though Home's MNEs enjoy more after-tax profits. The Home profit rate after taxes rises from $\frac{1}{2} K_H A$ to $\frac{1}{2} FB$.

Clearly, this outcome does not maximize Home's national income. From Home's viewpoint, its capital should be allocated so that the profit earned on the last unit placed abroad after paying Foreign's taxes equals the pretax return on the last unit placed at home. But the MNEs on their own will place capital to equalize after-tax profits in the two countries. The deduction method described earlier maximizes Home's national welfare, as Musgrave (1969) and others (e.g., Dutton, 1982) have pointed out. Feldstein (1994b) argued that the tax-credit system's case is understated by neglect of the MNE's ability (intramarginally) to borrow debt capital abroad at a cost below its after-tax return on foreign assets, yielding an arbitrage profit to its Home owners.

Foreign, the importer of direct investment, has a symmetrical interest under the prevailing tax convention in luring MNEs for the national-income gain that results when Foreign's treasury captures their tax payments. With the tax-credit system, the MNE pays the source or host tax rate, whichever is higher, and so Foreign obtains a pure transfer by raising its rate up to that of the source country. A higher rate might be optimal, depending on the distribution of pretax profit opportunities that MNEs perceive on Foreign's soil. Foreign might seek policy instruments that inflate MNEs' profit opportunities and thereby increase the tax rate that can be imposed without deterring them. Corden (1967) pointed out that raising Foreign's tariffs does the trick when it induces the MNE to shift from exporting to direct investment in Foreign.[3] The tariff is second best, however, because it distorts consumption patterns.[4] Gersovitz (1987) developed other aspects of the host's optimal policy.

---

[3] Svedberg (1982b) simulated the host country's choice between an optimal tariff on imported goods and a prohibitive tariff that generates income tax revenue from the tariff-jumping subsidiary (but loses the tariff revenue and some consumer surplus).

[4] Horst (1971) provided a more elaborate treatment of the effect of Foreign's tax on the MNE that can serve Foreign's market through local production, exports from Home, or some combination of the two. He found that the leverage Foreign has for promoting local production through manipulating its tax rate depends not only on the level of the tariff but also on whether or not the MNE's product pricing is constrained by arbitrage. That is, given its costs and the demand elasticities in Home and Foreign, some pair of

Taxing for monopoly gain

The simple account of national and international interests in taxing MNEs' net incomes has been extended in a number of important ways – by some authors in general and theoretical terms, by others in terms of the interests of particular countries. A general point first made by Macdougall (1960) concerns any effect that the quantity of foreign investment may have on its earnings. Assume that neither Home nor Foreign imposes a tax on corporation income, so as to put aside the problem of tax-collecting priority already discussed. Whatever the structure of Foreign's markets in which Home's MNEs compete, assume that additional capital invested in Foreign drives down the average rate of profit that they earn there, as in Figure 8.1. If the MNEs compete with each other (i.e., do not form a cartel to exploit Foreign's market), they will not take into account that each one's expanded foreign investment drives down the earnings of the others – a negative externality from Home's viewpoint. Home's potential monopoly power over its foreign investment goes unexploited, and to maximize national welfare Home's government should impose a tax on the earnings of foreign capital to retrieve this revenue. Home's motive for discriminating against foreign investment so as to maximize national monopoly profits is, it should be stressed, quite independent of the motive to deal with Foreign's priority in tax collection. The quest for monopoly gains can afflict the country receiving foreign investment as well as the source. Suppose that MNE capital is supplied competitively from abroad, but its supply price increases with the amount entering Foreign's economy (a conventional upward-sloping supply curve). Foreign raises its national welfare with a tax that exploits this monopsony power in foreign borrowing, reducing capital imports and driving down the supply price.[5]

Recent contributions have brought both the tax-priority problem and the monopoly issue to bear on Home's optimal tax strategy and have also taken account of the rivalrous relationship between Home's and Foreign's tax collectors. Hartman (1980) provided a useful reference point. His general-equilibrium model assigns to Home and Foreign each an endowment of capital and labor able to produce either of two commodities. However, his is not quite the Heckscher-Ohlin model (see Chapters 2, 5, and 7). Foreign investment results not from differences in the overall returns to capital in Home and Foreign

product prices will maximize the MNE's profits in Home and Foreign, but the differential between these profit-maximizing prices must not be so large that independent parties can profitably buy in the cheaper location and resell in the dearer. Horst showed that Foreign's tax rate may have considerable effect on the location of production when this arbitrage constraint is binding, but (under certain circumstances) not when the MNE's pricing is unconstrained. Also see Itagaki (1979).

[5] Depending on the shape of the demand curve, this maneuver can pay for Foreign even when dealing with a monopolistic MNE that operates with constant marginal costs.

but from a specific productivity advantage enjoyed by Home's MNEs when they go abroad. The MNEs might operate in either Home's export industry or its import-competing industry. The industrial site matters, because investment abroad in Foreign's import-competing sector expands world production of the good that Home exports, driving down its price and thus worsening Home's terms of trade; Home's income-maximizing tax on foreign investment is higher when the MNEs operate in Home's exportable-goods sector. Another feature of Hartman's model is that MNEs ship abroad only part of the capital they need in Foreign. They borrow a given fraction locally, perhaps because of the risk-spreading considerations discussed in Chapter 6. Each country imposes a general proportional tax on corporation incomes. When a tax change occurs, this model allows not just for the change induced in foreign investment but also for the reallocation of capital and labour within each country and the adjustment of flows of international trade.

Hartman's conclusions stem from simulating the effect on national income of Home's choice among the policies of exemption, credit for taxes paid abroad, and deductibility of taxes paid abroad. He confirmed that in general a deduction policy comes closest to maximizing Home's welfare, and Home's optimal tax on foreign investment can be even higher than that. The simulations allow Home's export (and MNE) industry to be either capital-intensive or labor-intensive. Home's welfare gain in moving from exemption to whatever tax on foreign investment is optimal is about the same in either case, but a much lower tax is optimal when the export good is capital-intensive. The optimal tax is higher the more of its funds does the MNE borrow abroad. Hartman also investigated the effects of these tax policies on income distribution. When Home's exportable good that the MNEs produce abroad is labor-intensive, Home's labor naturally gains as higher taxes discourage foreign investment. However, unlike some models discussed in Section 5.1, Hartman's model implies that labor benefits most from a policy that stops short of forcing the repatriation of all of Home's foreign investment. (The tax strategy that maximizes labor's real wage also maximizes the national income.) If the exportable sector in which foreign investment takes place is capital-intensive, a higher tax on foreign investment is not clearly in the interest of Home's labor. Thus, whether the taxation of foreign investment aims to raise national welfare or to redistribute income toward labor, the deduction policy may or may not be the best one – the results depending sensitively on which good MNEs produce abroad, how much capital they borrow locally, and how large is their cost advantage over native firms.

Nor did Hartman (1980) exhaust the factors complicating the simple conclusion that Home gains most from applying a deduction policy when taxing foreign investment. Beenstock (1977) pointed to the implications of two-way movements of direct investment for the nation's use of its monopoly power in taxing foreign capital. Home's government raises its tax on its MNEs' overseas profits in order to reduce their investment in Foreign and thus drive up their profit rate. But the return rises to all capital in Foreign, causing Foreign's own MNEs to repatriate some capital they had exported to Home. Because Home gets first crack at the profits of the overseas subsidiaries of Foreign's MNEs, the induced repatriation cuts Home's tax revenue, a loss that partly offsets Home's monopoly gains from taxing its MNEs' foreign profits. Home's tax collector can garner no monopoly profits at all from contracting its foreign investment if Home MNE capital repatriated from Foreign is matched dollar for dollar by Foreign MNE capital repatriated from Home.

Another complication surfaces in Heckscher-Ohlin models that allow for international movement of capital. These models emphasize the relationship between the factor endowment (capital and labor) of the country and its comparative advantage in international trade, implying that a change in the factor endowment when capital moves abroad induces a compensating adjustment in its international trade. Jones (1967) showed that this connection affects the process by which a country imposes a welfare-maximizing tax on international capital transactions. In this model, a flow of capital from Home to Foreign simply increases Foreign's overall stock of capital – MNE capital is not specific to a particular sector, nor does it carry any productivity advantage. Thus, when Home changes its tax on international capital movements, the resulting adjustment changes the overall equilibrium return to capital in Foreign. That shift in factor prices changes commodity outputs there, and the relative prices of commodities (Home's terms of trade) if Foreign is incompletely specialized and produces both of the two commodities. Jones showed that not only must Home set its optimal tariff on commodity trade and its optimal tax on international capital jointly, in this case, but also that either the optimal tariff or the optimal tax can be negative. That is, Home can gain by subsidizing its capital exports rather than by taxing them monopolistically if a capital subsidy works a sufficiently favorable change on the structure of product prices. If Foreign produces only its export good (completely specialized, in this two-good model), Home's optimal tariff and capital tax will be independent of each other, and both will be positive (zero in the limit).[6]

Strategic behavior and tax competition

The contributions discussed thus far have treated the optimal taxation of international capital as a problem that the single country solves taking tax

[6] Batra and Ramachandran (1980) explored some effects of taxes in the specific-factors version of the Heckscher-Ohlin model (capital is mobile internationally but not between sectors). They were uninterested in sectoral differences and terms-of-trade issues, but they did allow MNE capital (originating in Home) to be distinguished from Foreign's local capital. Foreign's tax on the income of its own capital, assumed in fixed supply, has no allocative effect. But Foreign's tax on MNE capital sends some of it back to Home. This tax raises Foreign's welfare, up to a point (Home does not tax corporate income), and reduces Home's welfare.

and other policies of the rest of the world as given. Feldstein and Hartman (1979; see also Hamada, 1966) considered the strategic aspects of capital taxation, in which Home makes some conjecture about how Foreign will react to Home's policy change. In their model, Home is a large country, in that its MNEs place enough capital abroad to affect wage rates in the receiving countries. Foreign can be thought of as a composite of identical small host economies, each setting its corporation income tax taking Home's tax as given. Home's officials observe this reaction function and set Home's own corporate income tax so as to maximize Home's welfare, with Foreign's reaction taken into account. Home's government also employs another policy instrument – the rate at which MNEs can take a credit against taxes paid to Foreign. The rest of the model is identical to that of Hartman (1980), described previously. Their basic-case conclusions are already familiar from research summarized earlier: Home should allow only a deduction for taxes its MNEs pay to Foreign; if the MNEs' investments are large enough to drive up wages abroad, Home should tax its capital exporters even more heavily. How do Foreign's tax authorities react to an increase in Home's tax on overseas capital? Feldstein and Hartman showed that under standard assumptions about production technology, a rise in Home's tax reduces Foreign's welfare-maximizing tax, making Home's optimal tax on overseas capital even higher than in the model's basic case.

Another aspect of strategic interaction arises over the effect of taxes on the production of the proprietary assets deployed by MNEs. Huizinga (1991) addressed the decision of a source country in a model styled after Helpman's (see Section 2.3), in which multinationals operate in a monopolistically competitive international manufacturing sector. Home's citizens benefit from tax revenues, which produce utility-yielding public goods, but the taxation of MNEs' profits exacts a cost by reducing the viable number of varieties of differentiated manufactures (in this model, everybody consumes all varieties). Part of this negative externality of taxation, however, falls on consumers in the other country. Foreign, itself not a source of MNEs, gains a strategic advantage from this asymmetry, in that Home rationally gives its MNEs a credit for taxes paid to Foreign. This endogenous derivation of the tax credit is the model's striking feature. Huizinga (1992; see also Grace and Berg, 1990) addressed the degree to which governments allow MNEs to charge their research and development expenditures (producing proprietary assets for worldwide use) against profits earned in the national economy. A high-tax country might actually attract MNEs if it allows deduction of a generous share of R&D outlays. When countries act noncooperatively, the global deductibility of the MNE's R&D spending will be less than the whole amount, and R&D will be underprovided in comparison to a global cooperative taxation regime.[7]

---

[7] Other strategic aspects of capital taxation in the open economy can be noted, although they are remote from the MNE; see Manning and Shea (1989) and Levinsohn and Slemrod (1993).

More general if less clearly relevant to the MNE is the literature on international tax competition (surveyed by Devereux, 1994). Suppose that each country taxes its factors of production (capital and labor) in order to produce public goods, and that capital is mobile internationally while labor is not. Each (host) country applies a single tax rate to capital working in its territory. Countries can then fall into competition with one another to offer lower tax rates to capital, with the possible implication that public goods are underprovided as a result. Gordon (1992) identified a Nash equilibrium in which capital's services are taxed at the source with a dominant capital exporter (as defined by Feldstein and Hartman, 1979) employing the partial-credit system and the other capital-importing countries setting their statutory tax rates equal to that of the leader. Gordon argued that actual taxation practice among the industrial countries resembled this model, at least until the United States ceased to be the dominant exporter in the 1980s.

Bond and Samuelson (1989) considered the same problem as Gordon but with different assumptions (about other taxes, and the elasticity of the supply of saving). The capital exporter again employs the partial-credit system. Although capital importers again wish to set their tax rates equal to that of the exporter, the exporter's incentive is to set a higher rate in order to restrict capital outflows. The model's only equilibrium occurs with tax rates high enough to choke off trade in capital. A more plausible equilibrium results if the capital exporter uses a deduction system.

Given the small role of net capital exports in MNEs' operations and the practice of taxing other capital income in the recipient's domicile, the tax-competition problem appears to have only modest relevance for MNEs. Whether tax rates are subject to international competition is an empirical question, however, and we shall see (Section 9.1) that governments indeed compete in a discriminatory way for individual foreign subsidiaries.

8.3. **National tax policies: empirical patterns**

Empirical research on national tax policies toward MNEs' incomes has focused on two questions: Do tax laws systematically violate the criteria of neutrality and distort the allocation of MNE capital? How do actual laws relate to the divergent goals of maximizing national and global welfare and to the division of gains from foreign investment between source and host countries?

Corporation income taxes and MNE location decisions

The effects of tax provisions on MNEs' location decisions can be examined in two ways – by measuring the sensitivity of foreign direct investment to tax incentives and by directly evaluating the neutrality of actual tax systems. A good deal of descriptive evidence bears on the latter; evidence of the former type is considered in Section 8.4. Descriptions of countries' taxes on MNE income have suggested that capital-export neutrality and capital-import neutrality are not too seriously violated, although with the qualification that effective rates vary more than do nominal ones. The major industrial countries levy the same tax rates on foreign subsidiaries operating within their borders as on domestic companies. They do commonly discriminate against foreign investors and violate capital-import neutrality by imposing withholding taxes on dividends and similar payments remitted to foreigners (often around 15 percent). However, a series of bilateral tax treaties commit host countries to nondiscrimination and result in reductions in or exemptions from these withholding taxes.[8]

The tax-credit system used by some principal source countries produces capital-export neutrality if source-country tax rates are no lower than those of host countries, but deferral violates neutrality when profits are ultimately repatriated. Thus, deferral violates capital-export neutrality when the host's rate lies below the source's rate. It encourages too much foreign investment.

Because capital export and import neutrality together require that all countries set the same corporate tax rate, the divergence of these rates provides evidence on the extent of violations. As of 1991 the basic statutory corporation tax rates of the OECD countries ranged from 30 to 56.5 percent, but with 16 of the 24 falling in the 35 to 45 percent range (OECD, 1991, p. 71). However, recent research has emphasized not these nominal rates but marginal effective tax rates, which take into account the integration of corporate and personal taxes on profit income, effects of the sources of financing of investment, inflation, depreciation rules, and the like. OECD (1991, pp. 138–43) expressed these rates as pretax rates of return that would have to be offered to attract capital from savers with an opportunity-cost yield on investments of 5 percent (with a 4.5 percent rate of inflation assumed). In the average OECD country a pretax yield of 5.9 percent is required to attract funds for domestic investments. Capital export and import neutrality are equally violated, in that higher pretax yields must be offered: An average return of 7.5 percent is required either to induce investments abroad or to attract funds from foreign savers.[9] The OECD study evaluated export neutrality among OECD host countries and import neutrality among sources by calculating for each country a standard deviation of required yields for foreign direct investments in all the other OECD countries.

[8] See OECD (1991). Earlier contributions include Musgrave (1969, 1975), Sato and Bird (1975), Kyrouz (1975), Ness (1975), Snoy (1975, Part IV), Kopits (1976a), Bergsten et al. (1978, Chapter 6), and Adams and Whalley (1977). The effect of withholding taxes on capital-import neutrality also depends on how the host taxes dividend income received by its own citizens (see Sato and Bird, 1975; Lent, 1977).

[9] These figures pertain to pairs of countries with bilateral tax treaties; without them, the average for both capital exports and imports rises to 9.7%. These treaties exist between all the OECD countries with large outflows and/or inflows but are spotty for the smaller countries (Iceland, Portugal, Greece, Turkey) (OECD, 1991, p. 64).

The average of these standard deviations is 1.2 percent (range 0.6–3.1). For import neutrality, the corresponding standard deviation of required yields across source countries is 1.3 percent (range 0.5 – 3.6) (OECD, 1991, p. 141).[10] These figures confirm the impression from earlier studies that the violations of capital export and import neutrality appear larger when marginal effective rates are analyzed rather than nominal corporation tax rates (also see Alworth, 1988, Chapter 3).

National policies and national interests

Tax arrangements that maximize individual countries' welfare do not, we have seen, generally maximize world welfare. One source of divergence, the tax priority issue, affects all countries: They need not be big enough for their policy changes to influence MNEs' marginal revenue or supply price. The second source, monopoly power in foreign investment, applies only to large countries. But MNEs' affinity for imperfectly competitive markets (see Chapters 1 and 4) does imply that even a small nation's MNEs might face downward-sloping demand curves in their external markets, giving the source government an incentive to act "large."

Host countries gain much from the prevailing tax-credit system, as several quantitative appraisals have indicated. Jenkins (1979) estimated the gains for Canada, a major recipient. Of the various refinements built into his estimates, one holds particular interest. What happens to native Canadian capital when foreign investment enters Canada, driving down the rate of return that would otherwise accrue to native capitalists? To make the worst case, Jenkins assumed that this depressant effect of inbound MNEs propels all the foreign investment that flows outward from Canada, so that the sums Canada forfeits to foreign tax collectors partially offset the gains from taxing foreign subsidiaries in Canada. Canada's gains from taxing foreign subsidiaries amount to no less than 2.5 percent of gross national product without this offset, 1.5 percent even with the offset. Similarly, Grubel (1974) (also see Rugman, 1980*b*, Chapter 6) evaluated the net social rate of return to the United States from its foreign direct investments in a number of industrial countries. He found that the average net rate of return was negative for the period 1960–9, −5.9 percent annually. It remains negative even if royalties and fees remitted by subsidiaries to their U.S. parents are assumed to add a pure "rent" component to the parents' profits. Grubel noted that including gross fees and royalties as profits is inappropriate if the marginal costs of transferring intangibles abroad are substantial, as Teece (1977) showed them to be. Rousslang and Pelzman (1983) estimated the effects

---

[10] These standard deviations can be compared to the mean difference between required returns on domestic and foreign investments, 7.5% − 5.9% = 1.6%. All figures quoted here are unweighted averages; OECD (1991, pp. 151–3) concluded that weighting by actual foreign-investment flows would lower the means and dispersions a little.

of deferral for U.S. MNEs. It does not necessarily reduce U.S. welfare (they demonstrated conditions under which its effects could be positive). However, their empirical estimate indicates that deferral lowers U.S. income while increasing rest-of-world income by only a little more.

The gains that host countries enjoy from taxing foreign investments have been sorely neglected in debates over MNEs (see Chapter 10). The various benefits and costs most commonly proclaimed either defy our best measuring instruments or are entirely conjectural; the substantial gains generated by the tax system often go unnoticed.[11] The point is particularly relevant to LDCs that have granted MNEs substantial tax concessions in order to lure foreign investment. As Musgrave (1969, p. 75) pointed out, they may thereby give up their biggest benefit from the inflow.[12] On the other hand, they might simply be victims of tax competition. In general the LDCs' policies toward MNEs have evolved into more rational forms (see Section 4.4 and Chapter 10). One example is the replacement of unfavorable tax treaties left over from colonial domination by treaties that effectively exploit the partial-credit tax systems of principal source countries (UNCTC, 1988a).

In principal source countries, such as the United States and the United Kingdom, concern about the effects of foreign investment first arose in the 1960s and 1970s in connection with the countries' balance-of-payments positions (see Section 6.4), but tax issues soon surfaced as well. In the United States the foreign tax credit and deferral were recognized as not sufficiently restrictive of foreign investment to maximize national welfare. Certain policies affecting taxation of dividends remitted by subsidiaries in developing countries and depressing MNEs' charges to their subsidiaries for R&D services (thus inflating their profits taxable overseas) were also seen to favor global rather than national welfare (Bergsten et al., 1978, pp. 206–7).

Horst (1977; also see Bergsten et al., 1978, Chapter 6 and Appendix B) undertook the most ambitious investigation of the resulting welfare effects, a model of the profit-maximizing MNE facing all the essential features of the U.S. tax system. The company can manipulate financial instruments such as the subsidiary's rate of dividend payout, transfers of new funds to the subsidiary, and the MNE's rate of capital formation at home and abroad. The model dis-

---

[11] A qualification is the need to net out the incremental cost of public services provided to foreign subsidiaries, omitted from the calculations just cited. That qualification is important in the context of local public finances and for LDCs' policies (Section 9.1), but probably not for industrial countries' receipts from corporation income taxes.

[12] Musgrave (1969, p. 94) noted that developing countries often combine a low corporation income tax with a high withholding rate on remitted dividends, so as to encourage MNEs to invest heavily and make maximum use of their deferral opportunities. Also, the tax giveaway is mitigated by the shakedown losses that leave a foreign subsidiary with slender taxable profits in its early years (see Hughes and You, 1969, pp. 158–60, 183–6).

plays, for example, the incentive that deferral provides the MNE to favor foreign over domestic investment and to slant its intracompany financing of the subsidiary toward equity rather than debt. Horst's simulations indicated the effect of repealing the deferral provision so that U.S MNEs would be liable for U.S taxes on their foreign profits as earned. Investments in the subsidiaries would fall by 8.5 percent, whereas the parents' investments at home would rise by 3.9 percent; a sharp drop in transfers of funds to the subsidiaries indicates that they would rely more on funds borrowed abroad. Domestic and foreign taxes paid by U.S. manufacturers would rise by 9.1 percent. Repealing both deferral and the tax-credit provision, so that foreign taxes would be only a deduction from income taxable in the United States, would raise U.S. tax receipts by 50 percent while cutting the MNEs' capital formation abroad by 56.2 percent and raising it in the United States by one-fourth. These data suggest that switching from a tax system that (roughly) maximizes global welfare to one that (roughly) maximizes U.S. domestic welfare would produce substantial changes in both the volume of foreign investment and tax revenue.[13]

Hufbauer (1992) took the controversial position that U.S. tax policy should be designed to capture rents from the proprietary assets of MNEs by exempting their overseas income from taxation and deterring (or at least not encouraging) their licensing of technologies to independent foreign parties. It is not clear how Hufbauer conceives the desirable "headquarters activities" that should be attracted: as outlays on R&D, marketing, and the like are required to create and maintain these assets, it is not clear that their direct private marginal revenue products exceed their opportunity costs (with their highly random outcomes duly noted). If they are believed to deliver positive domestic externalities, that makes a case for direct subsidy to the asset-creating activities. (Whatever one makes of Hufbauer's general proposals, the book contains much useful analysis of detailed issues of international tax policy.)

8.4. Effects of taxation on MNEs' behavior

The normative analysis of Section 8.3 assumed that the MNE arranges its affairs so as to minimize its tax burden. Now we consider the actual evidence on MNEs' responses to tax incentives. Negative commentary on MNEs often includes the charge that they seize available opportunities to minimize taxes. That motive hardly distinguishes them from other economic agents, but they might enjoy opportunities not open to single-nation enterprises. We first review

---

[13] Hartman (1977) pointed to a strategic consequence of ending the deferral provision. Because of deferral, foreign countries now have an incentive to hold their corporation tax rates on subsidiaries of U.S. MNEs below the U.S. rate in order to attract taxable U.S. investment. With deferral ended, however, the tax-credit provision would immediately siphon the subsidiary's tax benefit into the U.S. Treasury. The host country would therefore have no reason to keep its corporation tax below the U.S. level.

evidence on how taxation influences MNEs' resource allocations, then turn to transfer pricing practices.

Tax effects on transactions

The evidence reviewed in Chapter 6 indicated that MNEs apparently manage their financial flows so as to maximize expected posttax global profits, which implies that they should be sensitive to tax factors.[14] Surveys and interview studies of corporate motives usually have rated tax factors less important than key nontax factors governing pretax rates of return. Snoy's review (1975, Chapter 28) suggested that surveys giving attention to tax variables have ranked them below quantifiable costs and political stability in importance but ahead of some other influences. Wilson's (1993) recent field study reached similar conclusions. That tax factors do not contribute more to explaining key foreign-investment decisions might indicate only that they vary less among countries than the factors that govern pre-tax rates of return.

Snoy (1975, Chapters 26 and 27) pioneered a statistical investigation of investment flows over the years 1966–9 from several leading source countries to a number of host-country destinations. His explanatory variables included source-host tax differentials bearing on either retained earnings or remitted dividends of foreign subsidiaries, as well as other controls such as national growth-rate differentials. The tax variables are not very robust in their statistical significance, but their coefficients always take the predicted signs, and their magnitudes imply that tax changes would have large effects. For example, unifying the European host countries' tax rates would change the growth rate of U.S. foreign direct investment in the various individual countries by one-third or more. Root and Ahmed (1978) included corporation tax rates among the factors they employed to explain foreign-investment flows into 41 developing countries, finding a significant negative effect.

Numerous recent time-series studies have confirmed the finding that taxes strongly affect the location of foreign investment. Boskin and Gale (1987), studying aggregate U.S. inflows and outflows of foreign direct investment, found that a domestic tax policy change that increases domestic investment by $1 will prompt $0.08 to 0.27 of additional investment from abroad and deter $0.04 of U.S. investment abroad (the figures refer to rates of expenditure out

---

[14] That higher taxes on foreign income will repel foreign investment is a proposition not without its exceptions. When the government taxes foreign-source profits, it absorbs part of the profits but also part of the risk to which the MNE is exposed. Suppose, with Hartman (1979), that at the margin foreign investment is financed entirely from tax-deductible debt and that domestic debt is risk-free to borrowers. Then increased taxation of its foreign profits on equity causes the MNE to increase its borrowing and capital formation overseas. Similarly, an increased tax on profits from domestic investments could cut foreign investments through its effect on the MNE's total investment spending (Jun, 1990).

of retained earnings). Grubert and Mutti (1991*b*) analyzed foreign subsidiaries' behavior in Canada, observing that capital expenditures are more responsive to U.S. and Canadian tax factors than is foreign direct investment (the financial flow). Also, foreign subsidiaries account for all of the responsiveness of capital expenditures in Canadian manufacturing to this tax differential.[15] Cummins and Hubbard (1994) used panel data on U.S. MNE subsidiaries' capital expenditures in industrial host nations to show that a q-based model of investment fits much better when tax effects are incorporated than when they are ignored. And Harris (1993) demonstrated that a 1986 U.S. tax change that removed a favorable tax treatment of domestic capital expenditures raised U.S. MNEs' capital expenditures abroad.

Several recent investigators such as Jun (1990) and Slemrod (1990; see his summary of earlier contributions) focused on Hartman's distinction between tax incentives affecting the reinvestment of foreign subsidiaries' earnings and outflows of interaffiliate equity and debt. Jun's aggregated time-series models fit rather poorly, but he argued that the greater predictability of parents' transfers than of reinvested retentions gives some support to the view that parents' transfers are (contrary to Hartman) the predominant marginal source of funds. Slemrod also found that U.S. MNE parents' transfers of funds to subsidiaries could be well explained by their marginal rates of taxation (elasticity −1.4). He divided the principal source countries into those employing the exemption and tax-credit systems, expecting to find that foreign investment in the United States should depend only on the U.S. tax rate for the exemption countries, a more complicated tax differential for the tax-credit countries. U.S. taxes strongly deter funds transfers to the United States, he found, but the effect turned up in both exemption and tax-credit countries. Altshuler et al. (1994) exploited the implication that temporary but not permanent variations in repatriation taxes should affect MNEs' dividend receipts from their subsidiaries; using intercountry tax differences to capture the permanent component and intertemporal ones for the temporary component, they confirmed the proposition.

Similar findings come from cross-section studies that typically rely on the effect of different tax levels in various host or source countries. Grubert and Mutti (1991*a*) related the stock of U.S. foreign investment to host-country tax rates in cross section, again finding a significant and highly elastic relationship. Cross-section methods were also used by Hines and Rice (1994) to test the effects of host countries' taxes not only on MNEs' actual commitments of resources but also on the use of transfer pricing to shift reported profits to low-tax

[15] Grubert and Mutti (1991*b*) experimented with various tax measurements, concluding that the average effective rate outperforms the marginal rate that is commonly preferred on theoretical grounds. It is interesting that a case for the average rate can be built on the assumption that foreign investments are discrete projects rather than incremental changes in foreign-capital stocks (Devereux, 1994).

countries. In addition, given the labor and capital that U.S. MNEs utilize in various countries and the country's level of productivity, the MNEs report significantly more income, the lower is the tax rate (Hines and Rice noted that the share of total U.S. capital abroad located in these "tax haven" countries has increased rapidly).[16] Hines (1993a) also found that U.S. states' tax rates on corporate income have strong locational effects (a 1 percent higher tax rate yields a 7 to 9 percent lower share of manufacturing investment from source countries that use the exemption system). Investors from both exemption and tax-credit countries are sensitive to state taxes, but those from exemption countries more so.[17]

Various other transactions of MNEs are potentially sensitive to tax provisions, and of these dividend remittance has been studied extensively. The analysis is behavioral rather than based on value-maximization models because of the puzzle why firms pay dividends, given their adverse tax consequences for shareholders' wealth. Hines and Hubbard (1990) concluded that remittance practices of subsidiaries to their parents largely parallel the dividend-paying behavior of the parents themselves. Nonetheless, dividend-payment patterns are generally consistent with tax minimization: Most subsidiaries pay no dividends (or interest and royalties) to their parents; those that do pay out most of their profits; and dividends respond to the parent's (excess or deficit) tax-credit situation. Both Hogg and Mintz (1993) and Altshuler and Newlon (1993) found intrafirm dividend payments responsive to tax changes in various countries that altered the tax price of dividends. Earlier studies agree that subsidiaries' dividend remittances are tax-sensitive. Kopits (1972) found that the dividend flows from U.S. MNEs' foreign subsidiaries depend on their after-tax profits, interacted with a factor indicating the host country's differential tax rates on retained and distributed earnings. Ness (summarized in Kopits, 1976a, pp. 647–8) similarly found that the retention of earnings in various host countries depended on a measure of the opportunity cost of funds with tax incentives appropriately embedded. Ladenson (1972) detected no influence of tax-rate differentials on dividends, but aggregation of statutory tax rates across regions might have caused this. Hartman (1981) offered some tentative evidence that retentions abroad of profits earned by U.S. MNEs are sensitive to taxes because of the deferral provision.

[16] Although the use of tax havens is deplored as tax evasion, it has the property of reducing the locational distortion associated with other host countries' differing marginal tax rates.

[17] Plasschaert (1979, p. 115) described the tax-haven mechanism. In 1962 the United States changed its tax laws to deny the deferral privilege to MNE income reported in tax-haven countries. Musgrave (1969, pp. 85–8) pointed out that this reform's economic benefit to the United States was in fact dubious, because profits that would be remitted to the United States anyhow then had to be reported in higher-tax foreign jurisdictions, transferring real income to foreign countries through the tax-credit mechanism.

Tax incentives affect many decisions made by the MNE (Auerbach and Hassett, 1993). These include the mode by which subsidiaries are established (acquisition vs. green-field), the method of effecting acquisitions (cash vs. securities), and the location and means of any external financing of asset acquisitions (Hogg and Mintz, 1993). Hines (1993*b*, 1994*b*) showed that a less favorable tax treatment by the United States of U.S. MNEs' deductibility of the costs of R&D undertaken at home induced some companies to shift R&D activities abroad. Hines (1994*c*) demonstrated that withholding taxes on intrafirm royalty payments made by affiliates to MNE parents tend to increase R&D by the affiliates, consistent with local R&D being a substitute for technology transferred from the parent. Froot and Hines (1994) showed that a 1986 change in tax deductibility of interest for U.S.-based parents tended to reduce their borrowing and investing and cause substitution of leasing, likely as an alternative to capital ownership.

Transfer pricing

The possibility that MNEs avoid taxes and accomplish other unsavory deeds by manipulating the prices assigned to intracorporate transactions has received much attention. Casson (1979) urged that transfer-pricing maneuvers, undertaken solely to divert tax revenues away from governments, cause an overextension of foreign investment. And Vaitsos (1974) charged that MNEs siphon unduly large flows of purchasing power out of the developing countries through transfer-pricing practices (also see Lall, 1973).

In Section 8.1 we found that, unless tax minimization is curtailed by other constraints such as avoiding tariffs, MNEs have an incentive to use transfer prices to the maximum extent to place profits in low-tax jurisdictions. Companies' use of transfer pricing hence should be limited only by tax collectors' detection skills. The empirical studies definitely agree. Kopits (1976*b*) fastened on intracorporate royalty payments as a likely candidate for transfer pricing, because arm's-length standards for a "reasonable" price are largely lacking. MNEs should seek to conceal remitted profits as royalty payments from foreign countries with higher tax rates on dividends but lower tax rates on royalties than the U.S. corporate tax rate. The substitution of royalties for dividends is significant and seems to be almost dollar-for-dollar among some industrial countries. Kopits estimated that about one-fourth of royalty payments from industrial countries represent concealed profit remittances, about 13 percent from LDCs. More and Caves (1994), in the course of analyzing intracorporate royalties as indicators of proprietary assets' productivity abroad, confirmed a significant transfer-pricing component.

Other classes of transactions also yield evidence of transfer-price manipulation. Following Vaitsos (1974) various other researchers have detected the adjustment of the prices of intrafirm transfers of inputs (e.g., UNCTC, 1985, pp. 33–8). Müller and Morgenstern (1974) claimed to find the effect in foreign subsidiaries' exports from Argentina, but the research design is suspect. Stewart (1989) showed that the pricing of intrafirm exports from and imports to Ireland is consistent with incentives to move profits to this low-tax country. Lecraw (1985) found that MNEs operating in countries of Southeast Asia, in pricing goods transferred within the firm, use nonmarket methods of transfer pricing (more easily subject to manipulation) where the perceived extent of risk in the host country is great. Benvignati (1985) observed that the business units of large U.S. firms use market-based methods of pricing less commonly in their international than their domestic transactions (for which tax-related incentives to manipulate prices generally do not exist); she controlled for industry characteristics that affect the availability of market-based transfer-price criteria. The results of Al-Eryani et al. (1990) suggest that market-based methods are used more intensively by firms that are (for whatever reason) more concerned about satisfying legal requirements. The one exception to the typical positive findings of transfer-price adjustments is Bernard and Weiner's (1990) analysis of pricing in interaffiliate and arm's-length oil shipments; their large and accurate data set indicates pervasive differences between these prices, but the differences are not stable over time and yield only weak evidence of tax-motivated transfer pricing.

The other line of research on transfer pricing addresses overall reported profits rather than particular classes of transactions. Hines and Rice (1994) showed that the income reported by U.S. subsidiaries in various countries (given the local inputs and their productivity) decreases significantly with the square of the host-country tax rate, confirming that the profit gain from tax-motivated transfer pricing increases more than proportionally to the tax differentials involved. Harris et al. (1993) investigated whether taxes paid to the U.S. government by U.S. MNEs vary inversely with the extent of their operation in tax-haven countries (after controlling for other determinants of profitability); the effect appears but is substantial only for firms with extensive multinational operations. And Harris (1993) demonstrated that a large reduction in the basic U.S. rate of corporate income tax caused U.S. MNEs quickly to shift expenses to foreign jurisdictions and thus taxable income to the United States. The shift was most apparent for firms in industries intensive in spending on intangibles (research, marketing), whose site of benefit is in any case hard to determine.

The empirical evidence identifies organizational constraints on transfer pricing that have eluded the theoretical model builders. The prices attached to intrafirm transactions affect the profitability of the firm's various activities, and an accurate knowledge of opportunity costs is essential for its owners to know whether the firm carries out the optimal set of activities and conducts each of them in the profit-maximizing way.[18] Adjusting these transfer prices in order to reduce taxes therefore requires the MNE either to incur the fixed cost of main-

---

[18] Companies' quests for efficient transfer prices rather closely resemble the processes by which economists identify efficient shadow prices. An arm's-length price in a compet-

taining "two sets of books," or mandates a centralized system of control, evaluation, and reward that can work around tax-distorted transfer prices without sending wrong internal signals to the firm's divisional managers.

Some investigators of businesses' transfer-pricing practices have taken account of this interplay of tax and administrative considerations. Arpan's (1971, Chapter 4) survey of foreign MNEs with subsidiaries in the United States revealed a rough distinction between large companies in noncompetitive environments and small ones facing more competition. The former group both lack arm's-length bases for setting transfer prices and can justify the overhead expense of a complicated cost-based system of transfer pricing capable of compromise among administrative and tax-avoidance objectives. Overall, companies heed tax considerations and some other government fiscal incentives, but also they clearly employ transfer prices for internal-control objectives. Minimizing U.S. customs duties is not an important goal, partly because the possible savings are small, partly because costly litigation can result. Burns's (1980) survey of factors considered by U.S. MNEs agreed with Arpan's results in all important respects. Tax factors weigh in substantially, although with less force than does the need to motivate subsidiaries' managers effectively. The distinction between large, noncompetitive MNEs and small, competitive ones again appears in the transfer-pricing method that they use and the extent to which tax rates influence their policies.[19] Tang (1979, Chapter 6) sought from U.S. and Japanese MNEs rankings by importance of the factors influencing their methods of transfer pricing. The primary roles of global profit maximization, minimization of tax and tariff payments, and the need to motivate foreign-subsidiary managements were all confirmed. Several other studies have suggested more generally that many companies find the gains from transfer-pricing maneuvers to be small relative to the administrative costs and risks involved (Joachimsson, 1980; Rugman, 1980*b*, Chapter 7; Plasschaert, 1981), or that only large companies find the fixed cost worth incurring (Bernard and Weiner, 1992; Al-Eryani et al., 1990).

The most comprehensive study of organizational constraints on transfer pricing is by Yunker (1982). Large firms that can justify the fixed cost of tax-motivated transfer pricing tend to have relatively large numbers of autonomous subsidiaries, making tax-motivated transfer prices disruptive for internal con-

itive market is the ideal choice, but unlikely, in the nature of things, to be available for many intracorporate transactions. Alternatives constructed from the company's internal data have various strengths and weaknesses. See Arpan (1971, Chapter 2) for a survey. Tang (1979, Chapter 5) compared the practices of U.S. and Japanese MNEs' (they are quite similar).

[19] Lessard (1979) and Brooke and Remmers (1970, pp. 117–22) also commented from casual survey evidence on the degree to which administrative considerations constrain the unfettered use of transfer pricing to avoid taxes. Greene and Duerr (1970) provided more systematic evidence on the point.

trol and evaluation. Therefore, it is important to measure companies' situations carefully when seeking to predict transfer-pricing behavior. Yunker confirmed that firms with more autonomous subsidiaries are less likely to use strategic transfer pricing. Large overall size of the firm and uncertainty of the environments in which its subsidiaries operate deter strategic pricing; the higher the ratio of foreign to total sales, the greater the potential profit gain, and the more extensive the use of tax-motivated transfer pricing.[20]

Finally, some authors considered the effects of transfer pricing on the welfare of the affected nations. Jenkins and Wright (1975) examined the practices in the U.S. petroleum industry, which enjoyed a long-standing special incentive to transfer its profits upstream to crude-petroleum-producing countries, paying as a result almost no corporation income taxes to the United States. Jenkins and Wright sought to measure this profit transfer away from consuming countries other than the United States by assuming that the oil MNEs' investments in those nations should have earned profit rates as high as did the average manufacturing investment of U.S. MNEs in those countries. They concluded that in 1970, transfer pricing cost those consuming countries at least $240 million. Vaitsos (1974) undertook a detailed inquiry into transfer pricing by MNEs operating in four major sectors in South America. Transfer prices on components or intermediate goods imported to Latin American countries were carefully compared with market prices for identical goods elsewhere in the world. Vaitsos's (1974, Chapter 4) comparisons between sectors and between Latin American host countries confirmed a number of expectations about transfer pricing. For Colombia, imports were particularly overpriced in pharmaceuticals – a sector in which firms were subject to a limit on the nominal profits that they could repatriate. Overpricing of transferred merchandise was less in sectors where the MNEs compete more with each other; with competition there should be fewer excess profits for clandestine repatriation through transfer pricing.[21] Vaitsos (1974, pp. 73–4) also alluded to price controls, suggesting that intermediate imports are overpriced in order to establish a high cost base for determining permitted prices. Chile, a country with a high corporate tax rate, experienced proportionally high royalty remittances, and in Colombia royalty remittances were also high in the sectors with strong transfer-pricing incentives (Vaitsos, 1974, pp. 85–6; also see Lall and

---

[20] Yunker also provided evidence on firms' reasons for using "instrumental" (i.e., non-market) transfer pricing. Besides tax avoidance these include the avoidance of restrictions on profit remittance, maintenance of good relations with host countries, and stabilizing the competitive position of the subsidiary; about equal weights were assigned to these four motives.

[21] Tariffs were also set so as to encourage the overpricing of intermediate pharmaceuticals – low on intermediates, high on competing final goods (Vaitsos, 1974, pp. 90–1). Transfer pricing to conceal excess profits gleaned in the host-country market has been spotted in some industrial countries as well (see Greenhill and Herbolzheimer, 1980).

Streeten, 1977, pp. 146–7). Vaitsos's general discussion flirted with the idea that MNEs systematically transfer wealth away from the developing countries, as if this propensity were somehow built into the decision structure of a MNE. However, his evidence journeyed toward a different conclusion: MNEs' transfer-pricing maneuvers are due to a conjunction of motive with market opportunity and incentives based on the LDCs' own policies (also see Vernon, 1977, Chapter 7).[22]

8.5. Summary

Corporation income taxes on MNEs' investments abroad have distinct normative effects on world welfare and on the welfare of the source and host countries. The taxation of foreign-investment income affects world welfare if either of two forms of neutrality is violated. Capital-export neutrality prevails if taxes do not distort the market's incentives for allocating capital between domestic or overseas uses. Capital-import neutrality prevails if taxes do not distort the recruitment of capital services from domestic or imported sources to serve a given market. Both export neutrality and import neutrality can be achieved only if all countries employ the same tax rate. Conventionally, the host country's tax collector gets first priority at taxing the incomes of foreign subsidiaries. The source country's tax authority can then exempt the same income from further taxation (import neutrality is attained), give a credit against taxes paid abroad (either export or import neutrality, but not both), or allow the foreign tax as a deduction from income taxable at home (neither form of neutrality results). An important influence on effective tax rates is the practice of deferral, which permits the MNE to postpone paying taxes due to the source country until its host-country profits are actually repatriated. Effective tax rates also can be affected by the MNE's seizure of opportunities to move reported profits between countries through the pricing of interaffiliate transactions. The firm's incentive is to set such prices as high or as low as possible, until all reported profits are transferred to the low-tax location.

Effects on national welfare of taxing foreign income diverge from those on global welfare for two reasons. First, globally efficient taxes can be collected by either country, but each nation cares whether or not its treasury receives the tax revenue. Home wants MNE capital allocated so that the marginal pretax return at home equals the marginal return from foreign investment after foreign taxes are paid. This rule calls for the deduction method of treating foreign taxes. Foreign gains by attracting MNE capital so as to garner the tax proceeds. The second divergence between global welfare and national welfare stems from monopoly gains. If Home's MNEs compete among themselves in Foreign's

---

[22] A study by the U.S. Tariff Commission (1973, pp. 434–5), analyzing data for 1966 and 1970, concluded that average ex post tax rates on foreign income of U.S. MNEs exceeded that on income reported in the United States, which would indicate an inducement on average to move profits toward the United States through transfer pricing.

market and drive down their mutual rate of return, Home has an incentive to discriminate in its tax structure against foreign investment. If MNE capital is industry-specific, Home's motive for restricting the outflow is amplified if foreign investment expands world production of Home's exportable good, worsening its terms of trade. Similar conclusions follow from a Heckscher-Ohlin model in which MNE capital loses its sector-specific identity: Home's taxation of capital exports for monopoly gain may be tempered or reversed by any induced change in the structure of Foreign's production that tends to improve Home's commodity terms of trade.

The national interests of Home and Foreign are adversary to one another, in the light of both tax-priority and monopoly criteria for taxing foreign capital so as to raise national welfare. Some researchers have investigated strategic reactions between countries, discovering that (if Home is a leader and Foreign a collection of small follower economies) Home may wish to tax foreign-investment income even more heavily than domestic considerations would warrant, because Foreign rationally responds by reducing its own tax. It is possible that symmetrical tax competition among countries to attract mobile capital leads to the underprovision of public goods.

Actual tax systems of the industrial countries violate global-welfare criteria, but apparently not grossly. Export neutrality and import neutrality cannot both prevail unless all countries impose the same tax rate; actual rates vary, but they are rather bunched for the leading industrial countries. Import neutrality is impaired by withholding taxes on dividends abroad, but these are commonly waived or reduced under bilateral tax treaties. The prevalent tax-credit arrangement is potentially consistent with export neutrality, although deferral can introduce a bias toward excessive foreign investment. MNEs can react to tax provisions by rearranging their allocative decisions so as to maximize after-tax profits. Then one would expect a one-dollar change in expected profits due to tax changes to have the same effect as a one-dollar change from any other source. Foreign investors' decisions indeed do appear sensitive to taxes, not only in their basic investment decisions but also in recruiting funds, determining repatriations, allocating R&D, and the like.

MNEs manipulate the prices attached to intracorporate transactions (royalty payments, interaffiliate goods movements), moving taxable profits into jurisdictions where they pay a lower tax and reporting higher profits in such locations. However, transfer prices also serve internal needs of control and evaluation of the corporation's performance. Large companies whose internal transfer prices are not readily compared with market prices apparently do maintain complex transfer-pricing systems aimed in part at minimizing taxes. Smaller companies and those in more competitive environments, whose transfer prices the tax collector can readily check against market prices, do not find such maneuvers to their advantage. Decentralized internal control systems deter manipulative transfer pricing.

9

Multinationals in developing countries

MNEs have gone through a cycle in their encounters with host-country governments. They have met hostility and resentment in all countries that host substantial foreign investment, but nowhere more than in the LDCs from World War II through the 1970s. They were blamed for the national economy's manifest shortcomings, not to mention the historical sins of colonial domination, as well as genuine clashes of economic interest. With the waning of socialism and the coming of the LDCs' debt crisis, much of the acrimony vanished, but the issues that it raised continue to dominate the research literature.

The normative appraisal of MNEs' allocations in LDCs could be controversial even without this political background. Advocates of diverse policies toward development seem to concur on a diagnosis that key markets are malfunctioning, or important prices are misaligned to their shadow equivalents, so that saving and investment, the foreign-exchange rate, wage rates, returns to human capital, and other such important magnitudes can be far off the mark. Appropriate levels for them may therefore differ greatly from what the market signals to private decision makers, and not necessarily in unambiguous directions. The MNEs' allocative decisions both respond to and affect these imbalances and distortions. Does the MNE's presence mean more capital formation or productivity growth than otherwise? Can sticks and carrots be applied to the MNE to produce more desirable allocations? Our discussion will focus on these questions about the instruments of development policy, not its ends or the political and social processes by which they are defined.[1] This approach is not calculated to maximize the difference between LDCs and developed countries; on

---

[1] Those interested in a broader approach may consult the work of Biersteker (1978), who did a heroic job of lining up the "critics" of MNEs and the "neoconventionalists" on these large issues, and the analyses of Evans (1979), Hood and Young (1979, Chapter 8), Vernon (1971, Chapters 2, 5, and 7; 1977, Chapters 7–9), Lall and Streeten (1977, Part I), Kumar (1990), and Helleiner (1989).

the contrary, some industrial host countries' policies toward MNEs rest on these same perceived shadow-price discrepancies.

Another issue of procedure grows out of a problem that plagues much research on the effects of MNEs on LDCs' economies. Conditions in the host LDC affect the prevalence and character of MNEs' activities there. Hence, to test any hypothesis about the MNEs' effects on the performance of the host economy, one must control for this reverse causation. Therefore, we review the evidence on what determines MNEs' prevalence in the developing world, then turn to MNEs' effects. A final section addresses MNEs based in third-world countries.

9.1. **Determinants of MNEs' activities**

Foreign subsidiaries' operations in the LDCs tend to divide sharply into three categories. The exporters of natural resources and resource-based products need no explanation: They go where the resources are, if conditions in the sector call for vertical integration. The second class is made up of exporters of manufactured goods or components. The third class comprises producers largely engaged in serving the LDC's domestic market. An important point of fact is the sharpness of the distinction between the second and third groups. The theory of MNEs' locational choices (see Section 2.2) indicates that, given scale economies and the very small domestic markets of most LDCs, a foreign subsidiary will locate there either to serve the market or to export extensively, but it will not serve the domestic market and export "a little" (Horst, 1971, 1973). The data confirm this prediction. For example, the 80 projects analyzed by Reuber et al. (1973) were divided into export-oriented projects (26) and those serving the domestic market (54); the average proportion of output exported was 87 percent for the former group and 3 percent for the latter. This pattern is not intrinsic to LDCs but rather to small national markets generally; it also turns up in countries such as Ireland (Andrews, 1972; Buckley, 1974). Accordingly, generalizations that span the export and domestic-market subsidiaries are somewhat suspect.

Foreign subsidiaries serving domestic markets

The forces explaining MNEs' presence in the domestic markets of LDCs are about the same as those explaining their presence in industrial countries. Nankani (1979) confirmed that foreign investment in LDCs by various industrial source countries depends on the prevalence in the source countries of industries congenial to foreign investment. Morley and Smith (1971) suggested that MNEs respond to LDCs' tariff incentives in industries where proprietary assets are important. Juhl (1979) confirmed for West Germany Nankani's finding that foreign investment in LDCs increases with an industry's plant scale and expenditure on producing proprietary assets, and he did not find physical capital intensity to deter investing in LDCs.[2] Hughes and You (1969, pp. 179–83) pointed out that MNEs commonly have initial contact with LDC markets as exporters, and so import-substituting foreign investments reflect the comparative-advantage structure of the exporting country. Finally, students of Japanese foreign investment (Yoshihara, 1976, Chapter 4, 1978; Ozawa, 1979a, 1979b; Tsurumi, 1976) all stressed defensive investment by smaller-scale Japanese enterprises in unlikely industries such as textiles; these investments utilize managerial and capital assets of firms that lack opportunities for domestic growth and/or face threats in either their domestic or overseas market.

The extent of parallel between the interindustry determinants of investment in developed and LDC economies is illustrated by Lall and Mohammed's (1983a) study of Indian public companies. They found royalty payments a significant determinant, although not the usual domestic R&D/sales ratio. Other conventional results include positive influences for intensive use of skilled labor and scale economies in production. Unconventional results are the insignificance of the Indian firm's advertising/sales ratio and the significant negative influence of the capital intensity of the U.S. counterpart industry.

Similarly useful for perspective on differences associated with the LDCs' situations is Lecraw's (1991) intercountry analysis of GNP-normalized inflows of direct investment during 1974–86, especially its breakdown of those flows into investments oriented toward the domestic market, toward the processing of natural resources, and toward other export-processing activities. Certain factors affect the inflows of all three types of foreign direct investment: The riskiness of the country deters each, while the amplitude of domestic factor stocks and the openness of the host's policies toward MNEs promotes each. The growth of domestic demand and the height of protective tariffs affect only investments oriented toward the domestic market, while taxes and quality-adjusted labor costs affect only the export-oriented investments. Export-processing investments depend on the real exchange rate, while resource-extractive investments depend on the relative price of resource products. Lecraw's results strongly support the distinction among these types of investments.[3]

---

[2] As an exception, Koo (1985) argued that Korean government intervention had been so intrusive as to dominate Korea's pattern of interindustry distribution.

[3] Previous studies had supported many of these conclusions: Reuber et al. (1973, pp. 115–20), Nankani (1979, Chapter 3), and Evans (1979, Chapter 3). Nankani found that aggregate foreign investment in manufacturing shows at least a weak positive relationship to political stability and negative relationships to hostile investment climate and ideological orientation toward socialism, but his data did not distinguish between export-oriented and local-market investments. The evidence of Reuber et al. (1973, p. 95) suggests that these elements of political economy pose less uncertainty for export-oriented projects (also see Root and Ahmed, 1978, and Dunning, 1981a). Numerous studies (e.g., Reuber et al., 1973, pp. 113–14 and Appendix A) observed a strong positive correlation between countries' levels of GNP per capita and stocks of foreign investment per capita, perhaps reflecting the attraction of MNEs serving local markets to

Other investigators also addressed the effect of risk on foreign investment flows, an issue relevant to LDCs if not only to them. Nigh (1986) investigated the influence on U.S. investment in eight Latin American countries of indexes of conflict and of cooperation, both within the host nation and between it and the United States. Over a 21-year period the indexes of conflict wield a significant negative, and those of cooperation a significant positive influence, both intra- and international. A similar study by Nigh and Schollhammer (1989) of Japanese foreign direct investment found a negative influence of intranational conflict but not of the other indexes (for developed host countries Japanese MNEs' responses to intranational conflict proved asymmetrical, declining when conflict increases but ignoring reductions in conflict as well as changes in cooperation).

Export-processing activities

The MNEs' role in the export sectors is more distinctively an LDC question. Helleiner (1973) pointed out that these exports fall into four rough categories. Locally produced raw materials can be subjected to further processing, and MNEs sometimes undertake this role either as an economic choice or in response to host-country inducements. Second, some LDCs have become heavy exporters of simple manufactured goods whose production processes are suitable to their factor endowments. MNEs' involvement in these products will be discussed subsequently. Third, labor-intensive processes in manufacturing operations may be carried on in LDC facilities that import unfinished goods and reexport them after additional processing. Evidence summarized in Section 1.2 indicates that MNEs play a significant role in these offshore fabrications, but a good deal of business is also done at arm's length between industrial-country firms and local LDC enterprises (Hone, 1974; Sharpston, 1975; Sprietsma, 1978; Jarrett, 1979). Fourth, in some of the larger and more advanced LDCs, some import-competing manufacturing industries (both local firms and MNEs) have been transformed into successful exporters.[4]

Scattered information suggests that MNEs account for a moderate proportion (20–30 percent) of the manufactured exports from some successful LDC exporters, less from the other LDCs (Nayyar, 1978; Blomström, 1990). De la Torre (1972) showed that in several Latin American countries exports of differentiated manufactures encounter marketing barriers to entry in industrial-country markets, and so smaller proportions of these outputs are exported than the proportions of undifferentiated manufactures. But subsidiaries of MNEs enjoy advantages against these barriers, therefore exporting larger proportions of

countries with tastes and factor prices less distant from those of their industrialized home bases.

[4] Helleiner (1973, p. 26) noted that MNEs have been firm supporters of regional free-trade arrangements among LDCs because of the resulting opportunity to rationalize small-scale facilities and develop exports.

their outputs than local firms and accounting for larger shares of exports of such products. Lee (1986) confirmed this statistically by showing how the inter-industry determinants of offshore-processing activities differ between developed and LDC host countries. Distribution channels controlled by the manufacturer and quasi-contractual linkage between distributor and customer are more important positive predictors of offshore processing in the LDCs; also, the industry's labor intensity favors the LDCs.

The contrast between export-oriented and local-market subsidiaries extends to many facets of their activities. They of course differ in the general types of incentives that affect the MNE's investment decision. The export-oriented investments are footloose and are determined largely from unit labor costs (Reuber et al., 1973, pp. 115–20; Nankani, 1979).[5] Flamm (1984) modeled this footloose property in terms of portfolio adjustment by the parent MNEs, concluding that actual speeds of adjustment are indeed quite rapid, but expectations about relative costs of producing in different locations are not volatile.

Some differences appear in the financial flows of the two types of investments. Reuber et al. (1973, pp. 87–97) found that local-market subsidiaries rely more than do export-oriented projects on funds secured in the LDC. The funds supplied by local partners account for part of the difference, but it should also matter that export-oriented subsidiaries have little incentive for local borrowing to hedge assets whose yields ride on the real exchange rate of the local currency (Shapiro, 1975a). Reuber et al. found no robust difference in the average profitabilities of the two investment types. Export-oriented investments show higher nominal profitability (not robust, in their statistical analysis), but local-market subsidiaries remit much larger percentages of earnings as royalties and fees and surely face in greater measure the regulatory incentives for manipulative transfer pricing discussed in Section 8.4. Chen and Tang (1987), however, concluded from an analysis of frontier production functions that the average efficiency of export processing businesses in Taiwan (relative to inferred best-practice) is about one-fifth higher than the average efficiency of businesses serving local markets. Chen and Tang (1986) also showed that subsidiaries in Taiwan exporting most of their output are about the same size as those serving local markets but substantially more labor-intensive, as Taiwan's comparative advantage would suggest.

[5] Of course, low unit labor costs are not the same thing as low wages. Therefore, statistical studies of the relationship between foreign investments in host countries and their wage rates have yielded mixed results. Riedel (1975) found that foreign investment in Taiwan does depend on wage differentials between Taiwan and the investing country. Jarrett (1979, Chapter 8) did find that more offshore procurement tends to occur among low-wage countries. But studies of the intercountry distribution of foreign direct investment itself, such as those of Nankani (1979) and Dunning (1980), generally have found no relationship at all or even a positive relationship between foreign investments and host-country wage levels.

Export-oriented and local-market subsidiaries also differ in a few strategic operating characteristics. Reuber et al. (1973, pp. 82–7) found that the MNE parents hold significantly higher fractions of equity in the export-oriented subsidiaries. The difference arises partly from public policy, partly from the MNEs' own preferences. LDC governments frequently demand that MNEs take on local partners in joint ventures. MNE's generally resist this (more in some settings than in others, as we saw in Section 3.4), but local entrepreneurs obviously can prove more useful allies when the project aims to serve the local LDC market. Export-oriented MNEs are likely to be especially resistant if the subsidiary produces components or undertakes processing for transfer to the parent or other affiliates. Furthermore, MNEs situating footloose export-oriented subsidiaries surely enjoy a stronger bargaining position in dealing with potential host governments and so can avoid being bedded down with unwanted local partners.

LDC government incentives and requirements

The influence of government incentives on direct investments in LDCs is important for its potential to distort MNEs' location choices and affect the welfare of the LDCs themselves. Reuber et al. (1973, pp. 120–32) emphasized the variety and types of incentives that had been offered by host countries to the projects they surveyed.[6] The incidences of various incentives found by Reuber et al. were as follows: tariff protection, 34 of 76 cases (the mean tariff rate was 68 percent); import-quota protection, 34 of 77; tariff reduction on imported equipment, 43 of 78; tariff reduction on imported components, 29 of 75; tariff reduction on imported raw materials, 26 of 76; tax holiday, 37 of 80 (mean length five years); accelerated depreciation for tax purposes, 20 of 71; public provision of infrastructure investments, 18 of 70. The forms of assistance show some natural correlations with the type of investment. Export-oriented investments tend to receive the tax holidays and infrastructure investments, domestic-market projects protection from competing imports. Correspondingly, the MNE respondents often saw import protection as essential to inducing their local-market investments, and financial incentives as important for inducing export-oriented investments.

Overall, Reuber et al. (1973, pp. 127–32) did not accord these various inducements a vital role in inducing foreign investment, and they noted that previous empirical studies had led to a mixed evaluation.[7] For one thing, companies tend to discount inducements on the presumption that what the government gives with one hand it may well take away with the other. Also, some

---

[6] Indeed, 22 of the 80 projects surveyed were initiated because of requests from the host governments (pp. 77–80).

[7] See Reuber et al. (1973, p. 131, note 53) and Cohen (1975, Chapter 4). Bond (1981) pointed out that tax holidays induce firms to exhaust their capital services by the holiday's expiration, or to liquidate then and sell their secondhand assets to a new firm.

evidence suggests that government's efficiency and predictability in dealing with MNEs (something on which the government cannot readily bargain) weighs quite heavily relative to the specific inducements put forth. For example, Murtha (1991) demonstrated that foreign subsidiaries purchasing from suppliers who are beneficiaries of the host government's industrial targeting pay close attention to the government's reputation for policy consistency; the subsidiaries' investments in assets specific to transactions with these suppliers decrease with the frequency of disruptive interventions by the government. Nonetheless, the most thorough study of hosts' incentives to foreign investors, Guisinger and Associates (1985), concluded that 50 of 74 closely studied investments in 30 countries (not all LDCs) had been influenced by host-government incentives. The proportion is actually higher for investments oriented toward domestic markets (78 percent) than investments oriented toward export markets (58 percent), although the carrots offered to foreign investors serving local markets are usually accompanied by sticks of types described subsequently. The length of tax holidays significantly determines the locations of foreign investors among Caribbean nations, according to Woodward and Rolfe (1993).

A recent study (UNCTC, 1991a) documented the general relaxation of LDC hosts' controls on foreign direct investment over 1977–87. It also developed a panel-data analysis of the responses of aggregate foreign investment flows (new equity, retentions, and intracorporate loans) to these changes, finding significant positive effects of more favorable terms of both taxes and performance requirements. Indicators of other classes of policies were not statistically significant, consistent with those policies being applied in a discriminatory case-by-case fashion (among other explanations). Among control variables a risk indicator took a significant negative coefficient for LDCs other than the newly industrializing countries. UNCTC (1991a) also showed that the stringency of controls on foreign direct investment fluctuates with the country's rate of economic growth (i.e., foreigners are welcomed when economic conditions are poor).

Another contribution of Guisinger and Associates was to document the competition of host countries to attract foreign investors. Governments not only compete in the general classes of incentives that they offer (some portfolios contain as many as 30) but also get into bidding rounds for particular MNEs. Rivalry tends to be sharpest among similar and nearby countries. It favors foot-loose activities, and inducements increase with unemployment in the host and with the paucity of MNEs currently looking for sites. Hosts tend to favor subsidy instruments that can be tailored to discriminate among individual foreign investors.

A comprehensive inducement for foreign direct investment in exporting activities is the export-processing zone (EPZ). These zones are simply a device for bundling together many concessions from the host country's prevailing taxes, tariffs, labor regulations, and the like. The government can thereby relax onerous regulations that it does not wish to repeal outright (Wall, 1976). Baerresen (1971) described Mexico's experience, Warr (1987) evaluated the Philippines', and Fröbel et al. (1980, Part III) undertook an extensive international inquiry. In the countries for which data are available, garments, textiles, and electrical goods account for three-fourths of the activity. Fröbel et al. also described the West German garment industry's participation in these foreign investments, indicating a trend toward more and smaller German firms going abroad, and increasingly toward low-wage countries as recipients of these investments. Woodward and Rolfe (1993) determined that EPZ acreage is a significant determinant of the distribution of foreign investment among Caribbean host nations. Fröbel et al. (pp. 139–41) and Baerresen agree that worker productivity in EPZs closely approaches its level in the MNEs' national home bases. Ranis and Schive (1985) found that in Taiwan EPZs mobilized foreign direct investment to play an important catalytic role in the transition from import-competing to export-oriented industrialization.

Hamada (1974) analyzed the EPZ theoretically in the context of the two-sector Heckscher-Ohlin model of international trade. The small, labor-rich LDC exports the labor-intensive commodity and imports the capital-intensive one. The LDC that imposes a protective tariff on imports impairs its economic welfare, because it is too small to improve its terms of trade thereby. MNE capital flowing into the LDC's domestic economy simply shifts the output mix toward the import-competing capital-intensive good, leaving the private incomes of domestic factors of production unchanged but the country as a whole worse off (because the government would no longer collect customs duties on the displaced imports).[8] If the MNE capital instead enters the EPZ, exactly the same thing happens: Now it attracts labor out of the domestic factor endowment instead of adding capital to it, with the same unfavorable effect on welfare. One senses that the Heckscher-Ohlin model, with pure competition and all factors of production fully employed, captures little of the institutional setting of the LDC economy; in his survey of empirical evidence on EPZs, Balasubramanyam (1988) argued that the prevailing evidence of structural unemployment in LDCs and elevated wages in the EPZs suffices to put the negative welfare implications aside. Hamilton and Svensson (1980) tried to improve things by making capital sector-specific in what is otherwise the same simple two-sector model. An inflow of MNE capital to the LDC's export sector then will improve the LDC's economic welfare, and an inflow to the EPZ may do so, but the outcome depends on some hard-to-interpret technical conditions.

Another aspect of investment incentives that raises both theoretical and empirical questions is the performance requirements that are commonly linked with subsidies and incentives offered to import-competing foreign investments.

---

[8] Many extensions to this model are discussed in Section 9.2.

Half of the investments studied by Guisinger and Associates (1985) were subject to requirements that involve either export targets (or requirements to balance foreign-exchange earnings and uses) or minimum content levels for locally produced inputs. If these requirements impose binding constraints, they raise the costs of the foreign subsidiary (to purchase overpriced locally produced inputs, or to subsidize unprofitable exports). If the subsidiary competes against a domestic rival, the host country gets a profit-shifting gain, although it might suffer a net loss if the local inputs or the exports in fact are inefficient when valued at proper shadow prices (Davidson et al., 1985).[9]

Export-performance requirements were analyzed in general equilibrium by Rodrik (1987), who assumed that the subsidiary must export some fixed fraction of its output in a two-good, two-country model with specific factors of production. An increase in the mandated share of output exported then has various welfare effects for the host: The subsidiary reduces its output, which raises host welfare because the tariff-protected subsidiary's output itself generates a welfare loss; the associated reallocation of domestic factors of production can involve a gain (especially in a specific-factors model); profit-shifting to domestic enterprises competing with the subsidiary also involves a gain. Despite this net benefit, Rodrik showed that the increase of welfare with the export requirement eventually ceases (i.e., an optimal value exists).

Observers commonly deplore the redistributive effects of the competition among host governments to secure foreign investments (recall Chapter 8's discussion of tax competition). Their effect on global efficiency, however, is not necessarily negative. Given that governments engage in many surplus-redistributing transactions with firms (taxes, mandated activities, public services), under certain assumptions the government that can offer the sweetest deal to a foreign investor is controlling the site at which the investor's activity will be most productive (see Bond and Samuelson, 1986).

Local ownership requirements

Another policy common in LDCs and some industrial countries is that MNEs founding subsidiaries sell or provide some equity to local partners. This policy seems to stem from nationalistic preferences (see Chapter 10) and does not evidently recognize the trade-off for the host between tax revenue and nationals' control of business units (Katrak, 1983*b*). We saw in Section 3.3 that without policy intervention the MNE prefers a joint venture to a wholly owned subsidiary under some circumstances. Even without a local-ownership policy, the riskiness of LDC conditions can itself cause the MNE to forgo full ownership, as can sociocultural distance between source and host countries (Gatignon

---

[9] Again, evidence developed in UNCTC (1991*b*) suggests that these trade-performance requirements are used flexibly to extract surplus from MNEs, and thus imposed less frequently than their prevalence on the LDCs' statute books suggests.

and Anderson, 1988). Beyond this unconstrained choice the MNE might encounter requirements or incentives for a higher level of local participation. Statistical analyses by Fagre and Wells (1982), Lecraw (1984), and Gomes-Casseres (1990) are notable for distinguishing between the MNE's unconstrained preferences on ownership and the bargaining relationship that might induce it to settle for less (also see Grieco, 1984; Kobrin, 1987; and Contractor, 1990).

Fagre and Wells inferred the MNE's ownership preferences from its choice in host countries that impose no local ownership requirements, while Lecraw employed a refined definition of the bargaining range defined by the lowest local share the host government had accepted for any previous foreign subsidiary and the highest that the MNE had tolerated in any of its subsidiaries in the region (Southeast Asia). Within this bargaining range Lecraw found the MNE does better if it enjoys technological leadership, has a strong goodwill asset (advertising intensity), exports heavily from the host country, and finds the host country not a particularly attractive business location (the MNE manager's subjective evaluation).[10] The MNE does less well the more MNEs from its base industry had previously invested in Southeast Asia. Weak evidence suggests that larger subsidiaries do better. Fagre and Wells reported similar results, including the finding that the U.S. MNE does better, the fewer firms operate in its three-digit industry in the United States. Gomes-Casseres simply ran his cross-section analysis of joint-venture choices separately on subsidiaries in host countries that do and do not restrict full ownership by the MNE. Significant predictors of the joint-venture choice in the restricting countries are previous operating experience in the host country (positive) and the recent prosperity of the host economy (also positive). Interestingly in light of the obsolescing bargain discussed in Section 4.4, operation in a resource-extraction activity induces taking on local partners in all countries, not just those with policies of restricting foreign ownership.

These statistical studies of observed ownership patterns do not reveal dynamic aspects of the issue that appear in some case studies. Mytelka (1979) reviewed the experience of the Latin American Andean Group of countries with their Decision 24, which in effect sought to stiffen each member's resolve about confining MNEs to minority ownership positions. It specifically denied benefits of the group's trade liberalization to nondivesting subsidiaries. Those benefits were not large for most firms, and Mytelka concluded that Decision 24's effects on ownership and investment inflows were small. Martinussen (1988) analyzed experience with India's Foreign Exchange Regulation Act (1973), which put a ceiling of 40 percent foreign ownership on nonexempted sub-

---

[10] Regarding the higher MNE ownership shares in exporting subsidiaries, we note the theoretical result (Katrak, 1983b) that the MNE capable of serving a market from either a wholly owned or a partly owned subsidiary might discriminate against the latter.

sidiaries, attempting to drive foreign investors out of the consumer-goods industries. Companies' responses included increased remittance of dividends in order to repatriate some capital; also, equity was issued in such a way as to disperse holdings or place it in the hands of passive domestic investors and preserve control by the MNE. The inflow of new investment plunged as a result of the controls. Nonetheless, little contraction of the foreign-controlled sector took place. Martinussen (1988, pp. 83–4) quoted an interviewee: "It takes a long time to enter the system of licensing and controls, but once you are inside, you are protected and you can make very good returns."

9.2. **Effects on economic development**

The effects of foreign investment on the LDC host economy run from the narrowly microeconomic to the aggregative (savings, investment, growth of real income) to the political and social systems. We proceed along this array but stop short of the political and social, where neither economic analysis nor the organized stock of informed observation offers much help.

A common theme is the problem of second-best outcomes. Consider a foreign direct investment that is profitable and would raise world welfare if all markets in the host economy (and the source, as well) were largely free from distortions. When some distortion is present, however, the social evaluation of the MNE's investment can diverge from its private profitability. The distortion can go in either direction and is wholly specific to the situation: The MNE that invests to expand the output of a tariff-protected activity can reduce economic welfare; the MNE that invests and hires labor at a conventional or statutory minimum wage exceeding labor's opportunity cost generates greater social than private benefits (but cf. Batra, 1986). The literature on the effects of foreign direct investments in LDCs identifies many second-best problems but seldom supplies enough evidence to convince us that a substantial and confidently signed discrepancy exists.

Industrial structure and performance

The effects of MNEs on the structure and performance of LDC industries raise the same questions reviewed in Chapter 4, but their various weights differ to reflect LDC conditions. We draw on surveys of this diffuse literature by Lall (1978a) and Newfarmer (1985). Lall observed (pp. 226–9) that the correlation between the presence of MNEs and the concentration of sellers in the market, regularly seen in the industrial countries, prevails in the LDCs as well. It has the additional force of a historical basis in colonial powers' tendency to exclude or restrict entry by MNEs from other countries (Svedberg, 1981). However, most studies observing that correlation have not grappled with the problem of common causes giving rise to both foreign investment and high concentration, and so the conclusion usually stated that MNEs cause concentration is not automatically supported. Lall's (1979*a*) study of Malaysia did attempt this control. In consumer-good industries, the common-cause hypothesis prevails, but in producer-good industries, the presence of MNEs seems to wield a net positive influence on concentration.

The soundest way to determine the effects of MNE entrants on concentration is to follow industries over time. As Lall (1979*a*) pointed out, entry's initial effect of reducing concentration can be followed by an ultimate increase, and the normative significance of that increase depends on how it comes about. The best of the time-profile studies suggest several generalizations.[11] First, in some sectors the entry of MNEs (indeed, of modern industry generally) has brought the demise of artisan and small-scale local producers. This event resembles any displacement of a less efficient technology by a more efficient one, but of course the negative effects on the welfare of the displaced producers can attract national economic and cultural concern. The effects of MNEs' entry on local industrial competitors are largely consistent with Chapter 4's evidence about the market shares commanded by MNEs. In some industries MNEs hold decisive advantages, so local entrepreneurs either imitate them or are expelled; this pattern applies especially to advertising-intensive industries (Jenkins, 1990, 1991, pp. 125–8). In other sectors, MNEs might claim moderate market shares but settle into a market equilibrium along with viable domestic competitors. The MNEs' subsidiaries typically are larger firms than their domestic rivals (e.g., Lall, 1978*a*, p. 232; Kumar, 1991), a finding that also holds for the less industrialized and smaller developed countries (such as Canada and Australia). Also, studies of individual markets (Evans on Brazilian pharmaceuticals) suggest that MNEs and domestic firms commonly carry out different arrays of activities when they compete in the same general market.[12] Some evidence suggests that MNEs' shares in LDC markets may, on the average, be rising. However, the world's population of MNEs is also growing, including those originating in LDCs (see Section 9.3); put in that context, a rising trend in their aggregate share does not have any necessary implications for seller concentration in the markets tenanted by MNEs.

One element in LDCs' concerns over the market activities of MNEs is the displacement of domestic entrepreneurs. If natives can learn the entrepreneur-

---

[11] Biersteker (1978, Chapter 6) on Nigeria, Evans (1979, Chapter 3) on Brazil. Also see Newfarmer (1979, 1980, 1985).

[12] The question whether or not these differences exist should itself vary predictably from industry to industry. Cohen (1975, Chapter 3), for example, undertook a rather unmotivated comparison between paired foreign-controlled and domestic firms producing 11 narrowly defined commodities in Singapore, Taiwan, and South Korea. The sample leaned toward simple manufactures and export-oriented production. In these sectors Cohen found no obvious differences in terms of share of output exported, wages, employee turnover, thickness of the value-added slice, or other descriptive features. Also see Gershenberg and Ryan (1978) and Riedel (1975).

ial ropes in a softer environment without MNE competitors, the argument goes, they can then spread their skills throughout the economy. The argument has sharp limitations,[13] but it does flag certain empirical issues. MNEs have been entering LDC markets more and more frequently by buying out local firms; indeed, this mode of entry is more common the larger the supply of "good" local firms to buy.[14] Concern therefore arises about the fate of native entrepreneurs in "denationalized" enterprises. Evans (1979, Chapter 3) noted a handful of cases in which bought-out entrepreneurs transferred their skills to other industries in which local enterprise suffered less or no disadvantage. Vernon (1976*b*) suggested that since World War II local LDC enterprises have become more viable competitors by sending managers abroad for business training.

A similar issue arises in connection with R&D done by MNEs and local firms. Although MNEs decentralize some R&D to subsidiaries' locations (see Section 7.1), partly in response to host-government pressures, levels of local R&D spending often are perceived as low by host governments. The implicit model of market failure holds that the skills acquired by nationals in undertaking R&D yield greater value for the national economy than their opportunity cost, presumably because not all rents from new knowledge of special local relevance get collected by the R&D proprietors, or because R&D skills somehow yield spillover value for other activities. If national firms undertake R&D at all, the evidence from Chapter 7 leads us to expect that their spending rates will be higher than those of local foreign subsidiaries. In their study of subsidiaries in Latin America Fairchild and Sosin (1986) determined that subsidiaries are more likely to use foreign engineering consultants and to hold licenses from abroad than domestic firms, but all rely on imported equipment, and domestic firms depend more on their own research. Evans (1979, Chapter 4) concluded that Brazilian domestic pharmaceutical firms have done reasonably well in developing local products, whereas the foreign subsidiaries depend on their parents' innovations.

Numerous studies also address differences in productivity and profitability between MNEs and local firms. The various sources of rents to MNEs' activities, identified in preceding chapters, imply that MNEs will on average be more profitable than competing single-nation firms, although that margin will vary from sector to sector. Lall's (1978*a*) survey concluded that most studies have found this difference, although in the more careful inquiries it has not always

---

[13] Nationals also learn the ropes by working for MNEs before venturing on their own. Also, the fact that nationals may rise to the occasion when put on their own mettle does not preclude learning more by watching the successes (and mistakes) of foreign managers.

[14] One implication of MNEs' lower opportunity costs of capital is that they will discount the expected future cash flow of a national firm at a lower rate than will its LDC owners and hence will be willing to pay more than their asking price.

proved statistically significant.[15] Aggregate data for the United States indicate no difference in the profitability of subsidiaries between developed countries and LDCs once the petroleum sector has been omitted (Leftwich, 1974). Although there are reasons why MNEs' activities should be more profitable in LDCs (risk premia, monopoly positions in small markets), there are also reasons why actual or reported profits in LDCs may be lower (regulations, transfer-pricing incentives). In any case, the prevailing pattern is for subsidiaries to show higher profits; those can be regarded as stable rents, as well-controlled studies such as Fairchild and Sosin (1986) find no difference in rates of growth or technology adoption.

Productivity comparisons raise many complex issues, some of which will be developed later, but they yield a few generalizations. Among the more advanced LDCs, MNEs seem to enjoy no intrinsic productivity advantage independent of the transaction-cost advantages that make them MNEs in the first place. This was shown most elaborately for Argentina by Vendrell-Alda (1978). Similarly, Tyler (1978) found no differences within most Brazilian industrial sectors, although MNEs seem to enjoy higher residual productivity when all industries are lumped together. Tyler's results associate the advantage with scale economies enjoyed by the MNE rather than with intrinsic efficiency. Lim (1976) found for Malaysia that large raw differences in capital utilization favoring the MNEs disappear when controls are imposed for various factors including the professionalism of management, while Negandhi (1975) also found no difference between foreign subsidiaries and comparable local firms. In the studies assembled by Ramstetter (1991) foreign subsidiaries and local firms in Thailand appear to use identical technologies, but with the subsidiaries more efficient (pp. 89–92); no advantage appears in Korea, where a sufficient explanation is public policy on activities open to MNEs (pp. 111–23). Studies using the methodology of frontier production functions have found that, after controlling for such factors as size and age of firm, foreign control accounts for no statistically significant difference in a firm's efficiency (Tyler, 1979; Pitt and Lee, 1981).[16]

Skills, wages, and employment

The next group of issues concerns the wages that MNEs pay, the training that they provide, and the level of employment offered. Although MNEs'

---

[15] Gershenberg and Ryan (1978); Willmore (1976); Lall and Streeten (1977, Chapter 6). Yoshihara (1976) applied no statistical tests to his extensive data on Singapore, but they seem consistent with no significant difference.

[16] The utilization rate for physical capital is commonly an important component of industrial efficiency in LDCs. Gershenberg (1986) investigated this issue in Kenyan firms, finding no significant ownership-related differential after controlling for size and industry.

affiliates are expected to pay the going local wage for labor of given qualifications, the statistical evidence (see Chapter 5) suggests that they pay, on average, higher wages in the LDCs. The survey of Reuber et al. (1973, pp. 175–6)
found that the majority of MNE respondents pay the prevailing wage, but an
appreciable minority pay more, and national surveys (e.g., Markensten, 1972,
pp. 88–93, 102–10; Willmore, 1986) typically have reported higher wages in
MNEs. In a careful statistical analysis Lim (1977) found the MNEs' wages in
Malaysia to exceed those of national companies, even with many variables controlled, although the excess comes in fringe benefits rather than the basic wage.
The normative significance of the wage differential is an open question. It may
involve the transfer of rents to the LDC work force. It may reflect a preference
of alien entrepreneurs for better "quality" workers, or those already accustomed
to industrial work in local firms (which suggests that the local firms' lower
wages may partly reflect training benefits). Neither of these cases involves any
transfer of rents to the LDCs except to the extent that foreign investment
reduces structural unemployment. Also, a negative corollary of any tendency
of MNEs to pay high wages is their incentive to import labor-saving technology that could be welfare-reducing (Berry, 1974; also see Lapan and Bardhan, 1973).

Some sources (e.g., Chen, 1983c, pp. 51–63) suggested that MNEs invest
heavily in training LDC labor. But training does not appear to be a major or distinctive activity of MNEs, and it bestows no benefits on the host country if employees themselves finance it through apprentice wages. Reuber et al. (1973,
pp. 172–4) found no evidence of apprentice wages; since rates of labor turnover
are high in the foreign subsidiaries,[17] MNEs apparently cannot capture all the
rents of the training that they provide. However, Svedberg's (1977, pp. 123–32)
analysis of the limited evidence available indicates that the aggregate value of
the resulting externality is small. Reuber et al. (1973, pp. 169–72) also provided
evidence on the use of native employees in skilled and managerial positions,
where any significant training benefits should accrue. Managerial and engineering positions had only a bare majority of nationals when the average project began, but the proportion had risen to 70 percent by the time of the survey.
This survey also showed that the skilled proportion of the work force is
much lower for export-oriented subsidiaries than for those serving the domestic market.

In industrialized host countries, the main labor-force issue has been the stability of employment. McAleese and Counahan (1979) explored this issue for
Ireland. They found ad hoc reasons why employment in foreign subsidiaries

---

[17] Other investigators (Cohen, 1973) disagreed, finding low rates of labor turnover among
foreign subsidiaries. Diverse patterns are likely, but subsidiaries that pay higher wages
can expect to reduce turnover. Host-country gains from rents to labor therefore trade off
against any gains from the circulation of trained personnel.

might be either more or less stable over a recession period than in domestic companies, but no compelling factor running either way. They found employment to be more stable in larger plants and in firms that perform a marketing function locally (and perhaps thereby able to "manage" demand somewhat), but no difference associated with nationality.

Choice of technology

A suspicion commonly voiced in LDCs holds that MNEs create too few jobs because they fail to adapt their technologies, designed for industrial-country wages and capital costs, to the factor prices prevailing in LDCs. This issue has been extensively investigated, perhaps because the thought of capital and labor optimally combined can drive economists to ecstasies that other humans find baffling. It involves not just MNEs but also whether technology developed in the industrial countries gets adapted efficiently by whatever LDC firms employ it. As Lall (1978a) suggested, the issues boil down to whether or not the advanced-country technologies familiar to the MNEs (1) are economically adaptable to the LDCs' conditions of labor abundance, (2) are in fact adapted by MNEs, and (3) are adapted better than by local firms.[18]

The first question gets only a general answer here. The labor intensity of a production process can be quite inflexible: There is only one way to make x, or only one that is efficient over a wide range of factor prices. Alternatively, technologies might be adaptable to LDCs' factor prices, but only with an investment in devising and developing the technology that is large enough to deter the individual firm. Why, then, does some firm not make the adaptation and license the results profitably throughout the LDC world? The limitations of the market for proprietary technology (see Chapter 7) supply one answer. Also, technology can be specific to many local conditions besides relative factor prices.[19]

Some direct surveys address MNEs' adaptations to LDCs' local cost conditions. Reuber et al. (1973, Chapter 6) reported that MNEs make adaptations of technologies rather infrequently, the process technology being unchanged in 73 percent of their cases, quality-control systems being unchanged in 83 percent. Courtney and Leipziger (1975) employed an interesting statistical research design that compared the technology choices of foreign affiliates of U.S. MNEs in LDCs and in industrial host countries. They determined whether or not the two sets of subsidiaries appeared to operate from the same production function and, if they did, whether or not the LDC subsidiaries adopted more labor-intensive technologies appropriate to their surroundings. In most industries

---

[18] For more complete surveys, see Lall (1978a), Chudson and Wells (1974), Moxon (1979), and Jenkins (1990).

[19] Grossman and Razin (1985) presented a rather contrived model in which MNEs choose more capital-intensive techniques because holding capital in different countries is an effective way to spread risks

more labor-intensive technologies were chosen in the LDCs; in some cases the underlying production functions seemed to differ, in others only the equilibrium capital-labor ratio chosen along a common function. In a study similar to Courtney and Leipziger's, Lipsey et al. (1982) showed that foreign subsidiaries of U.S. and Swedish MNEs choose capital-intensities that increase with host countries' wage rates, after controlling for the industry and scale of operation.[20] Yeoman (1976) found the amount of adaptation to vary greatly from industry to industry, which could be due to intrinsic differences in technology.

Several results confirm that adaptations of technology are costly, so that only the inexpensive or the necessary ones get made. Yeoman (1976, Chapter 6) suggested that adaptation takes place only in activities where the potential effect on the product's unit cost is substantial. Reuber et al. (1973) and Martinussen (1988, pp. 153–4) found that adaptation frequently is to the smaller scale of operation in LDC markets rather than to different factor prices. Morley and Smith (1977a), Hughes and You (1969, pp. 193–4), and Chen (1983c, pp. 148–9) also found that a lot of adaptation takes place, but mostly to small scales of operation. Strassmann (1968) reported fairly widespread use of secondhand machinery by MNEs in Mexico and Puerto Rico – a low-cost way to access the lower capital-intensity of the last generation of industrial-country technology (Markensten, 1972, pp. 97–101). Both MNEs and domestic companies tend to stick with machinery from their own nations (Morley and Smith, 1977b; Lecraw, 1977), possibly due to the transactions costs of worldwide search for other wares. Forsyth (1972, pp. 124–7) suggested that the amount of adaptation increases with the subsidiary's age and experience. However, Chen (1983c, pp. 102–19) argued that in Hong Kong's efficient input markets there is no reason to expect different technology choices, and in a well-controlled study none appear except in the garment industry, where they can be ascribed to different products.

If MNEs do some (but not much) adopting of technology to LDCs' cost conditions, how do their input choices compare with those made by local firms? Numerous studies found differences, although only a few controlled for many contributing factors (Jenkins, 1990). Without control for industry mix, for example, MNE plants might be capital-intensive because they operate in more capital-intensive industries. Even with industry mix and perhaps other variables controlled, the results are still diverse. Morley and Smith (1977b) found foreign firms more capital-intensive in about half of the industries they analyzed, and size differences were not involved. Examining a small number of matched pairs of MNEs and local companies in Mexico and the Philippines,

---

[20] The factor-price conditions of the source country apparently can also matter. Ranis and Schive (1985, pp. 115–16) found that Japanese subsidiaries are more labor intensive than U.S. subsidiaries in every broad Taiwanese industry, and in both domestic-market and export-oriented investments.

Mason (1973) found the subsidiaries to be more capital-intensive on both stock and flow measures of capital. Wells (1973) identified specific technologies, so that the choices made by his Indonesian firms could be unambiguously classified; four-fifths of the foreign firms chose the capital-intensive technology, but only one-tenth of the local firms. Forsyth and Solomon (1977) (also see Solomon and Forsyth, 1977) found a similar difference for Ghana, as did Biersteker (1978, pp. 123–9) for Nigeria.[21] Most studies not reporting the result, such as Pack (1976), Cohen (1975, Chapter 3), Riedel (1975), and Chung and Lee (1980), were based on industries not heavily tenanted by MNEs or export sectors in which MNEs are expected to implant labor-intensive processes.

These studies suggest several explanatory factors. MNEs might face different factor prices. MNEs might rationally not base their technology choices on local capital costs, and several papers that found MNEs more capital-intensive also report that they pay higher wages (Wells, 1973; Mason, 1973; Forsyth and Solomon, 1977; Biersteker, 1978, pp. 137–42). Labor-intensive processes incur increased costs of supervision and coordination that can easily offset their ostensible advantages (Strassmann, 1968). A monopoly market position mutes the incentive to adapt efficient technology (Wells, 1973; Yeoman, 1976; White, 1976). Wells (1973) argued that an absence of market pressure allows playroom for "engineering man," who relishes technical sophistication for its own sake. However, monopoly cases blur into those for which capital intensity serves to maintain quality control of a product subject to a worldwide trademark (Wells, 1973; Keddie, 1976), and it is not clear that a technical-inefficiency explanation is needed.

Several studies classified the enterprise population more elaborately than MNE versus local. Forsyth and Solomon (1977) divided national enterprises in Ghana into those owned by natives and those owned by resident expatriates. What factor-intensity differences they found distinguished native-owned firms (less capital-intensive) from all others, suggesting that something other than entrepreneurial residence may be involved. Morley and Smith (1977*b*) made two-way comparisons among U.S., West German, other Western European, and national firms in Brazil. Value added per worker turned out to be greater for U.S. MNEs than for other MNEs, and greater for MNEs than for national firms. They concluded that these differences reflect some unknown combination of factor proportions and outright efficiency.

Linkages

A concept stressed in the literature on development is linkages of input-output relationships extending back from the purchases made by a firm and forward through the inputs that it supplies to other processes and activities.

---

[21] Lecraw (1977) concluded that LDC-based MNEs operating in Thailand make more efficient adaptations than do developed-country MNEs.

The implicit assumption is that many cells in the input-output table of a developing country are empty for lack of entrepreneurial effort or other requisites. Encouraged by a specific demand for an output or a concrete supply of an input, a viable activity may spring up. MNEs' critics in the developing countries claim that MNEs do not generate enough of these linkages (Singer, 1950). Although this proposition is not itself operational, some factual evidence does appear that can be related to the behavior that we expect of MNEs. Studies of foreign subsidiaries in industrial countries indicate that their purchases of inputs from the host-country market tend to increase as the subsidiary matures (Safarian, 1966, Chapter 5; Forsyth, 1972, p. 115; McAleese and McDonald, 1978). LDC governments take some of the rents they can extract from MNEs in the form of requiring more local inputs. Case studies such as UNCTC (1992*b*) on Mexico show that local subcontracting of inputs is undertaken largely to minimize costs, only partly under imposed obligations, and the main contractors extensively provide training in quality control and technical assistance (pp. 42–5). Activities undertaken by MNEs differ considerably in terms of linkage potential; MNEs doing labor-intensive processing of components for export buy few local inputs, only half as much as other projects according to Reuber et al. (1973, Chapter 5). Most of their respondents claim no forward linkages, but a substantial minority boast (perhaps self-serving) of encouraging numerous local distributors or sales organizations.

A few studies investigated these linkages statistically. Biersteker (1978, pp. 89–91) found that MNEs' affiliates in Nigeria purchase more inputs abroad than do native firms, but the difference stems mostly from MNEs' prevalence in newer products. Cohen (1973), who sampled closely paired foreign and domestic firms, also found that the foreign subsidiaries import more. Langdon's (1981) study of Kenya associated subsidiaries' reliance on imported inputs with quality control and determined that the inputs come principally from affiliates abroad. Buckley (1974), McAleese and McDonald (1978), and O'Loughlin and O'Farrell (1980) found that foreign subsidiaries in Ireland buy fewer local inputs than do national firms, especially if the subsidiary draws inputs from an overseas affiliate. Foreign subsidiaries make smaller (but increasing) proportions of their sales into the Irish economy (potential forward linkages) than do domestic firms.

Theoretical models have developed the point that foreign direct investment can raise productivity for the host LDC simply by enlarging its economy, in some models of underdevelopment. Rivera-Batiz and Rivera-Batiz (1990) assumed that the manufacturing sector (constant returns to scale) purchases business services as inputs, and each differentiated business service incurs a fixed cost of production (F). The productivity of the manufacturing sector increases with the number of business services available, which in turn is determined by the economy's (the manufacturing sector's) size relative to F. Inflows of direct investment then increase manufacturing productivity in two ways: By enlarging the manufacturing sector they make more business services viable; and by bidding down the economy's cost of capital they reduce the effective size of F. Malley and Moutos (1994) addressed the externality of increased employment that stems from inflows of direct investment (driven by the migration of new goods technologies as in Krugman, 1979) when the LDC host economy has an unlimited labor supply at a convention-driven opportunity wage. Lin (1993) estimated an econometric model across 23 semi-industrialized host countries to analyze linkages in a related model. Lin employed a two-sector model: an export-processing sector containing foreign affiliates and a domestic sector. The export-processing sector hosts MNEs' proprietary assets (their prevalence indicated by license and royalty fees remitted to the United States), and the growth of payments for those stocks (weighted by the export-processing sector's importance) indeed exerts a significant positive influence on aggregate output growth, with the growth of capital and labor controlled. The growth of the export-processing sector itself exerts an independent positive influence on aggregate economic growth, in the spirit of export-led growth models.[22]

Capital inflows, saving, and balance of payments

The next issue concerns the net contributions made by MNEs to the capital stocks of developing countries. Closely related is the effect of their financial activities on an LDC's balance of payments. The simple view of foreign investment as capital arbitrage contrasts sharply with the allegation made in LDCs that foreign affiliates borrow much capital locally, earn high profits, and soon are removing more capital from the LDCs than they imported at the outset. As we saw in Sections 5.2 and 6.4, drawing conclusions about these questions once again entails a tricky controlled-experiment issue. But the MNE is not primarily an arbitrager of capital, and risk-bearing considerations explain matching of local-currency assets and liabilities.

The qualitative finding that industrial MNEs are unimportant sources of net capital inflows is clearly established. The capital stock of the typical nonextractive subsidiary in a developing country is small (Cohen, 1975), and MNEs seem to account for only a small proportion of the capital inflow to some of the more successful LDCs, such as Korea (Westphal et al., 1979).

Whether the capital that MNEs bring to developing countries is "a lot" or "a little" may matter little for the LDC's welfare. If capital is indeed scarce and commands a high return, that reward tends to pass directly to the foreign investor (except for what the tax collector intercepts). The arbitrage premium does not raise the LDC's own national income. Indeed, an influx of MNE capital can lower the rate of return to domestic savers, depressing their rate of sav-

---

[22] The linkages investigated by Lin encompass the specific leakages and spillovers of MNEs' technologies, analyzed in Section 7.2.

ing and hence the growth rate of the LDC's national income. The same proposition can be stated in other ways: The reward to domestic labor might rise and that to domestic capitalists hence fall, reducing saving if only the capitalists save; or the MNE might preempt investment opportunities, discouraging local capitalists from saving in order to seize them. A number of studies investigated this relationship statistically. Using data for 21 developing countries, Areskoug (1976) related aggregate domestic fixed-asset investment to various sources of gross saving available to the economy – foreign private investment (including direct), government borrowing abroad, and domestic GNP (source of domestic saving). If a dollar of capital inflow is associated with less than one dollar of domestic investment, we can suppose that domestic saving was reduced somewhat and consumption increased. Areskoug found that for the typical LDC, both private foreign investment and government borrowing abroad produced a good deal less than a dollar of capital formation per dollar of inflow. This "leakage" appeared to be less in LDCs with more authoritarian governments, where agents in the private sector probably enjoyed less chance to make an economic response to the injection of capital from abroad.

Areskoug's results are generally consistent with those of a number of other studies that will not be reviewed in detail. However, one that holds particular interest is that of Weisskopf (1972). He accepted the familiar "two-gap" model of development planning, which suggests that the LDC's growth rate can be constrained either by the amount of savings available for investment or by the nation's foreign-exchange earnings available to buy development-related imports. Weisskopf identified those countries in which savings appear to be the binding constraint, and for them he estimated that a given net capital inflow from abroad prompts a 23 percent offset in the form of reduced domestic savings.

The two-gap model and the foreign-exchange constraint on development provide the basis for much critical discussion of the MNE's repatriation of profits and other payments (such as royalties). MNEs contribute foreign exchange when they first invest in the LDC, of course. The ongoing foreign subsidiary borrows locally, plows back its profits, but eventually remits cumulative earnings that may be large relative to its initial injection of foreign exchange. Its output may replace imports (and save foreign exchange), but its purchases of imports from abroad are a drain on foreign currency. Obviously, no general presumptions arise as to the effects of MNEs in the LDC that places a high shadow price on foreign exchange (see Section 6.4).[23]

Closely related to the foreign-exchange constraint is the body of literature investigating whether foreign subsidiaries or domestic firms import or export more (Willmore, 1986; Jenkins, 1990). This literature holds little interest for

---

[23] See Biersteker (1978, pp. 93–7) and Lall and Streeten (1977) for typical analyses. Bos et al. (1974) developed an ambitious model.

reasons implicit in Section 9.1: Whether a subsidiary does or does not import or export depends on the nature of the profit opportunity that it seeks to exploit, and without controlling for these opportunities one cannot predict any particular relationship of foreign ownership to trading activities. Willmore (1992) is a good example of a study that takes this conditionality problem seriously, to good effect. Petrochilas (1989, Chapter 7) modeled Greece's exports as depending on terms of trade and supply capability, with foreign direct investment contributing to supply along with domestic investment and technology inflows. Smits (1988) analyzed the cross-country association between direct-investment stocks and exports and imports (with GNP and population controlled): In small countries a significant positive relation exists between foreign investment and both exports and imports, although for the full sample of countries neither relationship is significant. The result presumably reflects MNEs' propensity to seek profit opportunities wherever they may be, with production for the local market holding greater attraction in large countries.

There is also evidence that MNEs respond with alacrity to both market and governmental incentives to shift their activities from the local to the export market. UNCTC (1992b) analyzed Mexico's 1982 reform, which removed many controls and regulations, imposed performance requirements on many foreign subsidiaries in the auto, computer, and office equipment industries, and at the same time heavily devalued the currency. During 1982–7 U.S. foreign subsidiaries increased their combined exports/sales ratio from 11 to 32 percent, much of this through interaffiliate trade. Survey respondents confirmed that the initiating change in public policy was accommodated by changes in strategy through the whole MNE.

Rate of growth

MNEs' effects on the LDC's rate of economic growth might seem to provide the ultimate relationship to be investigated. Unfortunately, it seems a rather ineffective focus for research. All the effects of foreign investment noted earlier can alter the LDC's real growth rate in various ways and pursuing the individual strands of influence beats trying to measure some amalgam of diverse effects, each with its own time structure of operation. No overall theoretical prediction connects the stock of foreign investment in the LDC to the rate at which its national income grows. Even if foreign investment should have spillover effects that raise the *level* of national income, these need not translate into an ongoing favorable effect on the rate of growth. If foreign investment generates a flow of investible tax revenues for the government, it can increase the growth rate. If it reduces the LDC private sector's rate of saving, it can lower the growth rate. Many other hypotheses are possible.

The empirical research on this topic has suffered both from this lack of theoretical guidance and in some cases from special pleading by the researchers.

It is generally agreed that the stock of foreign investment per capita is positively correlated among LDCs with GNP per capita, but that fact settles nothing about the causation involved or about the effect of today's stock of foreign capital on tomorrow's rate of national economic growth. An inflow of MNE capital, of course, enlarges the rate of growth as it affects gross domestic investment. Papanek (1973), for example, found that private capital inflows had about the same effect on growth (dollar for dollar) as did domestic saving and foreign short-term borrowing, although foreign aid seemed to have a substantially larger effect. But that direct effect of an inflow of MNE capital tells nothing about its indirect effects once in place.

The statistical studies of this issue, it must be said, bear strong imprints of their authors' prior beliefs about whether a negative or positive relationship would emerge. Kobrin (1977) postulated a positive influence of the foreign-investment stock on growth because avenues of progress are provided to nonelite nationals, and social modernization and progressive cultural borrowings are promoted. Numerous indicators of economic and social modernization for 57 LDCs were reduced by means of factor analysis to three components. There was no simple correlation between these factors (summarizing the degree of modernization) and the incidence of foreign investment. Nonetheless, when Kobrin (1977, Chapter 7) took account of the interaction between industrialization and foreign investment, he concluded that foreign investment "intensifies the relationship between social modernization and industrialization." But the methodology lacks control for the positive influence of modernization on the prevalence of direct investment, so that Kobrin's association (if we accept it) proves nothing about causation. Similarly, Blomström et al. (1992) confidently concluded that the growth of income per capita in LDCs (1960–85) is increased by the average ratio of the inflow of foreign direct investment to GDP over that period, on the basis of a significant positive regression coefficient in a model with reasonable controls for other influences. A limited analysis of lead-lag relations seems to support this finding, but the obvious two-way causation was not addressed directly.

Parallel problems arise in research of the doubters, such as Chase-Dunn (1975) and Bornschier (1980; also see Bornschier and Chase-Dunn, 1985). Both accept "dependency theory," which is a catchall term for all possible ways in which foreign investment might reduce host-country welfare and growth. Chase-Dunn related income per capita in 1970 (and several other measures of the level of development) across a number of LDCs to those countries' GNP levels per capita in 1950 and proxies for stocks of foreign capital per capita as of 1950–5. He indeed secured a positive relationship to 1950 income and a negative relationship to the stock of foreign investment. However, the levels of foreign investment and income per capita in 1950 are positively related to one another, and therefore this apparent negative relationship of subsequent development to foreign investment would emerge statistically even if there were no behavioral relationship between them at all. In short, the methodology is biased to produce the expected relationship. Bornschier (1980) recognized that an inflow of foreign investment produces an increase in real capital formation, but he expected that the established stock of foreign investment would negatively affect subsequent growth. His cross-sectional regression analysis, like that of Chase-Dunn, built in a statistical bias that tends to produce a negative relationship between nations' rates of growth of national income per capita (1965–75) and their stocks of foreign direct investment in 1965.[24] The relationship between a LDC's stock of foreign investment and its subsequent economic growth is a matter on which we totally lack trustworthy conclusions.

Tariff protection, import-competing foreign investment, and welfare

An issue that has attracted much theoretical research is the potential adverse effect on the small host country's welfare of inflows of foreign investment attracted to industries sheltered by tariffs. Inefficient production is enlarged, if foreign capital is paid its marginal product at tariff-inclusive domestic prices. Tariff revenue is lost to the government (although tax revenue might be gained). Welfare declines (Minabe, 1974). Brecher and Diaz Alejandro (1977) pointed out that this impairment of welfare will be reversed if the capital inflow proceeds far enough to affect domestic factor prices. Where the LDC's optimal tariff is positive, Svedberg (1977, pp. 43–52; 1979) showed that it might need to ban foreign investment in order to prevent welfare-reducing foreign investment (Markusen and Melvin, 1979, examined these issues in the context of a two-country model). On the other hand, Sechzer (1988) showed that a sufficiently high tariff can cause capital flows great enough that the overall effect is welfare-increasing. Other contributors to this large literature investigated the effects of trade restrictions other than tariffs (Buffie, 1985, 1987; Dei, 1985), other economic distortions such as unemployment (Brander and Spencer, 1987; Buffie, 1987; Grinols, 1991) or scale economies in the import-competing sector (Ishikawa, 1991), the presence of nontraded goods (Tsai, 1987), and strategic interactions between the tariff-setting country and a foreign monopolist (Levinsohn, 1989). Miyagiwa and Young (1986) addressed the problem in

---

[24] Bornschier included among his independent variables a measure of the cumulative inflow of direct investment (1967–73) relative to 1967 gross domestic product. But that inflow must have been positively correlated with the initial stock of foreign investment (also normalized by a variable closely related to national income). The growth rate of national income per capita was positively related to the growth of foreign investment, as Bornschier (and conventional analysts) expected. But, given that positive relationship between the growth of income and the foreign-investment inflow, the statistical method tends to produce a negative relationship between the growth rate and the initial foreign-investment stock, even if no behavioral relationship exists. The model in Bornschier and Chase-Dunn (1985) is similar.

the context of host countries with different economic structures joined in a customs union.

These theoretical models have their empirical counterpart in research on the benefits and costs of foreign direct investments. The analyses of Reuber et al. (1973) and Lall and Streeten (1977; see the summary and evaluation of Encarnation and Wells, 1986) concluded that substantial proportions of projects have negative social rates of return largely associated with tariff protection that attracts the MNE investors. Almost all export-oriented projects yield positive social rates of return. Encarnation and Wells (1986) themselves analyzed 50 projects, finding that all of the export-oriented ones yield positive benefits, 55 to 75 percent of the whole sample (depending on the assumptions made). The normative problem of tariff-induced foreign investments is thus a real one; its cause of course is not the MNEs themselves but the governmental decisions that distort price signals.

Consider instead a two-sector specific-factors model, with internationally mobile capital used only in manufactures, land used only in agriculture, and labor used in both. An exogenous inflow of capital under free trade is welfare-increasing. However, a tariff again causes it to reduce welfare, and the optimal tax on inflows of capital exceeds the (given) rate of tariff on imports of manufactures (Brecher and Findlay, 1983). If the exportable (agriculture) sector's specific asset were also internationally mobile, exogenous inflows would increase welfare even in the presence of tariff protection (Srinivasan, 1983). R. W. Jones (1984) pointed out that the result does not depend on the correspondence between home and foreign technology, the factor intensity of the imported commodity, or whether or not the inflowing capital is sector-specific.

9.3 Third-world multinationals

It was first recognized in the late 1970s that LDCs were beginning to sprout MNEs of their own. These apparently have expanded rapidly; no global data are available, but in Indonesia they recently accounted for 56 percent of foreign-investment projects approved by the government, while in 1967–77 they accounted for only 18 percent (Wells, 1993). A large literature has arisen on the properties of "third-world multinationals."[25]

Motives for foreign investment

The results are consistent with the transaction-cost analysis of the MNE amended with qualifications for the institutional conditions of LDCs. The

---

[25] Early investigations included Lecraw (1977), the chapters by Wells and Diaz Alejandro in Agmon and Kindleberger (1977, Chapters 5 and 6), Yoshihara (1976, Chapter 7), Heenan and Keegan (1979), Kumar and McLeod (1981), and Wells (1983). Aggarwal and Weekly (1982) and Agarwal (1985) provided literature surveys.

proprietary-assets approach on its face seems ill-attuned to LDCs as source countries, resting as it does on assets built up by research efforts and large investments in goodwill assets. The third-world MNEs do indeed possess proprietary assets, but with different properties from those common in industrialized countries. Some foreign investors possess technologies appropriate to third-world relative factor prices (Lall, 1983, pp. 51–61); Ferrantino (1992) found that the likelihood of Indian firms investing abroad increases with their own R&D expenditures but decreases with patenting activity in their industry in the United States.[26] The technology advantages of Hong Kong–based MNEs turn out to be product designs rather than technologies (Chen, 1983*b*). Those with marketing goodwill assets depend on capabilities for serving customers and not advertising-based goodwill (Lall, 1983, pp. 61–2). In general, third-world MNEs cluster in traditional manufacturing industries and not those associated with advanced technology or rapid growth. An exception is Arab MNEs, which tend to be capital-intensive and associated with the petroleum industry and the wealth that it generated (Nugent, 1986).

A second explanation of third-world MNEs' proprietary assets is entrepreneurial ability to operate in LDCs' institutional conditions (Euh and Min, 1986). Korean MNEs, for example, depend heavily on the ability to use cheap skilled labor to design and operate projects abroad at low cost (Kumar and Kim, 1984). Some evidence that supports this is indirect: Third-world MNEs move abroad when their growth opportunities run out in the source country due to market conditions (Katz and Kosacoff, 1983) or curbs imposed by the government (Aggarwal and Weekly, 1982). Foreign investment would not be attractive in such cases without some entrepreneurial advantage. A specific entrepreneurial capability important in export-processing activities is a reputation for prompt delivery of products meeting agreed standards of quality and/or uniformity (Wells, 1993). As a qualification of Chapter 1's transaction-cost model of the MNE, if entrepreneurial capability is a resource in inelastic supply (as in LDCs), foreign investment can occur simply because a nonnative entrepreneur can excel marginal native entrepreneurs.

Some foreign investments from LDCs fit the standard case of vertical integration either backward into securing raw materials or forward into the distribution of manufactured exports. Korea in this regard follows in Japan's footsteps (Euh and Min, 1986), and backward integration is also observed in Latin America (UNCTC, 1983*b*, p. 14).

A motive for foreign investment distinctly strong in LDCs is the spreading of risks. These include both political risks of governmental interference or instability and economic risks of exchange-rate and other disturbances. Some for-

---

[26] Ferrantino (1991) analyzed the advantage in technology adaptation theoretically.

eign investments substitute for forbidden outflows of personal capital to safe destinations; certain source countries permit foreign investments only by means of machinery exports, mandating a joint venture abroad to mobilize other inputs (Lall, 1983). On the other hand, Lecraw (1977) concluded that LDC-based MNEs are less sensitive to host-country risks than other MNEs, and that they have a comparative advantage in dealing with LDC-host governments.

Another distinctive feature of third-world MNEs is the occurrence of personal foreign investments, especially those of ethnic Chinese in Southeast Asia (Yoshihara, 1976, Chapter 7). Here the capitalists move with their capital, and the traits of the resulting enterprises are indistinguishable from those of host-country national firms (see Ranis and Schive, 1985, on Taiwan). At the opposite pole, Lecraw (1992) showed that foreign investment in export-oriented projects by Indonesian industrial groups is strongly complementary with each group's development in its home base as well: While foreign investments were occurring, the typical group also improved product quality, lowered costs relative to Indonesian rivals, and increased its capital intensity.

Destinations and activities in host countries

Strong regularities appear in the relationships between the source and host countries of third-world MNEs. These foreign investments flow from higher-income to lower-income developing countries. The host countries tend to be nearby and/or familiar nations: Indian firms to English-speaking and Argentine firms to Spanish-speaking countries. Ferrantino (1992) confirmed this and showed that the prevalence of source-country migrants in the host country is also a positive predictor. Several studies find source-country exports to the host a positive predictor of foreign investment, which could be for various reasons. Trade barriers are pervasively important influences on the location of third-world MNEs. These include not only the obvious host-country restrictions but also international regulatory regimes such as the Multifibre Arrangement in textiles, which induces firms in quota-constrained exporting countries to expand their outputs elsewhere (Chen, 1983*b*).

Joint ventures and minority participations seem to be much more common in the subsidiaries of third-world MNEs than among industrial nations' MNEs that possess strong proprietary assets (e.g., UNCTC, 1983*b*). Among the factors contributing to this are inexperience of the MNEs and thin administrative resources that cause subsidiaries to be left with considerable autonomy (Aggarwal and Weekly, 1982). Operating scales of the foreign subsidiaries are typically quite small – for this organizational reason and also the lack of scale economies in third-world MNEs' typical activities. This pattern holds despite the fact that large LDC firms are the ones most likely to make foreign investments (Lall, 1986). Comparison studies tend to find that foreign subsidiaries of third-world MNEs are less capital-intensive than subsidiaries of industrial countries' MNEs, and indistinguishable from local firms (Athukorala and Jaya-suriya, 1988).

9.4. Summary

This chapter addresses the causes and effects of foreign direct investments in LDCs. The foreign subsidiaries found in LDCs tend to divide sharply into those producing primarily for export and those serving the domestic market – a reflection of the small sizes of most LDC economies. MNEs are active in sectors where marketing entry barriers would otherwise limit LDCs' manufactured exports, as well as in sectors that undertake labor-intensive stages of processing. Subsidiaries that serve LDCs' domestic markets are found in about the same sectors as their developed-country counterparts. Export-oriented subsidiaries and domestic-market subsidiaries differ in various ways: The former are more likely to be wholly owned by the parents and less reliant on local capital markets; as expected, there are no systematic or average differences in their profitability levels.

Despite hostile rhetoric, LDC governments often offer substantial inducements to MNEs – tax holidays and infrastructure investments for the export-oriented, tariff protection for the import-competing. These inducements significantly affect locational choices. Economic theory casts a skeptical eye at LDCs' benefits from some of these concessions. If MNEs are lured into a small national market by an "inefficient" tariff, the investment inflow can reduce national welfare, but considerations of raising employment and host-country tax revenue can supply reasons for offering such inducements.

Systematic evidence on MNEs' effects on developing economies is not abundant. Foreign subsidiaries' relationships to surrounding market structures generally are similar to those found in industrialized countries. Although MNEs tend to populate concentrated sectors, they do not enjoy universal advantages over native entrepreneurs, nor do they always claim commanding market shares. National enterprises in the more advanced LDCs may do more R&D (if they do any at all), and native entrepreneurs who cannot compete successfully in sectors where MNEs are advantaged do flourish in other sectors.

MNEs on average pay higher wages in LDCs than do domestic enterprises, and they may provide some training for which the benefits accrue partly to nationals who receive it. But the evidence does not suggest that either the training or the extra wages provide a large stream of rents to LDC nationals.

LDC spokesmen voice concern that the technology of industrial countries is not adapted sufficiently to the labor-abundant conditions of most LDCs. Survey evidence indicates that MNEs do some adapting, but not a great deal, and it appears that the costs of adaptation commonly are high relative to the benefits expected by individual companies. Much adaptation takes inexpensive forms, such as the use of secondhand machinery, or occurs incidental to designing facilities for operation on a small scale. Some studies find that foreign subsidiaries use less labor-intensive techniques than their national competitors. They may adapt less where product quality depends on use of the parent's home technology, or where the market structure provides a less competitive spur.

MNEs' operations do not turn mainly on moving capital from where it is cheap to where it is dear, so they are not important sources of funds for capital-scarce LDC economies. Foreign direct investments, like other funds from abroad, tend to go partly into expanded consumption (reduced saving) in the host country, only partly into enlarging the host's capital stock.

Some researchers have tried to identify the overall effects of MNEs' presence in developing countries on the LDCs' subsequent rates of economic growth. The possible causal connections are numerous but speculative and ill-defined in terms of economic models. Empirical investigations, whether by those disposed to think good or ill of the MNE, have employed inadequate research procedures and have yielded no trustworthy conclusions.

Third-world MNEs differ from their industrial-country cousins in possessing proprietary assets well suited to LDC conditions, and in having the incentive to avoid risks or the ability to deal with them in LDC contexts. They are attracted to other (and nearby) LDCs, where they tend to operate at small scales in collaboration with local partners. They tend (especially the ethnic Chinese investments in Asia) to be little distinguished from local firms.

10

Public policy

The literature on public policy toward MNEs compels an approach different from that of previous chapters. To describe the policy issues and conflicts arising in each country touched by MNE activities would be a hopeless task. Therefore, we employ a telescopic approach that emphasizes not the substantive details of these issues but the behavioral context in which they arise. This chapter follows a two-pronged normative and positive strategy. First, the apparatus of neoclassical welfare economics supplies conclusions about what economic policies will maximize real income. The relevant results, most of them reported in the preceding chapters, are recapitulated in the first section of this chapter. In the following sections we shall attempt to apply economic models of political behavior to the actual dialogue over public policy toward MNEs.

10.1. National and international welfare

The preceding chapters set forth the neoclassical welfare economics of MNEs on the following assumptions: First, each national government seeks to maximize the real incomes of its citizens, taking other nations' policies as given. Second, decisions about distributing that income get made separately from decisions about maximizing the pie to be divided. (We did, however, note some theoretical connections between MNE activities and the functional distribution of income.) Third, each enterprise is assumed to have an unambiguous national citizenship, so that it maximizes its profits (or optimizes its profits and risks) in terms of one national currency and price set, and the nation's government can regard its maximized profit as a component of national income.[1]

---

[1] The third assumption has not been defended explicitly in this book. The great bulk of MNEs clearly keep their legal and administrative headquarters in single national locations where most of their beneficial shareholders also reside. A few well-known binational MNEs are exceptions. So are some individual proprietors of LDC-based MNEs,

Fourth, the MNE's proprietary assets lead it typically to face downward-sloping demand curves for its outputs (this assumption is sometimes applied to the source nation's competing MNEs as a group), and the host nation faces an upward-sloping supply curve of MNE resource commitments (in a sense that varies from model to model). Fifth, each country is assumed to make policy decisions on MNEs in its role as either source or host. The cross-hauling of direct investments makes many countries play both roles, but many policies can feasibly distinguish between domestic and foreign MNEs (subject to the equal-treatment obligations under treaties and the threat of retaliation by other countries).

The normative analyses presented previously, generally resting on these assumptions, lead to results that will be reviewed after a few preliminaries. Foreign investment indicates arbitraged resources. To the extent that the arbitragers seek profits, and market prices are undistorted, arbitrage is a productive activity until the margin is competed away. On that simple basis rests any general presumption that the actual allocation of MNE resources is efficient. The same conclusion flows in more qualified form from the transaction-cost model of the MNE. Where alternative methods of allocation – administrative or market – can compete freely, the resulting distribution of activity between MNEs and single-nation companies can make some claim to pursue an efficient outcome. The claim is qualified by sunk costs and transitory disturbances that can make the outcome path-dependent. At their best, the benefit-cost techniques of development planning can claim some usefulness for weighing the appropriateness of a foreign investment where shadow and market prices might diverge widely (e.g., Encarnation and Wells, 1986). Applications of benefit-cost analysis to MNEs, however, are seldom at their best. The approach usually dwindles into list-making, the listed items running to poorly defined economic benefits and politically defined costs.

A generally positive Darwinian assessment of MNEs is also qualified by the distinction between national and global welfare. Bhagwati and Brecher (1980) pointed out that the presence of MNEs qualifies the proper choice of many policies ostensibly unrelated to foreign investment, because the policy instruments redistribute income between domestic income recipients and foreign suppliers of equity capital. To take their simplest case, suppose that national policy aims to maximize national income, that the nation exports capital-intensive goods, that all workers are citizens, but that all capital is supplied by foreigners. Moving from autarky (no trade) to free trade will maximize domestic product, but it will reduce national income because the real wage falls while the real return to capital rises. Svensson (1981) assessed (rather negatively) the generality of

in that the entrepreneur may move with his capital when a foreign subsidiary is started. Finally, the increasing international diversification of securities portfolios chips away at the assumption.

their finding. Now we turn to a review of the normative conclusions from preceding chapters.

Taxation

Surely the most important case for positive government action toward MNEs lies in the field of taxation. Corden (1967), for example, stressed the density of assumptions needed to warrant a zero tax in a host country. If governments' revenue needs demand the taxation of profits, global-welfare maximization generally requires that all countries apply the same rate and that it apply to both foreign and domestic investments (see Chapter 8). For global welfare, it matters not which country, source or host, taxes the foreign investment income so long as the common effective rate applies. The divergence of national welfare from global welfare stems from two sources. The first grows from the host country's prior claim to tax the profits of resident subsidiaries. When investment flows to the host nation, tax revenue (and national income) is therefore transferred from source to host country. Optimal tax arrangements for the source require marginal equality between pretax returns to capital at home and returns abroad after payment of foreign taxes, which calls for giving MNEs a deduction rather than a credit for taxes paid abroad. Optimal policy for the host depends on the tax policies of source countries, but it generally involves setting a tax rate no lower than that (assumed common) of the source countries. One important qualification applies because the source country lets its MNEs defer taxes on foreign profits until they are repatriated. With deferral put in force, the host optimally lowers its tax rate below the source's but imposes a withholding tax on the dividends when they are paid to the parent. Tax competition can occur among countries, tending to cause underprovision of public goods and to shift tax burdens onto immobile factors. Alternatively, in countries that enjoy opportunities for exploiting monopoly/monopsony power in world markets for MNEs' services, optimal taxes will be higher, analogous to the "optimal tariff" on traded goods.

Taxes on capital interact importantly with tariffs on trade. Without the opportunity to annex tax revenue from abroad, the small nation (unable to improve its terms of trade) can lower its real income if its tariff induces a capital inflow to its capital-intensive import-competing sector, unless the capital inflow shifts its production structure enough to extinguish international trade (Brecher and Diaz Alejandro, 1977). This result is subject to many qualifications noted in Section 9.2. If all countries do tax capital, then the tariff becomes attractive for a small host country as a way to attract tax-paying capital,[2] although if capital is sector-specific, a particular tariff could fail by repelling more foreign investment from some industries than it attracts to

[2] The tariff is just one example of small profit-increasing market distortions that could play this role.

others (Corden, 1967). Finally, in the general-equilibrium context of the Heckscher-Ohlin model, the capital stock in a (large) country influences its terms of trade, and the individual country might either tax or subsidize foreign investment because of the indirect effect on the terms of trade (Jones, 1967). All these tax applications aim to improve national welfare at the expense of global welfare.

Transfer-pricing decisions by MNEs seek (among other things) to minimize the burden of taxes and tariffs paid by the company. Tax minimization redistributes real income between countries and will be condoned by one, condemned by another (their effect on global welfare depends on the optimality of the underlying taxes being avoided). A country whose taxes and tariffs create incentives for adverse transfer pricing makes an optimal outlay on policing transfer prices in relation to the extra revenue captured. An ad valorem tariff can deter strategic transfer pricing of imported goods or components.

Natural-resource rents

The economics of natural resources indicates that world welfare is maximized by the competitive extraction of nonrenewable natural resources by well-informed owners. Neither the owning country nor the using country gains from any different long-run program for extracting natural resources (although either would benefit from springing an unexpected monopoly or monopsony on the other). The efficient program for extracting resources leaves their owner with the maximum (present value of) scarcity rents. If the resource deposits are heterogeneous in quality or location, this same efficient allocation also yields differential rents to those deposits of better quality or more favorable location (than the worst in actual use). MNEs enter the picture as bargainers with owning governments over the terms of extraction (see Section 4.4). The MNEs have no general interest (barring global monopoly power) in departing from the efficient program for extracting the resource. But they gain from any rents they can capture from the resource-owning nation (as will the resource-using countries if they are the homes of the MNEs). For the resource owners, if the extracting MNEs are not their citizens, the problem is to capture all rents imputable to the resource, leaving only a normal rate of return for the MNE. A predetermined royalty rate is not efficient for this purpose because it distorts the operating firm's output decision. Other instruments include demanding a "free" equity share for the government at the outset, requiring a local joint-venture partner, taxing, or nationalizing the project once in place. Shifting rates of taxation – the obsolescing bargain – might offer the highest yield by annexing not just the rents but also the quasi rents (depreciation allowances) from the project, but the possibility of such expropriation halts the foresighted foreign investor in the first place, and the host has an incentive to commit not to use its taxing powers fully.[3]

Competition policy

Competition policy, like tax policy, encounters the dilemma of discordant national and international interests (Section 4.3). In the absence of other distortions, maximum world welfare requires competitive markets. National welfare is similarly maximized by competitive domestic markets. However, each nation gains if it can monopolize its sales abroad (exports, foreign subsidiaries, rental of proprietary assets) and monopsonize its foreign purchases (including those by its MNEs' foreign subsidiaries). Private-sector monopoly is as good for this purpose as taxes and tariffs, unless the current shadow price on government revenue is positive. However, the country might lack policy instruments to make an industry behave monopolistically in its foreign sales or purchases but competitively in domestic transactions. An intermediate degree of competition in both foreign and domestic markets is then optimal.

The nation has a parallel interest in fighting off exactions by foreign monopolists (monopsonists). A tax on monopolized imports might be helpful even if the foreign monopolist produces subject to constant costs (this depends sensitively on the shape of the demand curve); authorities should pay attention to whether or not the tariff induces the foreign seller to invest behind the tariff wall, which may or may not be desirable. If foreign subsidiaries take part in noncompetitive domestic industries, and competition policy is confined to high-priority situations, it should first attack MNE-dominated sectors if monopoly leads mainly to excess profits, but sectors dominated by domestic sellers if monopoly leads mainly to inflated costs (technical inefficiency).

An extensive literature from the past decade (surveyed by Krugman, 1989) addresses countries' opportunities for strategic profit-shifting policies in world oligopolies. Although most papers deal with trade policy rather than policy toward MNEs, the translation is typically straightforward. Core findings are that a country gains from any policy that can aid its national firm to shift to a higher-profit equilibrium in competition with a foreign rival. The policy instrument is (generally) a tax or subsidy applied to the home firm that modifies the home firm's behavior and indirectly causes the foreign rival either to reduce output

---

[3] The source country without monopsony power lacks any instruments to help its MNEs to capture rents overseas. We can note the discussion over what the source can do to avert the obsolescing bargain. In the United States this issue has related to the Overseas Private Investment Corporation and to the use of various threats and punishments against countries treating U.S. MNEs in ways deemed unacceptable to the United States. See Bergsten et al. (1978, Chapters 9 and 13) and Haendel (1979).

(in Cournot competition) or increase price (Bertrand competition). The action might aim to affect the market equilibrium either at home or abroad. This literature suffers from at least two major limitations. First, it addresses the policy option open to one country on the assumption that the foreign nation (which loses from the policy change) remains passive. Depending on the model, rivalry in industrial policy can leave both countries worse off and calls for a coalition on the globally optimal policies noted above. Second, as a practical matter, the policy prescription (tax or subsidy) depends on the mode of competition in the global industry, a matter that is not obvious empirically.

Technology creation and transfer

Technology policy toward the MNE can be regarded as either very simple or very complex. To make it simple, dwell on the analogy to the economics of the patent system. The outlays on innovation and the dissemination of innovative results that will maximize social surplus diverge from what profit-seeking firms will expend. The terms of the patent system can be optimized to minimize the discrepancy, although a discrepancy will remain. Buyers of innovative goods can, in principle, form a coalition to pay up as a lump sum the cost of investment in innovation, but the free-rider problem induces each to try to avoid payment. In relation to MNEs, the source country hopes to collect monopoly rents on technology sent abroad, the host country hopes to pay as little as possible, and no arrangement emerging from this interaction is likely to maximize world welfare. Specifically, each country underallows the tax deductibility of outlays on producing globally useful intangible assets. The presence of many source and host countries worsens the problem by amplifying the free-rider elements.

The complexities enter via the theoretical models described in Chapter 7, which suggest the following points: (1) The source country has a self-interest in establishing property rights in new industrial knowledge, which the free-riding host will tend to resist. (2) The source country should cheapen the dissemination of its knowledge stock if the resulting production changes will improve its terms of trade. (3) On restrictive assumptions the source country could command the same innovative rents whether it exports the innovation embodied in goods, lets its MNE monopolize the host's market, or licenses the technology; if production is subject to diminishing returns, however, using more than one of these instruments becomes attractive. (4) The source country can trust its national MNEs to maximize the foreign rents to the nation's technology unless they compete as suppliers of technology or they value incorrectly the probability of technology leaking from proprietary control when licensed abroad or used by a foreign subsidiary. (5) The level of foreign investment optimal for the host country is increased if the MNE's proximity raises the rate at which its technology leaks into natives' hands or induces the MNE to infuse technology faster to its subsidiary (see Katrak, 1994, on other welfare aspects of R&D performed by MNEs in host countries).

The discussion in this section certainly does not cover every normative issue bearing on MNEs; any close study of the questions affecting a particular country (e.g., Bergsten et al., 1978; Graham and Krugman, 1991) will expose many more. However, they bring out the form that those issues take and the prevailing divergence among global welfare, source-country welfare, and host-country welfare. This divergence, long a staple in the theory of tariffs, proves widely relevant, especially because MNEs tend to be prevalent in markets with few participants.

10.2. National policies: a behavioral approach

Traditional welfare economics assumes that the government wishes to maximize real income for its citizens and merely needs an economist's help with the technical details of its policies. The behavioral approach to public policy assumes, instead, that governmental decisions result from self-interested agents interacting in a political setting. This positive treatment of policy decisions leads to no single all-purpose model like that of neoclassical welfare economics, but the specific applications to date share a coherent general approach. Policy toward MNEs has not usually been treated behaviorally, so the following analysis is tentative.[4]

To propose an inductive behavioral approach to policies toward MNEs requires a brief sketch of the evidence that supports the induction. Host countries, especially developing nations, since World War II tended to hold a broadly suspicious approach to foreign subsidiaries that rested on a collection of both economic and noneconomic concerns (Vernon, 1977). In general this hostility receded since the 1970s, and regulatory policies manifestly took on a more clearly economic character (UNCTC, 1988a, pp. 239–329; 1991a). Several factors contributed to this major shift. In the LDCs the shift toward export-oriented development strategies, the pressures associated with the crisis over their governments' international debts, and the general retreat of interventionist ideologies were important factors. Among the industrial countries a significant factor was the increase in the symmetry of countries' positions as both sources and hosts of foreign investment. The United States illustrates this, having long seen its interest as a source country but quickly erupting in the standard suspicions of foreign investors as the country first became a major host nation in the 1980s (Kudrle, 1991, reviewed some major diatribes). Also sig-

---

[4] Writers such as Vernon (1977) and Stopford and Strange (1991, Chapter 4) would object that the following models overrationalize the political process and the coherence and consistency of government policy toward MNEs. The point is well taken for limiting one's expectations about how much policy toward MNEs can be explained from purposive models, but it does not rule out some systematic patterns.

nificant is the increasing density of alliances and agreements among MNEs of different nationalities, which effectively pools national interests (Cowhey and Aronson, 1993). The following treatment does not address these trends directly.

Host countries

We concentrate on countries in their host capacities, because policy toward resident foreign subsidiaries attracts more attention than policy toward overseas activities of the country's own MNEs. The policies implemented by or urged on industrialized host countries prove particularly suggestive. Many are not easily reconciled with the preceding prescriptions of neoclassical welfare economics, and so they cry out for other explanations.[5] They suggest two models:

1. *National preference.* The first model follows the research tradition by assuming a democratic political system in which the elected government, seeking to remain in power, proposes packages of measures expected to appeal to a majority of voters. Each vote goes for the package among those offered expected to yield the most utility to the voter. The voters as producers hold various equities in factor services that they supply, but one set of factor services, by assumption, yields income flows not reaching domestic voters: equities in the local subsidiaries of foreign MNEs. The government's package of measures can include various devices for redistributing income from the political minority to the majority, and these are expected to win approval up to the point where expected losses of income to the median voter due to inefficiencies of the redistributive devices offset that voter's gains from the redistributions. Because foreigners do not vote in national elections, pure redistributions away from foreign equity holders cause no negative votes and thus should proceed further than redistributions adverse to the interests of enfranchised minorities.[6]

A nationalistic preference can clearly enter into the voters' calculations. It might take various forms. In one formulation, voters experience disutility from perceiving that resource allocations in the national economy are influenced by foreigners (e.g., a foreign-subsidiary plant closes, costing workers their jobs). Freedom from perceived foreign influence thereby becomes a collective consumption good. The national electorate will then favor measures to reduce or

---

[5] Useful descriptions of these policies have been provided: Kindleberger (1969); Behrman (1970); Vernon (1971, Chapters 5–7; 1977, Chapters 6 and 8); Parry (1973); Hodges (1974); Safarian (1978); Organization for Economic Cooperation and Development (1978, 1980); Wallace (1982); Behrman and Grosse (1990); and Stopford and Strange (1991).

[6] Foreign interests do not vote in elections, but of course they make campaign contributions and exert political influence through other channels. Their successful rent-seeking subtracts from the national income (Graham and Krugman, 1991). In general the political influence of foreigners is sensibly regarded as discounted from that of equivalent domestic business units.

regulate this influence, again subject to the condition that real-income costs of the restriction do not outweigh the utility of the gain in perceived independence. In a slightly different formulation, citizens experience disutility when they see fellow nationals suffer losses from decisions made by foreigners, so that they will vote to reverse or regulate such decisions even when their welfare is not affected directly. Two arbitrary-sounding features of the model are in fact chosen advisedly. First, subjective perception of foreign influence is what matters; a disturbance emanating from an industry with many sellers, half foreign subsidiaries, could arouse less antipathy than the same one stemming from a duopoly with one foreign firm. Second, disutility from foreign influence on decisions could apply asymmetrically to the ones that impose losses on citizens, decisions that confer gains being ignored. This asymmetry accords with the general proposition that political decisions often seem to aim at preserving existing allocations (maintaining perceived equities) rather than maximizing the utility of the politically powerful (the so-called conservative social welfare function).

A different formulation of national preference holds that voters themselves prefer to deal with nationals and experience disutility from economic contact with foreigners. National preference in this version involves xenophobia, but not the aspect of collective goods invoked earlier. This form of preference could explain, say, a political decision to exclude foreigners from sectors bringing them into contact with large numbers of voters as stylers and sellers of consumer goods and services (broadcasting, publishing).

The national-preference model naturally leads into a consideration of interest groups, which provide an alternative way to think about political choice. MNEs (perhaps large companies in general) are commonly asserted to influence political decisions beyond their weight in voters' preferences. This proposition is best supported by the fixed cost of lobbying activities, which weighs less heavily on the large firm. In an inversion of this view, Hirschman (1969) argued that the political impotence of foreign entrepreneurs (undone by national preference) displaces the interest-group equilibrium from what would prevail if untainted native entrepreneurs sat in the same executive chairs. In this spirit, interest groups of domestic entrepreneurs may seek regulation or exclusion of MNEs as undesired competitors or, alternatively, may promote their expansion for rent-increasing effects on supply or demand in adjacent markets.

2. *Government policy.* The second model need not diverge much from the national-preference model, but we develop it differently in order to illustrate the analytical possibilities. Shift the focus from utility-maximizing electoral behavior to the utility of a coalition of government officials whose tenure in office is not explained within the model. Assume that the government pursues many policy objectives but lacks policy instruments that are reliably sufficient to attain them. Perhaps powerful interest groups prohibit or restrict policies that

unavoidably (if perhaps incidentally) harm their welfare. Perhaps norms of convention or constitution keep the government from imposing or fully enforcing theoretically sufficient policies. The government periodically wants to modify the economic allocations that result from market transactions, but the lack of instruments leaves it constantly shorthanded for making its allocative preferences stick. Private economic agents who can dodge its allocative designs become odious to the government. If MNEs enjoy better alternatives than nationals (they can spread the transaction cost of dealing with the government over more business, or when pressed can credibly threaten to cut back their local activities), they incur ill will with the government and invite overall restriction or special regulation of their activities.

The government-policy model can assume an electoral flavor if we suppose that the median voter prefers that the government's bidding be done, whatever its effect on that voter's welfare. Put simply, the median voter may believe that allocations sought by the government are intrinsically superior to those cast up by the market. In that case, any proposal to restrict or regulate MNEs wins approval, because the median voter's restraining concern with regulatory effects on real income (present in the national-preference model) is defined away.

These models of political behavior call for a systematic empirical test. Unfortunately, writers on policy toward the MNE generally have not considered the issue in this positivistic framework. Some simply offer descriptions, others polemics. Hence, the following assessment of the fit of these models is entirely tentative and impressionistic.

Both models seem to possess some explanatory power. The national-preference model accords particularly well with the cases in which a source government uses its MNEs to influence resource allocations within a host country. The invasion of sovereignty typically evokes a popular response in the host country that is quite disproportionate to the effect on real income, suggesting a preference for sovereignty per se. Similar resentment surrounds the MNE's decision to, say, reallocate production facilities from host A to host B; A's suffering at the hands of foreign decision makers begets a political reaction much exceeding what would occur if, instead, one independent national firm contracted in A and another expanded in B. The national-preference model also explains restrictions in some hosts (especially LDCs) on the foreign nationals employed by the MNE or the presence of MNEs in "nonessential" activity. All countries including the United States (Graham and Krugman, 1991, pp. 119–29) ban foreign control of firms in certain sectors: defense (obviously), but also others perceived to have broad significance for the economy or culture, such as banking and broadcasting. Chronicles of the controversies of MNEs' attempted acquisitions of domestic firms show repeated ad hoc instances of the targets claiming (or receiving) special status in the national interest; sometimes the claim has a clear basis in competition policy or other public interests, sometimes not (see the cases reviewed in Canada, Industry Canada, 1994). Exclusion of MNEs, however, can also respond purely to the preference of certain interest groups (local entrepreneurs) for shunning the competitive pressure of MNEs' rivalry in the market.[7]

The government-policy model also seems to hold a good deal of explanatory force. This fit is rather obvious for socialist governments openly disinclined to accept market allocations of resources. The model more interestingly explains behavior patterns of less interventionist governments that periodically find themselves short of policy instruments. One example is the exclusion of MNEs from policy-sensitive sectors, consistent with the government-policy model. Another is the policy of conditional national treatment currently popular among U.S. policy makers: Classes of benefits routinely provided to business firms are denied to those under foreign control unless the source government makes analogous benefits available to foreign subsidiaries of U.S. MNEs. Also consistent is the preference of some governments for using informal suasion on economic agents rather than laying down clear rules – a logical compromise when the policy goal in question is controversial or is in conflict with more general policies or precepts. The government then grows fearful that the foreign subsidiary may enjoy better alternatives than national firms to profit-reducing adherence to the policy, or that the MNE may simply hear the whispered hint less clearly. Observers such as Behrman and Grosse (1990) argued that host governments tend to hold rather stable neo-mercantilistic preferences that are implemented as opportunities permit. These preferences favor exports (and resist imports), the creation of jobs (especially in economically disadvantaged regions), and the development of technically sophisticated industries. The effort devoted to implementing these preferences tends to fluctuate widely in response to whatever perceived conditions drive the strengths of the preferences.

The government-policy model is consistent with the policy of screening individual foreign direct investments, implemented for a time by Canada and practiced in lesser (sporadic) degree in other industrial countries (Graham and Krugman, 1991, pp. 136–8).[8] Both as proposal and as practice, the screening of investments rests on no clear statutory criteria but simply requires the MNE to bargain with the government. If the host government has a well-defined welfare function (from whatever source), this bargain in principle permits it to capture surplus from the MNE in a Pareto-efficient fashion through an all-or-nothing offer. Practice appears vastly more ad hoc, with entirely nontransparent criteria and procedures. The bargaining in practice seems com-

---

[7] Japan's highly restrictive policies (now modified) contained both strands (Henderson, 1973).

[8] Consider Canada's regulatory practice in comparison with those employed by many developing countries. Compare Safarian (1978, 1985) and Robinson (1976). Also see Lombard's (1979) study of Colombia.

monly to turn on policy side-payments – exports, training or promotion of nationals, etc. – notably consistent with the government-policy model. Its expe-
dient character is confirmed in MNEs' own evaluations of the policy
interventions that they face (Poynter, 1985).

An empirical pattern of policy making related to both models is short-run
fluctuation of policies toward MNEs with the perceived state of the host economy. The government-policy model is consistent with unstable policies toward
MNEs: welcomed when policy instruments cannot conquer unemployment, restricted when conditions are good (UNCTC, 1991a). Such patterns were noted
in Canada's regulation of new foreign investments (Globerman, 1984) and
Venezuela's profit-threatening actions against U.S. MNEs (R. J. Jones, 1984).
The pattern emphasizes the paucity of instruments assumed by the government-
policy model but is not inconsistent with the national-preference model.

One good test of the national-preference and government-policy models is
their ability to explain a widespread host-country policy such as incentives or
requirements that the MNE take on local partners in its subsidiary, or yield control to nationals. The policy is seldom consistent with maximizing national income by the host country, because MNE is allowed to auction equity shares
in the subsidiary and thereby capitalize any rents it is earning (Wallace, 1982,
pp. 74–8).[9] Imposing a requirement of 50 percent or more control by nationals
is consistent with the national-preference model. Requiring local minority
shareholding or participation, however, is hard to explain, because it neither
maximizes the incomes of nationals nor mitigates foreign control. Perhaps governments believe that it sensitizes the subsidiary to informal suasion, thus serving the government-policy interest. In short, the policy of requiring equity
participation by nationals seems more consistent with the political-behavior
models than with the straight maximization of national income.

The national-preference model does not necessarily conflict with the assumption of neoclassical welfare economics that host governments maximize
national income. Therefore, the extent of inconsistency between host policies
and income maximization provides some evidence on the political-behavior
models. To hazard a bold generalization, LDCs' policies run toward consistency with income maximization, whereas developed hosts are more likely to
pursue noneconomic goals (Negandhi and Baliga, 1979). The evidence on the
rationality (or increasing rationality) of LDCs' policies was presented mainly
in Chapter 4 (the obsolescing bargain), Chapter 8 (maximum exploitation of
source countries' tax-credit policies), and Chapter 9 (use of policy commitments).[10] Developed-country policies that seem best explained by collective

---

[9] Sometimes the government itself demands a minority shareholding, which is simply an
alternative to taxation. See Section 8.3 and the suggestive but special-case models of
Svejnar and Smith (1984).

[10] Hawkins et al. (1976) argued that nationalizations of MNEs' subsidiaries in LDCs
during 1946–73 resulted from a left-wing shift of government in about half the cases,

preferences for nonmarket goals include pressures for local minority ownership and local performance of R&D and support for competing national firms ("national champions") in sectors deemed nationally important.[11] This difference between developed and less-developed hosts is consistent with collective nationalistic preferences for the economy's mixture of activities being an income-elastic (i.e., "normal") good that is consumed in greater amounts by wealthier societies.

Surveying companies' reactions to host-government policies is as impossible as surveying the policies themselves.[12] Copious evidence cited in previous chapters suggests that the MNE as a global profit maximizer tends to react to host-government policies so as to minimize their impairment of expected profits. Some may entirely shun countries imposing policies with a significant chance of leaving no positive return (see Grosse, 1980, on the effect of the Andean Foreign Investment Code). Others adapt in various ways that may affect quite intimately their corporate organizations and strategies (Doz, 1980).[13]

Source countries

Models of political behavior can also be applied to countries' policies toward their own MNEs. The basic voting model implies that a policy benefiting the nation's MNEs at the expense of foreigners will win favor with the median voter. If capital income (including equity shareholdings) is more concentrated than labor income, however, a voting model does imply that under some conditions source-country voters will approve restriction of foreign investment in order to redistribute income from capital to labor (see Chapter 5). This issue aside, source countries will also approve public measures to assist national MNEs in maximizing their rents from foreign markets, subject to conditions relating to the costs of these policies and how they are financed. It is not obvious that a nationalistic preference to avoid dealings with foreigners

but otherwise displayed considerable (and increasing) economic rationality. Also see Diaz Alejandro (1970), Truitt (1974), Williams (1975), Sigmund (1980), and UNCTC (1991a).

[11] Obviously there is ground for doubt whether market failures are involved, or only neo-mercantilist preferences. Behrman and Grosse (1990, pp. 203–4) did notice a general trend from minority ownership requirements to substantive performance requirements.

[12] A class of hosts omitted completely from this study is the former centrally planned economies. The literature on MNEs' joint ventures with the centrally planned regimes now seems irrelevant, and only a little experience has been observed systematically of MNEs' activities in the privatization process (Donges and Wieners, 1994).

[13] Doz found that companies that have rationalized their production internationally resist national intrusion more than those serving closed local markets. Competitive position influences the MNE's adaptation. A firm with unique assets attractive to host governments can take a tougher line, and the MNE without close international rivals tries to do so. The less advantaged MNE, however, may follow a policy of close cooperation with the host government in order to secure a local-market position from which stronger rivals cannot dislodge it.

leads the median voter to curb the MNE from dealing with them abroad, and so the national-preference model seems to predict no restrictions on the nation's MNEs and some basis for public assistance if needed to increase their overseas rents.

The government-policy model seems potentially more symmetrical between host and source countries than the national-preference model. A government acting to curb hard-to-control economic agents will find domestic MNEs no more appetizing than foreign ones. However, rational voters with a preference for public-sector allocations should appreciate that the national MNE itself provides the government with an instrument usable to affect resource allocations abroad, or that MNEs' rents from abroad should compensate for some disutility from any weakening of the government's ability to control. Therefore, the government-policy model predicts that MNEs' foreign activities will be subject to some constraint.

We do not pursue these suggestions in detail because countries recently have acted so much more passively as sources than as hosts.[14] The sporadic policies of the United States toward its MNEs have been consistent with a willingness to let nationals earn rents abroad so long as no obvious incidental costs result,[15] and government resources have at times been committed to increase or preserve these rents. Sigmund (1980) characterized the main line of U.S. policy, holding that because the market allocation of MNE activities yields benefit to both source and host, the host country should not act to increase its share of the pie. Such a posture seems stronger in its consistency with rational behavior by source-country voters than in its logical consistency. The United States and other source countries have occasionally sought to use their MNEs to influence allocations abroad, usually in support of objectives of foreign policy. This practice may connote some positive support for MNEs explained by the government-policy model. However, the consequent conflicts between MNEs and host countries points to severe limits on the MNE's usefulness on a policy instrument (Graham and Krugman, 1991, pp. 95–118).

[14] The debate over imperialism as a possible front for foreign investment will not be reviewed here, but note Rodman (1988) and Behrman and Grosse (1990, pp. 83–4) on the changing responses of source countries to host-country interventions.

[15] Bergsten et al. (1978, Chapter 9). Once more, thresholds of perception may be important. The costs of allowing favorable tax treatment to foreign-source income have received less attention from the voting public than issues on which much less real income rides. The same holds for the possible redistributive effects of MNEs, although these resist easy quantification even by subtle economic research (see Chapter 5). These patterns might suggest a model in which MNEs and other large corporations have privileged or cost-efficient access to political favor. (Helleiner, 1977, argued from U.S. trade policy for such a model.) However, U.S. companies have not secured or even sought protection against entry by foreign MNEs, although they repeatedly succeed in repelling competition from imports.

10.3. **International regulation**

Economic analysis points to a number of divergences between source and host countries' national interests in the MNE, and between any nation's interest and that of global welfare. One branch of public policy toward MNEs rests, however, on a different perception of the policy problem. What has been called the "sovereignty at bay" school argues that MNEs have escaped the regulatory reach of *any* national government. One cannot readily make sense of this, in that every business unit of a MNE is legally domiciled in a territory where some government is sovereign. The government-policy view that governments find themselves short of policy instruments offers some explanation, as does the competition among governments to attract foreign investors. Behrman and Grosse (1990) suggested that the MNE's bargaining power against the host nation is nothing more than its desirable attributes that makes the host perceive costs to exclude it. In any case, that the MNEs' power vis-à-vis governments calls for international regulation is widely urged. Is there an economic case for collective international commitments on policy toward MNEs? If so, does it bear any relation to the actual dialogue over international regulation?

Global and national interests

The analysis summarized in Section 10.1 made clear that the national policies consistent with maximum global welfare from MNEs' activities diverge from those that seek to maximize national welfare. This proposition holds if countries fail to recognize the interdependent effects of their policies, and there is no guarantee in the theory of bargaining and retaliation that recognition will bring consensus on policies that maximize joint (global) welfare. The problem is highlighted by comparison to the General Agreement on Tariffs and Trade (GATT, now transformed into the World Trade Organization) as a forum for mutual reduction of barriers to trade. One possible interpretation of GATT is that each nation acting independently imposes excessive tariff protection for some combination of two reasons: It thinks it can thereby improve its terms of trade, and it caters to domestic special interests for lack of any general principle or commitment for holding them at bay. GATT has attacked both problems over the years. By staging general rounds of coincident tariff reduction, it causes the global gains to be spread fairly evenly among the participating nations (because no country's terms of trade undergo much change when calculated at ex-tariff prices). And it gives the national government that really wants to maximize national welfare a commitment helpful to stand off domestic pressure groups.

One can imagine a similar international forum that would bargain toward global-welfare-maximizing policies on MNEs that were identified previously

(Rubin and Hufbauer, 1984). It could mediate or arbitrate cases in which the MNE serves as the alleged instrument for one country's incursions on another's sovereignty. These conflicts differ importantly from the economic ones emphasized earlier, because conflicting interests in international political or military (power) arrangements usually are intrinsically zero-sum and provide no basis for bargaining toward a global optimum.

Comparison to GATT reveals intrinsic difficulties with this idealized agenda for international coordination of policy toward MNEs. Countries' interests in efficient arrangements for international trade are made similar by the (at least approximate) balance that must prevail between exports and imports (they can differ only through a persistent net international flow of capital). That balance permits a general tariff reduction to distribute its benefits fairly evenly among the participants without any complicating side payments. But there is no comparable balance condition for a country's interests as source and host of MNEs. Therefore, no globally efficient change in policy that is not neutral between source and host can claim to spread its benefits equitably without the aid of side payments. The trend for more and more countries to play significant roles as both sources and hosts improves the prospect, but the difference remains. A package of globally optimal policy changes would likely contain some providing net benefits to source countries, others shifting gains to hosts; the result could be declared to balance, although only as an act of faith.

Moves toward international regulation

The preceding scenario bears little relation to actual steps toward international control of the MNE. Scholarly treatments have largely ignored the economic issues in favor of those of sovereignty and diplomacy.[16] The popular campaign has not sought international regulation so much as resolutions from international organizations urging national governments to regulate the activities of MNEs more intensively (Roberts and Liebhaberg, 1977, provided a convenient account). Much of the push came from trade unions in the industrial countries and from LDCs. In Chapter 5 we examined why national trade unions have reason to seek international support for their efforts to consolidate their bargaining power against MNEs: Otherwise the intrinsic clash of interest among unions in different countries comes to the fore. The LDCs similarly seek international support for their own regulatory efforts, perhaps partly to suppress competition among themselves in the terms offered to footloose MNEs, partly for help in minimizing the MNEs' opportunities to evade regulations already in force or to summon source-country aid.

---

[16] See Wallace (1976), Hellmann (1977), and Keohane and Ooms (1975). Exceptions include Vernon (1977, Chapter 8), who did appreciate the conflict between national welfare and global welfare, and Wallace (1982), who is strong in recognizing conflicting national interests.

The principal result of this was a set of guidelines for MNEs agreed upon by industrial-country members of the OECD (see OECD, 1986), partly as a foil to more drastic commitments sought by the LDCs. The guidelines reflect a deal between source-country and host-country interests. The former secured a commitment that hosts should (except in the defense sector) give foreign subsidiaries treatment no less favorable than that given to national firms. In exchange a nonbinding code of good behavior was pressed upon the MNEs: They should take account of the host's general economic objectives, especially those having to do with economic and social progress. They should make available any information needed by the host government (see Wallace, 1982, Chapter 8, for background on this point). They should cooperate with local community and business interests; they should eschew predatory practices toward local competitors, national citizens should be hired. Bribery or other inappropriate interferences with the host's political process should not take place. They should heed the goal of preserving the environment and obey regulations dealing with it.

The code has much of the flavor of the government-policy view of national relations with MNEs. It regards the national government as short on policy instruments to achieve broad objectives. It directly reflects the view that public regulation involves suasion and moral standards rather than clear-cut rules that define legal and illegal behavior.

10.4. **Summary**

Traditional welfare economics supplies rules for optimal policies in the many markets affected by the presence of MNEs. These policies' assumed goal is to maximize real income. A dilemma immediately arising is that policies to maximize the incomes of source countries, host countries, and the world as a whole are not identical. Conflict is therefore expected, and in the important case of taxation policy, the conflict does not depend on countries being "large" in world markets or on the MNEs themselves enjoying monopoly power. The principal areas of policy, besides taxation (explored in earlier chapters and summarized in this one), are natural-resource rents, competition policy for industrial markets, and the creation and transfer of industrial knowledge. These policy conclusions are qualified by the existence of multiple market distortions, which forces the analyst into second-best prescriptions and benefit-cost analyses of individual investments. The presence of MNEs also colors the formation of policy on matters ostensibly unrelated to MNEs, because a policy's redistributive effect between nationals and foreign investors can make national income decline even when domestic product rises.

The divergence of actual policy toward MNEs from the normative prescriptions calls for a behavioral approach. Two lines of analysis seem fruitful. One addresses national (nationalistic) preferences in the context of democratic government, emphasizing the consequences of voters seeking maximum benefits against investors domiciled abroad (who lack voting rights but can exert influence through other channels). The national preference itself can take several forms, such as a collective distaste for perceived influence by foreign companies on the nation's resource allocation. Another model concentrates on the means-end relationship in policy and the shortcomings of a government's policy options that are amplified by the superior alternatives open to MNEs. If the government's preferences for allocating resources are axiomatically superior to the market's, or if the median voter believes them superior, discriminatory restrictions on MNEs follow from the fact of their superior alternatives. No systematic empirical research has followed up these policy models, but casual evidence suggests that both command some explanatory power. The national-preference model holds few implications for source countries' policies, but the government-policy model does call attention to the home-based MNE's possible usefulness as a policy instrument for influencing allocations abroad.

International regulation of MNEs has sometimes been urged. A logical case can be built on the conflict between policies maximizing national welfare and global welfare, but a comparison to GATT stresses the improbability that such regulation could be realized. Actual international moves toward regulating MNEs grow largely from the efforts of host countries to legitimize and coordinate their own national regulations. The OECD guidelines compromise between this and source-country interests.

BIBLIOGRAPHY

Adams, J. D. R., and J. Whalley (1977). *The International Taxation of Multinational Enterprises in Developed Countries.* Westport, CT: Greenwood Press.

Adelman, M. A. (1972). *The World Petroleum Market.* Baltimore: Johns Hopkins University Press.

Adler, M. (1974). "The Cost of Capital and Valuation of a Two-Country Firm," *J. Finance,* 29 (March), 119–32.

Adler, M., and B. J. Dumas (1975). "The Long-Term Financial Decisions of the Multinational Corporation." In E. Elton and M. Gruber (eds.), *International Capital Markets,* pp. 360–87. Amsterdam: North-Holland.

  (1983). "International Portfolio Choice and Corporate Finance: A Synthesis," *J. Finance,* 38 (June), 925–84.

Adler, M., and G. V. G. Stevens (1974). "The Trade Effects of Direct Investment," *J. Finance,* 29 (May), 655–76.

Agarwal, J. P. (1985). "Intra-LDC Foreign Direct Investment: A Comparative Analysis of Third World Multinationals," *Devel. Econ.,* 33 (September), 236–53.

Agarwal, S., and S. N. Ramaswami (1992). "Choice of Foreign Market Entry Mode: Impact of Ownership, Location and Internalization Factors," *J. Int. Bus. Stud.,* 23 (First Quarter), 1–27.

Aggarwal, R., and L. A. Soenen (1987). "Changing Benefits of International Diversification of Real Assets," *Riv. Int. Scienza Econ. Comm.,* 34 (November), 1103–12.

Aggarwal, R., and J. K. Weekly (1982). "Foreign Operations of Third World Multinationals: A Literature Review and Analysis of Indian Companies," *J. Devel. Areas,* 17 (October), 13–30.

Agmon, T., and C. P. Kindleberger (eds.) (1977). *Multinationals from Small Countries.* Cambridge, MA: MIT Press.

Agmon, T., and D. Lessard (1977). "Investor Recognition of Corporate International Diversification," *J. Finance,* 32 (September), 1049–55.

Ågren, L. (1990). *Swedish Direct Investment in the U.S.* Stockholm: Institute of International Business, Stockholm School of Economics.

Aharoni, Y. (1966). *The Foreign Investment Decision Process.* Boston: Division of Research, Graduate School of Business Administration, Harvard University.

Aizenman, J. (1992). "Exchange Rate Flexibility, Volatility, and the Patterns of Domestic and Foreign Direct Investment." Working Paper No. 3953, National Bureau of Economic Research.

  (1994). "Foreign Direct Investment, Employment Volatility and Cyclical Dumping." Working Paper No. 4683, National Bureau of Economic Research.

261

Akhter, S. H., and R. F. Lusch (1991). "Environmental Determinants of U.S. Foreign Direct Investment in Developed and Developing Countries: A Structural Analysis," *Int. Trade J.*, 5 (Spring), 329–60.

Al-Eryani, M. F., P. Alam, and S. H. Akhter (1990). "Transfer Pricing Determinants of U.S. Multinationals," *J. Int. Bus. Stud.*, 21 (Third Quarter), 409–25.

Aliber, R. Z. (1970). "A Theory of Direct Foreign Investment." In C. P. Kindleberger (ed.), *The International Corporation: A Symposium*, pp. 17–34. Cambridge, MA: MIT Press.

(1978). *Exchange Risk and Corporate International Finance*. Somerset, NJ: Halsted Press.

(1993). *The Multinational Paradigm*. Cambridge, MA: MIT Press.

Alsegg, R. J. (1971). *Control Relationships between American Corporations and Their European Subsidiaries*. AMA Research Study No. 107. New York: American Management Association.

Altshuler, R., and T. S. Newlon (1993). "The Effects of U.S. Tax Policy on the Income Repatriation Patterns of U.S. Multinational Corporations." In Giovannini et al. (1993), pp. 77–115.

Altshuler, R., T. S. Newlon, and W. C. Randolph (1994). "Do Repatriation Taxes Matter? Evidence from the Tax Returns of U.S. Multinationals." Working Paper No. 4667, National Bureau of Economic Research.

Alworth, J. S. (1988). *The Finance, Investment and Taxation Decisions of Multinationals*. Oxford: Blackwell.

Amano, A. (1977). "Specific Factors, Comparative Advantage, and International Investment," *Economica*, 44 (May), 131–44.

Anderson, E., and H. Gatignon (1986). "Modes of Foreign Entry: A Transaction Cost Analysis and Propositions," *J. Int. Bus. Stud.*, 17 (Fall), 1–26.

Andersson, T., and T. Fredriksson (1993). "International Organization of Production and Variation in Exports from Associates." Working Paper No. 377, Industriens Utredningsinstitut, Stockholm.

Andrews, M. (1972). "A Survey of American Investment in Irish Industry." Senior honors thesis, Harvard College.

Antonelli, C. (1985). "The Diffusion of an Organisational Innovation: International Data Telecommunications and Multinational Industrial Firms," *Int. J. Ind. Org.*, 3 (March), 109–18.

Areskoug, K. (1976). "Foreign Direct Investment and Capital Formation in Developing Countries," *Econ. Devel. Cult. Change*, 24 (April), 539–47.

Ariga, M. (ed.) (1975). *International Conference on International Economy and Competition Policy*. Tokyo: Council of Tokyo Conference on International Economy and Competition Policy.

Arpan, J. S. (1971). *International Intracorporate Pricing*. New York: Praeger.

Arrow, K. J. (1975). "Vertical Integration and Communication," *Bell J. Econ.*, 6 (Spring), 173–83.

Arthur D. Little, Inc. (1976). "The Reasons and Outlook for Foreign Direct Investment in the United States." In U.S. Department of Commerce, *Foreign Direct Investment in the United States: Report of the Secretary of Commerce to the Congress in Compliance with the Foreign Investment Study Act of 1974*, Appendix G. Washington: U.S. Government Printing Office.

Athukorala, P., and S. K. Jayasuriya (1988). "Parentage and Factor Proportions: A Comparative Study of Third-World Multinationals in Sri Lankan Manufacturing," *Oxford Bull. Econ. Statist.*, 50 (November), 409–23.

Auerbach, A. J., and K. Hassett (1993). "Taxation and Foreign Direct Investment in the United States: A Reconsideration of the Evidence." In Giovannini et al. (1993), pp. 119–44.

Auquier, A. A., and R. E. Caves (1979). "Monopolistic Export Industries, Trade Taxes, and Optimal Competition Policy," *Econ. J.*, 89 (September), 559–81.

Auster, E. R. (1992). "The Relationship of Industry Evolution to Patterns of Technological Linkages, Joint Ventures, and Direct Investment between U.S. and Japan," *Manag. Sci.*, 38 (June), 778–92.

Baba, M. (1975). "Foreign-Affiliated Corporations and Concentration in Japanese Manufacturing Industry." In M. Ariga (ed.), *International Conference on International Economy and Com-*

petition Policy, pp. 172–82. Tokyo: Council of Tokyo Conference on International Economy and Competition Policy.

Baerresen, D. W. (1971). *The Border Industrialization Program of Mexico*. Lexington, MA: Lexington Books, D. C. Heath.

Baglini, N. A. (1976). *Risk Management in International Corporations*. New York: Risk Studies Foundation.

Balasubramanyam, V. N. (1988). "Export Processing Zones in Developing Countries: Theory and Empirical Evidence." In D. Greenaway (ed.), *Economic Development and International Trade*, pp. 157–65. New York: St. Martin's Press.

Balasubramanyam, V. N., and D. Sapsford (eds.) (1994). *The Economics of International Investment*. Aldershot: Edward Elgar.

Baldwin, J. R., and R. E. Caves (1991). "Foreign Multinational Enterprises and Merger Activity in Canada." In L. Waverman (ed.), *Corporate Globalization through Mergers and Acquisitions*, pp. 89–122. Calgary: University of Calgary Press.

Ball, C. A., and A. E. Tschoegl (1982). "The Decision To Establish a Foreign Bank Branch or Subsidiary: An Application of Binary Classification Procedures," *J. Fin. Quant. Analysis*, 17 (September), 411–24.

Bandera, V. N., and J. T. White (1968). "U.S. Direct Investments and Domestic Markets in Europe," *Econ. Int.*, 21 (February), 117–33.

Bane, W. T., and F.-F. Neubauer (1981). "Diversification and the Failure of New Foreign Activities," *Strategic Manag. J.*, 2 (July), 219–33.

Banks, R. F., and J. Stieber (eds.) (1977). *Multinationals, Unions, and Labor Relations in Industrialized Countries*. Cornell International Industrial and Labor Relations Report No. 9. Ithaca, NY: New York State School of Industrial and Labor Relations, Cornell University.

Baranson, J. (1978a). *Technology and the Multinationals: Corporate Strategies in a Changing World Economy*. Lexington, MA: Lexington Books, D. C. Heath.

(1978b). "Technology Transfer: Effects on U.S. Competitiveness and Employment." In U.S. Department of Labor, Bureau of International Labor Affairs, *The Impact of International Trade and Investment on Employment*, W. Dewald (ed.), pp. 177–203. Washington: U.S. Government Printing Office.

Bardhan, P. K. (1982). "Imports, Domestic Production, and Transnational Vertical Integration: A Theoretical Note," *J. Polit. Econ.*, 90 (October), 1020–34.

Barlow, E. R., and I. T. Wender (1955). *Foreign Investment and Taxation*. Englewood Cliffs, NJ: Prentice-Hall.

Barnet, R. J., and R. E. Muller (1974). *Global Reach: The Power of the International Corporations*. New York: Simon & Schuster.

Barrell, R., and N. Pain (forthcoming). "An Econometric Analysis of U.S. Foreign Direct Investment," *Rev. Econ. Statist.*

Barros, P. P. (1994). "Market Equilibrium Effects of Incentives to Foreign Direct Investment," *Econ. Letters*, 44 (Nos. 1–2), 153–7.

Basant, R., and B. Fikkert (forthcoming). "The Effects of R&D, Foreign Technology Purchase, and Domestic and International Spillovers on Productivity in Indian Firms," *Rev. Econ. Statist.*

Batra, R. N. (1986). "A General Equilibrium Model of Multinational Corporations in Developing Economies," *Oxford Econ. Pap.*, 38 (July), 342–53.

Batra, R. N., and J. Hadar (1979). "Theory of the Multinational Firm: Fixed versus Floating Exchange Rates," *Oxford Econ. Pap.*, 31 (July), 258–69.

Batra, R. N., and R. Ramachandran (1980). "Multinational Firms and the Theory of International Trade and Investment," *Amer. Econ. Rev.*, 70 (June), 278–90.

Baum, D. J. (1974). *The Banks of Canada in the Commonwealth Caribbean: Economic Nationalism and Multinational Enterprises of a Medium Power*. New York: Praeger.

Baumann, H. G. (1975). "Merger Theory, Property Rights, and the Pattern of U.S. Direct Investment in Canada," *Weltwirtsch. Arch.*, 111 (No. 4), 676–98.

Beamish, P. W. (1988). *Multinational Joint Ventures in Developing Countries*. London: Routledge.

Beamish, P. W., and J. C. Banks (1987). "Equity Joint Ventures and the Theory of the Multinational Enterprise," *J. Int. Bus. Stud.*, 18 (Summer), 1–16.

Beechler, S., and J. Z. Yang (1994). "The Transfer of Japanese-Style Management to American Subsidiaries: Contingencies, Constraints, and Competences," *J. Int. Bus. Stud.*, 25 (Third Quarter), 467–91.

Beenstock, M. (1977). "Policies towards International Direct Investment: A Neoclassical Reappraisal," *Econ. J.*, 87 (September), 533–42.

(1982). "Finance and International Direct Investment in the United Kingdom." In Black and Dunning (1982), pp. 122–39.

Behrman, J. N. (1969). *Some Patterns in the Rise of the Multinational Enterprise*. Research Paper No. 18. Chapel Hill: Graduate School of Business Administration, University of North Carolina.

(1970). *National Interests and the Multinational Enterprise: Tensions among the North Atlantic Countries*. Englewood Cliffs, NJ: Prentice-Hall.

Behrman, J. N., and W. A. Fischer (1980). *Overseas R&D Activity of Transnational Companies*. Cambridge, MA: Oelgeschlager, Gunn and Hain.

Behrman, J. N., and R. E. Grosse (1990). *International Business and Governments: Issues and Institutions*. Columbia: University of South Carolina Press. 1990.

Belderbos, R. A. (1992). "Large Multinational Enterprises Based in a Small Economy: Effects on Domestic Investment," *Weltwirtsch. Arch.*, 128 (No. 3), 543–57.

Belderbos, R., and L. Sleuwaegen (forthcoming). "Japanese Firms and the Decision to Invest Abroad: Business Groups and Regional Core Networks," *Rev. Econ. Statist.*

Benito, G. R. G., and G. Gripsrud (1992). "The Expansion of Foreign Direct Investments," *J. Int. Bus. Stud.*, 23 (Third Quarter), 461–76.

Benvignati, A. M. (1983). "International Technology Transfer Patterns in a Traditional Industry," *J. Int. Bus. Stud.*, 14 (Winter), 63–75.

(1985). "An Empirical Investigation of International Transfer Pricing by US Multinational Firms." In Rugman and Eden (1985), pp. 193–211.

(1987). "Domestic Profit Advantages of Multinational Firms," *J. Bus.*, 60 (July), 449–61.

(1990). "Industry Determinants and 'Differences' in U.S. Intrafirm and Arms-Length Exports," *Rev. Econ. Statist.*, 72 (August), 481–88.

Bergsten, C. F., T. Horst, and T. H. Moran (1978). *America Multinationals and American Interests*. Washington: Brookings Institution.

Bernard, J.-T., and R. J. Weiner (1990). "Multinational Corporations, Transfer Prices, and Taxes: Evidence from the U.S. Petroleum Industry." In Razin and Slemrod (1990), pp. 123–54.

(1992). "Transfer Prices and the Excess Cost of Canadian Oil Imports: New Evidence on Bernard vs. Rugman," *Can. J. Econ.*, 25 (February), 22–40.

Bernheim, B. D., and M. D. Whinston (1990). "Multimarket Contact and Collusive Behavior," *Rand J. Econ.*, 21 (Spring), 1–26.

Berry, A. (1974). "Static Effects of Technological Borrowing on National Income: A Taxonomy of Cases," *Weltwirtsch. Arch.*, 110 (No. 4), 580–606.

Bertin, G. Y. (1987). "Multinational Enterprises: Transfer Partners and Transfer Policies." In A. E. Safarian and G. Y. Bertin (eds.), *Multinationals, Governments and International Technology Transfer*, pp. 85–100. New York: St. Martin's Press.

Bertin, G. Y., and S. Wyatt (1988). *Multinationals and Industrial Property: The Control of the World's Technology*. Hemel Hempstead: Harvester-Wheatsheaf.

Bhagwati, J. N., and R. A. Brecher (1980). "National Welfare in an Open Economy in the Presence of Foreign-Owned Factors of Production," *J. Int. Econ.*, 10 (February), 103–15.

Bhagwati, J. N., R. W. Jones, R. A. Mundell, and J. Vanek (eds.) (1971). *Trade, Balance of Payments and Growth: Papers in International Economics in Honor of Charles P. Kindleberger.* Amsterdam: North-Holland.

Biersteker, T. J. (1978). *Distortion or Development: Contending Perspectives on the Multinational Corporation.* Cambridge, MA: MIT Press.

Black, J., and J. Dunning (eds.) (1982). *International Capital Movements.* London: Macmillan.

Blair, Andrew R. (1987). "The Relative Distribution of the United States Direct Investment: The U.K./EEC Experience," *Eur. Econ. Rev.*, 31 (July), 1137–44.

Blake, D. H. (1972). "The Internationalization of Industrial Relations," *J. Int. Bus. Stud.*, 3 (Fall), 17–32.

Blanchflower, D. (1984). "Comparative Pay Levels in Domestically-owned and Foreign-owned Manufacturing Plants: A Comment," *Brit. J. Ind. Relations*, 22 (July), 265–7.

Blodgett, L. L. (1991). "Partner Contributions as Predictors of Equity Share in International Joint Ventures," *J. Int. Bus. Stud.*, 22 (First Quarter), 63–78.

Blomström, M. (1983). "Foreign Investment, Technical Efficiency and Structural Change: Evidence from the Mexican Manufacturing Industry." Ph.D. dissertation, Gothenburg University.

  (1989). *Foreign Investment and Spillovers.* London: Routledge.

  (1990). *Transnational Corporations and Manufacturing Exports from Developing Countries.* New York: United Nations Centre on Transnational Corporations.

Blomström, M., A. Kokko, and M. Zejan (1992). "Host Country Competition and Technology Transfer by Multinationals." Working Paper No. 4131, National Bureau of Economic Research.

Blomström, M., and R. E. Lipsey (1989). "The Export Performance of U.S. and Swedish Multinationals," *Rev. Income Wealth*, 35 (September), 245–64.

  (1991). "Firm Size and Foreign Operations of Multinationals," *Scand. J. Econ.*, 93 (No. 1) 101–7.

  (1993). "Foreign Firms and Structural Adjustment in Latin America: Lessons from the Debt Crisis." In G. Hansson (ed.), *Trade, Growth and Development*, pp. 109–32. New York: Routledge.

Blomström, M., R. E. Lipsey, and K. Kulchycky (1988). "U.S. and Swedish Direct Investment and Exports." In R. E. Baldwin (ed.), *Trade Policy Issues and Empirical Analysis*, pp. 259–97. Chicago: University of Chicago Press.

Blomström, M., and E. Wolff (1994). "Multinational Corporations and Productivity Convergence in Mexico." In W. Baumol, R. Nelson, and E. Wolff (eds.), *Convergence of Productivity: Cross-national Studies and Historical Evidence*, pp. 243–59. New York: Oxford University Press.

Blomström, M., and M. Zejan (1991). "Why Do Multinational Firms Seek Out Joint Ventures?" *J. Int. Devel.*, 3 (No. 1), 53–63.

Boatwright, B. D., and G. A. Renton (1975). "An Analysis of United Kingdom Inflows and Outflows of Direct Foreign Investment," *Rev. Econ. Statist.*, 57 (November), 478–86.

Boddewyn, J. J. (1983). "Foreign Direct Divestment Theory: Is It the Reverse of FDI Theory?" *Weltwirtsch. Arch.*, 119 (No. 2), 345–55.

Boddewyn, J. J., M. B. Halbrich, and A.C. Perry (1986). "Service Multinationals: Conceptualization, Measurement and Theory," *J. Int. Bus. Stud.*, 17 (Fall), 41–57.

Bond, E. (1981). "Tax Holidays and Industry Behavior," *Rev. Econ. Statist.*, 63 (February), 88–95.

Bond, E. W., and L. Samuelson (1986). "Tax Holidays as Signals," *Amer. Econ. Rev.*, 76 (September), 820–6.

  (1989). "Bargaining with Commitment, Choice of Techniques, and Direct Foreign Investment," *J. Int. Econ.*, 26 (February), 77–97.

Booth, E. J. R., and O. W. Jensen (1977). "Transfer Prices in the Global Corporation under Internal and External Constraints," *Can. J. Econ.*, 10 (August), 434–46.

Bornschier, V. (1980). "Multinational Corporations and Economic Growth: A Cross-National Test of the Decapitalization Thesis," *J. Devel. Econ.*, 7 (June), 191–210.

Bornschier, V., and C. Chase-Dunn (1985). *Transnational Corporations and Underdevelopment.* Greenwich, CT: Praeger.

Bos, H. C., M. Sanders, and C. Secchi (1974). *Private Foreign Investment in Developing Countries: A Quantitative Study on the Evaluation of the Macroeconomic Effects.* Dordrecht: Reidel.

Boskin, M. J., and W. G. Gale (1987). "New Results on the Effects of Tax Policy on the International Location of Investment." In M. Feldstein (ed.), *The Effects of Taxation on Capital Accumulation*, pp. 201–19. Chicago: University of Chicago Press.

Brainard, S. L. (1993a). "A Simple Theory of Multinational Corporations and Trade with a Trade-off between Proximity and Concentration." Working Paper No. 4269, National Bureau of Economic Research.

(1993b). "An Empirical Assessment of the Factor Proportions Explanation of Multinational Sales." Working Paper No. 3624-93-EFA, Sloan School of Management, MIT.

(1993c). "An Empirical Assessment of the Proximity/Concentration Tradeoff between Multinational Sales and Trade." Working Paper No. 3625-93-EFA, Sloan School of Management, MIT.

Brander, J. S., and P. R. Krugman (1983). "A 'Reciprocal Dumping' Model of International Trade," *J. Int. Econ.*, 15 (November), 313–21.

Brander, J. S., and B. J. Spencer (1987). "Foreign Direct Investment with Unemployment and Endogenous Taxes and Tariffs," *J. Int. Econ.*, 22 (May), 257–79.

Brash, D. T. (1966). *American Investment in Australian Industry*. Cambridge, MA: Harvard University Press.

Brecher, R. A., and C. F. Diaz Alejandro (1977). "Tariffs, Foreign Capital and Immiserizing Growth," *J. Int. Econ.*, 7 (November), 317–22.

Brecher, R. A., and R. Findlay (1983). "Tariffs, Foreign Capital and National Welfare with Sector-Specific Factors," *J. Int. Econ.* 14 (May), 277–88.

Brewster, K. (1958). *Antitrust and American Business Abroad*. New York: McGraw-Hill.

Broll, U. (1992). "The Effect of Forward Markets on Multinational Firms," *Bull. Econ. Res.*, 44 (July), 233–40.

Broll, U., and I. Zilcha (1992). "Exchange-Rate Uncertainty, Futures Markets and the Multinational Firm," *Eur. Econ. Rev.*, 36 (May), 815–26.

Brooke, M. Z., and H. L. Remmers (1970). *The Strategy of Multinational Enterprise: Organisation and Finance*. New York: American Elsevier.

Buckley, P. J. (1974). "Some Aspects of Foreign Private Investment in the Manufacturing Sector of the Economy of the Irish Republic," *Econ. Soc. Rev.*, 5 (April), 301–21.

(1985). "New Forms of International Industrial Co-operation." In P. J. Buckley and M. Casson (eds.), *The Economic Theory of the Multinational Enterprise*, pp. 39–59. London: Macmillan.

Buckley, P. J., Z. Berkova, and G. D. Newbould (1983). *Direct Investment in the United Kingdom by Smaller European Firms*. London: Macmillan.

Buckley, P. J., and M. Casson (1976). *The Future of the Multinational Enterprise*. London: Macmillan.

(1981). "The Optimal Timing of a Foreign Direct Investment," *Econ. J.*, 91 (March), 75–87.

(1988). "A Theory of Cooperation in International Business." In Contractor and Lorange (1988), pp. 31–53.

Buckley, P. J., and J. Clegg (eds.) (1991). *Multinational Enterprises in Less Developed Countries*. Basingstoke: Macmillan.

Buckley, P. J., and H. Davies (1979). "The Place of Licensing in the Theory and Practice of Foreign Operations." Discussion Paper No. 47, University of Reading.

Buckley, P. J., J. H. Dunning, and R. D. Pearce (1978). "The Influence of Firm Size, Industry, Nationality, and Degree of Multinationality on the Growth of the World's Largest Firms, 1962–1972," *Weltwirtsch. Arch.*, 114 (No. 2), 243–57.

(1984). "An Analysis of the Growth and Profitability of the World's Largest Firms 1972 to 1977," *Kyklos*, 37 (No. 1), 3–26.

Buckley, P. J., and R. D. Pearce (1979). "Overseas Production and Exporting by the World's Largest Enterprises: A Study in Sourcing Policy," *J. Int. Bus. Stud.*, 10 (Spring), 9–20.

Buffie, E. F. (1985). "Quantitative Restrictions and the Welfare Effects of Capital Inflows," *J. Int. Econ.*, 19 (November), 291–303.

(1987). "Labor Market Distortions, the Structure of Protection and Direct Foreign Investment," *J. Devel. Econ.*, 27 (October), 149–63.

Burenstam Linder, S. (1961). *An Essay on Trade and Transformation*. Uppsala: Almqvist & Wiksells.

Burgess, D. F. (1978). "On the Distributional Effects of Direct Foreign Investment," *Int. Econ. Rev.*, 19 (October), 647–64.

Burns, J. M. (1976) *Accounting Standards and International Finance, with Special Reference to Multinationals*. Washington: American Enterprise Institute.

Burns, J. O. (1980). "Transfer Pricing Decisions in U.S. Multinational Corporations," *J. Int. Bus. Stud.*, 11 (Fall), 23–39.

Burton, F. N., and F. H. Saelens (1987). "Trade Barriers and Japanese Foreign Direct Investment in the Colour Television Industry," *Manag. Decision Econ.*, 8 (December), 285–93.

Business International (1981). *New Directions in Multinational Corporate Organization*. New York: Business International.

Calderon-Rossell, J. R. (1985). "Toward the Theory of Foreign Direct Investment," *Oxford Econ. Pap.*, 37 (June), 282–91.

Campa, J. M. (1993). "Entry by Foreign Firms in the United States under Exchange Rate Uncertainty," *Rev. Econ. Statist.*, 75 (November), 614–22.

(1994). "Multinational Investment under Uncertainty in the Chemical Processing Industries," *J. Int. Bus. Stud.*, 25 (Third Quarter), 557–78.

Campa, J. M., and S. Donnenfeld (1994). "Market Structure Consequences for Foreign Direct Investment in the U.S." Working paper, New York University.

Canada, Industry Canada (1994). *Formal and Informal Investment Barriers in the G-7 Countries*. Ottawa: Industry Canada.

Cantwell, J. (1988). "The Reorganization of European Industries after Integration: Selected Evidence on the Role of Multinational Enterprise Activities." In Dunning and Robson (1988), pp. 25–49.

(1989). *Technological Innovation and Multinational Corporations*. Oxford: Blackwell.

(ed.) (1992). *Multinational Investment in Modern Europe: Strategic Interaction in the Integrated Community*. Aldershot: Edward Elgar.

Cantwell, J., and F. Sanna-Randaccio (1992). "Intra-industry Direct Investment in the European Community: Oligopolistic Rivalry and Technological Competition." In Cantwell (1992), pp. 71–106.

(1993). "Multinationality and Firm Growth," *Weltwirtsch. Arch.*, 129 (No. 2), 275–99.

Carmichael, F. (1992). "Multinational Enterprise and Strikes: Theory and Evidence," *Scot. J. Polit. Econ.*, 39 (February), 52–68.

Casson, M. (1979). *Alternatives to the Multinational Enterprise*. London: Macmillan.

(ed.) (1983). *The Growth of International Business*. London: Allen & Unwin.

(1994). "Internationalization as a Learning Process: A Model of Corporate Growth and Geographic Diversification." In Balasubramanyam and Sapsford (1994), pp. 14–46.

Casson, M., and Associates (1986). *Multinationals and World Trade: Vertical Integration and the Division of Labour in World Industries*. London: Allen & Unwin.

Caves, R. E. (1971). "International Corporations: The Industrial Economics of Foreign Investment," *Economica*, 38 (February), 1–27.

    (1974*a*). "Multinational Firms, Competition, and Productivity in Host-Country Industries," *Economica*, 41 (May), 176–93.

    (1974*b*). "Causes of Direct Investment: Foreign Firms' Shares in Canadian and United Kingdom Manufacturing Industries," *Rev. Econ. Statist.*, 56 (August), 279–93.

    (1974*c*). "Industrial Organization." In J. H. Dunning (ed.), *Economic Analysis and the Multinational Enterprise*, pp. 115–46. London: Allen & Unwin.

    (1975). *Diversification Foreign Investment and Scale in North American Manufacturing Industries*. Ottawa: Economic Council of Canada.

    (1980*a*). "Productivity Differences among Industries." In R. E. Caves and L. B. Krause (eds.), *Britain's Economic Performance*, pp. 135–98. Washington: Brookings Institution.

    (1980*b*). "Investment and Location Policies of Multinational Companies," *Schweiz. Z. Volkswirtsch. Statist.*, 116 (No. 3), 321–38.

    (1989). "Exchange-Rate Movements and Foreign Direct Investment in the United States." In D. B. Audretsch and M. P. Claudon (eds.), *The Internationalization of U.S. Markets*, pp. 199–228. New York: New York University Press.

    (1990). "Growth of Large Enterprises and Their Market Environments." In P. de Wolf (ed.), *Competition in Europe: Essays in Honour of Henk W. de Jong*, pp. 61–83. Dordrecht: Kluwer.

    (1991). "Corporate Mergers in International Financial Integration." In A. Giovannini and C. Mayer (eds.), *European Financial Integration*, pp. 136–60. Cambridge: Cambridge University Press.

    (1995). "Growth and Decline in Multinational Enterprises: From Equilibrium Models to Turnover Processes." In E. K. Y. Chen and P. Drysdale (eds.), *Corporate Links and Foreign Direct Investment in Asia and the Pacific*, pp. 9–28. Pymble, Australia: Harper Educational.

Caves, R. E., H. Crookell, and J. P. Killing (1983). "The Imperfect Market for Technology Licenses," *Oxford Bull. Econ. Statist.*, 45 (August), 249–67.

Caves, R. E., and S. K. Mehra (1986). "Entry of Foreign Multinationals into U.S. Manufacturing Industries." In Porter (1986), pp. 449–81.

Caves, R. E., M. E. Porter, and A. M. Spence, with J. T. Scott (1980). *Competition in the Open Economy: A Model Applied to Canada*. Cambridge, MA: Harvard University Press.

Caves, R. E., and T. A. Pugel (1980). *Intraindustry Differences in Conduct and Performance*. Monograph Series in Finance and Economics, 1980–2. New York: Graduate School of Business Administration, New York University.

Chalmin, P. (1986). "The Strategy of a Multinational in the World Sugar Economy: The Case of Tate and Lyle, 1870–1980." In Teichova et al. (1986), pp. 103–15.

Chandler, A. D. (1980). "The Growth of the Transnational Industrial Firm in the United States and the United Kingdom: A Comparative Analysis," *Econ. History Rev.*, 2nd series, 33 (August), 396–410.

Chase-Dunn, C. (1975). "The Effects of International Economic Dependence on Development and Inequality: A Cross-National Study," *Amer. Soc. Rev.*, 40 (December), 720–38.

Chen, E. K. Y. (1983*a*). "Multinational Corporations in Technology Diffusion in Hong Kong Manufacturing," *Appl. Econ.*, 15 (June), 309–21.

    (1983*b*). "Multinationals from Hong Kong." In S. Lall and Associates (1983), pp. 88–136.

    (1983*c*). *Multinational Companies, Technology and Employment*. New York: St. Martin's Press.

Chen, T., and D. Tang (1986). "The Production Characteristics of Multinational Firms and the Effect of Tax Incentives: The Case of Taiwan's Electronics Industry," *J. Devel. Econ.*, 24 (November), 119–29.

    (1987). "Comparing Technical Efficiency between Import-Substitution-Oriented and Export-Oriented Foreign Firms in a Developing Economy," *J. Devel. Econ.*, 26 (August), 277–89.

Chipman, J. S. (1971). "International Trade with Capital Mobility: A Substitution Theorem." In Bhagwati et al. (1971), pp. 201–37.

Chudson, W. A., and L. T. Wells, Jr. (1974). *The Acquisition of Technology from Multinational Corporations by Developing Countries*. New York: United Nations.

Chung, B. S., and C. H. Lee (1980). "The Choice of Production Techniques by Foreign and Local Firms in Korea," *Econ. Devel. Cult. Change*, 29 (October), 135–40.

Clegg, L. J. (1987). *Multinational Enterprise and World Competition: A Comparative Study of the USA, Japan, the UK, Sweden, and West Germany*. London: Macmillan.

Coase, R. H. (1937). "The Nature of the Firm," *Economica*, 4 (November), 386–405.

Cohen, B. I. (1972). "Foreign Investment by U.S. Corporations as a Way of Reducing Risk." Discussion Paper No. 151, Economic Growth Center, Yale University.

(1973). "Comparative Behavior of Foreign and Domestic Export Firms in a Developing Economy," *Rev. Econ. Statist.*, 55 (May), 190–7.

(1975). *Multinational Firms and Asian Exports*. New Haven: Yale University Press.

Cole, H. L., and W. B. English (1991). "Expropriation and Direct Investment," *J. Int. Econ.*, 30 (May), 201–27.

Connor, J. M. (1977). *The Market Power of Multinationals: A Quantitative Analysis of U.S. Corporations in Brazil and Mexico*. New York: Praeger.

Contractor, F. J. (1980). "The 'Profitability' of Technology Licensing by U.S. Multinationals: A Framework for Analysis and an Empirical Study," *J. Int. Bus. Stud.*, 11 (Fall), 40–63.

(1990). "Ownership Patterns of U.S. Joint Ventures Abroad and the Liberalization of Foreign Government Regulations in the 1980s: Evidence from the Benchmark Surveys," *J. Int. Bus. Stud.*, 21 (First Quarter), 55–73.

Contractor, F. J., and Peter Lorange (eds.) (1988). *Cooperative Strategies in International Business*. Lexington, MA: Lexington Books.

Copithorne, L. W. (1971). "International Corporate Transfer Prices and Government Policy," *Can. J. Econ.*, 4 (August), 324–41.

Corden, M. (1967). "Protection and Foreign Investment," *Econ. Record*, 43 (June), 209–32.

Coughlin, C. C. (1983). "The Relationship between Foreign Ownership and Technology Transfer," *J. Compar. Econ.*, 7 (December), 400–14.

Coughlin, C. C., J. V. Terza, and V. Arromdee (1991). "State Characteristics and the Location of Foreign Direct Investment within the United States," *Rev. Econ. Statist.*, 73 (November), 675–83.

Courtney, W. H., and D. M. Leipziger (1975). "Multinational Corporations in LDCs: The Choice of Technology," *Oxford Bull. Econ. Statist.*, 37 (November), 297–304.

Cousineau, J.-M., R. Lacroix, and D. Vachon (1989). "Foreign Ownership and Strike Activity in Canada." Working Paper No. 8927, Department of Economics, University of Montreal.

Cowhey, P., and J. D. Aronson (1993). *Managing the World Economy: The Consequences of Corporate Alliances*. New York: Council on Foreign Relations.

Cowling, K., and R. Sugden (1987). *Transnational Monopoly Capitalism*. Brighton: Wheatsheaf Books.

Creamer, D. B. (1976). *Overseas Research and Development by United States Multinationals 1966–1975*. New York: Conference Board.

Creigh, S. W., and P. Makeham (1978). "Foreign Ownership and Strike-Proneness: A Research Note," *Brit. J. Ind. Relations*, 16 (November), 369–72.

Crispo, J. (1967). *International Unionism: A Study in Canadian-American Relations*. Toronto: McGraw-Hill.

Culem, C. G. (1988). "The Locational Determinants of Direct Investments among Industrialized Countries," *Eur. Econ. Rev.*, 32 (April), 885–904.

Cummins, J. G., and R. G. Hubbard (1994). "The Tax Sensitivity of Foreign Direct Investment: Evidence from Firm-Level Panel Data," Working Paper No. 4703, National Bureau of Economic Research.

Curhan, J. P., W. H. Davidson, and R. Suri (1977). *Tracing the Multinationals: A Sourcebook on U.S.-Based Enterprises*. Cambridge, MA: Ballinger.

Curtin, W. J. (1973). "The Multinational Corporation and Transnational Collective Bargaining." In D. Kujawa (ed.), *American Labor and the Multinationals*, pp. 192–222. New York: Praeger.

Cushman, D. O. (1985). "Real Exchange Rate Risk, Expectations, and the Level of Direct Investment," *Rev. Econ. Statist.*, 67 (May), 197–208.

(1987). "The Effects of Real Wages and Labor Productivity on Foreign Direct Investment," *So. Econ. J.*, 54 (July), 174–83.

(1988). "Exchange-Rate Uncertainty and Foreign Direct Investment in the United States," *Weltwirtsch. Arch.*, 124 (No. 2), 322–36.

d'Arge, R. (1969). "Note on Customs Unions and Foreign Direct Investment," *Econ. J.*, 79 (June), 324–33.

Das, S. (1987). "Externalities and Technology Transfer through Multinational Corporations," *J. Int. Econ.*, 22 (February), 171–82.

Davidson, C., S. J. Matusz, and M. E. Kreinin (1985). "Analysis of Performance Standards for Direct Foreign Investments," *Can. J. Econ.*, 18 (November), 876–90.

Davidson, W. H. (1976). "Patterns of Factor-Saving Innovation in the Industrialized World," *Eur. Econ. Rev.*, 8 (October), 207–17.

(1980). "The Location of Foreign Direct Investment Activity: Country Characteristics and Experience Effects," *J. Int. Bus. Stud.*, 11 (Fall), 9–22.

(1984). "Administrative Orientation and International Performance," *J. Int. Bus. Stud.*, 15 (Fall), 11–23.

Davidson, W. H., and D. G. McFetridge (1984). "International Technology Transfer and the Theory of the Firm," *J. Ind. Econ.*, 32 (March), 253–64.

(1985). "Key Characteristics in the Choice of International Technology Transfer," *J. Int. Bus. Stud.*, 16 (Summer), 5–21.

Davies, H. (1977). "Technology Transfer through Commercial Transactions," *J. Ind. Econ.*, 26 (December), 161–75.

Davies, S. W., and B. R. Lyons (1991). "Characterising Relative Performance: The Productivity Advantage of Foreign Owned Firms in the UK," *Oxford Econ. Pap.*, 43 (October), 584–95.

Davis, S. M. (1976). "Trends in the Organization of Multinational Corporations," *Columbia J. World Bus.*, 11 (Summer), 59–71.

de Bodinat, H. (1975). "Influence in the Multinational Corporation: The Case of Manufacturing." D.B.A. thesis, Graduate School of Business Administration, Harvard University.

de Kuijper, M. A. M. (1983). "The Unraveling of Market Regimes: In Theory and in Application to Copper, Aluminum, and Oil." Ph.D. dissertation, Harvard University.

de Meza, D., and F. van der Ploeg (1987). "Production Flexibility as a Motive for Multinationality," *J. Ind. Econ.*, 35 (March), 343–51.

De la Torre, J., Jr. (1972). "Marketing Factors in Manufactured Exports from Developing Countries." In L. T. Wells, Jr. (ed.), *The Product Life Cycle and International Trade*, pp. 223–57. Boston: Division of Research, Harvard Business School.

De la Torre, J., Jr., R. B. Stobaugh, and P. Telesio (1973). "U.S. Multinational Enterprises and Changes in the Skill Composition of U.S. Employment." In D. Kujawa (ed.), *American Labor and the Multinationals*, pp. 127–43. New York: Praeger.

De Melto, D., et al. (1980). "Innovation and Technological Change in Five Canadian Industries." Discussion Paper No. 176, Economic Council of Canada.

Deane, R. S. (1969). "Import Licensing: A Stimulus to Foreign Investment," *Econ. Record*, 45 (December), 526–43.

(1970). *Foreign Investment in New Zealand Manufacturing*. Wellington, N.Z.: Sweet and Maxwell.

Dei, F. (1985). "Voluntary Export Restraints and Foreign Investment," *J. Int. Econ.*, 19 (November), 305–12.

(1990). "A Note on Multinational Corporations in a Model of Reciprocal Dumping," *J. Int. Econ.*, 29 (August), 161–71.

Demirag, I. S. (1988). "Assessing Foreign Subsidiary Performance: The Currency Choice of UK MNCs," *J. Int. Bus. Stud.*, 19 (Summer), 257–75.

Denis, J.-E., and D. Depelteau (1985). "Market Knowledge, Diversification, and Export Expansion," *J. Int. Bus. Stud.*, 16 (Fall), 77–89.

Devereux, M. P. (1994). "Tax Competition and the Impact on Capital Flows." Working paper, Conference on Locational Competition in the World Economy, Institut für Weltwirtschaft, Kiel.

Diaz Alejandro, C. F. (1970). "Direct Foreign Investment in Latin America." In C. P. Kindleberger (ed.), *The International Corporation: A Symposium*, pp. 319–44. Cambridge, MA: MIT Press.

(1979). "International Markets for Exhaustible Resources, Less Developed Countries, and Multinational Corporations." In R. G. Hawkins (ed.), *Research in International Business and Finance: An Annual Compilation of Research. Vol. 1. The Economic Effects of Multinational Corporations*, pp. 319–44. Greenwich, CT: JAI Press.

Dietermann, G. J. (1980). "Evaluating Multinational Performance under FAS No. 8," *Manage. Account.*, 61 (May), 49–55.

Diewert, W. E. (1985). "Transfer Pricing and Economic Efficiency." In Rugman and Eden (1985), pp. 47–81.

Dollar, D. (1986). "Technological Innovation, Capital Mobility, and the Product Cycle in North-South Trade," *Amer. Econ. Rev.*, 76 (March), 177–90.

Donges, J. B., and J. Wieners (1994). "Foreign Investment in Eastern Europe's Transformation Process." In Balasubramanyam and Sapsford (1994), pp. 129–48.

Donsimoni, M.-P., and V. Leoz-Arguelles (1980). "Profitability and International Linkages in the Spanish Economy." Working paper, Université Catholique de Louvain.

Doukas, J., and N. G. Travlos (1988). "The Effect of Corporate Multinationalism on Shareholders' Wealth: Evidence from International Acquisitions," *J. Finance*, 43 (December), 1161–75.

Doz, Y. L. (1980). "Strategic Management in Multinational Companies," *Sloan Manage. Rev.*, 21 (Winter), 27–46.

Drake, T. A., and R. E. Caves (1992). "Changing Determinants of Japanese Foreign Investment in the United States," *J. Jap. Int. Econ.*, 6 (September), 228–46.

Droucopoulos, V. (1983). "International Big Business Revisited: On the Size and Growth of the World's Largest Firms," *Manag. Decision Econ.*, 4 (December), 244–52.

Dubin, M. (1976). "Foreign Acquisitions and the Spread of the Multinational Firm." D.B.A. thesis, Graduate School of Business Administration, Harvard University.

Dukes, R. E. (1980). "Forecasting Exchange Gains (Losses) and Security Market Response to FASB Statement Number 8." In R. M. Levich and C. G. Wihlborg (eds.), *Exchange Risk and Exposure: Current Developments in International Financial Management*, pp. 177–93. Lexington, MA: Lexington Books, D. C. Heath.

Dunning, J. H. (1958). *American Investment in British Manufacturing Industry*. London: Allen & Unwin.

(1970). *Studies in International Investment*. London: Allen & Unwin.

(ed.) (1971). *The Multinational Enterprise*. London: Allen & Unwin.

(1973a). "Multinational Enterprises and Domestic Capital Formation," *Manchester Sch. Econ. Soc. Stud.*, 40 (September), 283–310.

(1973b). "The Determinants of International Production," *Oxford Econ. Pap.*, 25 (November), 289–336.

(ed.) (1974a). *Economic Analysis and the Multinational Enterprise*. London: Allen & Unwin.

(1974*b*). "Multinational Enterprises, Market Structure, Economic Power and Industrial Policy," *J. World Trade Law*, 8 (November/December), 575–613.

(1977*a*). "Trade, Location of Economic Activity and the MNE: A Search for an Eclectic Approach." In B. Ohlin, P.-O. Hesselborn, and P. M. Wijkman (eds.), *The International Allocation of Economic Activity: Proceedings of a Nobel Symposium Held at Stockholm*, pp. 395–418. London: Macmillan.

(1977*b*). *European Industry in the U.S.* London: Wilton House.

(1980). "Toward an Eclectic Theory of International Production: Some Empirical Tests," *J. Int. Bus. Stud.*, 11 (Spring/Summer), 9–31.

(1981*a*). "Explaining the International Direct Investment Position of Countries: Towards a Dynamic or Developmental Approach," *Weltwirtsch. Arch.*, 117 (No. 1), 30–64.

(1981*b*). *International Production and the Multinational Enterprise.* London: Allen & Unwin.

(1984). "Non-Equity Forms of Foreign Economic Involvement and the Theory of International Production," *International Business Strategies in the Asia-Pacific Region: Environmental Changes and Corporate Responses. Res. Int. Bus. Fin.*, 4 (Part A), 29–61.

(ed.) (1985). *Multinational Enterprises, Economic Structure and International Competitiveness.* Chichester: Wiley.

(1986). *Japanese Participation in British Industry.* London: Croom Helm.

(1988). *Explaining International Production.* London: Unwin Hyman.

Dunning, J. H., and M. McQueen (1982). "The Eclectic Theory of the Multinational Enterprise and the International Hotel Industry." In Rugman (1982), pp. 79–106.

Dunning, J. H., and E. J. Morgan (1980). "Employee Compensation in U.S. Multinationals and Indigenous Firms: An Exploratory Micro/Macro Analysis," *Brit J. Ind. Relations*, 18 (July), 179–201.

Dunning, J. H., and R. D. Pearce (1977). *U.S. Industry in Britain.* Boulder: Westview Press.

Dunning, J., and P. Robson (eds.) (1988). *Multinationals and the European Community.* Oxford: Blackwell.

Dutton, J. (1982). "The Optimal Taxation of International Investment Income: A Comment," *Quart. J. Econ.*, 97 (May), 373–80.

Eastman, H. C., and S. Stykolt (1967). *The Tariff and Competition in Canada.* New York: St. Martin's Press.

Eaton, J., and M. Gersovitz (1984). "A Theory of Expropriation and Deviations from Perfect Capital Mobility," *Econ. J.*, 94 (March), 16–40.

Eden. L. (1983). "Transfer Pricing Policies under Tariff Barriers," *Can. J. Econ.*, 16 (November), 669–85.

(1985). "The Microeconomics of Transfer Pricing." In Rugman and Eden (1985), pp. 13–46.

Egelhoff, W. G. (1984). "Patterns of Control in U.S., U.K., and European Multinational Corporations," *J. Int. Bus. Stud.*, 15 (Fall), 73–93.

(1988). "Strategy and Structure in Multinational Corporations: A Revision of the Stopford and Wells Model," *Strategic Manag. J.*, 9 (January), 1–14.

Encarnation, D. J., and L. T. Wells (1986). "Evaluating Foreign Investment." In T. H. Moran et al., *Investing in Development: New Roles for Private Capital*, pp. 61–86. New Brunswick, NJ: Transaction Books.

Enderwick, P. (1985). *Multinational Business and Labour.* New York: St. Martin's Press.

Enderwick, P., and Associates (1989). *Multinational Service Industries.* London: Routledge.

Enderwick, P., and P. J. Buckley (1983). "The Determinants of Strike Activity in Foreign-Owned Plants: Inter-industry Evidence from British Manufacturing Industry 1971–1973," *Manag. Decision Econ.*, 4 (June), 83–8.

Engwall, L., and J. Johnson (eds.) (1980). *Some Aspects of Control in International Business.* Acta Universitatis Upsaliensis, Studia Oeconomiae Negotiorum No. 12, Uppsala.

Erdilek, A. (ed.) (1985). *Multinationals as Mutual Invaders: Intra-Industry Direct Foreign Investment*. London: Croom Helm.

Erland, O. (1980). "International Take-overs and Technology Intensity." In Engwall and Johnson (1980), pp. 17–29.

Errunza, V., and E. Losq (1985). "International Asset Pricing under Mild Segmentation: Theory and Test," *J. Finance*, 40 (March), 105–24.

Errunza, V. R., and L. W. Senbet (1984). "International Corporate Diversification, Market Valuation, and Size-Adjusted Evidence," *J. Finance*, 39 (July), 727–43.

Ethier, W. J. (1986). "The Multinational Firm," *Quart. J. Econ.*, 101 (November), 805–33.

Ethier, W. J., and H. Horn (1990). "Managerial Control of International Firms and Patterns of Direct Investment," *J. Int. Econ.*, 28 (February), 25–45.

Euh, Y.-D., and S. H. Min (1986). "Foreign Direct Investment from Developing Countries: The Case of Korean Firms," *Devel. Econ.*, 24 (June), 149–68.

Eun, C. S., and S. Janakiramanan (1986). "A Model of International Asset Pricing with a Constraint on the Foreign Equity Ownership," *J. Finance*, 41 (September), 897–914.

Evans, P. (1979). *Dependent Development: The Alliance of Multinational State and Local Capital in Brazil*. Princeton: Princeton University Press.

Evans, T. G., and W. R. Folks, Jr. (1979). *Contemporary Foreign Exchange Risk Management Practices at U.S. Multinationals: Implications for Exchange Markets*. Occasional Paper No. 10. Washington: Center for Multinational Studies.

Fagre, N., and L. T. Wells, Jr. (1982). "Bargaining Power of Multinationals and Host Governments," *J. Int. Bus. Stud.*, 13 (Fall), 9–23.

Fairchild, L., and K. Sosin (1986). "Evaluating Differences in Technological Activity between Transnational and Domestic Firms in Latin America," *J. Devel. Stud.*, 22 (July), 697–708.

Falvey, R. E. (1979). "Specific Factors, Comparative Advantage and International Investment: An Extension," *Economica*, 46 (February), 77–82.

Falvey, R. E., and H. O. Fried (1986). "National Ownership Requirements and Transfer Pricing," *J. Devel. Econ.*, 24 (December), 249–54.

Fatemi, A. M. (1984). "Shareholder Benefits from Corporate International Diversification," *J. Finance*, 39 (December), 1325–44.

Fatemi, A. M., and E. P. H. Furtado (1988). "An Empirical Investigation of Wealth Effects of Foreign Acquisitions." In S. J. Khoury and A. Ghosh (eds.), *Recent Developments in International Banking and Finance*, Vol. 2, pp. 363–79. Lexington, MA: Lexington Books.

Feldstein, M. (1994a). "The Effects of Outbound Foreign Direct Investment on the Domestic Capital Stock." Working Paper No. 4668, National Bureau of Economic Research.

(1994b). "Taxes, Leverage and the National Return on Outbound Foreign Direct Investment." Working Paper No. 4689, National Bureau of Economic Research.

Feldstein, M. S., and D. G. Hartman (1979). "The Optimal Taxation of Foreign Source Investment Income," *Quart. J. Econ.*, 93 (November), 613–30.

Ferrantino, M. J. (1991). "Appropriate Technology in a Model of Multinational Duopoly," *Can. J. Econ.*, 24 (August), 660–78.

(1992). "Transaction Costs and the Expansion of Third-World Multinationals," *Econ. Letters*, 38 (April), 451–6.

(1993). "The Effect of Intellectual Property Rights on International Trade and Investment," *Weltwirtsch. Arch.*, 129 (No. 2), 300–31.

Findlay, R. (1978). "Relative Backwardness, Direct Foreign Investment, and the Transfer of Technology: A Simple Dynamic Model," *Quart. J. Econ.*, 92 (February), 1–16.

Fishwick, F. (1982). *Multinational Companies and Economic Concentration in Europe*. Farnborough: Gower.

Flamm, K. (1984). "The Volatility of Offshore Investment," *J. Devel. Econ.*, 16 (December), 231–48.

Flanagan, R. J., and A. R. Weber (eds.) (1974). *Bargaining without Boundaries: The Multinational Corporation and International Labor Relations*. Chicago: University of Chicago Press.

Flowers, E. B. (1976). "Oligopolistic Reactions in European and Canadian Direct Investment in the United States," *J. Int. Bus. Stud.*, 7 (Fall/Winter), 43–55.

Forsgren, M. (1989). *Managing the Internationalization Process: The Swedish Case*. London: Routledge.

Forsyth, D. J. C. (1972). *U.S. Investment in Scotland*. New York: Praeger.

(1973). "Foreign-owned Firms and Labour Relations: A Regional Perspective," *Brit. J. Ind. Relations*, 11 (March), 20–8.

Forsyth, D. J. C., and R. F. Solomon (1977). "Choice of Technology and Nationality of Ownership in Manufacturing in a Developing Country," *Oxford Econ. Pap.*, 29 (July), 258–82.

Frank, R. H., and R. T. Freeman (1978). *Distributional Consequences of Direct Foreign Investment*. New York: Academic Press.

Franko, L. G. (1971). *Joint Venture Survival in Multinational Corporations*. New York: Praeger.

(1976). *The European Multinationals: A Renewed Challenge to American and British Big Business*. Stamford, CT: Greylock.

(1983). *The Threat of Japanese Multinationals*. New York: John Wiley.

(1989). "Use of Minority and 50-50 Joint Ventures by United States Multinationals during the 1970s: The Interaction of Host Country Policies and Corporate Strategies," *J. Int. Bus. Stud.*, 20 (Spring), 19–40.

Fröbel, F., J. Heinrichs, and O. Kreye (1980). *The New International Division of Labour: Structural Unemployment in Industrialised Countries and Industrialisation in Developing Countries*. Cambridge: Cambridge University Press.

Froot, K. (ed.) (1993). *Foreign Direct Investment*. Chicago: University of Chicago Press.

Froot, K. A., and J. R. Hines, Jr. (1994). "Interest Allocation Rules, Financing Patterns, and the Operations of U.S. Multinationals." Working Paper No. 4924, National Bureau of Economic Research.

Froot, K. A., and J. Stein (1991). "Exchange Rates and Foreign Direct Investment: An Imperfect Capital Markets Approach," *Quart. J. Econ.*, 106 (November), 119–217.

Galbraith, C. S., and N. M. Kay (1986). "Towards a Theory of Multinational Enterprise," *J. Econ. Behav. Organ.*, 7 (March), 3–19.

Garnaut, R., and A. Clunies Ross (1975). "Uncertainty, Risk Aversion and the Taxing of Natural Resource Projects," *Econ J.*, 85 (June), 273–89.

Gatignon, H., and E. Anderson (1988). "The Multinational Corporation's Degree of Control over Foreign Subsidiaries: An Empirical Test of a Transaction Cost Explanation," *J. Law Econ. Organ.*, 4 (Fall), 305–36.

Gehrels, F. (1983). "Foreign Investment and Technology Transfer: Optimal Policies," *Weltwirtsch. Arch.*, 119 (No. 4), 663–84.

Geringer, J. M. (1988). *Joint Venture Partner Selection: Strategies for Developed Countries*. New York: Quorum Books.

Geringer, J. M., and L. Hebert (1989). "Control and Performance of International Joint Ventures," *J. Int. Bus. Stud.*, 20 (Summer), 235–54.

Germidis, D. (ed.) (1977). *Transfer of Technology by Multinational Corporations. Vol. 1. A Synthesis and Country Case Study*. Development Centre Studies. Paris: Organization for Economic Cooperation and Development.

Gernon, H. (1983). "The Effect of Translation on Multinational Corporations' Internal Performance Evaluation," *J. Int. Bus. Stud.*, 14 (Spring), 103–12.

Geroski, P. A. (1991). "Domestic and Foreign Entry in the United Kingdom: 1983–1984." In P. A. Geroski and J. Schwalbach (eds.), *Entry and Market Contestability*, pp. 63–88. Oxford: Blackwell.

Gershenberg, I. (1986). "Labor, Capital, and Management Slack in Multinational and Local Firms in Kenyan Manufacturing," *Econ. Devel. Cult. Change*, 35 (October), 163–78.

Gershenberg, I., and T. C. I. Ryan (1978). "Does Parentage Matter? An Analysis of Transnational and Other Firms: An East African Case," *J. Devel. Areas*, 13 (October), 3–10.

Gersovitz, M. (1987). "The Effects of Domestic Taxes on Foreign Private Investment." In D. Newbery and N. Stern (eds.), *The Theory of Taxation for Developing Countries*, pp. 615–35. New York: Oxford University Press.

Ghemawat, P., M. E. Porter, and R. A. Rawlinson (1986). "Patterns of International Coalition Activity." In Porter (1986), pp. 345–65.

Ghertman, M., and J. Leontiades (eds.) (1978). *European Research in International Business*. Amsterdam: North-Holland.

Ghoshal, S., H. Korine, and G. Szulanski (1994). "Inter-unit Communication in Multinational Corporations," *Manag. Sci.*, 40 (January), 96–110.

Ghoshal, S., and N. Nohria (1989). "Internal Differentiation within Multinational Corporations," *Strategic Manag. J.*, 10 (July), 323–37.

Giddy, I. H. (1981). "The Cost of Capital in the International Firm," *Manag. Decision Econ.*, 2 (December), 263–71.

Gillis, M., and R. E. Beals, in collaboration with G. P. Jenkins, L. T. Wells, and U. Peterson (1980). *Tax and Investment Policies for Hard Minerals: Public and Multinational Enterprise in Indonesia*. Cambridge, MA: Ballinger.

Gilman, M. (1981). *The Financing of Foreign Direct Investment: A Study of the Determinants of Capital Flows in Multinational Enterprises*. London: Frances Pinter.

Giovannini, A., R. G. Hubbard, and J. Slemrod (eds.) (1993). *Studies in International Taxation*. Chicago: University of Chicago Press.

Glejser, H. (1976). "The Respective Impacts of Relative Income, Price and Technology Changes, U.S. Foreign Investment, the EEC and EFTA on the American Balance of Trade." In H. Glejser (ed.), *Quantitative Studies of International Economic Relations*, pp. 133–71. Amsterdam: North-Holland.

Glick, R. (1990). "Japanese Capital Flows in the 1980s," *Econ. Rev. Fed. Res. Bank of San Francisco* (Winter), 18–31.

Glickman, N. J., and D. P. Woodward (1988). "The Location of Foreign Direct Investments in the United States: Patterns and Determinants," *Int. Reg. Sci. Rev.*, 11 (No. 2), 137–54.

(1989). *The New Competitors: How Foreign Investors Are Changing the U.S. Economy*. New York: Basic Books.

Globerman, S. (1975). "Technological Diffusion in the Canadian Tool and Die Industry," *Rev. Econ. Statist.*, 57 (November), 428–34.

(1979a). "Foreign Direct Investment and 'Spillover' Efficiency Benefits in Canadian Manufacturing Industries," *Can. J. Econ.*, 12 (February), 42–56.

(1979b). "A Note on Foreign Ownership and Market Structure in the United Kingdom," *Appl. Econ.*, 11 (March), 35–42.

(1984). "The Consistency of Canada's Foreign Investment Review Process – A Temporal Analysis," *J. Int. Bus. Stud.*, 15 (Spring), 119–29.

(1985). "Canada." In Dunning (1985), pp. 187–215.

Globerman, S., J. C. Ries, and I. Vertinsky (1994). "The Economic Performance of Foreign Affiliates in Canada," *Can. J. Econ.*, 27 (February), 143–56.

Goedde, A. G. (1978). "U.S. Multinational Manufacturing Firms: The Determinants and Effects of Foreign Investment." Ph.D. dissertation, Duke University.

Goehle, D. G. (1980). *Decision Making in Multinational Corporations*. Ann Arbor: UMI Research Press.

Goldberg, L. S., and C. D. Kolstad (1994). "Foreign Direct Investment, Exchange Rate Variability and Demand Uncertainty." Working Paper No. 4815, National Bureau of Economic Research.

Goldsbrough, D. J. (1979). "The Role of Foreign Direct Investment in the External Adjustment Process," *IMF Staff Pap.*, 26 (December), 725–54.

(1981). "International Trade of Multinational Corporations and Its Responsiveness to Changes in Aggregate Demand and Relative Prices," *IMF Staff Pap.*, 28 (September), 573–99.

Gomes-Casseres, B. (1989). "Ownership Structures of Foreign Subsidiaries: Theory and Evidence," *J. Econ. Behav. Organ.*, 11 (January), 1–25.

(1990). "Foreign Ownership Preferences and Host Government Restrictions: An Integrated Approach," *J. Int. Bus. Stud.*, 21 (First Quarter), 1–22.

(1993). "Computers: Alliances and Industry Evolution." In D. B. Yoffie (ed.), *Beyond Free Trade: Firms, Governments, and Global Competition*, pp. 79–128. Boston: Harvard Business School Press.

Gordon, R. H. (1992). "Can Capital Income Taxes Survive in Open Economies?," *J. Finance*, 47 (July), 1159–80.

Gordon, S. L., and F. A. Lees (1986). *Foreign Multinational Investment in the United States*. New York: Quorum Books.

Gorecki, P. K. (1976). "The Determinants of Entry by Domestic and Foreign Enterprises in Canadian Manufacturing Industries: Some Comments and Empirical Results," *Rev. Econ. Statist.*, 58 (November), 485–8.

(1980). "The Determinants of Foreign and Domestic Enterprise Diversification in Canada: A Note," *Can. J. Econ.*, 13 (May), 329–39.

Grace, M. F., and S. V. Berg (1990). "Multinational Enterprises, Tax Policy, and R&D Expenses," *So. Econ. J.*, 57 (July), 125–38.

Graham, E. M. (1978). "Transatlantic Investment by Multinational Firms: A Rivalistic Phenomenon?" *J. Post-Keynes. Econ.*, 1 (Fall), 82–99.

Graham, E. M., and P. R. Krugman (1991). *Foreign Direct Investment in the United States*. 2nd ed. Washington: Institute for International Economics.

Grant, R. M. (1987). "Multinationality and Performance among British Manufacturing Companies," *J. Int. Bus. Stud.*, 18 (Fall), 79–89.

Greenberg, E., W. J. Marshall, and J. B. Yawitz (1978). "The Technology of Risk and Return," *Amer. Econ. Rev.*, 68 (June), 241–51.

Greene, J., and M. G. Duerr (1970). *Intercompany Transactions in the Multinational Firm: A Survey*. Managing International Business No. 6. New York: Conference Board.

Greenhill, C. R., and E. O. Herbolzheimer (1980). "International Transfer Pricing: The Restrictive Business Practices Approach," *J. World Trade Law*, 14 (May/ June), 232–41.

Greening, T. S. (1976). "Oil Wells, Pipelines, Refineries and Gas Stations: A Study of Vertical Integration." Ph.D. dissertation, Harvard University.

Greer, C. R., and J. C. Shearer (1981). "Do Foreign-Owned Firms Practice Unconventional Labor Relations?" *Monthly Labor Rev.*, 104 (January), 44–8.

Gresik, T. A., and D. R. Nelson (1994). "Incentive Compatible Regulation of a Foreign-Owned Subsidiary," *J. Int. Econ.*, 36 (May), 309–31.

Grieco, J. (1984). *Between Dependency and Autonomy: India's Experience with the International Computer Industry*. Berkeley: University of California Press.

Grinols, E. L. (1991). "Unemployment and Foreign Capital: The Relative Opportunity Costs of Domestic Labour and Welfare," *Economica*, 58 (February), 107–21.

Grosse, R. E. (1980). *Foreign Investment Codes and Location of Direct Investment*. New York: Praeger.

Grossman, G. M., and E. Helpman (1991). *Innovation and Growth in the Global Economy*. Cambridge, MA: MIT Press.

Grossman, G. M., and A. Razin (1985). "Direct Foreign Investment and the Choice of Technique under Uncertainty," *Oxford Econ. Pap.*, 37 (December), 606–20.

Grubaugh, S. G. (1987*a*). "Determinants of Direct Foreign Investment," *Rev. Econ. Statist.*, 69 (February), 149–52.

(1987*b*). "The Process of Direct Foreign Investment," *So. Econ. J.*, 54 (October), 351–60.

Grubel, H. G. (1974). "Taxation and Rates of Return from Some U.S. Asset Holdings Abroad, 1960–1969," *J. Polit. Econ.*, 82 (May/June), 469–87.

(1977). "A Theory of Multinational Banking," *Banca Naz. Lavoro Quart. Rev.*, No. 123 (December), 342–63.

Gruber, W., D. Mehta, and R. Vernon (1967). "The R&D Factor in International Trade and International Investment of U.S. Industries," *J. Polit. Econ.*, 75 (February), 20–37.

Grubert, H., and J. Mutti (1991*a*). "Taxes, Tariffs and Transfer Pricing in Multinational Corporate Decision Making," *Rev. Econ. Statist.*, 73 (May), 285–93.

(1991*b*). "Financial Flows versus Capital Spending: Alternative Measures of U.S.-Canada Investment and Trade in the Analysis of Taxes." In P. Hooper and J. D. Richardson (eds.), *International Economic Transactions: Issues in Measurement and Empirical Research*, pp. 293–317. Chicago: University of Chicago Press.

Guisinger, S. E., and Associates (1985). *Investment Incentives and Performance Requirements: Patterns of International Trade, Production, and Investment.* New York: Praeger.

Gunter, H. (1975). "Labor and Multinational Corporations in Western Europe: Some Problems and Prospects." In D. Kujawa (ed.), *International Labor and the Multinational Enterprise*, Chapter 7, New York: Praeger.

Gupta, A., et al. (1991). "Gains from Corporate Multinationalism: Evidence from the China Experience," *Fin. Rev.*, 26 (August), 387–407.

Habib, M. M., and B. Victor (1991). "Strategy, Structure, and Performance in U.S. Manufacturing and Service MNCs: A Comparative Analysis," *Strategic Manag. J.*, 12 (November), 589–606.

Haddad, M., and A. Harrison (1993). "Are There Positive Spillovers from Direct Foreign Investment? Evidence from Panel Data for Morocco," *J. Devel. Econ.*, 42 (October), 51–74.

Haendel, D. (1979). *Foreign Investments and the Management of Political Risk.* Boulder: Westview Press.

Håkanson, L. (1981). "Organization and Evolution of Foreign R&D in Swedish Multinationals," *Geografiska Annaler*, 63B, 47–56.

(1983). "R&D in Foreign-Owned Subsidiaries in Sweden." In W. H. Goldberg (ed.), *Governments and Multinationals: The Policy of Control vs. Autonomy*, pp. 163–76. Cambridge, MA: Oelgeschlager, Gunn & Hain.

Håkanson, L., and R. Nobel (1993). "Foreign Research and Development in Swedish Multinationals," *Res. Policy*, 22 (November), 373–96.

Hamada, K. (1966). "Strategic Aspects of Taxation on Foreign Investment Income," *Quart. J Econ.*, 80 (August), 361–75.

(1974). "An Economic Analysis of the Duty-Free Zone," *J. Int. Econ.*, 4 (August), 225–41.

Hamilton, C., and L. E. O. Svensson (1980). "Duty-Free Zones and the Choice between Capital Import and Labor Export." Discussion paper, Institute for International Economic Studies, University of Stockholm.

Harrigan, K. R. (1988). "Strategic Alliances and Partner Asymmetries." In Contractor and Lorange (1988), pp. 205–26.

Harrington, J. W., Jr., K. Burns, and M. Cheung (1986). "Market-Oriented Foreign Investment and Regional Development: Canadian Companies in Western New York," *Econ. Geog.*, 62 (April), 155–66.

Harris, D. G. (1993). "The Impact of U.S. Tax Law Revision on Multinational Corporations' Capital Location and Income-Shifting Decisions," *J. Account. Res.*, 31 (Supplement), 111–40.

Harris, D., et al. (1993). "Income Shifting in U.S. Multinational Corporations." In Giovannini et al. (1993), pp. 277–302.

Harris, R. S., and D. Ravenscraft (1991). "The Role of Acquisitions in Foreign Direct Investment: Evidence from the U.S. Stock Market," *J. Finance*, 46 (July), 825–44.

Hart, O., and J. Moore (1990). "Property Rights and the Nature of the Firm," *J. Polit. Econ.*, 98 (December), 1119–58.

Hartman, D. G. (1977). "Foreign Investment Taxation and Factor Returns in the Host Country." Working paper, Harvard University.

(1979). "Foreign Investment and Finance with Risk," *Quart. J. Econ.*, 93 (May), 213–32.

(1980). "The Effects of Taxing Foreign Investment Income," *J. Pub. Econ.*, 13 (April), 213–30.

(1981). "Domestic Tax Policy and Foreign Investment: Some Evidence." Working Paper No. 784, National Bureau of Economic Research.

(1985). "Tax Policy and Foreign Direct Investment," *J. Pub. Econ.*, 26 (February), 107–21.

Hawawini, G., and M. Schill (1994). "The Japanese Presence in the European Financial Services Sector." In M. Mason and D. Encarnation (eds.), *Does Ownership Matter? Japanese Multinationals in Europe*, pp. 235–87. Oxford: Clarendon Press.

Hawkins, R. G. (ed.) (1979). *Research in International Business and Finance: An Annual Compilation of Research. Vol. 1. The Economic Effects of Multinational Corporations.* Greenwich, CT: JAI Press.

Hawkins, R. G., and D. Macaluso (1977). "The Avoidance of Restrictive Monetary Policies in Host Countries by Multinational Firms," *J. Money, Credit, Banking*, 9 (November), 562–71.

Hawkins, R. G., N. Mintz, and M. Provissiero (1976). "Government Takeovers of U.S. Foreign Affiliates," *J. Int. Bus. Stud.*, 7 (Spring), 3–16.

Hay, G. A., and D. Kelley (1974). "An Empirical Survey of Price-Fixing Conspiracies," *J. Law Econ.*, 17 (April), 13–38.

Hayden, E. W. (1976). *Technology Transfer to East Europe: U.S. Corporate Experience.* New York: Praeger.

Healy, P. J., and K. G. Palepu (1993). "International Corporate Equity Acquisitions: Who, Where, and Why?" In Froot (1993), pp. 231–50.

Hedlund, G. (1981). "Autonomy of Subsidiaries and Formalization of Headquarters-Subsidiary Relationships in Swedish MNCs." In Otterbeck (1981), pp. 25–78.

Heenan, D. A., and W. J. Keegan (1979). "The Rise of Third World Multinationals," *Harvard Bus. Rev.*, 57 (January/February), 101–9.

Heinkel, R. L., and M. D. Levi (1992). "The Structure of International Banking," *J. Int. Money Finance*, 11 (June), 251–72.

Helleiner, G. K. (1973). "Manufactured Exports from Less Developed Countries and Multinational Firms," *Econ. J.*, 83 (March), 21–47.

(1977). "Transnational Enterprises and the New Political Economy of U.S. Trade Policy," *Oxford Econ. Pap.*, 29 (March), 102–16.

(1979). "Transnational Corporations and Trade Structure: The Role of Intra-Firm Trade." In H. Giersch (ed.), *On the Economics of Intra-Industry Trade: Symposium 1978*, pp. 159–81. Tübingen: J. C. B. Mohr (Paul Siebeck).

(1989). "Transnational Corporations and Direct Foreign Investment." In H. Chenery and T. N. Srinivasan (eds.), *Handbook of Development Economics*, Vol. 2, pp. 1441–80. Amsterdam: North-Holland.

Helleiner, G. K., and R. Lavergne (1979). "Intra-Firm Trade and Industrial Exports to the United States," *Oxford Bull. Econ. Statist.*, 41 (November), 297–311.

Hellmann, R. (1970). *The Challenge to U.S. Dominance of the International Corporation.* New York: Dunellen.

(1977). *Transnational Control of Multinational Corporations.* New York: Praeger.

Helpman, E. (1981). "International Trade in the Presence of Product Differentiation, Economics of Scale, and Monopolistic Competition: A Chamberlin-Heckscher-Ohlin Approach," *J. Int. Econ.*, 11 (August), 305–40.

 (1984). "A Simple Theory of International Trade with Multinational Corporations," *J. Polit. Econ.*, 92 (June), 451–71.

 (1985). "Multinational Corporations and Trade Structure," *Rev. Econ. Stud.*, 52 (July), 443–57.

Helpman, E., and P. R. Krugman (1985). *Market Structure and Foreign Trade: Increasing Returns, Imperfect Competition, and the International Economy.* Cambridge, MA: MIT Press.

Henderson, D. F. (1973). *Foreign Enterprises in Japan: Laws and Policies.* Chapel Hill: University of North Carolina Press.

Hennart, J.-F. (1982). *A Theory of Multinational Enterprise.* Ann Arbor: University of Michigan Press.

 (1988). "A Transaction Cost Theory of Equity Joint Ventures," *Strategic Manag. J.*, 9 (July), 361–74.

 (1989). "Can the 'New Forms of Investment' Substitute for the 'Old Forms'?: A Transaction Costs Approach," *J. Int. Bus. Stud.*, 20 (Summer), 211–34.

 (1991). "The Transaction Costs Theory of Joint Ventures: An Empirical Study of Japanese Subsidiaries in the United States," *Manag. Sci.*, 37 (April), 483–97.

Hennart, J.-F., and Y.-R. Park (1993). "Greenfield vs. Acquisition: The Strategy of Japanese Investors in the United States," *Manag. Sci.*, 39 (September), 1054–68.

Herring, R., and T. D. Willett (1972). "The Capital Control Program and United States Investment Activity Abroad," *So. Econ. J.*, 39 (July), 58–71.

Hershfield, D. C. (1975). *The Multinational Union Faces the Multinational Company.* Conference Board Report No. 658. New York: Conference Board.

Herskovic, S. (1976). *The Import and Export of Technological Know How Through Licensing Agreements in Israel 1966–1974.* Jerusalem: Office of the Prime Minister, National Council for Research and Development.

Hertner, P., and G. Jones (eds.) (1986). *Multinationals: Theory and History.* Aldershot: Gower.

Hewitt, G. (1980). "Research and Development Performed Abroad by U.S. Manufacturing Multinationals," *Kyklos*, 33 (No. 2), 308–26.

 (1983). "Research and Development Performed in Canada by American Manufacturing Multinationals." In A. M. Rugman (ed.), *Multinationals and Technology Transfer: The Canadian Experience*, pp. 36–49. New York: Praeger.

Hines, J. R., Jr. (1993a). "Altered States: Taxes and the Location of Foreign Direct Investment in America." Working Paper No. 4397, National Bureau of Economic Research.

 (1993b). "On the Sensitivity of R&D to Delicate Tax Changes: The Behavior of U.S. Multinationals in the 1980s." In Giovannini et al. (1993), pp. 149–87.

 (1994a). "Credit and Deferral as International Investment Incentives." Working paper, Kennedy School of Government, Harvard University.

 (1994b). "No Place Like Home: Tax Incentives and the Location of R&D by American Multinationals." In J. M. Poterba (ed.), *Tax Policy and the Economy*, pp. 65–104. Cambridge, MA: MIT Press.

 (1994c). "Taxes, Technology Transfer, and the R&D Activities of Multinational Firms." Working Paper No. 4932, National Bureau of Economic Research.

Hines, J. R., Jr., and R. G. Hubbard (1990). "Coming Home to America: Dividend Repatriations by U.S. Multinationals." In Razin and Slemrod (1990), pp. 161–200.

Hines, J. R., Jr., and E. M. Rice (1994). "Fiscal Paradise: Foreign Tax Havens and American Business," *Quart. J. Econ.*, 109 (February), 149–83.

Hipple, F. S. (1990). "The Measurement of International Trade Related to Multinational Companies," *Amer. Econ. Rev.*, 80 (December), 1263–70.

Hirsch, S. (1976). "An International Trade and Investment Theory of the Firm," *Oxford Econ. Pap.*, 28 (July), 258–69.

Hirschey, M. (1981). "R&D Intensity and Multinational Involvement," *Econ. Letters*, 7 (No. 1), 87–93.

Hirschey, R. C., and R. E. Caves (1981). "Internationalization of Research and Transfer of Technology by Multinational Enterprises," *Oxford Bull. Econ. Statist.*, 42 (May), 115–30.

Hirschman, A. O. (1969). *How to Divest in Latin America and Why.* Essays in International Finance No. 76. Princeton: International Finance Section, Princeton University.

Hisey, K. B., and R. E. Caves (1985). "Diversification Strategy and Choice of Country: Diversifying Acquisitions Abroad by U.S. Multinationals, 1978–1980," *J. Int. Bus. Stud.*, 16 (Summer), 51–64.

Hjerppe, R., and J. Ahvenainen (1986). "Foreign Enterprises and Nationalistic Control: The Case of Finland Since the End of the Nineteenth Century." In Teichova et al. (1986), pp. 286–98.

Hladik, K. J. (1985). *International Joint Ventures: An Economic Analysis of U.S. Foreign Business Partnerships.* Lexington, MA: Lexington Books.

Hodder, J. E. (1982). "Exposure to Exchange-Rate Movements," *J. Int. Econ.*, 13 (November), 375–86.

Hodder, J. E., and L. W. Senbet (1990). "International Capital Structure Equilibrium," *J. Finance*, 45 (December), 1495–516.

Hodges, M. (1974). *Multinational Corporations and National Governments: A Case Study of the United Kingdom's Experience 1964–1970.* Lexington, MA: Lexington Books, D. C. Heath.

Hogg, R. D., and J. M. Mintz (1993). "Impacts of Canadian and U.S. Tax Reform on the Financing of Canadian Subsidiaries of U.S. Parents." In Giovannini et al. (1993), pp. 47–74.

Hone, A. (1974). "Multi-National Corporations and Multi-National Buying Groups: Their Impact on the Growth of Asia's Manufactured Exports," *World Devel.*, 2 (February), 145–9.

Hood, N., and J. Vahlne (eds.) (1988). *Strategies in Global Competition.* London: Croom Helm.

Hood, N., and S. Young (1976). "U.S. Investment in Scotland-Aspects of the Branch Factory Syndrome," *Scot. J. Polit. Econ.*, 23 (November), 279–94.

(1979). *The Economics of Multinational Enterprise.* London: Longmans Group.

(1988). "Note on Exchange Rate Fluctuations and the Foreign-Owned Sector in Scotland," *Scot. J. Polit. Econ.*, 35 (February), 77–83.

Horiuchi, T. (1989). "The Flexibility of Japan's Small and Medium-Sized Firms and Their Foreign Direct Investment." In K. Yamamura (ed.), *Japanese Investment in the United States: Should We Be Concerned?*, pp. 151–81. Seattle: Society for Japanese Studies, University of Washington.

Hörnell, E., and J. Vahlne (1986). *Multinationals: The Swedish Case.* London: Croom Helm.

Horst, T. (1971). "The Theory of the Multinational Firm: Optimal Behavior under Different Tariff and Tax Rules," *J. Polit. Econ.*, 79 (September/October), 1059–72.

(1972a). "The Industrial Composition of U.S. Exports and Subsidiary Sales to the Canadian Market," *Amer. Econ. Rev.*, 62 (March), 37–45.

(1972b). "Firm and Industry Determinants of the Decision to Invest Abroad: An Empirical Study," *Rev. Econ. Statist.*, 54 (August), 258–66.

(1973). "The Simple Analytics of Multinational Firm Behaviour." In M. B. Connolly and A. K. Swoboda (eds.), *International Trade and Money*, pp. 72–84. London: Allen & Unwin.

(1974a). *At Home Abroad: A Study of the Domestic and Foreign Operations of the American Food-Processing Industry.* Cambridge, MA: Ballinger.

(1974b). "The Theory of the Firm." In J. H. Dunning (ed.), *Economic Analysis and the Multinational Enterprise*, pp. 31–46. London: Allen & Unwin.

(1977). "American Taxation of Multinational Firms," *Amer. Econ. Rev.*, 67 (June), 376–89.

(1980). "A Note on the Optimal Taxation of International Investment Income," *Quart. J. Econ.*, 93 (June), 793–8.

Horstmann, I., and J. R. Markusen (1987*a*). "Licensing versus Direct Investment: A Model of Internationalization by the Multinational Enterprise," *Can. J. Econ.*, 20 (August), 464–81.

(1987*b*). "Strategic Investments and the Development of Multinationals," *Int. Econ. Rev.*, 28 (February), 109–21.

(1989). "Firm-specific Assets and the Gain from Direct Foreign Investment," *Economica*, 56 (February), 41–8.

(1992). "Endogenous Market Structures in International Trade (Natura Facit Saltum)," *J. Int. Econ.*, 32 (February), 109–29.

Hu, Y. S. (1973). *The Impact of U.S. Investment in Europe: A Case Study of the Automotive and Computer Industries*. New York: Praeger.

Hufbauer, G. C. (1966). *Synthetic Materials and the Theory of International Trade*. Cambridge, MA: Harvard University Press.

(1975). "The Multinational Corporation and Direct Investment." In P. B. Kenen (ed.), *International Trade and Finance: Frontiers for Research*, pp. 253–319. Cambridge. Cambridge University Press.

(1992). *U.S. Taxation of International Income: Blueprint for Reform*. Washington: Institute for International Economics.

Hufbauer, G. C., and F. M. Adler (1968). *Overseas Manufacturing Investment and the Balance of Payments*. Tax Policy Research Study No. 1. Washington: U.S. Treasury Department.

Hughes, H., and P. S. You (eds.) (1969). *Foreign Investment and Industrialisation in Singapore*. Canberra: Australian National University Press.

Hughes, J. S., D. E. Logue, and R. J. Sweeney (1975). "Corporate International Diversification and Market Assigned Measures of Risk and Diversification," *J. Fin. Quant. Analysis*, 10 (November), 627–37.

Hughes, K., and C. Oughton (1992). "Foreign and Domestic Multinational Presence in the UK," *Appl. Econ.*, 24 (July), 745–9.

Huizinga, H. (1990). "Unions, Taxes, and the Structure of Multinational Enterprises," *Econ. Letters*, 34 (September), 73–5.

(1991). "National Tax Policies Towards Product-Innovating Multinational Enterprises," *J. Pub. Econ.*, 44 (February), 1–14.

(1992). "The Tax Treatment of R&D Expenditures of Multinational Enterprises," *J. Pub. Econ.*, 47 (April 1992), 343–59.

Hulbert, J. M., and W. Brandt (1980). *Managing the Multinational Subsidiary*. New York: Holt Rinehart and Winston.

Hymer, S. H. (1960). "The International Operations of National Firms: A Study of Direct Foreign Investment." Ph.D. dissertation, MIT (published by MIT Press, 1976).

(1968). "The Large Multinational Corporation: An Analysis of Some Motives for the International Integration of Business," *Revue Economique*, 19 (No. 6), 949–73. Translated in M. Casson (ed.), *Multinational Corporations*, pp. 3–31. Aldershot: Edward Elgar, 1990.

Hymowitz, S. C. (1986). "Exterritorial Application of the Sherman Act to Foreign Corporations," *Delaware Law J.*, 11 (No. 2), 513–34.

International Labour Organization (1976*a*). *Multinationals in Western Europe: The Industrial Relations Experience*. Geneva: International Labour Organization.

(1976*b*). *Wages and Working Conditions in Multinational Enterprises*. Geneva: International Labour Organization.

Ishikawa, J. (1991). "Capital Inflows and Economic Welfare for a Small Open Economy with Variable Returns to Scale," *Econ. Letters*, 35 (April), 429–33.

Itagaki, T. (1979). "Theory of the Multinational Firm: An Analysis of Effects of Government Policies," *Int. Econ. Rev.*, 20 (June), 437–48.

(1981). "The Theory of the Multinational Firm under Exchange Rate Uncertainty," *Can. J. Econ.*, 14 (May), 276–97.

(1987). "International Trade and Investment by Multinational Firms under Uncertainty," *Manchester Sch. Econ. Soc. Res.*, 55 (December), 392–406.

(1989). "The Multinational Enterprise under the Threats of Restriction on Profit Repatriation and Exchange Control," *J. Devel. Econ.*, 31 (October), 369–77.

(1991). "A Two-Step Decision Model of the Multinational Enterprise under Foreign Demand Uncertainty," *J. Int. Econ.*, 30 (February), 185–90.

Jacquillat, B., and B. Solnik (1978). "Multinational Firms' Stock Price Behavior: An Empirical Investigation." In M. Ghertman and J. Leontiades (eds.), *European Research in International Business*, pp. 215–37. Amsterdam: North-Holland.

Jarillo, J. C., and J. S. Martinez (1990). "Different Roles for Subsidiaries: The Case of Multinational Corporations in Spain," *Strategic Manag. J.*, 11 (November), 501–12.

Jarrett, J. P. (1979). "Offshore Assembly and Production and the Internalization of International Trade within the Multinational Corporation." Ph.D. dissertation, Harvard University.

Jedel, M. J., and D. Kujawa (1976). "Management and Employment Practices of Foreign Direct Investors in the United States." In U.S. Department of Commerce, *Foreign Direct Investment in the United States: Report of the Secretary of Commerce to the Congress in Compliance with the Foreign Investment Study Act of 1974*, Appendix 1. Washington: U.S. Government Printing Office.

Jenkins, G. P. (1979). "Taxes and Tariffs and the Evaluation of the Benefit from Foreign Investment," *Can. J. Econ.*, 12 (August), 410–25.

Jenkins, G. P., and B. D. Wright (1975). "Taxation of Income of Multinational Corporations: The Case of the United States Petroleum Industry," *Rev. Econ. Statist.*, 57 (February), 1–11.

Jenkins, R. (1990). "Comparing Foreign Subsidiaries and Local Firms in LDCs: Theoretical Issues and Empirical Evidence," *J. Devel. Stud.*, 26 (January), 205–28.

(1991). "The Impact of Foreign Investment on Less Developed Countries: Cross-Section Analysis versus Industry Studies." In P. J. Buckley and J. Clegg (1991), pp. 111–30.

Jeon, Y.-D. (1992). "The Determinants of Korean Foreign Direct Investment in Manufacturing Industries," *Weltwirtsch. Arch.*, 128 (No. 3), 527–42.

Jilling, M. (1978). *Foreign Exchange Risk Management in U.S. Multinational Corporations*. Research for Business Decisions No. 6. Ann Arbor: UMI Research Press.

Joachimsson, R. (1980). "Taxation of International Corporations." In Engwall and Johnson (1980), pp. 31–42.

Johanson, J., and L.-G. Mattsson (1988). "Internationalisation in Industrial Systems – A Network Approach." In N. Hood and J.-E. Vahlne (eds.), *Strategies in Global Competition*, pp. 287–314. Beckenham: Croom Helm.

Johanson, J., and J.-E. Vahlne (1978). "A Model for the Decision Making Process Affecting Pattern and Pace of the Internationalization of the Firm." In M. Ghertman and J. Leontiades (eds.), *European Research in International Business*, pp. 9–27. Amsterdam: North-Holland.

Johnson, H. G. (1968). *Comparative Cost and Commercial Policy Theory for a Developing World Economy*. Wicksell Lectures. Stockholm: Almqvist & Wiksell.

(1970). "The Efficiency and Welfare Implications of the Multinational Corporation." In C. P Kindleberger (ed.), *The International Corporation: A Symposium*, pp. 35–56. Cambridge, MA: MIT Press.

Jones, G. (1986a). "The Performance of British Multinational Enterprise, 1890–1945." In Hertner and Jones (1986), pp. 96–112.

(ed.) (1986*b*). *British Multinationals: Origins, Management, and Performance*. Aldershot: Gower.

Jones, R. J., Jr. (1984). "Empirical Models of Political Risks in U.S. Oil Production Operations in Venezuela," *J. Int. Bus. Stud.*, 15 (Spring), 81–95.

Jones, R. W. (1967). "International Capital Movements and the Theory of Tariffs and Trade," *Quart. J. Econ.*, 81 (February), 1–38.

(1970). "The Role of Technology in the Theory of International Trade." In R. Vernon (ed.), *The Technology Factor in International Trade*, pp. 73–92. Universities-National Bureau Conference Series No. 22. New York: National Bureau of Economic Research.

(1971). "A Three-Factor Model in Theory, Trade, and History." In Bhagwati et al. (1971), pp. 3–21.

(1979). *International Trade: Essays in Theory*. Amsterdam: North-Holland.

(1980). "Comparative and Absolute Advantage," *Schweiz. Z. Volkswirtsch. Statist.*, 116 (No. 3), 235–60.

(1984). "Protection and the Harmful Effects of Endogenous Capital Flows," *Econ. Letters*, 15 (Nos. 3–4), 325–30.

Jones, R. W., and F. Dei (1983). "International Trade and Foreign Investment: A Simple Model," *Econ. Inquiry*, 21 (October), 449–64.

Jones, R. W., P. J. Neary, and F. Ruane (1983). "Two-Way Capital Flows: Cross-Hauling in a Model of Foreign Investment," *J. Int. Econ.*, 14 (May), 357–66.

Jorgenson, D. W. (1963). "Capital Theory and Investment Behavior," *Amer. Econ. Rev.*, 53 (May), 247–59.

Jorion, P. (1990). "The Exchange-Rate Exposure of U.S. Multinationals," *J. Bus.*, 63 (July), 331–45.

Juhl, P. (1979). "On the Sectoral Patterns of West German Manufacturing Investment in Less Developed Countries: The Impact of Firm Size, Factor Intensities and Protection," *Weltwirtsch. Arch.*, 115 (No. 3), 508–19.

(1985). "The Federal Republic of Germany." In Dunning (1985), pp. 127–54.

Jun, J. (1990). "U.S. Tax Policy and Direct Investment Abroad." In Razin and Slemrod (1990), pp. 55–74.

Kant, C. (1988*a*). "Endogenous Transfer Pricing and the Effects of Uncertain Regulation," *J. Int. Econ.*, 24 (February), 147–57.

(1988*b*). "Foreign Subsidary, Transfer Pricing and Tariffs," *So. Econ. J.*, 55 (July), 162–70.

Kassalow, E. M. (1978). "Aspects of Labour Relations in Multinational Companies: An Overview of Three Asian Countries," *Int. Lab. Rev.*, 117 (May/June), 273–87.

Katrak, H. (1977). "Multi-national Monopolies and Commercial Policy," *Oxford Econ. Pap.*, 29 (July), 283–91.

(1983*a*). "Global Profit Maximisation and Export Performance of Foreign Subsidiaries in India," *Oxford Bull. Econ. Statist.*, 45 (May), 205–22.

(1983*b*). "Multinational Firms' Global Strategies, Host Country Indigenisation of Ownership and Welfare," *J. Devel. Econ.*, 13 (December), 331–48.

(1984). "Pricing Policies of Multinational Enterprises: Host Country Regulation and Welfare," *Int. J. Ind. Org.*, 2 (December), 327–40.

(1985). "Imported Technology, Enterprise Size and R&D in a Newly Industrialising Country: The Indian Experience," *Oxford Bull. Econ. Statist.*, 47 (August), 213–30.

(1994). "R&D Activities of Multinational Enterprises and Host Country Welfare." In Balasubramanyam and Sapsford (1994), pp. 47–64.

Katz, J. M. (1969). *Production Functions, Foreign Investment and Growth: A Study Based on the Argentine Manufacturing Sector 1946–1961*. Contributions to Economic Analysis No. 58. Amsterdam: North-Holland.

Katz, J., and B. Kosacoff (1983). "Multinationals from Argentina." In Lall and Associates (1983), pp. 137–219.

Katz, M. L., and C. Shapiro (1985). "On the Licensing of Innovations," *Rand J. Econ.*, 16 (Winter), 504–20.

Keddie, J. (1976). "Adoption of Production Technique in Indonesian Industry." Ph.D. dissertation, Harvard University.

Kelly, M. W. (1981). *Foreign Investment Evaluation Practices of U.S. Multinational Corporations.* Ann Arbor: UMI Research Press.

Keohane, R. O., and V. D. Ooms (1975). "The Multinational Firm and International Regulation." In C. F. Bergsten and L. B. Krause (eds.), *World Politics and International Economics*, pp. 169–209. Washington: Brookings Institution.

Kim, W. C., and P. Hwang (1992). "Global Strategy and Multinationals' Entry Mode Choice," *J. Int. Bus. Stud.*, 23 (First Quarter), 29–53.

Kim, W. C., P. Hwang, and W. P. Burghers (1993). "Multinationals' Diversification and the Risk-Return Trade-Off," *Strategic Manag. J.*, 14 (May), 275–86.

Kim, W. S., and E. O. Lyn (1987). "Foreign Direct Investment Theories, Entry Barriers, and Reverse Investment in U.S. Manufacturing Industries," *J. Int. Bus. Stud.*, 18 (Summer), 53–66.

Kimura, Y. (1989). "Firm-Specific Strategic Advantages and Foreign Direct Investment Behavior of Firms: The Case of Japanese Semiconductor Firms," *J. Int. Bus. Stud.*, 20 (Summer), 296–314.

Kindleberger, C. P. (1969). *American Business Abroad: Six Lectures on Direct Investment.* New Haven: Yale University Press.

(ed.) (1970). *The International Corporation: A Symposium.* Cambridge, MA: MIT Press.

Klein, B. (1974). "The Role of U.S. Multinational Corporations in Recent Exchange Crises," Occasional Paper No. 6. Washington: Center for Multinational Studies.

Klein, M. W., and E. Rosengren (1992). "Foreign Direct Investment Outflow from the United States: An Empirical Assessment." In Klein and Welfens (1992), pp. 91–103.

(1994). "The Real Exchange Rate and Foreign Direct Investment in the United States: Relative Wealth vs. Relative Wage Effects," *J. Int. Econ.* 36 (May), 373–89.

Klein, M. W., and P. J. J. Welfens (eds.) (1992). *Multinationals in the New Europe and Global Trade.* Berlin: Springer-Verlag.

Klepper, S., and E. Graddy (1990). "The Evolution of New Industries and the Determinants of Market Structure," *Rand J. Econ.*, 21 (Spring), 27–44.

Knickerbocker, F. T. (1973). *Oligopolistic Reaction and Multinational Enterprise.* Boston: Division of Research, Graduate School of Business Administration, Harvard University.

(1976). "Market Structure and Market Power Consequences of Foreign Direct Investment by Multinational Companies," Occasional Paper No. 8. Washington: Center for Multinational Studies.

Kobrin, S. J. (1977). *Foreign Direct Investment Industrialization and Social Change.* Contemporary Studies in Economic and Financial Analysis No. 9. Greenwich, CT: JAI Press.

(1982). *Managing Political Risk Assessment: Strategic Response to Environmental Change.* Berkeley and Los Angeles: University of California Press.

(1987). "Testing the Bargaining Hypothesis in the Manufacturing Sector in Developing Countries," *Int. Org.*, 41 (Autumn), 609–38.

(1994). "Is There a Relationship between a Geocentric Mind-Set and Multinational Strategy?" *J. Int. Bus. Stud.*, 25 (Third Quarter), 493–511.

Koechlin, T. (1992). "The Determinants of the Location of USA Direct Foreign Investment," *Int. Rev. Appl. Econ.*, 6 (No. 2), 203–16.

Kogut, B. (1983). "Foreign Direct Investment as a Sequential Process." In C. P. Kindleberger and D. B. Audretsch (eds.), *The Multinational Corporation in the 1980s*, pp. 38–56. Cambridge, MA: MIT Press.

(1988a). "A Study of the Life Cycle of Joint Ventures." In Contractor and Lorange (1988), pp. 169–85.

(1988*b*). "Joint Ventures: Theoretical and Empirical Perspectives," *Strategic Manag. J.*, 9 (July), 319–32.

(1989). "The Stability of Joint Ventures: Reciprocity and Competitive Rivalry," *J. Ind. Econ.*, 38 (December), 183–98.

(1992). "National Organizing Principles of Work and the Erstwhile Dominance of the American Multinational Corporation," *Indust. Corp. Change*, 1 (No. 2), 285–325.

Kogut, B., and S. J. Chang (1991). "Technological Capabilities and Japanese Foreign Direct Investment in the United States," *Rev. Econ. Statist.*, 73 (August), 401–13.

Kogut, B., and N. Kulatilaka (1994). "Operating Flexibility, Global Manufacturing, and the Option Value of a Multinational Network," *Manag. Sci.*, 40 (January), 123–39.

Kogut, B., and H. Singh (1988). "The Effect of National Culture on the Choice of Entry Mode," *J. Int. Bus. Stud.*, 19 (Fall), 411–32.

Kogut, B., and U. Zander (1993). "Knowledge of the Firm and the Evolutionary Theory of the Multinational Corporation," *J. Int. Bus. Stud.*, 24 (Fourth Quarter), 625–45.

Kohlhagen, S. W. (1977). "Exchange Rate Changes: Profitability, and Direct Foreign Investment," *So. Econ. J.*, 44 (July), 42–52.

Koizumi, T., and K. J. Kopecky (1977). "Economic Growth, Capital Movements and the International Transfer of Technical Knowledge," *J. Int. Econ.*, 7 (February), 45–65.

(1980). "Foreign Direct Investment, Technology Transfer and Domestic Employment Effects," *J. Int. Econ.*, 10 (February), 1–20.

Kojima, K. (1975). "International Trade and Foreign Investment: Substitutes or Complements," *Hitotsubashi J. Econ.*, 16 (June), 1–12.

(1978). *Direct Foreign Investment: A Japanese Model of Multinational Business Operations.* New York: Praeger.

Kokko, A. (1992). *Foreign Direct Investment, Host Country Characteristics, and Spillovers.* Stockholm: Economic Research Institute, Stockholm School of Economics.

Koo, B.-Y. (1985). "Korea." In Dunning (1985), pp. 281–307.

Kopits, G. F. (1972). "Dividend Remittance Behavior within the International Firm: A Cross-Country Analysis," *Rev. Econ. Statist.*, 54 (August), 339–42.

(1976*a*). "Taxation and Multinational Firm Behavior: A Critical Survey," *IMF Staff Pap.*, 23 (November), 624–73.

(1976*b*). "Intrafirm Royalties Crossing Frontiers and Transfer Pricing Behaviour," *Econ. J.*, 86 (December), 791–805.

(1979). "Multinational Conglomerate Diversification," *Econ. Int.*, 32 (February), 99–111.

Krainer, R. E. (1967). "Resource Endowment and the Structure of Foreign Investment," *J. Finance*, 22 (March), 49–57.

Krause, L. B., and K. W. Dam (1964). *Federal Tax Treatment of Foreign Income.* Washington: Brookings Institution.

Kravis, I. B., and R. E. Lipsey (1980). "The Location of Overseas Production and Production for Export by U.S. Multinational Firms." Working Paper No. 482, National Bureau of Economic Research.

(1982). "The Location of Overseas Production and Production for Export by U.S. Multinational Firms," *J. Int. Econ.*, 12 (May), 201–23.

(1992). "Sources of Competitiveness of the United States and of Its Multinational Firms," *Rev. Econ. Statis.*, 74 (May), 193–201.

Krugman, P. (1979). "A Model of Innovation, Technology Transfer, and the World Distribution of Income," *J. Polit. Econ.*, 87 (April), 253–66.

(1989). "Industrial Organization and International Trade." In R. Schmalensee and R. D. Willig (eds.), *Handbook of Industrial Organization*, Vol. 2, pp. 1179–223. Amsterdam: North-Holland.

Kudrle, R. T. (1975). *Agricultural Tractors: A World Industry Study.* Cambridge, MA: Ballinger.

(1991). "Good for the Gander? Foreign Direct Investment in the United States," *Int. Org.*, 45 (Summer), 397–424.

Kujawa, D. (1971). *International Labor Relations Management in the Automotive Industry: A Comparative Study of Chrysler, Ford, and General Motors.* New York: Praeger.

(ed.) (1973). *American Labor and the Multinationals.* New York: Praeger.

(ed.) (1975). *International Labor and the Multinational Enterprise.* New York: Praeger.

(1979). "Collective Bargaining and Labor Relations in Multinational Enterprise: A U.S. Public Policy Perspective." In R. G. Hawkins (ed.), *Research in International Business and Finance: An Annual Compilation of Research. Vol. 1. The Economic Effects of Multinational Corporations*, pp. 25–51. Greenwich, CT: JAI Press.

Kumar, K., and K. Y. Kim (1984). "The Korean Manufacturing Multinationals," *J. Int. Bus. Stud.*, 15 (Spring), 45–61.

Kumar, K., and M. G. McLeod (eds.) (1981). *Multinationals from Developing Countries.* Lexington, MA: Lexington Books, D. C. Heath.

Kumar, M. S. (1984). "Comparative Analysis of UK Domestic and International Firms," *J. Econ. Stud.*, 11 (No. 3), 26–42.

Kumar, N. (1990). *Multinational Enterprises in India: Industrial Distribution, Characteristics, and Performance.* London: Routledge.

(1991). "Mode of Rivalry and Comparative Behaviour of Multinational and Local Enterprises: The Case of Indian Manufacturing," *J. Devel. Econ.*, 35 (April), 381–92.

Kwack, S. Y. (1972). "A Model of U.S. Direct Investment Abroad: A Neoclassical Approach," *Western Econ. J.*, 10 (December), 376–83.

Kyrouz, M. E. (1975). "Foreign Tax Rates and Tax Bases," *Nat. Tax J.*, 28 (March), 61–80.

Ladenson, M. L. (1972). "A Dynamic Balance Sheet Approach to American Direct Foreign Investment," *Int. Econ. Rev.*, 13 (October), 531–43.

Lake, A. W. (1979). "Technology Creation and Technology Transfer by Multinational Firms. In R. G. Hawkins (ed.), *Research in International Business and Finance: An Annual Compilation of Research. Vol. 1. The Economic Effects of Multinational Corporations*, pp. 137–77. Greenwich, CT: JAI Press.

Lall, R. (1986). "Third World Multinationals: The Characteristics of Indian Firms Investing Abroad," *J. Devel. Econ.*, 20 (March), 381–97.

Lall, S. (1973). "Transfer Pricing by Multinational Manufacturing Firms," *Oxford Bull. Econ. Statist.*, 35 (August), 179–95.

(1978*a*). "Transnationals, Domestic Enterprises, and Industrial Structure in Host LDCs: A Survey," *Oxford Econ. Pap.*, 30 (July), 217–48.

(1978*b*). "The Pattern of Intra-Firm Exports by US Multinationals," *Oxford Bull. Econ. Statist.*, 40 (August), 209–22.

(1979*a*). "Multinationals and Market Structure in an Open Developing Economy: The Case of Malaysia," *Weltwirtsch. Arch.*, 115 (No. 2), 325–50.

(1979*b*). "The International Allocation of Research Activity by U.S. Multinationals," *Oxford Bull. Econ. Statist.*, 41 (November), 313–31.

(1980). "Monopolistic Advantages and Foreign Involvement by U.S. Manufacturing Industry," *Oxford Econ. Pap.*, 32 (March), 102–22.

(1983). "Multinationals from India." In Lall and Associates (1983), pp. 21–87.

Lall, S., and Associates (1983). *The New Multinationals: The Spread of Third World Enterprises.* Chichester: Wiley.

Lall, S., and S. Mohammed (1983*a*). "Multinationals in Indian Big Business: Industry Characteristics of Foreign Investments in a Heavily Regulated Economy," *J. Devel. Econ.*, 13 (August), 143–57.

(1983*b*). "Foreign Ownership and Export Performance in the Large Corporate Sector of India," *J. Devel. Stud.*, 20 (October), 56–67.

Lall, S., and N. S. Siddharthan (1982). "The Monopolistic Advantages of Multinationals: Lessons from Foreign Investment in the US," *Econ. J.*, 92 (September), 668–83.

Lall, S., and P. Streeten (1977). *Foreign Investment, Transnationals and Developing Countries*. London: Macmillan.

Langdon, S. W. (1981). *Multinational Corporations in the Political Economy of Kenya*. New York: St. Martin's Press.

Lapan, H., and P. Bardhan (1973). "Localized Technical Progress and Transfer of Technology and Economic Development," *J. Econ. Theory*, 6 (December), 585–95.

Lecraw, D. (1977). "Direct Investment by Firms from Less Developed Countries," *Oxford Econ. Pap.*, 29 (November), 445–57.

(1983). "Performance of Transnational Corporations in Less Developed Countries," *J. Int. Bus. Stud.*, 14 (Spring/Summer), 15–33.

(1984). "Bargaining Power, Ownership, and Profitability of Transnational Corporations in Developing Countries," *J. Int. Bus. Stud.*, 15 (Spring), 27–43.

(1985). "Some Evidence on Transfer Pricing by Multinational Corporations." In Rugman and Eden (1985), pp. 223–39.

(1991). "Factors Influencing FDI by TNCs in Host Developing Countries: A Preliminary Report." In P. J. Buckley and J. Clegg (1991), pp. 163–80.

(1992). "Third World MNEs Once Again: The Case of Indonesia." In P. J. Buckley and M. Casson (eds.), *Multinational Enterprises in the World Economy: Essays in Honour of John Dunning*, pp. 115–33. Aldershot: Edward Elgar.

Lee, C. L., and C. C. Y. Kwok (1988). "Multinational Corporations vs. Domestic Corporations: International Environmental Factors and Determinants of Capital Structure," *J. Int. Bus. Stud.*, 19 (Summer), 195–217.

Lee, J. (1986). "Determinants of Offshore Production in Developing Countries," *J. Devel. Econ.*, 20 (January), 1–13.

Lee, J.-Y., and E. Mansfield (forthcoming). "Intellectual Property Protection and U.S. Foreign Direct Investment," *Rev. Econ. Statist.*

Lee, W. Y., and K. S. Sachdeva (1977). "The Role of the Multinational Firm in the Integration of Segmented Capital Markets," *J. Finance*, 32 (May), 479–92.

Leechor, C., and J. Mintz (1993). "On the Taxation of Multinational Corporate Investment When the Deferral Method Is Used by the Capital Exporting Country," *J. Pub. Econ.*, 51 (May), 75–96.

Lees, F. A. (1976). *Foreign Banking and Investment in the United States: Issues and Alternatives*. New York: Halsted Press.

Leftwich, R. B. (1974). "U.S. Multinational Companies: Profitability, Financial Leverage, and Effective Income Tax Rates," *Surv. Curr. Bus.*, 54 (May), 27–36.

Leksell, L. (1981). *Headquarters-Subsidiary Relationships in Multinational Corporations*. Stockholm: Stockholm School of Economics.

Lent, G. E (1977). "Corporation Income Tax Structure in Developing Countries," *IMF Staff Pap.*, 24 (November), 722–55.

Leonard, J. S., and R. McCulloch (1991). "Foreign Owned Business in the United States." In J. M. Abowd and R. B. Freeman (eds.), *Immigration, Trade, and the Labor Market*, pp. 261–83. Chicago: University of Chicago Press.

Leroy, G. (1976). *Multinational Product Strategy: A Typology for Analysis of Worldwide Product Innovation and Diffusion*. New York: Praeger.

Lessard, D. G. (1979). "Transfer Prices, Taxes, and Financial Markets: Implications of Internal Financial Transfers within the Multinational Corporation." In R. G. Hawkins (ed.), *Research in International Business and Finance: An Annual Compilation of Research Vol. 1. The Economic Effects of Multinational Corporations*, pp. 101–25. Greenwich, CT: JAI Press.

(1986). "Finance and Global Competition: Exploiting Financial Scope and Coping with Volatile Exchange Rates." In Porter (1993), pp. 147–84.

Levinsohn, J. (1989). "Strategic Trade Policy When Firms Can Invest Abroad: When Are Tariffs and Quotas Equivalent?" *J. Int. Econ.*, 27 (August), 129–46.

Levinsohn, J., and J. Slemrod (1993). "Taxes, Tariffs, and the Global Corporation," *J. Pub. Econ.*, 51 (May), 97–116.

Levy, B. (1988). "The Determinants of Manufacturing Ownership in Less Developed Countries: A Comparative Analysis," *J. Devel. Stud.*, 28 (March), 217–31.

Levy, H., and M. Sarnat (1970). "International Diversification of Investment Portfolios," *Amer. Econ. Rev.*, 60 (September), 668–75.

Li, J., and S. Guisinger (1992). "The Globalization of Service Multinationals in the 'Triad' Regions: Japan, Western Europe and North America," *J. Int. Bus. Stud.*, 23 (Fourth Quarter), 675–96.

Liang, A. Y.-W. (1994). "Spillover Effects of Foreign Direct Investment on the Productivity of Chinese State-Owned Enterprises." Senior honors thesis, Harvard College.

Lim, D. (1976). "Capital Utilisation of Local and Foreign Establishments in Malaysian Manufacturing," *Rev. Econ. Statist.*, 58 (May), 209–17.

(1977). "Do Foreign Companies Pay Higher Wages than Their Local Counterparts in Malaysian Manufacturing," *J. Devel. Econ.*, 4 (March), 55–66.

Lin, S. A. Y. (1993). "Multinationals' Intra-Firm Trade and Technology Transfer's Effects on LDCs' Growth." In H. P. Gray (ed.), *Transnational Corporations and International Trade and Payments*, pp. 166–81. London: Routledge.

Lindert, P. H. (1970). "The Payments Impact of Foreign Investment Controls," *J. Finance*, 26 (December), 1083–99.

Lippman, S. A., and R. P. Rumelt (1982). "Uncertain Imitability: An Analysis of Interfirm Differences in Efficiency under Competition," *Bell J. Econ.*, 13 (Autumn), 418–38.

Lipsey, R. E. (1993). "Foreign Direct Investment in the United States: Changes over Three Decades." In Froot (1993), pp. 113–70.

(1994). "Outward Direct Investment and the U.S. Economy." Working Paper No. 4691, National Bureau of Economic Research.

Lipsey, R. E., I. B. Kravis, and R. A. Roldan (1982). "Do Multinational Firms Adapt Factor Proportions to Relative Factor Prices?" In A. O. Krueger (ed.), *Trade and Employment in Developing Countries*. Vol. 2. *Factor Supply and Substitution*, pp. 215–55. Chicago: University of Chicago Press.

Lipsey, R. E., and M. Y. Weiss (1981). "Foreign Production and Exports in Manufacturing Industries," *Rev. Econ. Statist.*, 63 (November), 488–94.

Little, J. S. (1981). "The Financial Health of U.S. Manufacturing Firms Acquired by Foreigners," *New England Econ. Rev.* (July/August), 5–18.

Litvak, I. A., and C. J. Maule (1977). "Transnational Corporations and Vertical Integration: The Banana Case," *J. World Trade Law*, 11 (November/December), 537–49.

Lombard, F. J. (1979). *The Foreign Investment Screening Process in LDCs: The Case of Colombia.* Boulder: Westview Press.

Lubitz, R. (1971a). "Direct Investment and Capital Formation." In R. E. Caves and G. L. Reuber, *Capital Transfers and Economic Policy: Canada 1951–62*, pp. 146–95. Cambridge, MA: Harvard University Press.

(1971b). "A Note on United States Direct Investment and Human Capital," *J. Polit. Econ.*, 79 (September/October), 1171–5.

Lucas, R. E. B. (1993). "On the Determinants of Direct Foreign Investment: Evidence from East and Southeast Asia," *World Devel.*, 21 (March), 391–406.

Luehrman, T. A. (1990). "The Exchange Rate Exposure of a Global Competitor," *J. Int. Bus. Stud.*, 21 (No. 2), 225–42.

Lunn, J. (1980). "Determinants of U.S. Direct Investment in the E.E.C.: Further Evidence," *Eur. Econ. Rev.*, 13 (January), 93–101.

Lupo, L. A., A. Gilbert, and M. Liliestedt (1978). "The Relationship between Age and Rate of Return of Foreign Manufacturing Affiliates of U.S. Manufacturing Parent Companies," *Surv. Curr. Bus.*, 58 (August), 60–6.

MacCharles, D. C. (1987). *Trade among Multinationals: Intra-Industry Trade and National Competitiveness*. London: Croom Helm.

Macdougall, G. D. A. (1960). "The Benefits and Costs of Private Investment from Abroad: A Theoretical Approach," *Econ. Record*, 36 (March), 13–35.

Machlup, F., W. S. Salant, and L. Tarshis (eds.) (1972). *The International Mobility and Movement of Capital*. Universities-National Bureau Conference Series No. 24. New York: Columbia University Press for National Bureau of Economic Research.

Magee, S. P. (1977*a*). "Information and Multinational Corporations: An Appropriability Theory of Direct Foreign Investment." In J. Bhagwati (ed.), *The New International Economic Order*, pp. 317–40. Cambridge. MA: MIT Press.

　(1977*b*). "Application of the Dynamic Limit Pricing Model to the Price of Technology and International Technology Transfer." In K. Brunner and A. H. Meltzer (eds.), *Optimal Policies Control Theory and Technology Exports*, pp. 203–24. Amsterdam: North-Holland.

Mahini, A., and L. T. Wells, Jr. (1986). "Government Relations in the Global Firm." In Porter (1986), pp. 291–312.

Maki, D. R., and L. N. Meredith (1986). "Production Cost Differentials and Foreign Direct Investment: A Test of Two Models," *Appl. Econ.*, 18 (October), 1127–34.

Makin, J. H. (1989). "The Effects of Japanese Investment in the United States." In K. Yamamura (ed.), *Japanese Foreign Investment in the United States: Should We Be Concerned?*, pp. 41–62. Seattle: Society for Japanese Studies, University of Washington.

Makinen, G. E. (1970). "The 'Payoff' Period of Direct Foreign Investment by the United States Automobile Industry," *J. Bus.*, 43 (October), 395–409.

Malley, J., and T. Moutos (1994). "A Prototype Macroeconomic Model of Foreign Direct Investment," *J. Devel. Econ.*, 43 (April), 295–315.

Manning, R., and K. L. Shea (1989). "Perfectly Discriminatory Policy towards International Capital Movements in a Dynamic World," *Int. Econ. Rev.*, 30 (May), 329–48.

Mansfield, E. (1984). "R&D and Innovation: Some Empirical Findings." In Z. Griliches (ed.), *R&D, Patents, and Productivity*, pp. 127–48. Chicago: University of Chicago Press.

Mansfield, E., and A. Romeo (1980). "Technology Transfer to Overseas Subsidiaries by U.S.-Based Firms," *Quart. J. Econ.*, 95 (December), 737–50.

Mansfield, E., A. Romeo, and S. Wagner (1979). "Foreign Trade and U.S. Research and Development," *Rev. Econ. Statist.*, 61 (February), 49–57.

Mansfield, E., D. J. Teece, and A. Romeo (1979). "Overseas Research and Development by US-Based Firms," *Economica*, 46 (May), 187–96.

Mantel, I. M. (1975). "Source and Uses of Funds for a Sample of Majority-Owned Foreign Affiliates of U.S. Companies, 1966–72," *Surv. Curr. Bus.*, 55 (July), 29–52.

Marion, B. W., and H. J. Nash (1983). "Foreign Investment in U.S. Food-Retailing Industry," *Amer. J. Agric. Econ.*, 65 (May), 413–20.

Mariti, P., and R. H. Smiley (1983). "Co-operative Agreements and the Organization of Industry," *J. Ind. Econ.*, 31 (June), 437–51.

Markensten, K. (1972). *Foreign Investment and Development: Swedish Companies in India*. Scandinavian Institute of Asian Studies Monograph No. 8. Lund: Studentlitteratur.

Markusen, J. R. (1983). "Factor Movements and Commodity Trade as Complements," *J. Int. Econ.*, 14 (May), 341–56.

(1984). "Multinationals, Multi-plant Economies and the Gains from Trade," *J. Int. Econ.*, 16 (May), 205–26.

Markusen, J. R., and J. R. Melvin (1979). "Tariffs, Capital Mobility, and Foreign Ownership," *J. Int. Econ.*, 9 (August), 395–409.

Martin, S. 1991. "Direct Foreign Investment in the United States," *J. Econ. Behav. Organ.*, 16 (December), 283–94.

Martinez, J. I., and J. C. Jarillo (1989). "The Evolution of Research on Coordination Mechanisms in Multinational Companies," *J. Int. Bus. Stud.*, 20 (Fall), 489–514.

Martinussen, J. (1988). *Transnational Corporations in a Developing Country: The Indian Experience*. New Delhi: Sage Publications.

Mason, R. H. (1973). "Some Observations on the Choice of Technology by Multinational Firms in Developing Countries," *Rev. Econ. Statist.*, 55 (August), 349–55.

Mathewson, G. F., and G. D. Quirin (1979). *Fiscal Transfer Pricing in Multinational Corporations*. Toronto: University of Toronto Press for Ontario Economic Council.

Mauer, L. J., and A. E. Scaperlanda (1972). "Remittances from United States Direct Foreign Investment in the European Economic Community: An Exploratory Estimate of Their Determinants," *Econ. Int.*, 25 (February), 3–13.

McAleese, D., and M. Counahan (1979). " 'Stickers' or 'Snatchers'? Employment in Multinational Corporations during the Recession," *Oxford Bull. Econ. Statist.*, 41 (November), 345–58.

McAleese, D., and D. McDonald (1978). "Employment Growth and the Development of Linkages in Foreign-Owned and Domestic Manufacturing Enterprises," *Oxford Bull. Econ. Statist.*, 40 (November), 321–39.

McClain, D. S. (1974). "Foreign Investment in United States Manufacturing and the Theory of Direct Investment." Ph.D. dissertation, Massachusetts Institute of Technology.

(1983). "Foreign Direct Investment in the United States: Old Currents, 'New Waves,' and the Theory of Direct Investment." In C. P. Kindleberger (ed.), *The Multinational Corporation in the 1980s*, pp. 276–333. Cambridge, MA: MIT Press.

McCulloch, R., and J. L. Yellen (1976). "Technology Transfer and the National Interest," Discussion Paper No. 526, Harvard Institute of Economic Research, Harvard University.

McFetridge, D. G. (1987). "The Timing, Mode and Terms of Technology Transfer: Some Recent Findings." In A. Safarian and G. Y. Bertin (eds.), *Governments, Multinationals, and International Technology Transfer*, pp. 135–50. New York: St. Martin's Press.

McKern, R. B. (1976). *Multinational Enterprise and Natural Resources*. Sydney: McGraw-Hill.

McManus, J. C. (1972). "The Theory of the International Firm." In G. Paquet (ed.), *The Multinational Firm and the Nation State*, pp. 66–93. Don Mills, Ontario: Collier-Macmillan.

McMullen, K. E. (1983). "Lags in Product and Process Innovation Adoption by Canadian Firms." In A. M. Rugman (ed.), *Multinationals and Technology Transfer: The Canadian Experience*, pp. 50–72. New York: Praeger.

McQueen, D. L. (1975). "Learning, the Multinational Corporation and the Further Development of Developed Economies." In M. Ariga (ed.), *International Conference on International Economy and Competition Policy*, pp. 118–34. Tokyo: Council of Tokyo Conference on International Economy and Competition Policy.

Meredith, L. (1984). "U.S. Multinational Investment in Canadian Manufacturing Industries," *Rev. Econ. Statist.*, 66 (February), 111–19.

Michalet, C.-A., and M. Delapierre (1976). *The Multinationalization of French Firms*. Chicago: Academy of International Business.

Michel, A., and I. Shaked (1986). "Multinational Corporations vs. Domestic Corporations: Financial Performance and Characteristics," *J. Int. Bus. Stud.*, 17 (Fall), 89–100.

Mikesell, R. F. (1962). *US Private and Government Investment Abroad*. Eugene, OR: University of Oregon Press.

(1975). *Foreign Investments in Copper Mining: Case Studies of Mines in Peru and Papua, New Guinea.* Baltimore: Johns Hopkins Press for Resources for the Future.

Miller, J. C., and B. Pras (1980). "The Effects of Multinational and Export Diversification on the Profit Stability of U.S. Corporations," *So. Econ. J.*, 46 (January), 792–805.

Millington, A. I., and B. T. Bayliss (1991). "Non-Tariff Barriers and U.K. Investment in the European Community," *J. Int. Bus. Stud.*, 22 (Fourth Quarter), 695–710.

Minabe, N. (1974). "Capital and Technology Movements and Economic Welfare," *Amer. Econ. Rev.*, 64 (December), 1088–100.

Mirus, R., and B. Yeung (1987). "The Relevance of the Invoicing Currency in Intra-Firm Transactions," *J. Int. Money Finance*, 6 (December), 449–64.

Mitchell, W., J. M. Shaver, and B. Yeung (1992). "Getting There in a Global Industry: Impacts on Performance of Changing International Presence," *Strategic Manag. J.*, 13 (September), 419–32.

(1993). "Performance Following Changes of International Presence in Domestic and Transition Industries," *J. Int. Bus. Stud.*, 24 (Fourth Quarter), 647–69.

(1994). "Foreign Entrant Survival and Foreign Market Share: Canadian Companies' Experience in United States Medical Sector Markets," *Strategic Manag. J.*, 15 (September), 555–67.

Miyagiwa, K. F., and L. Young (1986). "International Capital Mobility and Commercial Policy in an Economic Region," *J. Int. Econ.*, 20 (May), 329–41.

Mohtadi, H. (1990). "Expropriation of Multinational Firms: The Role of Domestic Market Conditions and Domestic Rivalries," *Econ. Inquiry*, 28 (October), 813–30.

Molle, W., and R. Morsink (1991). "Intra-European Direct Investment." In B. Bürgenmeier and J. L. Muccielli (eds.), *Multinationals and Europe 1992: Strategies for the Future*, pp. 81–101. London: Routledge.

Morck, R., and B. Yeung (1991). "Why Investors Value Multinationality," *J. Bus.*, 64 (April), 165–87.

(1992). "Internalization: An Event Study Test," *J. Int. Econ.*, 33 (August), 41–56.

More, A., and R. E. Caves (1994). "Intrafirm Royalties in the Process of Expansion of U.S. Multinational Enterprises." In Balasubramanyam and Sapsford (1994), pp. 65–84.

Morley, S. A., and G. W. Smith (1971). "Import Substitution and Foreign Investment in Brazil," *Oxford Econ. Pap.*, 23 (March), 120–35.

(1977a). "The Choice of Technology: Multinational Firms in Brazil," *Econ. Devel. Cult. Change*, 25 (January), 239–64.

(1977b). "Limited Search and the Technology Choices of Multinational Firms in Brazil," *Quart. J. Econ.*, 91 (May), 263–88.

Motta, M. (1992). "Multinational Firms and the Tariff-Jumping Argument: A Game Theoretic Analysis with Some Unconventional Conclusions," *Eur. Econ. Rev.*, 36 (December), 1557–71.

Mowery, D. C. (1987). *Alliance Politics and Economics: Multinational Joint Ventures in Commercial Aircraft.* Cambridge, MA: Ballinger.

Moxon, R. W. (1979). "The Cost, Conditions, and Adaptation of MNC Technology in Developing Countries." In R. G. Hawkins (ed.), *Research in International Business and Finance: An Annual Compilation of Research. Vol. 1. The Economic Effects of Multinational Corporations*, pp. 189–222. Greenwich, CT: JAI Press.

Mueller, D. C., and J. E. Tilton (1969). "Research and Development Costs as a Barrier to Entry," *Can. J. Econ.*, 2 (November), 570–9.

Müller, R., and R. Morgenstern (1974). "Multinational Corporations and Balance of Payments Impacts in LDCs: An Econometric Analysis of Export Pricing Behavior," *Kyklos*, 27 (No. 2), 304–21.

Mundell, R. A. (1957). "International Trade and Factor Mobility," *Amer. Econ. Rev.*, 47 (June), 321–35.

Murtha, T. P. (1991). "Surviving Industrial Targeting: State Credibility and Public Policy Contingencies in Multinational Subcontracting," *J. Law Econ. Organ.*, 7 (Spring), 117–43.

Musgrave, P. B. (1969). *United Stares Taxation of Foreign Investment Income: Issues and Arguments*. Cambridge, MA: International Tax Program, Harvard Law School.

(1975). *Direct Investment Abroad and the Multinationals: Effects on the United States Economy*. U.S. Senate, Committee on Foreign Relations, Subcommittee on Multinational Corporations, Committee Print, 94th Congress, first session. Washington: U.S. Government Printing Office.

Mytelka, L. K. (1979). *Regional Development in a Global Economy: The Multinational Corporation, Technology, and Andean Integration*. New Haven: Yale University Press.

(ed.) (1991). *Strategic Partnerships: States, Firms, and International Competition*. London: Pinter.

Mytelka, L. K., and M. Delapierre (1988). "The Alliance Strategies of European Firms in the Information Technology Industry and the Role of ESPRIT." In Dunning and Robson (1988), pp. 129–51.

Nankani, G. T. (1979). *The Intercountry Distribution of Direct Foreign Investment in Manufacturing*. New York: Garland.

Naumann-Etienne, R. (1974). "A Framework for Financial Decisions in the Multinational Corporations: Summary of Recent Research," *J. Financial Quant. Anal.*, 9 (November), 859–74.

Nayyar, D. (1978). "Transnational Corporations and Manufactured Exports from Poor Countries," *Econ. J.*, 88 (March), 59–84.

Neary, J. P. (1978). "Short-Run Capital Specificity and the Pure Theory of International Trade," *Econ. J.*, 88 (September), 488–510.

(1980). "International Factor Mobility, Minimum Wage Rates and Factor Price Equalization: A Synthesis." Seminar Paper No. 158, Institute for International Economic Studies, University of Stockholm..

Negandhi, A. R. (1975). *Organization Theory in an Open System: A Study of Transferring Advanced Management Practices to Developing Nations*. New York: Dunellen.

(1983). "External and Internal Functioning of American, German, and Japanese Multinational Corporations: Decisionmaking and Policy Issues." In W. H. Goldberg (ed.), *Governments and Multinationals: The Policy of Control vs. Autonomy*, pp. 21–41. Cambridge, MA: Oelgeschlager, Gunn & Hain.

Negandhi, A. R., and B. R. Baliga (1979). *Quest for Survival and Growth: A Comparative Study of American, European, and Japanese Multinationals*. New York: Praeger.

Nelson, R. R., and S. G. Winter (1982). *An Evolutionary Theory of Economic Change*. Cambridge, MA: Harvard University Press.

Ness, W. L., Jr. (1975). "U.S. Corporate Income Taxation and the Dividend Remittance Policy of Multinational Corporations," *J. Int. Bus. Stud.*, 6 (Spring), 67–77.

Newbould, G. D., P. J. Buckley, and J. C. Thruwell (1978). *Going International: The Experience of Smaller Companies Overseas*. Somerset, NJ: Halsted Press.

Newfarmer, R. S. (1979). "TNC Takeovers in Brazil: The Uneven Distribution of Benefits in the Market for Firms," *World Devel.*, 7 (January), 25–43.

(1980). *Transnational Conglomerates and the Economics of Dependent Development: A Case Study of the International Electrical Oligopoly and Brazil's Electrical Industry*. Contemporary Studies in Economic and Financial Analysis No. 23. Greenwich, CT: JAI Press.

(ed.) (1985). *Profits, Progress and Poverty: Case Studies of International Industries in Latin America*. Notre Dame, IN: University of Notre Dame Press.

Newfarmer, R. S., and W. F. Mueller (1975). *Multinational Corporations in Brazil and Mexico: Structural Sources of Economic and Noneconomic Power*. U.S. Senate, Committee on Foreign Relations, Subcommittee on Multinational Corporations, 94th Congress, first session. Washington: U.S. Government Printing Office.

Newman, H. H. (1978). "Strategic Groups and the Structure-Performance Relationship," *Rev. Econ. Statist.*, 60 (August), 417–28.

Nicholas, S. (1983). "Agency Contracts, Institutional Modes, and the Transition to Foreign Direct Investment by British Manufacturing Multinationals before 1939," *J. Econ. History*, 43 (September), 675–86.

(1986). "The Theory of Multinational Enterprise as a Transactional Mode." In Hertner and Jones (1986), pp. 64–95.

Nieckels, L. (1976). *Transfer Pricing in Multinational Firms: A Heuristic Programming Approach and a Case Study*. Stockholm: Almqvist & Wiksell.

Nigh, D. (1986). "Political Events and the Foreign Direct Investment Decision: An Empirical Examination," *Manag. Decision Econ.*, 7 (June), 99–106.

Nigh, D., K. R. Cho, and S. Krishnan (1986). "The Role of Location-Related Factors in U.S. Banking Involvement Abroad: An Empirical Examination," *J. Int. Bus. Stud.*, 17 (Fall), 59–72.

Nigh, D., and H. Schollhammer (1987). "Foreign Direct Investment, Political Conflict and Co-operation: The Asymmetric Response Hypothesis," *Manag. Decision Econ.*, 8 (December), 307–12.

Norman, G., and J. H. Dunning (1984). "Intra-Industry Foreign Direct Investment: Its Rationale and Trade Effects," *Weltwirtsch. Arch.*, 120 (No. 3), 522–39.

Northrup, H. R., and R. L. Rowan (1979). *Multinational Collective Bargaining Attempts: The Record, the Cases, and the Prospects*. Multinational Industrial Relations Series No. 6. Philadelphia: Industrial Research Unit, The Wharton School, University of Pennsylvania.

Nugent, J. B. (1986). "Arab Multinationals: Problems, Potential and Policies." In K. M. Khan (ed.), *Multinationals of the South*, pp. 165–83. New York: St. Martin's Press.

O'Loughlin, B., and P. N. O'Farrell (1980). "Foreign Direct Investment in Ireland: Empirical Evidence and Theoretical Implications," *Econ. Soc. Rev.*, 11 (April), 155–85.

Oblak, D. J., and R. J. Helm, Jr. (1980). "Survey and Analysis of Capital Budgeting Methods Used by Multinationals," *Fin. Manag.*, 9 (Winter), 37–41.

Olsson, U. (1993). "Securing the Markets: Swedish Multinationals in a Historical Perspective." In G. Jones and H. G. Schröter (eds.), *The Rise of Multinationals in Continental Europe*, pp. 99–127. Cheltenham: Edward Elgar.

Oman, C. (1984). *New Forms of International Investment in Developing Countries*. Paris: OECD.

Ondrich, J., and M. Wasylenko (1993). *Foreign Direct Investment in the United States: Issues, Magnitudes, and Location Choice of New Manufacturing Plants*. Kalamazoo, MI: Upjohn Institute.

Onida, F., and G. Viesti (eds.) (1988). *The Italian Multinationals*. London: Croom Helm.

Organization for Economic Cooperation and Development (1974). *Export Cartels*. Paris: OECD.

(1977). *Restrictive Business Practices of Multinational Enterprises: Report of the Committee of Experts on Restrictive Business Practices*. Paris: OECD.

(1978). *National Treatment for Foreign-Controlled Enterprises Established in OECD Countries*. Paris: OECD.

(1980). *International Direct Investment: Policies, Procedures and Practices in OECD Member Countries, 1979*. Paris: OECD.

(1986). *The OECD Guidelines of Multinational Enterprises*. Paris: OECD.

(1991). *Taxing Profits in a Global Economy: Domestic and International Issues*. Paris: OECD.

Orr, D. (1975). "The Industrial Composition of U.S. Exports and Subsidiary Sales to the Canadian Market: Comment," *Amer. Econ. Rev.*, 65 (March), 230–4.

Orr, J. (1991). "The Trade Balance Effects of Foreign Direct Investment in U.S. Manufacturing," *Fed. Res. Bank of New York Quart. Rev.*, 16 (Summer), 63–76.

Otterback, L. (ed.) (1981). *The Management of Headquarters-Subsidiary Relationships in Multinational Corporations*. Aldershot: Gower

Owen, R. F. (1982). "Interindustry Determinants of Foreign Direct Investments: A Canadian Perspective." In Rugman (1982), pp. 238–53.

Ozawa, T. (1979*a*). "International Investment and Industrial Structure: New Theoretical Implications from the Japanese Experience," *Oxford Econ. Pap.*, 31 (March), 72–92.

(1979*b*). *Multinationalism, Japanese Style: The Political Economy of Outward Dependency.* Princeton: Princeton University Press.

Pack, H. (1976). "The Substitution of Labour for Capital in Kenyan Manufacturing," *Econ. J.*, 86 (March), 45–58.

Panagariya, A. (1986). "Increasing Returns, Dynamic Stability, and International Trade," *J. Int. Econ.*, 20 (February), 43–63.

Papanek, G. F. (1973). "Aid, Foreign Private Investment, Savings, and Growth in Less Developed Countries," *J. Polit. Econ.*, 81 (January/February), 120–30.

Parry, T. G. (1973). "The International Firm and National Economic Policy," *Econ. J.*, 83 (December), 1201–21.

(1974*a*). "Size of Plant, Capacity Utilization and Economic Efficiency: Foreign Investment in the Australian Chemical Industry," *Econ. Rec.*, 50 (June), 218–44.

(1974*b*). "Technology and the Size of the Multinational Corporation Subsidiary: Evidence from the Australian Manufacturing Sector," *J. Ind. Econ.*, 23 (December), 125–34.

(1978). "Structure and Performance in Australian Manufacturing, With Special Reference to Foreign-Owned Enterprises." In W. Kasper and T. G. Parry (eds.), *Growth, Trade and Structural Change in an Open Australian Economy*, pp. 173–99. Kensington, Australia: Centre for Applied Economic Research, University of New South Wales.

Parry, T. G., and J. F. Watson (1979). "Technology Flows and Foreign Investment in the Australian Manufacturing Sector," *Austral. Econ. Pap.*, 18 (June), 103–18.

Pastré, O. (1981). *Multinationals: Bank and Corporate Relationships.* Contemporary Studies in Economic and Financial Analysis No. 28. Greenwich, CT: JAI Press.

Pearce, R. D. (1989). *The Internalisation of Research and Development by Multinational Enterprises.* New York: St. Martin's Press.

(1993). *The Growth and Evolution of Multinational Enterprise: Patterns of Geographical and Industrial Diversification.* Cheltenham: Edward Elgar.

Pearce, R. D., and S. Singh (1992). *Globalizing Research and Development.* New York: St. Martin's Press.

Pearson, C. S. (ed.) (1987). *Multinational Corporations, Environment, and the Third World.* Durham, NC: Duke University Press.

Peck, M. J. (1976). "Technology." In H. Patrick and H. Rosovsky (eds.), *Asia's New Giant: How the Japanese Economy Works*, pp. 525–85. Washington: Brookings Institution.

Pennie, T. E. (1956). "The Influence of Distribution Costs and Direct Investments on British Exports to Canada," *Oxford Econ. Pap.*, 8 (October), 229–44.

Penrose, E. T. (1956). "Foreign Investment and the Growth of the Firm," *Econ. J.*, 66 (June), 220–35.

(1959). *The Theory of the Growth of the Firm.* Oxford: Blackwell.

(1968). *The Large International Firm in Developing Countries: The International Petroleum Industry.* London: Allen & Unwin.

(1973). "International Patenting and the Less-Developed Counties," *Econ. J.*, 83 (September), 768–86.

Perlmutter, H. V., and D. A. Heenan (1986). "Cooperate to Compete Globally," *Harvard Bus. Rev.*, 64 (March), 136–52.

Perry, M. K. (1989). "Vertical Integration: Determinants and Effects." In R. Schmalensee and R. D. Willig (eds.), *Handbook of Industrial Organization*, Vol. 1, pp. 183–255. Amsterdam: North-Holland.

Petrochilas, G. A. (1989). *Foreign Direct Investment and the Development Process: The Case of Greece.* Aldershot: Averbury/Gower.

Phillips-Patrick, F. J. (1991). "Political Risk and Organizational Form," *J. Law Econ.*, 34 (October), Part 2, 675–93.

Picht, H., and V. Stüven (1991). "Expropriation of Foreign Direct Investments: Empirical Evidence and Implications for the Debt Crisis," *Public Choice*, 69 (February), 19–38.

Pindyck, R. S. (1978). "Gains to Producers from the Cartelization of Exhaustible Resources," *Rev. Econ. Statist.*, 60 (May), 238–51.

Pitt, M. M., and L.-F. Lee (1981). "The Measurement and Sources of Technical Inefficiency in the Indonesian Weaving Industry," *J. Devel. Econ.*, 9 (August), 43–64.

Pitts, R. A., and J. D. Daniels (1984). "Aftermath of the Matrix Mania," *Columbia J. World Bus.*, 19 (Summer), 48–55.

Plasschaert, S. (1979). *Transfer Pricing and Multinational Corporations: An Overview of Concepts, Mechanisms and Regulations.* Farnborough: Saxon House.

(1981). "The Multiple Motivations for Transfer Pricing Modulations in Multinational Enterprises and Governmental Counter-Measures: An Attempt at Clarification," *Manage. Int. Rev.*, 21 (No. 1), 49–63.

Porter, M. E. (ed.) (1986). *Competition in Global Industries.* Boston: Harvard Business School Press.

(1990). *The Competitive Advantage of Nations.* New York: Free Press.

Porter, M. E., and M. B. Fuller (1986). "Coalitions and Global Strategy." In Porter (1986), pp. 315–43.

Poynter, T. A. (1985). *Multinational Enterprises and Government Intervention.* New York: St. Martin's Press.

Prachowny, M. F. J., and J. D. Richardson (1975). "Testing a Life-Cycle Hypothesis of the Balance-of-Payments Effects of Multinational Corporations," *Econ. Inquiry*, 13 (March), 81–98.

Prahalad, C. K., and Y. L. Doz (1987). *The Multinational Mission: Balancing Local Demands and Global Vision.* New York: Free Press.

Prindl, A. R. (1976). *Foreign Exchange Risk.* New York: Wiley.

Prusa, T. J. (1990). "An Incentive Compatible Approach to the Transfer Pricing Problem," *J. Int. Econ.*, 28 (February), 155–72.

Pugel, T. A. (1978). *International Market Linkages and U.S. Manufacturing: Prices, Profits, and Patterns.* Cambridge, MA: Ballinger.

(1980a). "Profitability, Concentration and the Interindustry Variation in Wages," *Rev. Econ. Statist.*, 62 (May), 248–53.

(1980b). "Endogenous Technical Change and International Technology Transfer in a Ricardian Trade Model." International Finance Discussion Papers No. 167, Board of Governors of the Federal Reserve System, Washington, D.C.

(1981a). "The Determinants of Foreign Direct Investment: An Analysis of US Manufacturing Industries," *Manag. Decision Econ.*, 2 (December), 220–8.

(1981b). "Technology Transfer and the Neoclassical Theory of International Trade." In R. G. Hawkins and A. J. Prasad (eds.), *Technology Transfer and Economic Development*, pp. 11–37. Greenwich, CT: JAI Press.

(1985). "The United States." In Dunning (1985), pp. 57–90.

Purvis, D. D. (1972). "Technology, Trade and Factor Mobility," *Econ. J.*, 82 (September), 991–9.

Raff, H. (1992). "A Model of Expropriation with Asymmetric Information," *J. Int. Econ.*, 33 (November), 245–65.

Ramachandran, V. (1993). "Technology Transfer, Firm Ownership, and Investment in Human Capital," *Rev. Econ. Statist.*, 75 (November), 664–70.

Ramstetter, E. D. (ed.) (1991). *Direct Foreign Investment in Asia's Developing Economies and Structural Change.* Boulder: Westview Press.

Rangan, S., and R. Z. Lawrence (1993). "The Responses of U.S. Firms to Exchange Rate Fluctuations: Piercing the Corporate Veil," *Brookings Pap. Econ. Activity*, 2, 341–72.

Ranis, G., and C. Schive (1985). "Direct Foreign Investment in Taiwan's Development." In W. Galenson (ed.), *Foreign Trade and Investment: Economic Development in the Newly Industrializing Asian Countries*, pp. 85–137. Madison: University of Wisconsin Press.

Ratnayake, R. (1993). "Factors Affecting the Inter-industry Variation of Foreign Ownership of Manufacturing Industry," *Appl. Econ.*, 25 (May), 653–59.

Ray, E. J. (1977). "Foreign Direct Investment in Manufacturing," *J. Polit. Econ.*, 85 (April), 283–97.

(1989). "The Determinants of Foreign Direct Investment in the United States, 1979–85." In R. C. Feenstra (ed.), *Trade Policies for International Competitiveness*, pp. 53–77. Chicago: University of Chicago Press.

Razin, A., and J. Slemrod (eds.) (1990). *Taxation in the Global Economy*. Chicago: University of Chicago Press.

Read, R. (1983). "The Growth and Structure of Multinationals in the Banana Export Trade." In Casson (1983), pp. 180–213.

Reddaway, W. B. (1967). *Effects of U.K. Direct Investment Overseas: An Interim Report*. University of Cambridge, Department of Applied Economics, Occasional Papers No. 12. Cambridge: Cambridge University Press.

(1968). *Effects of U.K. Direct Investment Overseas: Final Report*. University of Cambridge, Department of Applied Economies, Occasional Papers No. 15. Cambridge: Cambridge University Press.

Reuber, G. L., with H. Crookell, M. Emerson, and G. Gallais-Hamonno (1973). *Private Foreign Investment in Development*. Oxford: Clarendon Press.

Reuber, G. L., and F. Roseman (1972). "International Capital Flows and the Takeover of Domestic Companies by Foreign Firms: Canada, 1945–61." In F. Machlup, W. S. Salant, and L. Tarshis (eds.), *The International Mobility and Movement of Capital*, pp. 465–503. Universities-National Bureau Conference Series No. 24. New York: Columbia University Press for National Bureau of Economic Research.

Richardson, J. D. (1971). "Theoretical Considerations in the Analysis of Foreign Direct Investment," *Western Econ. J.*, 9 (March), 87–98.

Richman, P. B. (1963). *Taxation of Foreign Investment Income*. Baltimore: Johns Hopkins Press.

Riedel, J. (1975). "The Nature and Determinants of Export-Oriented Direct Foreign Investment in a Developing Country: A Case Study of Taiwan," *Weltwirtsch. Arch.*, 111 (No. 3), 505–28.

Rivera-Batiz, F. L., and L. A. Rivera-Batiz (1990). "The Effects of Direct Foreign Investment in the Presence of Increasing Returns Due to Specialization," *J. Devel. Econ.*, 34 (November), 287–307.

Robbins, S. M., and R. B. Stobaugh (1973). *Money in the Multinational Enterprise: A Study of Financial Policy*. New York: Basic Books.

Roberts, B. C. (1972). "Factors Influencing the Organization and Style of Management and Their Effect on the Pattern of Industrial Relations in Multi-national Corporations." In H. Günther (ed.), *Transnational Industrial Relations*, pp. 109–32. London: Macmillan.

(1973). "Multinational Collective Bargaining: A European Prospect?" *Brit. J. Ind. Relations*, 11 (March), 1–19.

Roberts, B. C., and B. Liebhaberg (1977). "International Regulation of Multinational Enterprises: Trade Union and Management Concerns," *Brit. J. Ind. Relations*, 15 (November), 356–73.

Roberts, B. C., and J. May (1974). "The Response of Multi-National Enterprises to International Trade Union Pressures," *Brit. J. Ind. Relations*, 12 (November), 403–16.

Robinson, R. D. (1976). *National Control of Foreign Business Entry: A Survey of Fifteen Countries*. New York: Praeger.

Rodman, K. A. (1988). *Sanctity vs. Sovereignty: The United States and the Nationalization of Natural Resource Investments*. New York: Columbia University Press.

Rodriguez, C. A. (1975). "Trade in Technological Knowledge and the National Advantage," *J. Polit. Econ.*, 83 (February), 121–35.

Rodriguez, R. M. (1980). *Foreign-exchange Management in U.S. Multinationals*. Lexington, MA: Lexington Books, D. C. Heath.

Rodrik, D. (1987). "The Economics of Export-Performance Requirements," *Quart. J. Econ.*, 102 (August), 633–50.

Ronstadt, R. (1977). *Research and Development Abroad by U.S. Multinationals*. New York: Praeger.

Root, F. R., and A. A. Ahmed (1978). "The Influence of Policy Instruments on Manufacturing Direct Foreign Investment in Developing Countries," *J. Int. Bus. Stud.*, 9 (Winter), 81–93.

Rosenblatt, S. M., and T. W. Stanley (1978). *The Multinational Enterprise in North-South Technology Transfer*. Occasional Paper No. 9. Washington: Center for Multinational Studies.

Rosenbluth, G. (1970). "The Relation between Foreign Control and Concentration in Canadian Industry," *Can. J. Econ.*, 3 (February), 14–38.

Roth, K., and A. J. Morrison (1990). "An Empirical Analysis of the Integration-Responsiveness Framework in Global Industries," *J. Int. Bus. Stud.*, 21 (Fourth Quarter), 541–64.

Rousslang, D., and J. Pelzman (1983). "The Benefits and Costs of the Deferral of U.S. Taxes on Retained Earnings of Controlled Foreign Corporations," *Eur. Econ. Rev.*, 20 (January), 79–94.

Rowthorn, R. E. (1992). "Intra-Industry Trade and Investment under Oligopoly: The Role of Market Size," *Econ. J.*, 102 (March), 402–14.

Rowthorn, R., with S. Hymer (1971). *International Big Business, 1957–1967: A Study of Comparative Growth*. University of Cambridge, Department of Applied Economics, Occasional Paper No. 24. Cambridge: Cambridge University Press.

Rubin, S. J., and G. C. Hufbauer (eds.) (1984). *Emerging Standards of International Trade and Investment: Multinational Codes and Corporate Conduct*. Totawa, NJ: Rowman & Allanheld.

Ruffin, R. J., and F. Rassekh (1986). "The Role of Foreign Direct Investment in U.S. Capital Outflows," *Amer. Econ. Rev.*, 76 (December), 1126–30.

Rugman, A. M. (1979). *International Diversification and the Multinational Enterprise*. Lexington, MA: Lexington Books.

(1980a). "Internalization as a General Theory of Foreign Direct Investment: A Re-appraisal of the Literature," *Weltwirtsch. Arch.*, 116 (No. 2), 365–79.

(1980b). *Multinationals in Canada: Theory, Performance, and Economic Impact*. Boston: Martinus Nijhoff.

(ed.) (1982). *New Theories of the Multinational Enterprise*. London: Croom Helm.

(ed.) (1983). *Multinationals and Technology Transfer: The Canadian Experience*. New York: Praeger.

(1985). "Internalization Is Still a General Theory of Foreign Direct Investment," *Weltwirtsch. Arch.*, 121 (No. 3), 570–75.

(1987). "The Firm-Specific Advantages of Canadian Multinationals," *J. Int. Econ. Stud.*, 2, 1–14.

Rugman, A. M., and L. Eden (eds.) (1985). *Multinationals and Transfer Pricing*. New York: St. Martin's Press.

Rutenberg, D. P. (1970). "Maneuvering Liquid Assets in a Multi-National Company: Formulation and Deterministic Solution Procedures," *Manage. Sci.*, 16 (June), B-671–84.

Safarian, A. E. (1966). *Foreign Ownership of Canadian Industry*. Toronto: McGraw-Hill.

(1978). "Policy on Multinational Enterprises in Developed Countries," *Can. J. Econ.*, 11 (November), 641–55.

(1985). *FIRA and FIRB: Canadian and Australian Policies on Foreign Direct Investment*. Toronto: Ontario Economic Council.

(1993). *Multinational Enterprise and Public Policy: A Study of the Industrial Countries.* Aldershot: Edward Elgar.

Sagari, S. B. (1992). "United States Foreign Direct Investment in the Banking Industry," *Transnat. Corp.*, 1 (No. 3), 93–123.

Saham, J. (1980). *British Industrial Investment in Malaysia, 1963–1971.* Kuala Lumpur: Oxford University Press.

Samuelson, L. (1982). "The Multinational Firm with Arm's Length Transfer Price Limits," *J. Int. Econ.*, 13 (November), 365–74.

(1986). "The Multinational Firm and Exhaustible Resources," *Economica*, 53 (May), 191–207.

Sanyal, R. N. (1990). "An Empirical Analysis of the Unionization of Foreign Manufacturing Firms in the U.S.," *J. Int. Bus. Stud.*, 21 (First Quarter), 119–32.

Sato, M., and R. M. Bird (1975). "International Aspects of the Taxation of Corporations and Shareholders," *IMF Staff Pap.*, 22 (July), 384–455.

Saunders, R. S. (1978). "The Determinants of the Productivity of Canadian Manufacturing Industries Relative to That of Counterpart Industries in the United States." Ph.D. dissertation, Harvard University.

(1982). "The Determinants of Interindustry Variation of Foreign Ownership in Canadian Manufacturing Industries," *Can. J. Econ.*, 15 (February), 77–84.

Savary, J. (1984). *French Multinationals.* London: Frances Pinter.

(1992). "Cross-Investments between France and Italy and the New European Strategies of Industrial Groups." In Cantwell (1992), pp. 150–91.

Scaperlanda, A. (1992). "Direct Investment Controls and International Equilibrium: The U.S. Experience," *East. Econ. J.*, 18 (Spring), 157–70.

Scaperlanda, A. E., and R. S. Balough (1983). "Determinants of US Direct Investment in the EEC Revisited," *Eur. Econ. Rev.*, 21 (May), 381–90.

Scaperlanda, A. E., and L. J. Mauer (1972). "The Determinants of U.S. Direct Investment in the E.E.C.: Reply," *Amer. Econ. Rev.*, 62 (September), 700–4.

Scherer, F. M., A. Beckenstein, E. Kaufer, and R. D. Murphy, with F. Bougeon-Maassen (1975). *The Economics of Multiplant Operation: An International Comparisons Study.* Harvard Economic Studies No. 145. Cambridge, MA: Harvard University Press.

Schmitz, A. (1970). "The Impact of Trade Blocs on Foreign Direct Investment," *Econ. J.*, 80 (September), 724–31.

Schmitz, A., and J. Bieri (1972). "E.E.C. Tariffs and United States Direct Investment," *Eur. Econ. Rev.*, 3 (October), 259–70.

Schneider, F., and B. S. Frey (1985). "Economic and Political Determinants of Foreign Direct Investment," *World Devel.*, 13 (February), 161–75.

Schroath, F. et al. (1993). "Origin Effects of Foreign Investment in the People's Republic of China," *J. Int. Bus. Stud.*, 24 (Second Quarter), 277–90.

Sciberras, E. (1977). *Multinational Electronic Companies and National Economic Policies.* Contemporary Studies in Economic and Financial Analysis No. 6, Greenwich, CT: JAI Press.

Sechzer, S. L. (1988). "The Welfare Effect of Foreign Investment in Trade Distorted Economies," *J. Int. Econ.*, 25 (November), 379–83.

Segerstrom, P. S., T. C. A. Anant, and E. Dinopoulos (1990). "A Schumpeterian Model of the Product Life Cycle," *Amer. Econ. Rev.*, 80 (December), 1077–91.

Sekiguchi, S. (1979). *Japanese Direct Foreign Investment.* Atlantic Institute for International Affairs Series No. 1. Montclair, NJ: Allenheld, Osmun.

Severn, A. K. (1972). "Investment and Financial Behavior of American Direct Investors in Manufacturing." In F. Machlup, W. S. Salant, and L. Tarshis (eds.), *The International Mobility and Movement of Capital*, pp. 367–96. Universities-National Bureau Conference Series No. 24. New York: Columbia University Press for National Bureau of Economic Research.

Severn, A. K., and M. M. Laurence (1974). "Direct Investment, Research Intensity, and Profitability," *J. Financial Quant. Anal.*, 9 (March), 181–90.

Shaked, I. (1986). "Are Multinational Corporations Safer?" *J. Int. Bus. Stud.*, 17 (Spring), 83–106.

Shank, K. S., Jesse F. Dillard, and Richard J. Murdock (1979). *Assessing the Economic Impact of FASB No. 8*. New York: Financial Executives Research Foundation.

Shapiro, A. C. (1975a). "Exchange Rate Changes, Inflation and the Value of the Multinational Corporation," *J. Finance*, 30 (May), 485–502.

——— (1975b). "Evaluating Financing Costs for Multinational Subsidiaries," *J. Int. Bus. Stud.*, 6 (Fall), 25–32.

——— (1978). "Financial Structure and Cost of Capital in the Multinational Corporation," *J. Financial Quant. Anal.*, 13 (June), 211–26.

Shapiro, D. M. (1980). *Foreign and Domestic Firms in Canada: A Comparative Study of Financial Structure and Performance*. Toronto: Butterworths.

——— (1983). "Entry, Exit, and the Theory of the Multinational Corporation." In C. P. Kindleberger and D. B. Audretsch (eds.), *The Multinational Corporation in the 1980s*, pp. 103–22. Cambridge, MA: MIT Press.

Sharpston, M. (1975). "International Sub-contracting," *Oxford Econ. Pap.*, 27 (March), 94–135.

Siddharthan, N. S., and N. Kumar (1990). "The Determinants of Inter-Industry Variations in the Proportion of Intra-Firm Trade: The Behaviour of US Multinationals," *Weltwirtsch. Arch.*, 126 (No. 4), 581–90.

Siddharthan, N.S., and S. Lall (1982). "The Recent Growth of the Largest U.S. Multinationals," *Oxford Bull. Econ. Statist.*, 44 (February), 1–13.

Siegel, M. H. (1983). *Foreign Exchange Risk and Direct Foreign Investment*. Ann Arbor: UMI Research Press.

Sigmund, P. E. (1980). *Multinationals in Latin America: The Politics of Nationalization*. Madison: University of Wisconsin Press.

Singer, H. W. (1950). "The Distribution of Gains between Investing and Borrowing Countries," *Amer. Econ. Rev.*, 40 (May), 473–85.

Sinn, H.-W. (1993). "Taxation and the Birth of Foreign Subsidiaries." In H. Herberg and N. V. Long (eds.), *Trade, Welfare, and Economic Policies: Essays in Honor of Murray C. Kemp*, pp. 325–52. Ann Arbor: University of Michigan Press.

Slemrod, J. (1990). "Tax Effects on Foreign Direct Investment in the United States: Evidence from a Cross-Country Comparison." In Razin and Slemrod (1990), pp. 79–117.

Sleuwagen, L. (1984). "Location and Investment Decisions by Multinational Enterprises." Ph.D. dissertation, Catholic University of Leuven.

——— (1985). "Monopolistic Advantages and the International Operations of Firms: Disaggregated Evidence from U.S. Based Multinationals," *J. Int. Bus. Stud.*, 16 (Fall), 125–33.

——— (1988). "Multinationals, the European Community and Belgium: Recent Developments." In Dunning and Robson (1988), pp. 153–70.

Sleuwaegen, L., and H. Yamawaki (1991). "Foreign Direct Investment and Intrafirm Trade: Evidence from Japan." In A. Koekkoek and L. B. M. Mennes (eds.), *International Trade and Global Development: Essays in Honour of Jagdish Bhagwati*, pp. 114–61. London: Routledge.

Smith, A. (1987). "Strategic Investment, Multinational Corporations and Trade Policy," *Eur. Econ. Rev.*, 31 (February), 89–96.

Smith, D. N., and L. T. Wells, Jr. (1975). *Negotiating Third World Mineral Agreements*. Cambridge, MA: Ballinger.

Smits, W. J. B. (1988). "Foreign Direct Investment and Export and Import Value," *De Economist*, 136 (No. 1), 91–117.

Snoy, B. (1975). *Taxes on Direct Investment Income in the EEC: A Legal and Economic Analysis*. New York: Praeger.

Soenen, L. A. (1979). "Efficient Market Implications for Foreign Exchange Exposure Management," *De Economist*, 127 (No. 2), 330–9.

Solomon, R. F., and D. J. C. Forsyth (1977). "Substitution of Labour for Capital in the Foreign Sector: Some Further Evidence," *Econ. J.*, 87 (June), 283–9.

Solomon, R. F., and K. P. D. Ingham (1977). "Discriminating between MNC Subsidiaries and Indigenous Companies: A Comparative Analysis of the British Mechanical Engineering Industry," *Oxford Bull. Econ. Statist.*, 39 (May), 127–38.

Southard, F. A., Jr. (1931). *American Industry in Europe*. Boston: Houghton Mifflin.

Sprietsma, H. B. (1978). "International Subcontracting and Developing Countries," *De Economist*, 126 (No. 2), 220–42.

Srinivasan, T. N. (1983). "International Factor Movements, Commodity Trade and Commercial Policy in a Specific Factor Model," *J. Int. Econ.*, 14 (May), 289–312.

Steuer, M. D., et al. (1973). *The Impact of Foreign Direct Investment on the United Kingdom*. London: Her Majesty's Stationery Office.

Steuer, M., and J. Gennard (1971). "Industrial Relations, Labour Disputes and Labour Utilization in Foreign-Owned Firms in the United Kingdom." In J. H. Dunning (ed.), *The Multinational Enterprise*, pp. 89–144. London: Allen & Unwin.

Stevens, G. V. G. (1969). "Fixed Investment Expenditures of Foreign Manufacturing Affiliates of United States Firms: Theoretical Models and Empirical Evidence," *Yale Econ. Essays*, 9 (Spring), 137–206.

  (1972). "Capital Mobility and the International Firm." In F. Machlup, W. S. Salant, and L. Tarshis (eds.), *The International Mobility and Movement of Capital*, pp. 323–53. New York: Columbia University Press for National Bureau of Economic Research.

  (1974). "The Determinants of Investment." In J. H. Dunning (ed.), *Economic Analysis and the Multinational Enterprise*, pp. 47–83. London: Allen & Unwin.

Stevens, G. V. G., and R. E. Lipsey (1992). "Interactions between Domestic and Foreign Investment," *J. Int. Money Finance*, 11 (February), 40–62.

Stewart, J. C. (1989). "Transfer Pricing: Some Empirical Evidence from Ireland," *J. Econ. Stud.*, 16 (No. 3), 40–56.

Stobaugh, R. B. (1970). "Financing Foreign Subsidiaries of U.S. Controlled Multinational Enterprises," *J. Int. Bus. Stud.*, 1 (Summer), 43–64.

  (1972). "The Neotechnology Account of International Trade: The Case of Petrochemicals." In L. T. Wells (ed.), *The Product Life Cycle and International Trade*, pp. 81–105. Boston: Division of Research, Graduate School of Business Administration, Harvard University.

Stobaugh, R. B., et al. (1976). *Nine Investments Abroad and Their Impact at Home: Case Studies on Multinational Enterprises and the U.S. Economy*. Boston: Division of Research, Harvard Business School.

Stonehill, A. (1965). *Foreign Ownership in Norwegian Enterprises*. Samfunnsokonomiske Studier No. 14. Oslo: Central Bureau of Statistics.

Stopford, J. M. (1976). "Changing Perspectives on Investment by British Manufacturing Multinationals," *J. Int. Bus. Stud.*, 7 (Fall/Winter), 15–27.

Stopford, J., and C. Baden-Fuller (1988). "Regional-Level Competition in a Mature Industry: The Case of European Domestic Appliances." In Dunning and Robson (1988), pp. 71–90.

Stopford, J. M., and K. O. Haberich (1978). "Ownership and Control of Foreign Operations." In Ghertman and Leontiades (1978), pp. 141–67.

Stopford, J. M., and S. Strange (1991). *Rival States, Rival Firms: Competition for World Market Shares*. Cambridge: Cambridge University Press.

Stopford, J. M., and L. Turner (1985). *Britain and the Multinationals*. Chichester: John Wiley.

Stopford, J. M., and L. T. Wells, Jr. (1972). *Managing the Multinational Enterprise: Organization of the Firm and Ownership of the Subsidiaries*. New York: Basic Books.

Strassmann, W. P. (1968). *Technological Change and Economic Development: The Manufacturing Experience of Mexico and Peru*. Ithaca, NY: Cornell University Press.

Stubenitsky, R. (1970). *American Direct Investment in the Netherlands Industry*. Rotterdam: Rotterdam University Press.

Stuckey, J. A. (1983). *Vertical Integration and Joint Ventures in the Aluminum Industry*. Cambridge, MA: Harvard University Press.

Stulz, R. M. (1984). "Pricing Capital Assets in an International Setting: An Introduction," *J. Int. Bus. Stud.*, 15 (Winter), 55–73.

Stulz, R. M., and W. Wasserfallen (1992). "Foreign Equity Investment Restrictions and Shareholder Wealth Maximization." Working Paper No. 4217, National Bureau of Economic Research.

Svedberg, P. (1977). *Foreign Investment and Trade Policies in an International Economy with Transnational Corporations: A Theoretical and Empirical Study with References to Latin America*. Stockholm: privately printed.

 (1979). "Optimal Tariff Policy on Imports from Multinationals," *Econ. Record*, 55 (March), 64–7.

 (1981). "Colonial Enforcement of Foreign Direct Investment," *Manchester Sch. Econ. Soc. Stud.*, 48 (March), 21–38.

 (1982*a*). "Colonialism and Foreign Direct Investment Profitability." In J. Black and J. H. Dunning (eds.), *International Capital Movements*, pp. 172–94. London: Macmillan.

 (1982*b*). "Multinational Enterprise Investment and Import Substitution in Latin America," *Austral. Econ. Pap.*, 21 (December), 321–31.

Svejnar, J., and S. C. Smith (1984). "The Economics of Joint Ventures in Less Developed Countries," *Quart. J. Econ.*, 94 (February), 149–67.

Svensson, L. (1981). "National Welfare in the Presence of Foreign Owned Factors of Production: An Extension," *Scand. J. Econ.*, 83 (No. 4), 497–507.

Swann, D., D. P. O'Brien, W. P. J. Maunder, and W. S. Howe (1974). *Competition in British Industry: Restrictive Practices Legislation in Theory and Practice*. London: Allen & Unwin.

Swedenborg, B. (1979). *The Multinational Operations of Swedish Firms: An Analysis of Determinants and Effects*. Stockholm: Industrial Institute for Economic and Social Research.

 (1985). "Sweden." In Dunning (1985), pp. 217–48.

Swenson, D. L. (1993). "Foreign Mergers and Acquisitions in the United States." In Froot (1993), pp. 255–81.

Taira, K., and G. Standing (1973). "Labor Market Effects of Multinational Enterprises in Latin America," *Nebr. J. Econ. Bus.*, 12 (Autumn), 103–17.

Tallman, S. B. (1988). "Home Country Political Risk and Foreign Direct Investment in the United States," *J. Int. Bus. Stud.*, 19 (Summer), 219–34.

Tang, R. Y. W. (1979). *Transfer Pricing Practices in the United States and Japan*. New York: Praeger.

Taylor, C. T., and Z. A. Silberston (1973). *The Economic Impact of the Patent System: A Study of the British Experience*. University of Cambridge, Department of Applied Economics, Monograph No. 23. Cambridge: Cambridge University Press.

Teece, D. J. (1976). *Vertical Integration and Vertical Divestiture in the U.S. Oil Industry*. Stanford: Institute for Energy Studies, Stanford University.

 (1977). "Technology Transfer by Multinational Firms: The Resource Cost of Transferring Technological Knowhow," *Econ. J.*, 87 (June), 242–61.

 (1986). "Transaction Cost Economics and the Multinational Enterprise: An Assessment," *J. Econ. Behav. Organ.*, 7 (March), 25–45.

Teichova, A., M. Levy-Leboyer, and H. Nussbaum (eds.) (1986). *Multinational Enterprise in Historical Perspective*. Cambridge: Cambridge University Press.

Telesio, P. (1979). *Technology Licensing and Multinational Enterprises*. New York: Praeger.

Terpstra, V., and C.-M. Yu (1988). "Determinants of Foreign Investment of U.S. Advertising Agencies," *J. Int. Bus. Stud.*, 19 (Spring), 33–46.

Terrell, H. S., and S. J. Key (1978). "U.S. Offices of Foreign Banks: The Recent Experience." International Finance Discussion Papers No. 124. Washington: Board of Governors of the Federal Reserve System.

Thomas J., and T. Worrall (1994). "Foreign Direct Investment and the Risk of Expropriation," *Rev. Econ. Stud.*, 61 (January), 81–108.

Thompson, R. S. (1985). "Risk Reduction and International Diversification: An Analysis of Large UK Multinational Companies," *Appl. Econ.*, 17 (June), 529–41.

Thurow, L. C. (1976). "International Factor Movements and the American Distribution of Income," *Intermountain Econ. Rev.*, 2 (Spring), 13–24.

Tilton, J. E. (1971). *The International Diffusion of Technology: The Case of Semi-conductors*. Washington: Brookings Institution.

Tomlinson, J. W. C. (1970). *The Joint Venture Process in International Business: India and Pakistan*. Cambridge, MA: MIT Press.

Torneden, R. L. (1975). *Foreign Disinvestment by U.S. Multinational Corporations, with Eight Case Studies*. New York: Praeger.

Trevor, M. (1983). *Japan's Reluctant Multinationals: Japanese Management at Home and Abroad*. London: Frances Pinter.

Truitt, J. F. (1974). *Expropriation of Private Foreign Investment*. International Business Research Series No. 3. Bloomington: Graduate School of Business, Indiana University.

Tsai, P. (1987). "The Welfare Impact of Foreign Investment in the Presence of Specific Factors and Non-Traded Goods," *Weltwirtsch. Arch.*, 123 (No. 3), 496–507.

Tsurumi, Y. (1976). *The Japanese Are Coming: A Multinational Spread of Japanese Firms*. Cambridge, MA: Ballinger.

Tyebjee, T. T. (1988). "Japan's Joint Ventures in the United States." In Contractor and Lorange (1988), pp. 457–72.

Tyler, W. G. (1978). "Technical Efficiency and Ownership Characteristics of Manufacturing Firms in a Developing Country: A Brazilian Case Study," *Weltwirtsch. Arch.*, 114 (No. 2), 360–79.

(1979). "Technical Efficiency in Production in a Developing Country: An Empirical Examination of the Brazilian Plastics and Steel Industries," *Oxford Econ. Pap.*, 31 (November), 477–95.

United Nations, Centre on Transnational Corporations (UNCTC) (1982). *Alternative Arrangements for Petroleum Development*. New York: United Nations.

(1983a). *Main Features and Trends in Petroleum and Mining Agreements*. New York: United Nations.

(1983b). *Measures Strengthening the Negotiating Capacity of Governments in Their Relations with Transnational Corporations: Joint Ventures among Firms in Latin America*. New York: United Nations.

(1985). *Transnational Corporations and International Trade: Selected Issues*. New York: United Nations.

(1988a). *International Income Taxation and Developing Countries*. New York: United Nations.

(1988b). *Transnational Corporations in World Development: Trends and Prospects*. New York: United Nations.

(1989). *Foreign Direct Investment and Transnational Corporations in Services*. New York: United Nations.

(1990). *Regional Economic Integration and Transnational Corporations in the 1990s: Europe 1992, North America and Developing Countries*. New York: United Nations.

(1991a). *Government Policies and Foreign Direct Investment*. UNCTC Current Series A/17. New York: United Nations.

(1991*b*). *The Impact of Trade-Related Investment Measures on Trade and Development*. New York: United Nations.

(1992*a*). *The Determinants of Foreign Direct Investment: A Survey of the Evidence*. New York: United Nations.

(1992*b*). *Foreign Direct Investment and Industrial Restructuring in Mexico*, UNCTC Current Series A/18. New York: United Nations.

U.S. Department of Commerce (1976). *Foreign Direct Investment in the United States: Report of the Secretary of Commerce to the Congress in Compliance with the Foreign Investment Study Act of 1974*. Washington: U.S. Government Printing Office.

U.S. Department of Labor, Bureau of International Labor Affairs (1978). *The Impact of International Trade and Investment on Employment*, W. Dewald (ed.). Washington: U.S. Government Printing Office.

U.S. Senate, Foreign Relations Committee, Subcommittee on Multinational Corporations (1975). *Multinational Corporations in the Dollar-Devaluation Crisis: Report on a Questionnaire*. Washington: U.S. Government Printing Office.

U.S. Tariff Commission (1973). *Implications of Multinational Firms for World Trade and Investment and for U.S. Trade and Labor*. Washington: U.S. Government Printing Office.

Vaitsos, C. V. (1974). *Intercountry Income Distribution and Transnational Enterprises*. Oxford: Clarendon Press.

Van den Bulcke, D. (1985). "Belgium." In Dunning (1985), pp. 249–80.

Van den Bulcke, D., and P. de Lombaerde (1992). "The Belgian Metalworking Industries and the Large European Internal Market: The Role of Multinational Investment." In Cantwell (1992), pp. 107–49.

Van den Bulcke, D., et al. (1980). *Investment and Divestment Policies in Multinational Corporations in Europe*. New York: Praeger.

Van Loo, F. (1977). "The Effect of Foreign Direct Investment on Investment in Canada," *Rev. Econ. Statist.*, 59 (November), 474–81.

Vendrell-Alda, J. L. M. (1978). *Comparing Foreign Subsidiaries and Domestic Firms: A Research Methodology Applied to Efficiency in Argentine Industry*. New York: Garland.

Verlage, H. C. (1975). *Transfer Prices for Multinational Enterprises*. Rotterdam: Rotterdam University Press.

Vernon, R. (1966). "International Investment and International Trade in the Product Cycle," *Quart. J. Econ.*, 80 (May), 190–207.

(1970). "Organization as a Scale Factor in the Growth of Firms." In J. W. Markham and G. F. Papanek (eds.), *Industrial Organization and Economic Development*, pp. 47–66. Boston: Houghton Mifflin.

(1971). *Sovereignty at Bay: The Multinational Spread of U.S. Enterprises*. New York: Basic Books.

(1974*a*). "Competition Policy toward Multinational Companies," *Amer. Econ. Rev.*, 64 (May), 276–82.

(1974*b*). "The Location of Industry." In J. H. Dunning (ed.), *Economic Analysis and the Multinational Enterprise*, pp. 89–114. London: Allen & Unwin.

(1976*a*). *The Oil Crisis*. New York: W. W. Norton.

(1976*b*). "Multinational Enterprises in Developing Countries: Issues in Dependency and Interdependence." In D. E. Apter and L. W. Goodman (eds.), *The Multinational Corporation and Social Change*, pp. 40–62. New York: Praeger.

(1977). *Storm Over the Multinationals: The Real Issues*. Cambridge, MA: Harvard University Press.

(1979). "The Product Cycle Hypothesis in a New International Environment," *Oxford Bull. Econ. Statist.*, 41 (November), 255–67.

Vernon, R., and W. H. Davidson (1979). "Foreign Production of Technology-Intensive Products by U.S.-Based Multinational Enterprises." Working Paper No. 79–5, Division of Research, Graduate School of Business Administration, Harvard University.

Vernon, R., and B. Levy (1980). "State-owned Enterprises in the World Economy: The Case of Iron Ore." Working Paper No. 80–24, Division of Research, Graduate School of Business Administration, Harvard University.

Veugelers, R. (1991). "Locational Determinants and Ranking of Host Countries: An Empirical Assessment," *Kyklos*, 44 (No. 3), 363–82.

(1993). "Reputation as a Mechanism Alleviating Opportunistic Host Government Behavior against MNEs," *J. Ind. Econ.*, 41 (March), 1–18.

Viesti, G. (1988). "Size and Trends of Italian Direct Investment Abroad: A Quantitative Assessment." In F. Onida and G. Viesti (eds.), *The Italian Multinationals*, pp. 30–48. London: Croom Helm.

Wagner. K. (1980). "Competition and Productivity: A Study of the Metal Can Industry in Britain, Germany and the United States," *J. Ind. Econ.*, 29 (September), 17–35.

Wakasugi, R. (1994). "On the Determinants of Overseas Production: An Empirical Study of Japanese FDI." Working Paper 94–2, Center for International Trade Studies, Faculty of Economics, Yokohama National University.

Wall, D. (1976). "Export Processing Zones," *J. World Trade Law*, 10 (September/October), 478–89.

Wallace, C. D. (1982). *Legal Control of the Multinational Enterprise: National Regulatory Techniques and the Prospects for International Controls*. The Hague: Martinus Nijhoff.

Wallace, D., Jr. (ed.) (1976). *International Control of Investment*. New York: Praeger.

Wang, J.-Y. (1990). "Growth, Technology Transfer, and the Long-Run Theory of International Capital Movements," *J. Int. Econ.*, 29 (November), 255–71.

Wang, J.-Y., and M. Blomström (1992). "Foreign Investment and Technology Transfer: A Simple Model," *Eur. Econ. Rev.*, 36 (January), 137–55.

Warr, P. G. (1987). "Export Promotion via Industrial Enclaves: The Philippines' Bataan Export Processing Zone," *J. Devel. Stud.*, 23 (January), 220–41.

Weinberg, P. J. (1978). *European Labor and Multinationals*. New York: Praeger.

Weisskopf, T. E. (1972). "The Impact of Foreign Capital Inflow on Domestic Savings in Underdeveloped Countries," *J. Int. Econ.*, 2 (February), 25–38.

Wells, L. T. (ed.) (1972). *The Product Life Cycle and International Trade*. Boston: Division of Research, Graduate School of Business Administration, Harvard University.

(1973). "Economic Man and Engineering Man: Choice in a Low-Wage Country," *Public Policy*, 21 (Summer), 319–42.

(1983). *Third World Multinationals*. Cambridge, MA: MIT Press.

(1993). "Mobile Exporters: New Foreign Investors in East Asia." In K. Froot (1993), pp. 173–95.

Wesson, T. J. (1993). "An Alternative Motivation for Foreign Direct Investment." Ph.D. dissertation, Harvard University.

Westphal, L. E., Y. W. Rhee, and G. Pursell (1979). "Foreign Influences on Korean Industrial Development," *Oxford Bull. Econ. Statist.*, 41 (November), 359–88.

Wheeler, D., and A. Mody (1992). "International Investment Location Decisions: The Case of U.S. Firms," *J. Int. Econ.*, 33 (August), 57–76.

Whichard, O. G. (1978). "Employment and Employee Compensation of U.S. Affiliates of Foreign Companies, 1974," *Surv. Curr. Bus.*, 58 (December), 23–34.

White, L. J. (1976). "Appropriate Technology and a Competitive Environment: Some Evidence from Pakistan," *Quart. J. Econ.*, 90 (November), 575–89.

Wickham, E., and H. Thompson (1989). "An Empirical Analysis of Intra-Industry Trade and Multi-national Firms." In P. K. M. Tharakan and J. Kol (eds.), *Intra-Industry Trade: Theory, Evidence, and Extensions*, pp. 121–44. New York: St. Martin's Press.

Wilkins, M. (1970). *The Emergence of Multinational Enterprise: American Business Abroad from the Colonial Era to 1914.* Cambridge, MA: Harvard University Press.

  (1974). *The Maturing of Multinational Enterprise: American Business Abroad from 1914 to 1970.* Cambridge, MA: Harvard University Press.

  (1986). "Defining a Firm: History and Theory." In Hertner and Jones (1986), pp. 80–95.

Williams, M. D. (1987). "European Antitrust Law and Its Application to American Corporations and Their Subsidiaries," *Whittier Law J.*, 9 (No. 3), 517–35.

Williams, M. L. (1975). "The Extent and Significance of the Nationalization of Foreign-owned Assets in Developing Countries 1956–1972," *Oxford Econ. Pap.*, 27 (July), 260–73.

Williamson, O. E. (1985). *The Economic Institutions of Capitalism.* New York: Free Press.

Williamson, P. J. (1986). "Multinational Enterprise Behaviour and Domestic Industry Adjustment under Import Threat," *Rev. Econ. Statist.*, 68 (August), 359–68.

Williamson, P. J., and H. Yamawaki (1991). "Distribution: Japan's Hidden Advantage," *Bus. Strategy Rev.*, 2 (Spring), 85–105.

Willmore, L. (1976). "Direct Foreign Investment in Central American Manufacturing," *World Devel.*, 4 (June), 499–517.

  (1986). "The Comparative Performance of Foreign and Domestic Firms in Brazil," *World Devel.*, 14 (April), 489–502.

  (1992). "Transnationals and Foreign Trade: Evidence from Brazil," *J. Devel. Stud.*, 28 (January), 314–35.

Wilson, B. D. (1979). "Divestment of Foreign Subsidiaries." D.B.A. thesis, Graduate School of Business Administration, Harvard University.

  (1980). "The Propensity of Multinational Companies to Expand through Acquisitions," *J. Int. Bus. Stud.*, 11 (Spring/Summer), 59–65.

Wilson, G. P. (1993). "The Role of Taxes in Location and Sourcing Decisions." In Giovannini et al. (1993), pp. 195–231.

Wilson, R. W. (1977). "The Effect of Technological Environment and Product Rivalry on R&D Effort and Licensing of Inventions," *Rev. Econ. Statist.*, 59 (May), 171–8.

Wolf, B. N. (1975). "Size and Profitability Among U.S. Manufacturing Firms: Multinational versus Primarily Domestic Firms," *J. Econ. Bus.*, 28 (Fall), 15–22.

  (1977). "Industrial Diversification and Internationalization: Some Empirical Evidence," *J. Ind. Econ.*, 26 (December), 177–91.

Wong, K. (1986). "Are International Trade and Factor Mobility Substitutes?" *J. Int. Econ.*, 21 (August), 25–43.

Wonnacott, R. J., and P. Wonnacott (1967). *Free Trade between the United States and Canada: The Potential Economic Effects.* Cambridge, MA: Harvard University Press.

Woodward, D. P. (1992). "Locational Determinants of Japanese Manufacturing Start-ups in the United States," *So. Econ. J.*, 58 (January), 690–708.

Woodward, D. P., and R. J. Rolfe (1993). "The Location of Export-Oriented Foreign Direct Investment in the Caribbean Basin," *J. Int. Bus. Stud.*, 24 (First Quarter), 121–44.

Yamawaki, H. (1985). "International Trade and Foreign Direct Investment in West German Manufacturing Industries." In J. Schwalbach (ed.), *Industry Structure and Performance*, pp. 247–86. Berlin: Edition Sigma.

  (1990). "Locational Decisions of Japanese Multinational Firms in European Manufacturing Industries." Working paper, Wissenschaftszentrum Berlin.

  (1991). "Exports and Foreign Distributional Activities: Evidence on Japanese Firms in the United States," *Rev. Econ. Statist.*, 73 (May), 294–300.

(1994*a*). "Entry Patterns of Japanese Multinationals in US and European Manufacturing." In M. Mason and D. Encarnation (eds.), *Does Ownership Matter? Japanese Multinationals in Europe*, pp. 91–121. Oxford: Clarendon Press.

(1994*b*). "Exit of Japanese Multinationals in U.S. and European Manufacturing Industries." Working paper, Catholic University of Louvain.

Yang, H. C., J. W. Wansley, and W. R. Lane (1990). "A Direct Test of the Diversification Service Hypothesis of Foreign Direct Investment," *Advances in Financial Planning and Forecasting*, 4, part A, 215–38.

Yannopoulos, G. N. (1983). "The Growth of Transnational Banking." In Casson (1983), pp. 236–57.

(1990). "Foreign Direct Investment and European Integration: The Evidence from the Formative Years of the European Community," *J. Common Market Stud.*, 28 (March), 235–59.

Yeoman, W. A. (1976). *Selection of Production Processes for the Manufacturing Subsidiaries of U.S.-Based Multinational Corporations*. New York: Arno Press.

Yoffie, D. B. (1993). "Foreign Direct Investment in Semiconductors." In K. Froot (1993), 197–228.

Yoshida, M. (1987). *Japanese Direct Manufacturing Investment in the United States*. New York: Praeger.

Yoshihara, K. (1976). *Foreign Investment and Domestic Response: A Study of Singapore's Industrialization*. Singapore: Eastern Universities Press.

(1978). *Japanese Investment in Southeast Asia*. Monographs of the Center for Southeast Asian Studies, Kyoto University, No. 11. Honolulu: University Press of Hawaii.

Yoshino, M. Y. (1976). *Japan's Multinational Enterprises*. Cambridge, MA: Harvard University Press.

Young, S., N. Hood, and S. Dunlop (1988). "Global Strategies, Multinational Subsidiary Roles and Economic Impact in Scotland," *Reg. Sci.*, 22 (December), 487–97.

Yu, C.-M. J. (1990). "The Experience Effect and Foreign Direct Investment," *Weltwirtsch. Arch.*, 126 (No. 3), 561–80.

Yu, C.-M. J., and K. Ito (1988). "Oligopolistic Reaction and Foreign Direct Investment: The Case of the U.S. Tire and Textile Industries," *J. Int. Bus. Stud.*, 19 (Fall), 449–60.

Yunker, P. J. (1982). *Transfer Pricing and Performance Evaluation in Multinational Corporations: A Survey Study*. New York: Praeger.

Zejan, M. C. (1989). "Intra-Firm Trade and Swedish Multinationals," *Weltwirtsch. Arch.*, 125 (No. 4), 814–33.

(1990*a*). "New Ventures or Acquisition: The Choice of Swedish Multinational Enterprises," *J. Ind. Econ.*, 38 (March), 349–55.

(1990*b*). "R&D Activities in Affiliates of Swedish Multinational Enterprises," *Scand. J. Econ.*, 92 (No. 3), 487–500.

Zenoff, D. B. (1966). "The Determinants of Dividend Remittance Practices of Wholly Owned European and Canadian Subsidiaries of American Multinational Corporations." D.B.A. thesis, Graduate School of Business Administration, Harvard University.

Name index

Subject index